Imaginary Citizens

Imaginary Citizens

Child Readers and the Limits of
American Independence, 1640–1868

COURTNEY WEIKLE-MILLS

The Johns Hopkins University Press
Baltimore

© 2013 The Johns Hopkins University Press
All rights reserved. Published 2013
Printed in the United States of America on acid-free paper

2 4 6 8 9 7 5 3 1

The Johns Hopkins University Press
2715 North Charles Street
Baltimore, Maryland 21218-4363
www.press.jhu.edu

Library of Congress Cataloging-in-Publication Data

Weikle-Mills, Courtney.
Imaginary citizens : child readers and the limits of American independence, 1640–1868 /
Courtney Weikle-Mills.
p. cm.
Includes bibliographical references and index.
ISBN 978-1-4214-0721-0 (hdbk. : acid-free paper) —
ISBN 978-1-4214-0807-1 (electronic) — ISBN 1-4214-0721-3 (hdbk. : acid-free paper) —
ISBN 1-4214-0807-4 (electronic)
1. Children—Books and reading—United States—History. 2. Children's literature,
American—History and criticism. 3. Citizenship—United States—History. I. Title.
PS490.W44 2013
810.9'9282—dc23   2012013045

A catalog record for this book is available from the British Library.

*Special discounts are available for bulk purchases of this book. For more information, please
contact Special Sales at 410–516–6936 or specialsales@press.jhu.edu.*

The Johns Hopkins University Press uses environmentally friendly book materials,
including recycled text paper that is composed of at least 30 percent post-consumer
waste, whenever possible.

To my son, Soren, who came into the world
as I was sending this book forth
And to my husband, Ryan, who endured its entire gestation

CONTENTS

Acknowledgments   ix

INTRODUCTION From Subjects to Citizens: *The Politics of
Childhood and Children's Literature*   1

1 Youth as a Time of Choice: *Children's Reading in
Colonial New England*   32

2 Affectionate Citizenship: *Educating Child Readers
for a New Nation*   63

3 Child Readers of the Novel: *The Problem of Childish Citizenship*   95

4 Reading for Social Profit: *Economic Citizenship as
Children's Citizenship*   131

5 Natural Citizenship: *Children, Slaves, and the Book of Nature*   168

CONCLUSION The Legacy of the Fourteenth Amendment: *Limited
Thinking on Children's Citizenship*   206

Notes   219
Index   257

ACKNOWLEDGMENTS

In writing about the limits of independence, I have been constantly reminded of my dependence on others. The intellectual contributions of this book would not have been possible without a trip to the American Antiquarian Society, where I held a short-term Reese fellowship on the History of the Book. I met many wonderful folks at AAS and would like to especially thank Bill Reese, Paul Erickson, Laura Wasowicz, Gigi Barnhill, and Elizabeth Pope, as well as fellow-fellows Robin Bernstein and David Nord. My appreciation also goes to Thomas G. Knoles for giving me permission to print excerpts of child diaries from AAS's manuscript collection and Jaclyn Penny for providing me with images and the licenses for them. I also thank the Library of Congress and Paul Hogroian for providing me with images from their collection.

I am incredibly grateful to my mentors at the Ohio State University, Jared Gardner, Elizabeth Hewitt, Roxanne Wheeler, and Susan Williams, for encouraging me to take on a project about children and for providing guidance during my first explorations of the topic. I would also like to thank Martha-Lynn and Jason Corner, Merry Guerrera, Christy Minard, Glenda Insua, and Natalie Giannini who have also been there from the beginning and provided insight, perspective, merriment, and distraction when I needed it. I am extremely fortunate to have found an intellectual home at the University of Pittsburgh and am indebted to my colleagues for their thoughtful readings of my work, especially Marah Gubar, Nancy Glazener, Troy Boone, Jonathan Arac, and Jean Carr. I would like to thank the University of Pittsburgh Humanities Center for a generous fellowship and attendees at my colloquium there for their questions and criticisms, including Todd Reiser, Kieran Setiya, Daniel Morgan, Clark Muenzer, Don Bialostosky, Amy Robin Hoffman, and Alexandra Valint. I am grateful for the graduate students of my Imagining U.S. Citizenship seminar for their help in teasing out the meanings of the Dutiful Child's Promises, especially Julia Strusienski, Schuyler Chapman, Alicia Williamson, and

Kathleen Davies. I also thank the University of Pittsburgh School of Arts and Sciences for a third-term research grant, which allowed me to work in Pitt's Nietz Collection and Elizabeth Nesbitt Room, and for money from the Richard D. and Mary Jane Edwards Endowed Publication Fund to pay for the indexing and images. Outside of my university, I have enjoyed having feedback on my work from other scholars of childhood, including Karen Sánchez-Eppler, Pat Crain, Beverly Lyon Clark, Julia Mickenberg, and Anna Mae Duane.

I am grateful to acquisitions editor Matthew McAdam at the Johns Hopkins University Press for his support and advocacy for this project. I appreciate the work of senior editor Michele Callaghan in helping me streamline and clarify my prose. I thank Cathy Hannabach for providing the index. I also thank the editors of *Early American Literature*, David Shields and Sandra Gustafson, for allowing me to use " 'Learn to Love Your Book': The Child Reader and Affectionate Citizenship," 43 (2008): 35–61, in revised form in chapter 2.

For unconditional encouragement, I express my appreciation to Betsy Greer (who first taught me to "love my book"), Robert and Linda Weikle, Marsha Mills, and Randy and Roxanne Mills, who have all heard my ideas with varying degrees of interest but unvarying degrees of support. Last, but not least, I thank my husband, Ryan, for helping me survive and understand the humbling process that writing always is, for helping me make all my best arguments better, and for keeping me focused and fed; and my son, Soren Keith, for general wonderfulness, for "helping" me type, and for sleeping on my shoulder as I finished my editing.

Imaginary Citizens

From Subjects to Citizens
The Politics of Childhood and Children's Literature

In 1845, the prolific author and publisher Samuel Goodrich presented his readers with a new edition of the first children's book that he had published, *The Tales of Peter Parley about America*. In his preface to this final revision, Goodrich looks back on the work's reception and makes a compelling statement about children's position in early America: "It is now several years since this little work was given to the public . . . The public—I mean the world of children—have bestowed upon it their favor, and I ask no more."[1] Goodrich's identification of "the public" with "the world of children" seems at first to be a simple clarification; children were the intended audience of the Parley tales and therefore *his* public: a group of individuals brought together by reading the stories and attending the speaking tours that Goodrich did in conjunction with the series. Yet Goodrich's assertion goes further than this; by claiming that children could give an opinion on matters related to America's political history, he implies that the world of child readers functions in a way that approximates the public entity known as "the people." Underlying Goodrich's humble statement is the profound notion that children can ratify national narratives.

Parley's tales about the fledgling nation corroborate the idea that children are an important part of the American public by telling the story of the country's political origins from the point of view of a child, the young Peter Parley. Goodrich, in the voice of an older Parley, claims that children are not merely witnesses and inheritors of American history but figures for "the people" in general; he explains that the president is "like a father, and the people are like his children. He watches over them . . . and he takes care that the laws are obeyed and the people protected."[2] While this image associates the people with protection and obedience, the culture surrounding the Parley tales also gave rise to images of children performing civic actions in their role as the people. Just a short time after Goodrich's retrospective edition was published, the editor of the *Youth's Casket*, Harley Thorne, nominated Parley for president on the "children's ticket."[3] Editor Hiram Hatchett likewise encouraged the child readers of *Robert Merry's Museum and Peter Parley's Magazine* to view themselves as participants in the political process; for instance, he answers one child correspondent by saying, "If you begin to vote when you are six years old . . . you [will] be able to muster a strong party."[4]

It may be tempting to dismiss these images of citizenship as oversimplifications designed for immature readers, but they become more significant when we consider that American citizens have often been aligned with children. Metaphors related to childhood were prevalent during the American Revolution, informing the debate about whether the colonists were British subjects or American citizens. Basing their expectations of colonial loyalty on patriarchal traditions of obedient subjecthood, loyalists cast the rebelling colonists as unruly boys and savage daughters who had shirked their duty to mind their English parents. Seizing on these metaphors, patriots used Enlightenment theories of citizenship and child rearing to style themselves as "sons of liberty" with a natural right to self-determination. The centrality of the child to Revolutionary politics set in motion a larger cultural obsession with childhood; as Caroline F. Levander and Carol J. Singley note in their recent anthology, the American nation has "since its inception . . . been identified with and imagined as a child."[5]

Yet post-Revolutionary metaphors of both the nation and its citizens as children tend to reflect ambivalence about childhood as a model for political identity. In recent years, Lauren Berlant has decried the rise of what she calls "infantile citizenship," a cultural ideal of political subjectivity as passive, innocent, and naively patriotic, which she claims animates the national imaginary and stifles the critical functioning of adult citizens.[6] President Barack Obama, whose message of change mobilized a historic youth vote, has also attempted to distance himself from a childish form of politics, remarking at his 2009 inauguration: "We remain a young nation. But . . . the time has come to set aside childish things."[7] Even in the nation's early years, Americans portrayed the emergence of the new republic both as the free birth of an infant nation and as the difficult maturation of a youth, struggling to cut itself from the apron strings of mother Britain and be a child no more.[8]

As the inconsistency of these metaphors suggests, it has been unclear what kind of citizenship children represent and how they are supposed to fit into the nation as citizens, a status that I take to mean that one is understood as a member of a political community with obligations and entitlements, including some measure of political agency. On the one hand, the prominent metaphors of American citizens as liberated children suggest that young people were included in discussions about liberty and that they enjoyed more political influence as the result of revolutionary efforts. Jay Fliegelman has argued that the war was not only a military revolt against Britain but also an ideological struggle "against patriarchal authority," which was reflected in the many novels from the period that depict the dangers of tyrannical

Matthew Darley published this cartoon between 1770 and 1774. The caption reads, "Poor Old England endeavoring to reclaim his wicked American children—And therefore is England maim'd & forced to go about with a staff." The British frequently portrayed the colonists seeking their independence as unruly children rebelling against their parents. Courtesy of the Library of Congress.

parenting and the need for children to choose their own loyalties.[9] Gillian Brown has claimed that revolutionary narratives of children's freedom had a noticeable effect on children's lives, as seen through books that encouraged young people to claim their natural right to independence.[10] Historians Steven Mintz, Caroline Cox, and Vincent DiGiromalo have shown that children participated in the activities of the Revolution by joining mob protests, boycotting British goods, serving in the militia, and writing enthusiastically about liberty.[11]

On the other hand, as childhood was coming to be defined by new theories of human development, children did not easily fit new definitions of citizenship. John Locke claimed that children were born with a right to independence, while simultaneously excluding them from civic rights and responsibilities on the basis of their immature reason and supposedly natural subjection to their parents. His seemingly radical argument that a *"Child is born a subject of no Country and Government"* and is therefore free to choose an affiliation is tempered by his simultaneous contention that "he is under his Father's Tuition and Authority, till he comes to Age of Discretion."[12] Though Americans also adopted English common law, which insisted that children were in fact subjects who owed loyalty to the state, Holly Brewer has shown that Lockean theory caused children to lose freedoms that they might have held under the British system of inherited power.[13] During the Revolution some politicians argued that children could not be tried as traitors and that they could inherit foreign property without charge of disloyalty because they were not yet capable of political choice.

In the young nation, children's political standing remained uncertain, as the Constitution did not define the requirements for citizenship. As a result of the ongoing tensions between common law and contract theory, early American lawmakers and court judges were inconsistent about whether children's political duties and privileges began at birth or at the age of consent.[14] Persons under age twenty-one were increasingly excluded from actions related to citizenship. In this sense, the evolving concept of childhood helped to define the limits, margins, and boundaries of citizenship.

The simultaneous emergence of a concept of citizenship based on free birth and a concept of childhood as a deficient state has meant that a defining feature of modern political identity has been a gap between the abstract right to political freedom and the specific right to exercise it. In early America, this gap was particularly significant because persons under age twenty-one made up more than half of the U.S. population during the period from 1776 to 1868.[15] To reconcile this problem, a large portion of the people came to be understood as "imaginary citizens": individuals who could not exercise civic rights but who figured heavily in literary depictions of citizenship and were often invited to view themselves as citizens despite their limited political franchise.

Although imaginary citizenship was not limited to children—women, slaves, and sometimes even animals shared this status—this age group was even more frequently addressed by early American texts than other excluded groups and, when these others were addressed, it was often through the lens of childhood. In his 1810 history of printing in America, Isaiah Thomas notes that before the Revolution an edition of most books might consist of 500 copies, while primers and spelling books might be printed in editions of 5,000, 10,000, 15,000, and 20,000.[16] Novels too were usually addressed to children and youth, specifically young women or girls. Newspapers and other periodicals might have been the province of adult male citizens, but children emerged as an audience for even these publicly aware texts. Child diarists Sally Ripley and Edmund Quincy Sewall, for instance, recorded their newspaper reading.[17] Periodicals quickly emerged that directly targeted a young audience. By the end of the nineteenth century, *The Youth's Companion* had the widest circulation of any periodical.[18] Therefore, literary and print versions of citizenship were often based on evolving cultural assumptions about what kind of citizen a child could be. These assumptions were, in turn, shaped by a variety of texts, including philosophical treatises regarding human history and development, fictional texts centering on themes of maturity and dependence, and children's books designed to teach their readers how to interact with language, nation, and law.

That children were among those addressed as imaginary citizens is significant because it changes the way that literary versions of citizenship can be understood. For instance, Cathy N. Davidson's claim that early American novels subversively call for the enfranchisement of their readers is complicated by the fact that many specifically claim that children and youth are their readership.[19] The rise of the American novel and its attention to child readers coincided with the emergence of developmental theories that made it difficult to argue that children had the rational capacities necessary to exercise political rights. As a result, many novelists actively struggled with the political problems presented by childhood. While these works used conventions associated with education, suggesting that authors wanted to promote their readers' entrance into active citizenship, they also expressed skepticism about the competencies of those who read such books. Even though a wider audience than children and youth read novels, the overt addresses to young people meant that other readers, especially women, were positioned as children while reading. Thus, the kind of citizenship novels promoted was often informed by concerns about children. Novels oscillated between trying to deal with the problem of how to include in the nation those who were deficient of reason and attempting to write away their childishness and establish an adult nation.

Other imaginary versions of citizenship for children lampooned the idea that texts could enfranchise alternative populations of citizens. In addition to imagining children in citizenship roles, *Parley's Magazine* attributes political agency to an elephant, an orangutan, and a cow, who reportedly led a political convention on human rights, and to a herd of cattle that staged a revolution to rival the slave insurrections in the south (cattle being a play on chattel).[20] These fictional animal protests give voice to those who are not legal citizens, but they also dramatize the limitations of the periodical's ability to grant citizenship privileges, instead imagining versions of political and literary representation that are not backed by rights or direct participation in politics. Similarly addressing those who, due to their infancy, could not be granted with most of the legal rights of citizenship, many early American texts offered forms of citizenship that were imaginary at their core.

Theorizing Imaginary Citizenship

By using the term *imaginary citizenship*, I do not mean that the citizenship represented by these texts was in any way make-believe—at least in the sense that these words connote playful immersion in a fantastical unreality or dreamy association with identities that are fully distant from one's own identity. Rather, I adopt a broader meaning of imagination, explained by Nathan Tierney (following Ludwig Wittgenstein) as "seeing as" or "a peculiar experience halfway between perception and conceptual thought."[21] While children no doubt used ideas related to citizenship to structure their play, reading often allowed individuals not just to pretend that they were citizens but to understand themselves as citizens: to see the social contract as an expression of their own consent even when it could not be given, to understand the law as an expression of their own sense of justice even when they had not participated in the making of it, to view the nation and the state as representing their own interests even when they had no direct political voice.[22]

These activities could be done in the absence of actual participation in the political process. As such, children's imaginary citizenship to some extent resembles the type of political identification that Michael Warner has associated with the emergence of a nationalist imaginary: "Imaginary participation in the civic order is . . . a precondition for modern nationalism . . . You can be a member of the nation, attributing its agency to yourself in imaginary identification, without . . . exercising any agency in the public sphere."[23] Warner claims that early Americans understood this imaginary identification as a degraded form of civic identity, available to excluded individuals by virtue of its difference from an earlier republican ideal that permitted only the participation of "non-particularized" adult men. I suggest, however, that this division disguises the ways in which children's imaginary citizenship could overlap with, resemble, and inform adult citizenship.

As Warner points out, even the citizenship of rights bearers had a major imaginary component. Political action in the early republic required the imaginary apparatus of print, in that reading and writing were understood as engaging in a public and approximating the social contract. While these printed interactions were supposed to constitute meaningful civic action and to require the prerequisite of adult reason, this fantasy of print as political action already marked its difference from the republican ideal of face-to-face adult male interaction. As Benedict Anderson has famously stated, not only is the nation necessarily an imagined community because "the members of even the smallest nation will never know most of their fellow-members, meet them, or even hear of them, yet in the minds of each lives the image of their communion," but "in fact, all communities larger than primordial villages of face-to-face contact (and perhaps even these) are imagined."[24] For these reasons, if Americans have at times considered the imaginary citizenship of children as a corrupted version of some prior, assumedly *real* citizenship, this both overestimates the autonomy of the adult republican citizen and underestimates the cultural power of the child and imagination.

In important political texts such as Thomas Paine's *Common Sense* (1776), the child was sometimes the ideal republican citizen: the wronged party who applied to redress from Britain and the watchdog who would judge the actions of the new government. In Paine's mind, the Revolution was informed by its imaginary as well as actual participants: "'tis not the concern of a day, a year, or an age; posterity are virtually involved in the contest."[25] It was on behalf of this posterity composed of hypothetical child citizens that many of the political struggles of early America were waged, with adult men acting as their representatives. Indeed, the nation's early citizens talked about themselves and their nation using terms related to childhood and infancy. Children were arguably included in the textual publics created by documents such as the Constitution, which required that freeholding men identify with its contents and that each new generation be included.

I therefore suggest that imaginary citizenship is not merely a token or symbolic form of mini-citizenship for children, nor is it a diminished version of a grander political ideal. Rather, it does powerful cultural work as a supplement to dominant notions of citizenship, often supplanting them in the cultural imagination. Modes of children's imaginary citizenship frequently eclipsed other understandings of citizenship, causing other excluded adults and even rights-holders to be represented metaphorically as children. The notion of a child citizen was so powerful in structuring citizenship for all individuals because childhood offered a way to explain and balance citizenship's limits and potentials as a political model meant to produce freedom. The idea that the child could be a citizen was significant for rights-bearing citizens because the idea that rights inhered in birth supported the concepts of equality and popular sovereignty. At the same time, the concept of childhood as a state characterized by limitations helped Americans address necessary limitations on citizens' freedoms. For instance, metaphors that encouraged rights-bearing citizens to imagine themselves as affectionate children of a parental state prompted them to recognize their own interests in the law even when they had not directly participated in its making. For non-rights-bearing members of society, the concept of childhood provided a rationale for exclusion at the same time that the idea that the child could be some kind of a citizen represented the potential for excluded individuals to imagine themselves as citizens and make up for this exclusion. Imaginary citizenship—both representations of children's citizenship and metaphors of citizens as children—allowed Americans to consider the limits and potentials of imagination, *and* the limits and potentials of rights, as aspects of citizenship.

Keeping in mind these multiple layers of meaning attached to childhood, *Imaginary Citizens* traces the history of imaginary citizenship as it developed alongside the first laws limiting children's political rights in the 1640s to the first constitutional definition of citizenship ratified in 1868. By beginning my study in Puritan New England around the time of the English Civil War, I do not seek to reenshrine Puritanism as the origin of U.S. politics or to suggest that citizenship was only influenced by English ideas but rather to suggest that debates about children's potential as citizens predate nationhood.[26] Assumptions about the politics of childhood strongly shaped the emergence of modern citizenship as a form of political identity distinct from patriarchal subjecthood. Because in the Anglo-American context these debates were happening within a period of civil war and migration on the part of dissenters who nonetheless still viewed themselves as members of the parent culture, ideas about citizenship were not at first directly related to having a distinct nationality. Instead, they emerged in a variety of contexts where authority was being redefined. Relationships between parents and children, church leaders and their flocks, and readers and their books, in addition to more directly political relationships, all provided situations in which the concepts of free birth, individual choice, rational thought, voluntary commitment, and consent that were coming to be the defining characteristics of citizens could be more fully elaborated.

The concept of "the citizen" continued to develop amorphously in the United States through a variety of laws, relationships, and texts, in part because citizenship was not officially defined by the Constitution until the ratification of the Fourteenth Amendment in 1868. This law—which attempted to establish a more concrete and universal basis for national citizenship after the American Civil War by making nationality a feature of the child's birth on U.S. soil—marks the end point of my study. However, the fact that I am writing this book amidst tensions between conservatives and liberals over the application of the Fourteenth Amendment suggests that, although the boundaries between imaginary and legal citizens have shifted over time, disputes over extralegal imaginary requirements for citizens persist despite moves toward a more concrete and inclusive legal definition of citizenship. Definitional crises involving children and citizenship continue to arise in times of internal conflict, despite this shared constitutional standard for determining national identity.

Debates about citizenship exceed nationhood and nationality, but it is no coincidence the American national imaginary and the nation's literature have been profoundly shaped by images and metaphors related to childhood. Literary metaphors of the nation and its citizens as children have been so prevalent in the United States because the contrast between the ideal of free birth and the assessment of children's capacities caused a split between legal and literary forms of citizenship, causing children's citizenship to be elaborated in the realm of the imagination. Though such a split is not unique to this country, it has been particularly significant due to the nation's youth. While the English were redefining political identity in the context of an existing political system, Americans were beginning political history afresh and were therefore particularly aware of the conflicts between legal rights and the ideal of natural rights inhering in birth. Some American politicians wanted to directly address the gap between birth and the onset of participation rights by creating a renewable social contract. Thomas Jefferson proposed that the laws should frequently expire, requiring new express consent on the part of each generation, since "by the law of nature, one generation is to another as one independent nation is to another."[27] Since Jefferson's impractical proposal did not come to fruition, the goal of a consenting body of citizens paradoxically required both more fictions about childhood and a sense of anxiety about their fictionality. In addition, the nation's infant status meant that Americans were all the more likely to have strong feelings about images of childhood and to identify the status of children with the health of the nation.[28]

The continued need to address children as imaginary citizens significantly informed the nation's literary forms and practices, including the rise and development of a literature designed specifically for children, as well as a broader preoccupation with childhood in literary texts. In this volume, I focus on how a variety of texts addressed child readers who, while learning to read, were also learning to negotiate between the material realities of the nation and its imagination of itself in language. These texts present an opportunity to understand how their authors encouraged individuals to collectively imagine citizenship, tried to control how citizenship was imagined, explored the possibilities and limitations of imaginary citizenship as a viable form of political representation, and attempted to translate imaginary citizenship into reality.

Pedagogical theories, methods, and texts associated with learning language often tell us as much about U.S. citizenship as the official positions of lawmakers and politicians. For instance, early American citizenship was strongly shaped by children's storybooks that encouraged young people to "love [their] books" as a way of forming patriotic attachments to the nation's laws.[29] Subsequently, during the period of rapid economic expansion in the early nineteenth century, children's miscellanies, which bind together various kinds of texts and images, tried to integrate the concepts of responsible republican citizenship with self-interested economic participation. During and after the Civil War, natural history books designed for teaching reading encouraged Americans to see citizenship as a natural impulse, rather than a learned habit.

These examples suggest that, although some versions of imaginary citizenship might be said to feed into what Berlant calls a "national fantasy politics" based on collective identification rather than critical engagement, children's imaginary citizenship has taken many different forms throughout the nation's history.[30] Goodrich's work, for instance, gives rise to images of childlike citizens that illustrate both deference to a father-like ruler and the extension of representative democracy to even the youngest members of society. At other times, images of child citizens have represented the fearful possibility of radical rebellion, the sentimental fantasy of an economically driven nation that benefits even its most disadvantaged citizens, and the notion that citizenship is a natural state available to all, regardless of race.

Narratives and practices associated with children's citizenship had an increasing impact on dominant ideas of citizenship as the nation expanded to include a more diverse population and as adults contended with limits on their knowledge, reason, and independence. Most dramatically, the Fourteenth Amendment officially declared the citizenship of all by making it a natural feature of birth rather than a contractual agreement, but stories and images of children's citizenship encroached upon adult citizenship long before this legal shift. Echoing Obama's speech, childhood was continually evoked and dismissed, defining the meaning and boundaries of American citizenship.

A Political History of Childhood

To explain why childhood came to have such a significant influence on formulations of citizenship, it is useful to trace the origins of both concepts in the seventeenth century, a period that has been associated with the transition from subjecthood to citizenship as well as the more precise designation of childhood as a stage of life. Philippe Ariès has controversially stated that childhood was invented in this period.[31] While many critics have rightly challenged Ariès's claim that "in medieval society the idea of childhood did not exist," it is true that the seventeenth century gave rise to an increased focus on childhood in nearly all aspects of European and American society.[32] Discussions of children (actual, hypothetical, and metaphorical) figured centrally in religious doctrine and political theory, educational treatises were written by authors with strong political investments, and a higher percentage of books were dedicated especially to child readers.

A new account of this increased emphasis on childhood can be seen by tracing how these changes can be linked to political history. The emergence of a more extensive Anglo-American discourse surrounding childhood was closely connected to the redefinition of political identity in the wake of the Protestant Reformation, the English Civil War (1642–51), and the migration to the new world.[33] These historical events, which gave rise to modern theories of citizenship, involved a struggle over the boundaries of childhood, culminating in what Brewer has called "a fundamental shift . . . in the legal assumptions about childhood, adulthood, and responsibility."[34] Specifically, children were increasingly excluded from political activities in which they had formerly participated such as voting, serving on juries, signing indentures and other contracts, and holding office (if they met property requirements) because they were not thought to have the mature rational capacities necessary to function as citizens. Most important, these events also produced a seemingly contradictory shift in literary and educational expectations of children, which emphasized their ability to perceive the laws of God and man and to make choices about their allegiances. These two changes, and the gap between them, begin the story of children's imaginary citizenship.

Assumptions about children (their political status and capacities) have long figured into theories of power and authority. Patriarchy, a social system in which fathers exercise power over their children and other similarly subjected persons such as women and slaves, dates to the ancient world. But the sixteenth and seventeenth centuries gave rise to new attempts to theorize patriarchal power and to extend its reach beyond the family. These attempts can be said to begin with the Protestant reformation. While Protestant leaders challenged hierarchies in the established Catholic Church, they simultaneously strengthened hierarchies in the home and political sphere by putting new doctrinal emphasis on the Ten Commandments, especially the fifth commandment to "honor thy father and mother." Martin Luther, for instance, regularly used the fifth commandment to teach deference to all superiors.[35]

In seventeenth-century England, prior to and during the English Civil War, patriarchal authority became more explicitly associated with a political position. Supporters of the monarchy borrowed from ancient and religious understandings of this type of authority to justify state power, using childhood as a metaphor for all political subjects. Most famously, Sir Robert Filmer supported divine right in *Patriarcha* (1680) by claiming that the fifth commandment referred not just to parents, but also to all authorities, especially the king. Filmer argued that rulers were literal fathers in their succession from Adam, but this patriarchal power was less about being distinctly parental and more about being unquestionably authoritative. For instance, Filmer emphasized parents' right to kill their children, something that few parents were likely to do, but that kings might. Due to the rights of succession, it was even possible that a child could gain patriarchal power and become a father:

"By this means it comes to pass that many a child, by succeeding a king, hath the right of a father over many a greyheaded multitude."[36] Images of subjects as children did not signify a distinctively childlike position as much as a God-granted position of subjection that cut across age boundaries. Although Filmer made his case for patriarchal power by exploiting the widespread belief that children were naturally subjected, pointing out that even rival philosophers could not deny this natural fact, he extended this subjection to nearly all persons within English society.

Patriarchal theory thus created purposeful blurring between adults and children. There were few people who, in Filmer's eyes, would not have been understood as children in need of protection, instruction, or discipline. Even if one was a parent to someone, one was a child to someone else, with God as the ultimate Father. This lack of a stable boundary between childhood and adulthood did not happen because ideas about childhood did not exist in previous eras or because children were primarily understood as "miniature adults."[37] Rather, childhood was purposefully made an indeterminate category so that it could be used to justify political subjection for a larger number of people. At the beginning of this period, metaphors of childhood do not seem to have been unevenly applied to women, servants, the lower classes, or people of color but instead were applied to all subjects. Patriarchal ideas about childhood directly shaped English legal decisions requiring subjects' inviolable bonds of loyalty to a monarch. For instance, jurist Sir Edward Coke ruled that "people's allegiance to their monarchs was natural, because it was natural to be indebted to the one whose power protected them in their helpless infancy and childhood."[38]

Yet these attempts to broaden patriarchal authority and to attach it to royalist ideology ultimately destabilized this form of authority by placing it at the center of a political debate. Although few thinkers in this period were entirely against patriarchal authority in the home, parliamentarians and dissenters mounted their attacks on the absolute power of the monarchy by challenging patriarchal justifications for authority, such as the idea that protection compels obedience. Locke, for instance, argues that protection by a parent-like ruler does not make a man "a subject or member" of a "commonwealth."[39] Rather, "nothing can make any man so, but his actually entering into it by positive engagement, and express promise and consent."[40] While protection continued to factor into popular understandings of citizenship, notions of subjecthood based on protection and familial belonging were coming to be challenged by theories emphasizing consent to and participation in the government as the defining features of political membership.

With these challenges came new attempts to solidify the boundaries of childhood and to differentiate the rule of the nursery from the rule of the nation. To preserve some sense of patriarchal right outside of politics, opponents of monarchical power came to distinguish religious, familial, and political understandings of what it meant to be a child and to identify a clearer age-based notion of childhood from within a larger range of metaphorical childhoods. The most fervent of dissenters claimed that one could be a dutiful child to one's parents or to God, as the "absolute Soveraign," without necessarily being the dutiful subject of the king.[41]

Arguments against political forms of patriarchy seemed to deemphasize childhood as a relevant aspect of political identity, because the child was no longer an all-purpose category of subjecthood. However, these changes actually gave rise to a more intense focus on childhood than ever before, since the weakening of patriarchal power meant that children's loyalties were thought to be unsure and available for shaping. Gradually, patriarchal concerns about childhood as a metaphor for all readers, believers, and political subjects gave way to concerns about the child as a *specific* kind of reader, believer, and political subject. This shift may explain why this period is associated with the discovery of childhood even though childhood as a dependent and subjected state was clearly not a new idea (and in fact dates as least as far back as the fifth commandment). Rather than *inventing* childhood, seventeenth-century thinkers reconsidered the definition and boundaries of childhood, as part of a politically motivated transition away from subjecthood toward citizenship.

Scholars have disagreed about how this shift affected children themselves. As a legal historian, Brewer traces how the rise of political theories that established "experience and reason as requirements for the exercise of political power" led to decreased rights for children.[42] She has shown that prior to the seventeenth century, suffrage was usually based on property ownership rather than age, making it possible for individuals as young as twelve to vote. Some elite children even held political offices. Most obviously, a number of child monarchs sat on the English throne, including Henry VI, who became king at nine months old, but teenagers with inherited wealth were also regularly elected to parliament seats until a law limited this practice in 1696.[43] The fact that children could have some power within a system based on inherited rights was a major argument against monarchical rule for authors of the Revolution such as Paine. This is because the legal concept of children and their capacities was changing. Brewer writes, "Modern childhood is a by-product of the Age of Reason, which designated children as those without reason" and gave new rationales for children's exclusion.[44] Brewer's argument matches what many political theorists were claiming at the time. Posing theories of children's development, Locke declared that adult citizens were not children. Notably, though, childhood retained metaphorical flexibility even as it was being defined as a specific concept; women and slaves, for instance, were excluded from participatory citizenship and came to be compared to children.

But at the same time that childhood was used as a rationale for limiting civic freedoms, liberal-democratic theory claimed that all people had the right to independence from birth—a right that literary scholars such as Brown and Fliegelman maintain was necessarily extended to children. Recognizing that a new definition of children's political status was needed, Locke claimed that children's minds were "blank slates" and that they were "born free," even though they did not yet have the full ability to understand this freedom or the right to exercise it legally.[45] As Anna Mae Duane has observed, "the child of the revolutionary age" came to represent "a form of radical choice."[46] Brown and Fliegelman have examined the consequences of this shift by looking at a variety of literary texts, from *The New England Primer* (1687) to *Robinson Crusoe* (1719), arguing that these texts celebrate the limits of patriarchal power and encourage children to make their own political decisions. When combined with Brewer's insights, this critical history reveals a divergence between the historical-legal and the literary consequences of liberal-democratic theory—one deeming children irrational and incapable of action, the other depicting children's political actions, capacities, and responsibilities in an imaginary, literary realm.

For Brown, the shifting status of children was not a contradiction. She claims that literary and instructional texts attempt to reconcile children's natural freedom with their legal exclusion by educating children to become citizens in a future time, creating citizenship as a potentiality rather than an actual right from birth. Yet, as I trace in detail throughout this book, this postponed citizenship also produced a long period in which children's loyalties were unsure and their rights unrecognized: a gap, to paraphrase Locke, between the birth of freedom and the exercise of it. Elaborating on and reconsidering the work of Fliegelman and Brown, I show how children were understood in this interim not just as noncitizens trying to become citizens but also as imaginary citizens. Children's books depict children, for instance, making political decisions, forming their own social contracts, and consenting to be ruled. They also pose alternate understandings of citizenship as benevolence or affection toward one's fellow man. This imaginary citizenship can actually be said to arise in concert with the loss of actual political status that Brewer discusses, since children suddenly had to be included in ways that were different from other kinds of individuals.

The Political Rise of Children's Literature

While children's imagined civic activities sometimes transcended the page and shaped their actions in the public and private spheres, literary texts were a key medium through which their claims to citizenship were encouraged. Not coincidentally, a more fully developed literature for children, as well as a fuller imaginative literature about childhood, arose at the very moment that childhood was no longer consonant with other forms of subjecthood. For much of the seventeenth century (and for many years prior to that period), child readership was seen as an expansive category, not necessarily limited by age. Catechisms were addressed to "children in age and children in understanding." Though these particular texts focus on readers who are lacking in religious learning, the reigning patriarchal ideology of the period made it difficult to distinguish children from other subjects of God's power. In Protestant religious culture, for instance, all believers were in some sense "children in Christ," because they were dependent on God and they had limited knowledge of his Will. As Elisa New points out, the idea that Puritan children were understood as miniature adults is complicated by "works which also make adults nothing but outsize children."[47] To the extent that this dependence was willed by God, it was not considered problematic for aged individuals to be understood as children. As New argues, "the adult attains to the pinnacle of development when she at last knows what a pygmy she is."[48]

But these comparisons were becoming increasingly troublesome as the result of the political use of childhood as a symbol of subjection not only to God but also to the king.[49] In contrast to the religious texts addressed to "children in age and in understanding," John Bunyan's *Divine Emblems: or, Temporal Things Spiritualized* (1686) uses this trope, but expresses anxiety about the overlap between children and adults:

> The title page will shew if thou wilt look,
> Who are the proper subjects of this book.
> They're boys and girls, of all sorts and degrees,
> From those of age, to children on the knees.
> Thus comprehensive am I in my notions,
> They tempt me to it by their childish motions
> We now have boys with beards and girls that be
> Huge as old women, wanting gravity.[50]

Although Bunyan was responding to a general lack of seriousness among his readers, it is no coincidence that, as a member of the parliamentarian army, Bunyan saw these transgressions of the boundaries between adulthood and childhood as particularly unnatural and troubling.[51] Bunyan addresses this problem by educating "boys with beards" about how not to be childish (though he is also teaching his younger readers not to be childish as well, further complicating the boundary). It is perhaps because he attempts to solidify the boundary between adulthood and childhood that Bunyan's work is often considered the first children's poetry book, despite his inclusive inscription.

The rise of a more extensive literature dedicated specifically to children, which began around the time that Bunyan was writing, can be said to result from the need to differentiate "children in years" from other kinds of metaphorical children and to consider the specific problems raised by young people's political status, religious beliefs, and reading habits. Readers of the seventeenth and eighteenth centuries witnessed a dramatic increase in children's books and child-rearing texts, often written by the same figures that were calling for a new understanding of political authority. Locke, for instance, wrote a popular child-rearing treatise, *Some Thoughts Concerning Education* (1693), in which he argued that educators should create entertaining books designed especially for young children.[52]

Though adults and children have continued to share texts throughout the history of children's literature, more distinctions were made between books that understood *all* readers as metaphorical children and books that addressed young people as a distinct class of readers and assumed that children would navigate traditionally shared texts, such as the Bible, differently from adults. Precise ideas about children's capacities first appeared in religious texts. For instance, Benjamin Keach's dissenting Baptist catechism *Instructions for Children: or, The Child's & Youth's Delight* (1695), which was published widely in the colonies, begins not with the common claim that it was written for children "in years and understanding" but with the question, "Child, how old art thou?" and the answer, "I am told, Father, that I am between three and four years Old."[53] This text emphasizes children's lack of knowledge, supporting arguments that children must be excluded from political and religious membership until their understandings develop. Another section of Keach's catechism, addressed to a "youth" of age ten, has the child reflect, on being asked how much he knows about God, "I am a Child, and know but a little; I understand as a Child and think as a Child."[54] Yet the text also emphasizes children's capacity to know. Keach's three-year-old shows better knowledge than his ten-year-old "brother," complicating age-based notions of rational and religious capacity.

Following these religious texts, a number of little books appeared that were dedicated to young readers. Books for children were especially integral to the development of book culture in the new world, reflecting the interest early Americans had in political and religious challenges to patriarchal authority and their efforts to forge new ways of integrating children into society. Books for young people, such as catechisms and primers, gained a wider circulation than many other publications. Children's story books, such as James Janeway's and Cotton Mather's *A Token for Children* (first American edition 1700), were what David D. Hall calls "steady sellers" or widely circulated books that had a long shelf life among the reading public.[55] During and after the Revolution, the children's book market expanded with Isaiah Thomas's adaption of John Newbery's playbooks, such as *The History of Goody Two Shoes* (1765, first American edition 1775), and with educational texts such as Noah Webster's *American Spelling Book* (1800). The centrality of such works to the republic of letters suggests that they taught American readers how to read. It also allows the possibility that the foremost American reader was, quite literally as well as imaginatively, a child, a detail that makes the frequent metaphorical references to American citizens as children all the more striking. Claims about the importance of children's reading would come to figure centrally in the American revolt against monarchical privilege; Benjamin Rush, educator and signer of the Declaration of Independence, believed that teaching children to read was "favorable to liberty."[56]

Perhaps counterintuitively, given the general trend of separating adults' and children's books during this time, many early American literary works that were read by adults were also explicitly addressed to children, suggesting that the shape of the nation's imaginative literature in general derived from the problem of children's inclusion. Novels of the period, considered by many scholars to represent adult potentials for citizenship, were explicitly addressed to adolescent girls—Susanna Rowson's *Charlotte Temple* (1794) claims "dear girls" as its "true" audience and Catharine Maria Sedgwick's *Hope Leslie* (1827) refers to "misses in their teens.[57] Many early novels record lingering anxieties about the difficulties of distinguishing between children and adults, as well as the difficulties of telling the difference between imagination and reality.

As Goodrich's association of the reading public with the world of children suggests, the nation's literature came by the nineteenth century to be linked with child readers. While both American and English publishers had long sold children's versions of novels, including Samuel Richardson's *Clarissa* (1747) and Daniel Defoe's *Robinson Crusoe* (1719), the miniaturization of English texts did not seem to create the fear that English literature and its readers were "childlike" (despite Virginia Woolf's later tongue-in-cheek comment that *Middlemarch* was the only English novel for "grown-up people").[58] Instead, it was later American books such as James Fenimore Cooper's Leatherstocking Tales (1823–41), Washington Irving's *The Sketch Book of Geoffrey Crayon, Gent.* (1820), Maria Susan Cummins's *The Lamplighter* (1854), Susan Warner's *The Wide, Wide World* (1850), and Mark Twain's *The Adventures of Huckleberry Finn* (1884) that became lumped in with children's books. While *Charlotte Temple* and other early American novels record anxieties that the nation's infant status had spawned an infantile citizenship, a juvenile national literature, and an unsophisticated reading populace, the popularity of these later texts suggests that these anxieties gave way to a sense of acceptance that children and adults might often work from the same imaginary models—at least until the latter part of the century when, as Beverly Lyon Clark has argued, another backlash against children's literature occurred.[59] An 1853 review of *The Wide, Wide World*, for instance, proclaims that the text was first read by children, who only later initiated adult women's reading: "As far as we know the early history of *The Wide, Wide World*, it was, for some time, bought to be presented to nice little girls . . . Elder sisters were soon poring over the volumes, and it was very natural that mothers next should try the spell."[60]

Literary works were often shared between children and adults, suggesting that ideas about childhood significantly informed the nation that was created through language. The emerging legal rhetoric of citizenship emphasized the adult qualities of reason, rights, and property ownership. However, children represented other qualities that were central to the ways that citizens were understood, such as affection and patriotism. Thus, even though children and citizens were being pulled apart in the transition away from patriarchal subjecthood, one of the major arguments of *Imaginary Citizens* is that childhood and citizenship are nonetheless understood better when they are not seen as mutually exclusive categories. Metaphors and narratives associated with childhood still provided the imaginative foundations for the political identity of many citizens, even though citizens were not as often understood as equivalent to children in a patriarchal sense. Looking at literary texts that included children as imaginary citizens allows us to notice the ways that concepts and practices related to childhood continued to inform citizenship in general, despite the legal and historical changes that excluded children from official versions of citizenship.

Citizen-Subjects

One reason that childhood continued to shape American notions of citizenship so strongly was that, although emerging ideas of childhood worked to differentiate between the subject and the citizen, subjecthood and citizenship were not so easy to separate. While citizens were no longer commonly understood as patriarchal subjects in the sense of being the supposedly *literal* children of a monarchical ruler, they were identified with subjecthood of a different kind, especially in relation to language and law. This new form of subjecthood coincided historically with the emergence of the concept of "subjectivity," or the idea that individuals could freely and autonomously make decisions and govern themselves based on their perceptions and knowledge. In his essay, "Citizen-Subject" Étienne Balibar points out, "the moment at which Kant produces . . . the [thinking, perceiving] 'subject' is precisely that moment at which politics destroys the 'subject' of the prince, in order to replace him with the republican citizen."[61]

For Balibar, the seeming neatness of this historical shift masks a variety of tensions within citizenship that were created by ongoing frictions between subjecthood and subjectivity. Even though the citizen "is that 'nonsubject' who comes after the subject, and whose constitution and recognition put an end (in principle) to the subjection of the subject," the citizen was nonetheless understood as a legal, psychological, and transcendental subject, or what Balibar calls "the Citizen-Subject." While the citizen-subject is differentiated from a patriarchal subject by "his participation in the formation and application of the decision" to enter the social contract, he is nonetheless torn between being "the citizen who makes the law" and "a subject of the law."[62] Emerging ideas of the citizen's subjectivity made it possible to argue that he participates in his own governance. At the same time the problem of being subjected to an authority distanced from oneself remained, whether that authority was a king, a text, or a state supposedly based on the will of the people.

Children, in a legal sense, would not be considered citizen-subjects since they encounter no such tension: they are subject to following most laws but do not have the right to make them. If we take literally Locke's view of childhood as having no country, which was adopted by some early American jurists, they would not even be subjects of the nation, remaining only under the control of their parents. Nonetheless, in the imaginary realm of citizenship, children were often portrayed as the ideal citizen-subjects. As Balibar points out, the very idea that the legitimacy of the state is created by the consent of its people is dependent on philosophical imaginings about the natural status of "man," not just of the citizen: "[popular] sovereignty must be founded retroactively on . . . the inscription of equality in human nature as equality 'of birth.' "[63] Although Balibar notes that such universal equality is improbable due to social hierarchies, the concept of subjectivity on which citizenship depends reaches imaginatively back into childhood for its narrative of citizenship's beginnings and for its rationale for how citizens are able to carry out their most basic functioning. As Levander has also argued, the idea that equal political rights "inhere in the condition of being human and are . . . universal despite differences among individuals" makes the child "a point of origin" for the citizen.[64]

Balibar does not discuss children explicitly in his essay. However, his work implies that it is because of a fantasy of children's free and equal birth that citizens can be seen as capable of contracting and making laws as part of one sovereign body. Moving from theories of citizenship to practices, we might note that it is this more abstract or imaginative potential for citizenship *rather* than a legal one that must be the underpinning of social order in most democratic-republics, since most individuals do not explicitly consent to the social contract, possess equal legal rights to govern, or participate fully in creating new laws. In early America, many were not even legally allowed to vote, though they might have been considered citizens in other ways. Even so-called rational, equal, and consenting white male adult citizens have to face compromises on their liberties and limits on their participation, while simultaneously believing in their full sovereignty and freedom. Because of this, all citizenship begins to look something like imaginary citizenship; the citizen-subject is a subject who imagines himself a citizen.

In this way, *how* individuals are encouraged to imagine citizenship, beginning with the most basic elements of learning language, becomes a significant part of how citizenship is legitimized, understood, practiced, and lived. As Balibar mentions in another context, "Let us dispense right away with the antithesis . . . between the 'real' and the 'imaginary' community. *Every social community reproduced by the functioning of institutions is imaginary.* . . . But this comes down to accepting that, under certain conditions, *only* imaginary communities are real."[65] Some narratives of imaginary citizenship are based on an approximation of consent. For instance, Warner points out that in the "We the People" of the Constitution, readers are imagined as consenting and participating.[66] Similar scenes are approximated in literature for children, but these texts also reveal other narratives that are meant to reconcile the two halves of the individuals' citizen-subjecthood. For instance, as I argue more fully in chapter 2, children's affection for the nation and its laws often motivate and sometimes replace consent. In the words of Noah Webster, children were meant to "know and *love*" the law.[67] This affection inculcated in childhood was a crucial supplement to the social contract. Specifically, narratives related to children's affectionate citizenship shore up ideologies of citizenship as consensual and free of subjection, since imagining laws as affectionate makes it desirable (and also reasonable) to consent to them. In their quest to reconcile the ideal of consent with the reality of being governed by other people, Americans often chose to imagine the bond between *all* citizens and the state as an affectionate relationship, like a child for a parent.

Although imaginary ideas of citizenship sometimes yielded images that were similar to those of patriarchal subjecthood—for instance, it is hard to miss that the same nation that rejected "mother Britain" created a legacy of "founding fathers"— children's imaginary citizenship was not just a reiteration of patriarchal ideas. Affectionate citizenship was not about securing individuals' obedience to a parent-like ruler but rather about encouraging them to imagine that the law was a legitimate object of affection and obedience: a symbolic extension of the parent and also of the self and its collective, the people. The legacy of affectionate citizenship continues to appear in current political discourse that sees attachments to the nation as both obligatory and voluntary. As Berlant puts it, "The infantile citizen's ingenuousness frequently seems like a bad thing, a political subjectivity based on . . . default social membership . . . But the infantile citizen's faith in the nation, which is based on a belief in the state's commitment to representing the best interests of ordinary people, is also said to be what vitalizes a person's patriotic and practical attachment to the nation and to other citizens."[68] Though Berlant is rightly suspicious of how affection has contributed to the "death" of the citizen's critical function in the post-Reagan era, the cultural emphasis on children's affectionate attachments can be tied to a longer and more varied history of imaginary citizenship and first became important due to the very idea of the citizen's representation in government.

Unlike in patriarchal theory, where the king was portrayed as a literal parent through the mechanisms of succession, the republican state was not a literal instantiation of either parent or people and thus needed imaginary narratives for its creation and functioning. These imaginary narratives were promoted by what Louis Althusser calls "ideological state apparatuses" such as schools, as well as by children's books.[69] Citizen-subjecthood ultimately required that individuals become subjects of language, the representational quality of which was the means through which the state could present itself as representative of the people. Bunyan's project of differentiating children from adults, for instance, has the goal of making its readers "subjects of this book," rather than political subjects of a monarch. The process of teaching children to read offered early Americans a chance to practice the movements between the literal and the representative that were so central to the shift from subjecthood to citizenship.

These connections—through which language represented the nation, which in turn represented the people—were not straightforward or automatic. Rather, because they were dependent on imagination, they were frequently unstable, requiring continual work on the part of readers to recognize both types of representations as truly representative and consequently legitimate. It may indeed be misleading to see the law as an affectionate representation of one's own agency reflected back to oneself in abstract form, as eighteenth-century children were encouraged to do. However, the idea that authority should be affectionate also gave rise to objections when laws failed to meet this ideal. In the nineteenth century, images of children as affectionate citizens further helped Americans recast the nation as worthy of attachment despite growing economic inequalities and racial divisions. Literature, then, represented a future citizenry in which all Americans could imaginatively invest. Though these images were sentimental and ultimately relied on a future in which inequality could continue to exist, they also competed with other emerging forms of citizenship that more shamelessly privileged the welfare of the few over the many.

One important consequence of imaginary citizenship was that childlike subjection was not eradicated by the shift from patriarchal subjecthood to citizenship, but it is important to emphasize that the citizen's subjecthood, while still tied to childhood, did not necessarily render the citizen passive or powerless in the face of ideologies of citizenship. As Brook Thomas has pointed out, the idea that "citizens are ideological subjects" has been a favorite topic of cultural and literary critics.[70] Thomas observes that many of these arguments are based implicitly or explicitly on Althusser's claim that individuals are "always already" subjects of ideology from birth and that they are specifically "*interpellated as . . . (free) subject*[s]" (i.e. citizens) only "*in order that* [they] *shall (freely) accept* [their] *subjection.*"[71] Thomas disparages such studies, arguing that attempts to "expose . . . links between subjects and citizens" do not often account for different kinds of subjecthood or for how "citizens differ from other types of subjects."[72] As the above quotations suggest, Althusser rolls together at least three different kinds of subjects: those entrenched in imaginary narratives from childhood, those specifically interpellated as "free subjects," and those freely accepting their subjection. But the transition from patriarchal subjecthood to citizenship, which seeks to differentiate the positions that various kinds of individuals might have under the law, denies the ease of such equations. To Thomas, the emergence of a concept of citizenship required that citizen-subjects be distinguished from other non-free subjects such as slaves, opening up "new possibilities for subjectivity."[73] Specifically, citizen-subjects were understood as participating in the making of law and as helping to construct the imaginary apparatuses related to national identity. While this might mean that citizens freely accept their subjection, citizen-subjecthood does not imply unthinking hesitation in response to a hail, but a conscious (if not always rational) decision to turn around and a sense that the hail is legitimate.

Despite the importance of narratives of children's "free birth" in the emergence of a citizen-subject, not all subjects were thought to be instantly capable of conscious participation. Though children may "always already" be subjects in the sense that social customs and narratives frame their experiences, they are not immediately recognized as *free* subjects, capable of choosing their political loyalties. Although many narratives of citizenship begin with birth, the fundamental importance of consent to notions of citizenship suggests that it required more than just birth for children to be hailed as citizen-subjects. Children had to be understood as taking part in the process of accepting social narratives. Their participation had to be seen as at least partially volitional, even when it could not be seen as fully rational, informed, or free. The ways that children were further taught and persuaded through imaginative narratives to accept ideologies of nationhood and citizenship were fundamental to the emergence of citizen-subjecthood as a distinct form of political identity.

Studying Child Readers

This book inevitably focuses to a large degree on how children's books addressed *implied* readers and represented ideal (or not so ideal) readers within their pages. I have also used archival materials to gauge child readers' responses when possible to show the ways that child readers interacted with these representations. Though all ways of reaching historical readers are mediated and any representation of a historical reader involves some imaginative leaps, I agree with the perspective recently expressed by Marah Gubar, who has argued that it is worth attempting to "find out as much as [we] can" about child responses even though we must "openly admit the impossibility of attaining anything close to complete, decisive knowledge."[74]

M. O. Grenby has claimed that there are reasons to see actual children's reading as different from the usual eighteenth-century imagination of reading as citizenship in the "republic of letters," because children are not usually independent consumers of printed materials and are less prepared to understand texts rationally. He writes, "Children were certainly deeply affected by their books, but not always in ways that can be straightforwardly ascribed to the persuasive powers of comprehended text."[75] More work is needed in this area, especially in the United States, as Grenby focuses on British materials. Still, as Grenby suggests, no single alternative model of reading can account for the ways that "childhood varied not only according to class, gender, location, religion, and across time, but also from family to family."[76] When it comes to actual readers, one must focus on "a multiplicity of individual experiences," contextualized within other existing data.[77]

What scant evidence we have from early American child readers suggests that children did claim to be participants in the national community—though in ways that are difficult to schematize or even fully catalogue. As just one example, readers from all over the nation participated in the correspondence section of *Robert Merry's Museum,* a readerly community that Pat Pfieger has described as "essentially democratic."[78] The child correspondents, many of whom wrote in several times, saw themselves as representatives of various parts of the country. When it was discovered that several readers bore the same name as one of the regular contributors, William H. Coleman, two Colemans were designated "North" and "South" and a discussion ensued about whether the Colemans were sufficiently representing their constituents. A reader from Springfield, Illinois, ponders, "Where is our Willie H. Coleman, West? We have no representative in the fight" and another proposes that they traverse Illinois to "electioneer" for the *Museum*.[79] In addition to indicating their awareness of the political process, readers regularly discussed national politics and events. The original William Hoyt Coleman, who started writing to the journal when he was eleven years old and who was dubbed Coleman North, describes his participation in the activities of the Fourth of July: "C-r-r-r-a-a-c-k!—fizz!—pop!—bang!—'The day we celebrate'—bang!—'our nation's birthday'—fiz-z-z!—whis-s-s-h! —'Bunker Hill and the spirit of '76'—bang!—crack!—'the Star-Spangled Banner and long may it wave'—pop!—fizz!"[80] In its image of a boy distracted from the speechifying by his excitement at the sounds of the firecrackers, this passage demonstrates that citizenship was among many topics that were of interest to child readers and suggests that their attention to texts and ideas related to citizenship was more or less intensive depending on what else was going on around them.

The child diary writers whom I cite in the individual chapters discussed their reading and national identifications often in sketchy ways against a backdrop of other more common and constant topics, such as death, work, school, and the weather, and in conjunction with more exciting themes, such as holidays and love interests. Some children, like young apprentice David Clapp, weighed in heavily on the importance of reading and thinking about politics; in his journal he often commented on holidays such as Washington's birthday and even wrote an essay about how newspapers prevent "Monarchy, Tyranny, and usurpation."[81] Others were not so interested. Ten-year-old Edmund Quincy Sewell conversely remarks, "The last *Messenger* was very dry, nothing but politics and such stuff."[82] Even so, all of these examples show children's awareness of political themes and conventions.

The correspondents' attempts to assign different William H. Colemans to represent political territories also illustrate child readers' careful attention to issues surrounding political representation. Coleman North was frequently chastised by other correspondents for taking up too much space in the forum while other readers' letters were consigned to the trash basket. For instance, a girl named Lina queries whether the chat is a "public institution" and whether Coleman is a "real live person," suggesting that if he is, she would like to join in sometime.[83] It is true that even if the chat could somehow represent all readers, it would only be an imaginative government, since none of the child readers could yet vote and be represented in Congress. Indeed, Hatchett wrote to Coleman South that he was "getting rather too near to politics" in suggesting that Texas be included as a state and that "if you go much further, we shall have to build a platform" when the *Museum* "should be enough, without any other."[84] Yet Lina's attention to whether Coleman and the others were "real live persons" suggests that child readers could also be savvy about trying to investigate what was only imaginary and what was real.

Though the question of whether Coleman or even Lina was a "real life person" is a tricky one also for scholars, since the correspondence section no doubt involved some degree of performance, it is nonetheless important to think about how actual readers responded to the images of citizenship that were circulating and participated in its imagination. Imaginary depictions of citizenship could promote political fantasies—for instance, of a truly representative government. However, I would like to think that imaginary citizenship is not just about false legitimization of a state that did not and could not represent all of its members (though this was certainly part of its appeal). While the idea that imagination might lead individuals into a foolish belief in untruths became a central concern in the modern era, imagination does not equal delusion.[85] Imaginary citizenship could also provide the basis for a community (such as that created by the correspondents of *Merry's Museum*) that could try to fill the gaps left open by the limitations of the social contract and its realization in government. Imaginary citizenship is what happens when political ideals come up against their practical limitations, causing crises of legitimization. But, rather than settling on one way of preserving these ideals indefinitely, authors and readers were inventive and resourceful in seeking new ways to merge the ideal and actual. As long as some individuals are excluded from making the laws, imagination brings up the possibility of identifying a more just relationship between citizens and government. Imaginary citizenship is both the marker of a government that cannot be fully legitimated by the consent of all and the drive that allows citizens to continually reconsider its legitimacy.

Recognizing that children consciously negotiated specific ideas of citizen-subjecthood is also important because anxieties represented by the child as a holdover of patriarchal subjecthood have shaped critical assessments of the politics of childhood, past and present. The need to distinguish citizens from childlike subjects has often resulted in children's exclusion from important works on citizenship. For instance, scholarship on early American citizenship has long been influenced by Davidson's claim that novels of the time extended political agency to readers who were not included in the original contract.[86] Though the child reader is included in this claim because many of the texts Davidson studies were explicitly dedicated to the "youth of Columbia," she does not discuss children at length, perhaps because children do not easily fit into her paradigms of political agency and dissidence.

Scholars who have studied children's relationship to citizenship have tended to perpetuate some of the same critical blind spots that led to children's exclusion from earlier studies, evading the problems that children bring to citizenship by misleadingly de-infantilizing or, in some cases, over-infantilizing the child. For instance, Brown, Mintz, and Fliegelman generally argue for children's political importance using an idealistic adult model of democratic citizenship, attributing to them the same capacities for independence, subversion, and rebellion that Davidson grants to adult novel readers. Lorinda B. Cohoon's work on boys' "serialized citizenships" from 1840 to 1911, which helpfully focuses on the diverse potentials of children's citizenship, does not deal with the fundamental problem of how and whether children are citizens, largely assuming that they were uncomplicatedly recognized as such (or, at least, that boys were).[87] Other scholarship has overplayed the incompatibility of childhood with meaningful citizenship. Berlant, as an example, has usefully criticized the ways that the concept of an infantile citizen has been used to promote reactionary agendas and to "erase the complexities of aggregate national memory."[88] However, she does not often entertain the possibility that child readers themselves might signify a group with their own complex imaginative identifications, conflicting loyalties, or unrealized claims to rights. Rather, for her, the prevalent images of children as citizens almost always signify the removal of agency and authenticity from citizenship, resulting in infantilized subjects who are enmeshed in an imaginary world removed from real political awareness.

In her recent work in childhood studies, Karen Sánchez-Eppler has challenged both critical tendencies, claiming that children's activities, such as play, had complex and meaningful social impact despite children's dependent status and their relegation to imaginary rather than legally recognized forms of citizenship.[89] By tracing the specific potentials represented by children's imaginary citizenship over time, my work attempts to further dislodge the deceptive binary that has arisen in American studies between an autonomous public adult citizen and an infantilized private subject who inevitably fails to engage in real political action. These extremes fail to capture how a large portion of the people experienced citizenship throughout U.S. history and ultimately present an unrealistic standard for political participation. Children's citizenship is neither a subversive consequence of democratic theory nor an aberration from it. Rather, children's imaginary citizenship helped create the idea of a responsible, consenting citizen, while also highlighting the limitations of this concept and the need for supplementary narratives about citizenship.

In the chapters that follow, I look at how childhood informed American citizenship from its colonial beginnings to its first constitutional definition in 1868. Chapter 1 shows how colonial struggles over children's church membership and their attendant political status gave rise to a divergence between the legal and literary notions of belonging that would come to shape American ideas of citizenship. Due to the

Protestant emphasis on religious knowledge as a precondition for conversion, children were increasingly excluded from full church membership and, consequently, from political rights. Yet children's books made a case for children's capacities. One of the most popular literary genres of the time, the child conversion narrative, depicted young children adopting religious beliefs independently of their parents. Religious leaders such as Cotton Mather and Jonathan Edwards also encouraged children to make choices about their loyalties, often through reading. By relocating children's modes of belonging in the realm of the imagination, colonial New Englanders began to construct the basis for children's imaginary citizenship, though their reliance on patriarchal theories of language kept them from fully recognizing the potentially radical effects of this shift.

Chapter 2 examines children's ambiguous status in relation to Lockean social contract theory and traces the ways that they were incorporated into the early nation as imaginary citizens. Although Fliegelman, Brown, and Mintz have convincingly argued that the revolutionary fervor involved children as well as adults, young people were not granted participation rights in the new republic. This gap between the rhetoric of children's freedom and the reality of their social status is a consequence of Locke's claim that "we are born free, as we are born Rational . . . not that we have actually the Exercise of either."[90] Though scholars of Locke have emphasized *either* his claims about the child's free birth *or* his denial of freedom until adulthood, the interim period between freedom and the exercise of it, which he addresses in his pedagogical works, made children's education a crucial supplement to the social contract. To explain why rational adult citizens ultimately consent to restrictions on their natural freedom, Locke relies not only on reason and property but also on affection and learning inculcated in childhood, which soften the fact of subjection and give it the feeling of freedom. The notion that children should "*love* their laws" became particularly important in the United States because the notion of popular rule meant that citizens needed to see the law as personal and familiar, even if they had not participated directly in the social contract. Imported children's books featuring affectionate governess characters, such as *The History of Little Goody Two Shoes* (1765) and Sarah Fielding's *The Governess* (1749), helped Americans to realize this vision of an affectionate republic by prompting children to transfer their affections from their parents to representative figures and finally to the abstractions of nation and law. Building on these narratives by narrating the process by which children's *own* authority becomes textual, Hannah Webster Foster's American school story *The Boarding School* (1798) further reinforces the imagined links between the personal and political by training children to recognize laws as the embodiments of their own opinions and desires—a lesson that was crucial in a democratic republic.

As the eighteenth century came to a close, Americans became preoccupied with delineating citizenship's limits. In the shadow of the French Terror and concerns about similar unrest at home, the Federalist government feared that children and other imaginary citizens might misread the meanings of liberty and equality, letting their emotions be carried away with unrealistic fantasies of freedom. In chapter 3, I argue that many early American novels highlight children's deficiencies as citizens, representing attempts to foreclose on the subversive potentials of children's imaginary citizenship and to reestablish citizenship as a rational adult activity. Young people who offer unsanctioned readings of ideas like equality and independence are often portrayed in novels as bad, or naïvely impressionable, readers, whose vulnerability to narrative seduction makes them equally amenable to rebellious plots and excessive subjugation. In order to eradicate this potential for childish citizenship, novels by William Hill Brown, Hannah Webster Foster, and Tabitha Gilman Tenney attempt (and record their own failure) to reassert the boundary between childhood and adulthood and to narrate a "coming of age" for their characters and readers. This attempt to make imaginary citizens grow up was complicated by a competing cultural desire for the citizen's perpetual, childlike subjection, which found expression in the novel's motifs of dead babies and childlike adults, as well as in the novel's status as reading material for children. The sketch, as a non-novelistic form explored by Washington Irving in *The Sketch Book of Geoffrey Crayon, Gent.* (1819), parodies the bad reader narrative and openly ventures skepticism about the American citizen's adulthood.

Chapter 4 addresses the shift in American understandings of citizenship that accompanied the rapid expansion of capitalism in the nineteenth century. While early republicans encouraged citizens to sacrifice their interests for the good of the commonwealth, nineteenth-century Americans sought a political ideology in which individuals could profit from the social compact. Profit incentives quickly complicated the notion that citizenship must be based on rational independence. During the financial panics of 1819 and 1837, the public witnessed the ways in which economic participation threatened to reduce anyone to the status of dependent child. Since most individuals could not maintain full rationality or independence in the volatile world of the market, Americans often needed to return to models of imaginary citizenship as they integrated capitalist incentives with political participation. As one result of this shift, children's imaginary citizenship became less publicly differentiated from adult political participation and was held up as a sentimental ideal of citizenship. Children's books of the period provided a fantasy of economic citizenship in which the multiple interests of dependent citizens could be combined to create social returns for all, even in the face of growing class disparities.

The vision of an affectionate republic of imaginary child citizens went a long way toward reconciling political ideals with the limits of American independence and equality, but it became increasingly dissatisfying as the nation contended with the inequalities associated with slavery. Ultimately a more inclusive notion of citizenship was needed to resolve the gap between imaginary citizenship and legally recognized political rights. My study ends with the Fourteenth Amendment, which declared that "all persons born or naturalized in the United States . . . are citizens of the United States and of the State wherein they reside." Though the law was designed to include former slaves after the Civil War, its language designates childhood as the entry point through which most non-immigrant people would become citizens. The association between children and slaves was not new: in the "patriarchal institution" of slavery, slaveholders made specific use of the concept of children's non-citizenship—and their imaginary citizenship—to rationalize restrictions on slaves' liberties. The Fourteenth Amendment contests these narratives by building on an alternative history of children's natural citizenship, including not only remnants of English common law but also a series of more radical visions of children's citizenship by thinkers such as Jean-Jacques Rousseau and Ralph Waldo Emerson. To make nature capable of creating and sustaining citizens, these thinkers looked to the medieval tradition of the "book of nature," which saw the physical world as legible to humans and especially children. By elaborating this vision of nature as a language, both Rousseau and Emerson tried to imagine a universal citizenship that was free of abstract words and artificial constraints and revealed the difficulties of separating natural citizenship from imaginary citizenship. The problem of slavery brought natural arguments for citizenship to national attention, resulting in the Fourteenth Amendment's declaration of the citizenship of all through the citizenship of children. Yet the ties between natural and imaginary citizenship have meant that the amendment has failed to fully settle the problems related to children's citizenship.

In the conclusion, I argue that problems surrounding children's political power have continued to generate political conflicts, such as the recent outcry over "anchor babies." Despite the lip service these debates pay to children's citizenship, the seeming finality of the amendment has actually deflected away from inquiries into the real meaning of its declaration of children's citizenship—specifically, what it means to declare the citizenship of a class of people who do not and probably cannot have full political rights. The fact that the United States is one of only two countries in the world that has signed, but not ratified, the 1989 Convention on the Rights of the Child suggests our deep cultural avoidance of this issue. The rights of children have ultimately become a much more live issue on the global stage than they were

in the infant nation, but even the Convention's comprehensive elaboration of children's rights does not explicitly discuss children's active citizenship, though it does
discuss their right to "acquire a nationality" and many other rights that parallel
citizenship such as the right to free expression and the right to assemble. All of these
circumstances suggest that the issue of children's citizenship is not easily resolved.
Nonetheless, childhood and imagination are concepts that are, by their very definitions, open-ended, and it is perhaps only by having a clear picture of how ideas of
citizenship have developed in relation to these concepts that we can begin to think
about this issue in more detail.

Throughout the book, I focus less on radical possibilities than on how children's
imaginary citizenship functioned in early America to underwrite and supplement the
concepts of rational, participatory, and consenting citizenship that often excluded
them by creating imaginary narratives of equality, free birth, natural citizenship, and
affectionate subjection. Nonetheless, one potential outcome of my historical work
might be to consider what would happen if children's citizenship was taken at face
value and embraced as a means for positing alternative models of both imaginary
and even legal citizenship. As the history of the transition from subjecthood to citizenship shows, children's supposed incompetence as participating citizens is socially
produced, not innate. In fact, children have the potential to raise more imaginative
possibilities regarding the future of politics than adults can offer since, as current
philosophers such as Alison Gopnik have shown, children are actually not irrational
as early developmental theorists claimed.[91] Rather, their brains offer more possibilities for imagining the world than adults' do. Furthermore, so-called adult consent is
often motivated by the same feelings of affection and dependence that supposedly
disqualify children from the legally recognized rights of citizenship.

While the consequences of the Fourteenth Amendment for children have been
mixed at best, the notion of children's imaginary citizenship, in that case, arguably helped change the law. Consequently, citizenship actually expanded to include
people who were formerly excluded, even though the meaning of this inclusion
via childhood has not been fully elaborated. Especially following the Fourteenth
Amendment, it makes even less sense to try and preserve a false sense of separation between children and citizens, since the official definition of citizenship now
explicitly assigns children a nationality, even though their rights do not equal those
of adults. If children are now to some extent legal, not just imaginary, citizens, as
the Fourteenth Amendment claims they are, it behooves us to think about how they
might be recognized and respected as such. For instance, should the gap between
legal and imagined versions of children's citizenship be further narrowed? What
might children's citizenship add to the current practice of that right?

Though consent, equality, independence, and reason are certainly important concepts related to citizenship, the history of children's imaginary citizenship especially prompts us to confront the limits of these ideas and to think about what might be required from active citizenship in addition to rational adult consent and independence. Feminist critics and advocates of children's rights have both contended that citizenship does not have to require an "illusory self-sufficiency" and that this illusion has more often been a source of unfair exclusion than the actual empowerment of citizens.[92] Annette C. Baier, for instance, offers an alternative model of citizenship based on an ethics of care and trust, claiming that being in a relationship that is not a social contract and not chosen does not necessarily meant that it is coercive, even though it may have the danger of being so.[93] Baier returns to a familial model of political relations, though it is best understood as a parental rather than a patriarchal one, noting that "the unequal infant does not choose its place in a family or nation, nor is it treated as free to do what it likes until some association is freely entered into." She contends that if we reconsider parental responsibility as a viable model for political relationships, "Contract soon ceases to seem the paradigm source of moral obligation . . . and justice as a virtue of social institutions [seems only as important as] the virtue, whatever its name, that ensures that the members of each new generation are made appropriately welcome and prepared for their adult lives."[94] While fictions of government based on the ideal of rational consenting adults have their use, recognizing that they have always required supplemental narratives might help us figure out to do when these narratives and we, those adults, come up short.

CHAPTER I

Youth as a Time of Choice

Children's Reading in Colonial New England

[A] young Dove is as compleat a Dove as an old one, tho' it be not
so large, nor has so many Feathers.

Solomon Williams, 1751

Thoughts about children's political identity in England and colonial America, especially in New England, were closely tied to changing notions of when religious belonging and church membership were thought to begin, since these were considered prerequisites to political participation. As patriarchal metaphors of subjects as children were being contested, thinkers of the period struggled with an abundance of new questions regarding children's religious and community membership. Since religious beliefs and political loyalties were no longer considered to be inherited, were children able to be church members or political subjects in their own right? How could they become so, if they were not obligated to follow their parents' choices? Would the current generation of children choose to continue existing traditions? As a result of these uncertainties, parents and educators expressed anxiety about children. The prevalent concern with infant damnation, perhaps most poignantly rendered in Jonathan Edwards's description of children as "young vipers," does not express indifference or hatred of children but rather a newfound belief in children's importance and uncertainty about their loyalties.[1]

Colonists devised a series of compromises regarding children's capacities, which gave rise to a divergence between legal and literary notions of citizenship. In the years 1641 and 1642 respectively, Massachusetts adopted *both* the first law (in England or the Americas) barring those under twenty-one from being elected to office *and* a literacy law requiring that children learn to read the Bible and recite the catechism.[2] The literacy law also declared that children must learn to read the "capital lawes" (those common to the Bible and the state), so that they could follow them, a major shift from the idea that obedience was required for all individuals simply by being child-subjects. These laws show the double attitude toward children occasioned by the shift from subjecthood to citizenship: in one sense, children were excluded from the political sphere because they were thought not to possess mature reason, but in another, they were included in a widespread social move toward making *the people* interpreters of the law rather than the king or the priests.

Though this greater emphasis on children's reading initially came from the Protestant belief that there should be no mediation between the individual believer and God, it also had political consequences in that individuals were thought to be bound by their direct consent to written laws, rather than a monarch. Children's ability to read was supposed to prepare them to participate on reaching the legal age, but the literacy law also had the effect of complicating the age restrictions on political participation by encouraging children's immediate civic and religious awareness through reading. There is evidence that literacy in seventeenth-century America was fairly high as a result of these laws. Kenneth Lockridge estimates that about half of the men and one-quarter of the women could read in the mid-seventeenth century, while other scholars have even argued that Lockridge's figures are low because he relies on signatures from wills to determine literacy.[3] E. Jennifer Monaghan notes that in 1668 officials in Beverly, Massachusetts, said they could not find any child over age nine who could not read. The political attention given to children's ability to read, while perhaps hyperbolic, suggests that the public was intensely concerned with their ability to comprehend, not just blindly follow, the law.

Children's political status was further complicated in Puritan New England by tensions between patriarchal traditions and Puritan doctrine. According to patriarchal theory, children inherited the beliefs and allegiances of their parents, but many Protestants were coming to believe that church membership was an individual commitment that could not be determined at birth.[4] This change was tied to the idea of a covenant of grace. This doctrine stated that God was responsible for the decision of whether an individual would be saved, but the covenant was also a contract. Recognizing one's status as "elect," which was a prerequisite for membership in most New England churches, required the ability to rationally understand and contract to God's covenant and, for this, individuals needed to know how to read God's word.

This doctrine conflicted with the longstanding practice of infant baptism, which implied that children became members through the salvation of their parents. Unable to fully break with this tradition, New Englanders debated when church membership began and whether baptism could be extended to the children of nonmembers, who could not claim salvation by inheritance or consent. These tensions led to the Halfway Covenant (1657–62). This controversial revision of Puritan doctrine held that children could be half-members of the church, which gave them the rights to partake in baptism and own property but not to take communion or vote on church or civic matters. They would be promoted to full membership only when they reached age fourteen and could testify to their conversion.

The Halfway Covenant had direct political consequences, since civic rights were limited to church members. It also corresponded to debates about who could act politically. Brewer explains, "The interwoven church and state . . . made the religious debates over church membership resonate in the debates over civil membership and authority."[5] Brewer argues that the Halfway Covenant reflected widespread attempts to differentiate children and adults by declaring children's reason to be immature.[6] Yet it did not exclude children entirely and instead positioned them as partial, nonvoting members.[7] The Halfway Covenant thus introduced the question of what a member of society who did not have full rights might look like. Over the course of the seventeenth and eighteenth centuries, especially during the Great Awakening, questions related to children's church membership remained in debate, and various arguments were made for how children might participate in religious matters even without full reason.

Literary texts of the period often went further than the law in imaginatively including children, recognizing their capacities for elective belonging outside of legal definitions of community membership. Although most church leaders did not believe that children were capable of full church standing, one of the most popular literary genres of the time, the child conversion narrative, contested the idea that children could not understand religion by depicting children converting independently of their parents. Many primers and catechisms similarly emphasized children's religious capacities, even as they addressed their perceived deficiencies. A poem at the end of the *New England Primer* proclaims that "God will lend a gracious Ear / To what a Child can say."[8] A number of religious authors encouraged children to read independently. Cotton Mather promoted children's reading by writing and distributing an enormous array of printed tracts and encouraging even the most unpracticed readers to read them alone. During the Great Awakening, children were encouraged to conduct their own religious meetings, a practice that led critics of the revivalist movement to complain that children were given too much autonomy as believers and as readers.

Children's religious reading had political implications. As Brewer explains, debates about religious comprehension extended to political inclusion, in that the "confidence in the ability to interpret the Bible extended to the ability to understand political principles."[9] Just as children were losing rights, efforts to encourage children's reading pushed against these restrictions by suggesting that children could indeed understand religion and politics. Yet these arguments rarely sought to regain rights for children. By relegating children's religious and political belonging to the realm of the imagination, colonial Americans began to form the basis for children's imaginary citizenship through reading. Since children were increasingly excluded (or at least half-excluded) from official forms of political and church membership, children's belonging came to be dependent partially on reading. Sermons, conversion narratives, and other texts asked their readers to engage in imaginative practices, which supplemented and even sometimes replaced their direct participation and contact with religious authorities. To further encourage young people to imaginatively identify as part of a religious community, the texts present fictionalized stories of children engaging in secret religious activities, creating a fantasy that individuals who are not officially recognized as members are nonetheless invested in perpetuating existing customs.

These imaginary relationships resemble those that were later needed to form the nation, which extended national identity to those who were not granted legal rights. While God's flock was limited by worldly concerns (who had the reason necessary to understand religion) and spiritual ones (who was actually saved by divine grace), the imaginative boundaries of his kingdom were extended to a much larger group: those who could imagine that they were saved. In Puritan New England, imaginary membership efforts focused on children because adults were assumed to have already passed through this imaginary stage and to have actualized their membership through election in the church. Adults also would have moved on to participating in local decision making, because those with full church membership could vote. As the country grew and direct participation in government was not always possible, imaginary membership became important for adults as well as children. Children's religious identification was one model that Americans could draw on for understanding how belonging could work in the realm of the imaginary, as well as in the realm of the legal or actual.

Still, as we shall see in this chapter, imaginary citizenship was not yet fully developed in colonial America—and not only because citizenship still had not replaced religious belonging as the dominant way that colonists understood their community. Prominent thinkers of the period, particularly Cotton Mather, did not totally distinguish new forms of religious belonging from older forms of subjecthood. While Mather challenged a strict patriarchal hierarchy by focusing on children as distinct believers capable of having their own relationship with God and his word, he nonetheless viewed language and its interpretation as largely controlled by patriarchal authority figures. In doing so, he failed to anticipate the radical consequences of imaginary membership. Independent reading opens up the interpretation of texts to common people, who must then *choose* to identify with the narratives with which they are presented. While Mather is careful to present children's reading as unambiguously pious activity in his own narratives about children, unconventional applications of religious language began to appear in similar narratives that parents wrote about their children, demonstrating the destabilization of traditional authorities.

The events of the Great Awakening, beginning with the wave of conversions in Northampton under the leadership of Reverend Jonathan Edwards, further destabilized patriarchal authority and gave rise to heated debates about children's status. Because Edwards initially linked religious belonging to emotional display rather than rational understanding, children and youths became central figures in the events of the Awakening. Later, after other ministers protested that children lacked the mature reason that was needed to be authentically religious, Edwards reacted by limiting communion and declaring scriptural reading an adult activity. Yet emotional and imaginative claims to belonging persisted, as did claims for children's autonomy, ultimately causing Edwards to be removed from his own church. While the historical argument that the Awakening contributed to the Revolution is likely overstated, I argue that the Awakening's model of a kind of community membership that transcended reason and rights was reconfigured into an alternative model of citizenship, existing alongside official understandings of its being a rational activity for privileged adult men.

Father Tongue

In addition to requiring new theories of childhood, the shift from subjecthood to citizenship involved new theories of language and reading—but these new ideas were slow to emerge. During the Reformation, one of the first objectives was to print the Bible in vernacular languages, which reformers argued was a divine process ordained by God to spread religion to the masses. But although Protestantism attempted to wrest the control of language away from the hierarchical structures of the Catholic Church, leaders quickly backed away from a democratic idea of interpretation and attempted to maintain patriarchal control of texts. Although Martin Luther initially "insist[ed] that children should receive daily lessons in the New Testament, so that they could become familiar with all its books by the age of nine or ten," he later made arguments for tighter church control over access to the Bible and argued that it was a "dead letter" if not transmitted by preaching.[10] As Jean-François Gilmont has concluded, "reformers were not interested in inviting the faithful to discover new messages, but rather in guaranteeing the stability of an elementary Christian doctrine."[11]

In line with these views, much of children's contact with language still happened within patriarchal traditions, which assumed that language was best controlled by fathers, whether of the church or family. The most common form of children's reading was drilling in the catechism, a practice that was initially done by clergymen.[12] Catechizing sessions emphasized the Ten Commandments, especially the fifth commandment demanding children's deference to parental authorities on all matters, including the interpretation of texts.

Beginning in the mid- to late-seventeenth century, catechizing became even more strongly connected to patriarchal political theory. Patriarchal theorists were well aware that controlling language was an important part of supporting monarchical power. Sir Robert Filmer's argument for divine right in *Patriarcha* is based not just on a theory of government but also of language. For him, the two were connected by God's division of his people into separate nations at the tower of Babel. To lend patriarchal support for the monarchy, Filmer insisted that the fatherly prerogative descended directly from the first patriarch, Adam, to the current ruler. It was thus important for him to claim that patriarchy survived the division of the world into separate nations and languages. He explains therefore "that even in the confusion God was careful to preserve the fatherly authority by distributing the diversity of languages according to the diversity of families."[13] He thereby aligns control over "families," "tongues," and "nations," under the rule of fathers and, ultimately, the king.

The patriarchal control over language was important to Filmer because he wanted to claim that the laws, as language given to the people, were not independent of the king whose will was represented by those laws: "the people have the law as a familiar admonisher and interpreter of the king's pleasure which being published throughout the kingdom doth represent the presence and majesty of the king." He points out that the *Magna Carta* limiting the power of the king "had only the form of the king's letters-patents . . . testifying those great liberties to be the sole act and bounty of the king."[14] The language of the law, he argues, cannot be separated from the royal ruler.

Filmer implies that patriarchs are the only persons who may exercise authority through language, but reflecting Protestant ideas, he also suggests that common readers can trace the king's authority in both the law and the Bible. Filmer's theory of hermeneutics emphasizes the literal meaning of the Bible over the interpretation of priests. He mocks those who are arguing for man's natural freedom as "papists" and as practicing "school divinity." This comment is significant in that the church traditions taught in medieval divinity schools would have taught allegorical interpretations of the Bible, which Protestants saw as misguided. Though Filmer's argument that Adam's power had been passed down to the current rulers seems equally dubious, he insists that he is only taking the "literal sense of the text," while accusing his opponents of "strain[ing]" verses about royal power "to signify the laws of the land, or else to mean the highest power."[15] In other words, Filmer claims that the literal sense is patriarchal. Readers were not barred from interpreting the Bible and laws, but they were to remember that patriarchal rulers determined the meanings of these texts. Metaphorically speaking, readers, like subjects, were children.

Patriarchal modes of reading were enforced in England through the expansion of rituals surrounding the catechism. As Brewer writes, "The Reformation in England introduced a national program of religious instruction . . . [and] formed one of the first conscious ways by which children learned norms of obedience to authority."[16] Increasingly, catechizing happened in multiple public and semipublic spaces, including schools and households, establishing parallels among parental, religious, and civic "fathers." Reciting the catechism was understood as a way for subjects to perform their acceptance of their place in this patriarchal web of authority. Brewer cites the standard catechism from the Anglican prayer book of 1549, in which readers promise "to love, honour, and succor my father and mother. To honour and obey the kyng and his ministers. To submitte my selfe to all my governours, teachers, spirituall pastours and maisters. To ordre my selfe lowly and reverentelye to all my betters."[17] Catechizing allowed ministers, teachers, governors, and parents to work as a multilateral force for stabilizing interpretation, keeping any one part of the chain of authorities from deviating from the orthodox meanings. This ritual connected the church to the state. The 1642 law in Massachusetts gave selectmen, as well as ministers, the power to catechize.

Printed texts were supposed to reinforce the chain of authority as well. The best-known colonial children's book, *The New England Primer*, linked the act of reading with obedience to patriarchal authorities. The famous alphabetic couplet from the *Primer*, "In Adam's Fall / We Sinned All," prefaces the child's learning of literacy with patriarchal claims regarding language. By associating the first letter, *A*, with the first patriarch, the *Primer* suggests that language is under the control of fathers.[18] Since, in Filmer's view, Adam was the source not only of sin but also of subjection, reading was understood as an act of accepting this subjection, seeing it as a foundational part of using language. The *Primer* also promoted patriarchal control of reading through its frontispieces. A frontispiece from as late as 1790 shows two children kneeling first to God, and then to their parents, suggesting that patriarchal deference was an important aspect of literacy. While other mock-frontispieces lampooned the idea of Catholic control of texts, such as a frontispiece depicting the pope as a "man of sin," the majority of frontispieces evoke patriarchal authority figures. A common image at

Frontispiece, *The New England Primer*, 1789. Children's textbooks often began with a picture of the king. Once the Revolutionary War was successful in overthrowing him, images of the founding fathers took its place. Courtesy of the American Antiquarian Society.

the beginning of the *Primer* was of the king or, later, of American founding father, George Washington. As in Filmer's interpretation of the king's stamp on the *Magna Carta*, these images suggest that the act of reading was supposed to reinforce the power of metaphorical fathers over their civic children.

Yet the seventeenth and eighteenth centuries witnessed multiple challenges to the patriarchal transmission of texts that followed from their initial popularization in the Reformation. Individual families, especially Puritans and dissenters, began replacing traditional catechizing sessions with family worship services, where fathers transmitted beliefs independently from civic and church authorities.[19] In *Cares about the*

Nurseries (1702), Mather suggests that catechizing can occur as "table talk" between parents and children. Although these catechizing sessions still granted interpretive power to fathers, there was the increasing likelihood that different families, groups, sects, or individuals would come up with different interpretations, breaking the chain of patriarchal political authority. Certainly an even more dissenting attitude was found among the Society of Friends, also known as Quakers, who believed that the Holy Spirit could speak through anyone, including women and children.

Political disagreements, as well as doctrinal ones, found their way into the catechisms and into the *Primer*, which as a heavily redacted, composite text cannot be said to have a simple message regarding politics. John Cotton's *Milk for Babes* catechism, which was first published in London in 1646 and included later in the *New England Primer*, transmits patriarchal authority in all but one important respect. Cotton claims that the fifth commandment applies to "all our superiours, whether in family, church, school, and commonwealth," but not explicitly to the king, even though Cotton tried to keep in good favor of the crown and did not express his admiration for Oliver Cromwell until after the establishment of Puritan commonwealth rule.[20] What appears as an adamant patriarchal command might thus be seen as an early and subtle attempt to delineate the limits of patriarchy.[21] As a more radical extension of the argument that obedience to the king was not implied by the fifth commandment, John Locke's *Two Treatises of Government* (1689) famously argued that the king was not a father and that political subjects were not the same as children, an assertion that became influential in America at the time of the Revolution.[22] In this light, the frontispieces of George Washington rather than the king can also be viewed as a critique of patriarchal political authority, notwithstanding his later establishment as the "father" of the country.

Reflecting the transitional period in which it was produced, parts of the *Primer* contain subtle moments in which readers are encouraged to act more like comprehending citizens than like patriarchal subjects. For instance, the "Dutiful Child's Promises," which were included beginning with the 1727 *New England Primer*, preserve a relentless patriarchal parallelism between various authorities, but they attribute to each authority a *different* ruling passion, progressing from compelled fear to honor, which was coming to be understood as a duty that had to be earned by the authority figure to which it was owed and finally to love, a reciprocal feeling of citizenship. Therefore, while the promises seem at first to align patriarchal authorities and to make "dutiful childhood" a category for every kind of obedient subject, they ultimately challenge the idea that all forms of authority are equally parental and that to be a child *was to be* dutiful. Instead, the verses elicit the child's promises, making "dutiful" a modifier that is chosen by certain children. The "Promises" also suggest

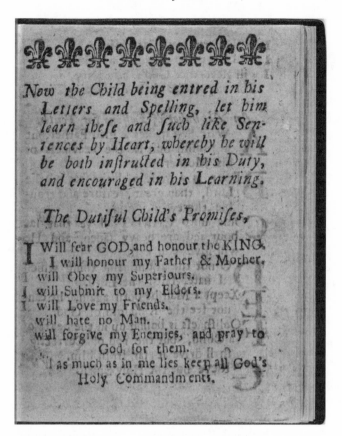

"The Dutiful Child's Promises," *The New England Primer*, 1727.
This series of promises was found in the beginning of primers in
colonial times. Once a child had "entred in his Letters and Spelling," he vowed to fear God but to honor human authority figures
from the king to his elders in society. Courtesy of the American
Antiquarian Society.

that the choice to be dutiful was contingent on children's ability to understand their
duties. The preface to the "Promises" specifies that it is only after "being entred into
his Letters and Spelling" that the child can make these oaths.

The Child Reader's Growing Independence

Another challenge to patriarchal theories of reading was that catechisms and other
texts were coming to be read independently, since strictures on public religious
practices meant that dissenters saw private rather than public worship as the mark

of true religious devotion. Cotton Mather assumes that the first part of catechizing is to give children a printed text and have them read it on their own: "First, then, 'tis to be taken for granted, *O Parents*, that you have put an agreeable *Catechism* into the Hands of your *Children*, and charged them to get it by heart."[23] In addition to suggesting that catechizing could be an independent as well as a public activity, Mather encouraged children to engage in a set of independent devotional reading practices known as "the religion of the closet," named for small rooms that people increasingly used for their private prayers.[24] The religion of the closet, a dissenting religious tradition that built on older religious rituals emphasizing seclusion, referred to more than just a physical space.[25] The closet also acted as a metaphor for an individual self, capable of independent thought, feeling, and judgment.

Although this type of contemplative reading practice had formerly involved only the most educated men, Mather actively encouraged unpracticed readers to participate in the religion of the closet as soon as they could "speak plain." In a 1712 sermon preached to the children of his church and also printed in pamphlet form, Mather demands, with more than a little urgency: *"Young Man, Run, Run into thy Closet and there Speak and Pray; and Weep unto thy Savior . . .* Children, I Demand your *Immediate Compliance."*[26] Elsewhere he claimed that children must *"Take up and Read! Take up and Read!"* in order to leave the "state of nature"—a phrase that would have been associated at this point in history not only with original sin but also with the chaos that motivates people to consent to government.[27]

Many children's books, such as primers, were traditionally used for drilling, but they also elicited children's independent reading.[28] A poem that appeared in a 1750 version of the *New England Primer* envisions the child reading alone: "Though I am young, a little one / If I can speak and go alone / Then I must learn to know the Lord / And learn to read his holy word." Although most of children's reading in this period is meant to promote religious rather than political identity, the practices had potentially destabilizing political implications. Filmer claimed that common reading did not pose a challenge to patriarchal control of language because the "literal sense" was in support of patriarchal rule. However, others maintained that—because all people, not just priests and kings, could understand the laws of God and man—the people should be the rightful arbiters of the law.

Mather, long seen as a transitional figure in between old world and new, characteristically stands in between these two positions. The author of more than 400 religious works, which he often distributed for free to his congregations, Mather revived the Protestant faith in the divinity of texts and the importance of lay readership, suggesting that even the most untested readers, such as children, were capable of understanding and reading independently. Mather was so taken with print culture and its possibilities that he called himself a "press master" for God.[29] In taking up this role, he made it clear that the power to apply God's law was in the hands of common people, including children. At the same time, because of his patriarchal understanding of language as controlled by fathers and ultimately God, he did not anticipate the potentially subversive consequences of this push for lay readership, emphasizing rather the divine transparency of texts and their marvelous ability to replicate themselves in their readers.

In eliciting children's independent reading, Mather was following the work that his father, Increase Mather, had begun in the years following the Halfway Covenant. Because the covenant allowed children to be baptized at birth and to become half members of the church, the Mathers encouraged them to own the covenant that they had begun with their baptism, so that their religious membership would be more than just a formality. Cotton's interest was also related to the Salem witch trials, during which he wrote that "'tis to be feared, The Children of *New-England* have *Secretly* done many things that have been pleasing to the Devil."[30] To recover from these events, he launched one of the largest attempts at early religious conversion that had ever been tried, including prayer meetings in which adults prayed for children's souls, special services for young people, study groups for children, and religious books designed for young people. This work, while not often recognized, predated the larger and more widely studied wave of child conversions of the Great Awakening by several years.

Mather's *Early Religion* (1694), the first of many sermons that he printed urging children's swift conversion, emphasizes that youth is a time in which allegiances can be made: "The Dayes of your *Youth*, are the Days of your *Choice*."[31] Making it clear that by "youth" he means young children as well as young adults, Mather continues, "Plainly then, There is not so much as one Reasoning *Babe* among you to be Excused from the Work of *Praising the Lord*. . . Tho' our God Loves not that any should be *Babes in Religion*, yet He Loves well to have *Religion in Babes*."[32] In this passage, the patriarchal metaphor of all believers as metaphorical children gives way to the question of how actual children can be religious. Amidst arguments that children lacked rational capacities, Mather asserts that young children do have the capacity for reasoned religious choice. He claims that in a span as short as eight years from birth, children could become full, *consenting* religious beings: "And why should it be *Too Soon*, for you in the *First Year*, and in the *First Month*, of your Reason, to open the *Doors* of your Hearts unto the Lord? When the Lord Jesus was but *Eight Dayes* old, He parted with some of His *Blood* for us. And can it then be, *Too Soon*, even for you that are *Eight Years* old, now to part with your *Sin* for Him? . . . I once again ask the Consent of your Souls."[33] In addition to claiming that children could consent with some degree of reason, Mather argues that religious feeling is essentially equal to reason as an indicator of capable decision making, allowing him to make even more of a case for children's inclusion.

Seen in this light, the most popular children's materials of the period, child conversion narratives (or stories of pious children who die young), can be understood as part of a larger political argument that young people are capable beings, worthy of some degree of autonomy and choice. One of the most popular collections of such narratives was James Janeway's *A Token for Children* (1671, first American edition 1700). "Token," in this case, has at least two meanings: first, the book contained signs—one might even say evidence—of God's presence in the lives of the children whose stories were included, and second, it was a memorial used to remember the deceased. The primary function of the text, however, was to educate child readers and thereby motivate them to also convert. To this end, although Janeway includes a preface for adults, entreating them to encourage their children to read the book, he largely presents children's reading as an independent activity that will aid them in determining their beliefs. It is not to be done because "because your good Mother will make you do it," but rather to be done on one's own initiative. The child's deliberation was to involve feeling as much as reasoned choice. Janeway asks his readers, "How art thou affected, poor Child, in the Reading of this Book . . . Have you been by your self upon your knees?"[34] By making children's affective reading the defining factor in their conversions, Janeway places religious membership in the hands of children. Although he asks children to honor their parents and respect their wishes, the entire preface reads as an attempt to gain children's religious loyalties, often with means that go beyond rational argument. Janeway writes, "Are you resolved by the strength of Christ to be a good Child? Are you indeed? nay, but are you indeed? . . . Now tell me, my pretty dear Child, what will you do?"[35] While Janeway is clearly trying to help things along by asking rhetorical questions and manipulating the reader's emotions, the decision to be godly belongs to the child, whose promises are elicited. Furthermore, he suggests that children's answers to the questions while reading constitute meaningful choices and allow them to imaginatively join the community of pious children that the text constructs.

Mather, who imported Janeway's text and added to it in 1700, also granted children an extraordinary amount of independence as readers. In addition to encouraging all children to "run into their closets," he had his own children's rooms fitted for reading, writing, and praying and encouraged them to collect key passages in commonplace books. Though at times Mather decided he wanted more control over his children's closet practices and devised ways to monitor them, Monaghan suggests that, overall, these activities created a "slight shift . . . in the power relationship in the family; Cotton was no longer to be the sole authority over the Word, but was diffusing some of his control among his children."[36]

While this was undoubtedly the case, Mather's writing oddly betrays little aware-ness of the ways that closet reading was a potentially radical activity that shifted the power of interpretation from kings to the people, ministers to congregations, and fathers to children. Though an innovator in a period of major transitions, Mather's traditional understanding of language does not allow him to see the full conse-quences of his conversion endeavors. Closet reading had the potential to challenge existing family, church, and political systems because it was a relatively ungoverned practice in which individuals were not accessible or accountable to authorities. In this light, while the urgency of Mather's insistence that the child become a closet reader is not strange, given the new religious necessities for individual literacy, it is odd that he does not seem to be particularly anxious about children's autonomy in the closet, only insisting that they get there as quickly as possible. Indeed, he argued that the child should be thrust into the closet and into texts without a moment's pause on achieving the ability to walk and speak. He insisted that children "get alone" as soon as they could first "go alone."[37]

Perhaps Mather was so entirely confident in the safety and desirability of closet reading for children because he subscribed to a patriarchal Protestant theory of language that posits that the Bible is subject to only one interpretation and that it has the power to replicate itself fully in the minds of readers. As sixteenth-century Protestant reformer, William Tyndale similarly put it: "Though shalt understand . . . that the scripture hath but one sense, which is the literal."[38] Mather's notion that the literal sense of the Bible could not be misinterpreted allowed him to see the individual worship pursued in the closet as compatible with existing patriarchal hierarchies. In Mather's eyes, this model of reading spread the authority of God to a wider range of persons and spaces. Although the Bible was a special sort of book, Mather tends to extend its power to convey one meaning to most texts, including ones that he wrote himself, meaning that books can become a form of patriarchal governance in the absence of authority figures.

While Mather's sermons for children and other popular children's texts of the period include multiple references to the child's inheritance of original sin and po-tential punishment before and after death, there are far fewer injunctions against faulty interpretation of texts than would be found only a few decades later. This omission can be partially explained by the lack of diversity of reading materials in New England; there were fewer chapbooks and ballads published and circulated there than in England, for instance, where Thomas White found it necessary to caution children against reading these "foolish books."[39] But, even though print was still in its foundational stages in colonial America, the reading imperatives for children created more books designed for young people, suggesting that reading was seen primarily as a social good. Among Mather's publications are at least twenty-five different books that address young people specifically. These books likely found their audience due to Mather's habit of gifting his books to his congregations. As Monaghan points out, "By 1700 he was regularly leaving books as gifts . . . Six years later he was claiming that he gave away each year some 600 books of his own author-ships."[40] Mather seems to have believed that writing was a privileged way of talking about touchy subjects such as sex, a topic about which he wrote a text for "young people," *The Pure Nazarite*, in 1723, and which he suggested that they take into their closets with them to read whenever they felt sexually tempted. Oddly, Mather does not seem particularly troubled that the child reader would be all alone reading texts about sexual deviance.

Instead, Mather conceives of closet reading as a means to promote the repli-cation of texts in as many spaces and minds as possible. His body of work is a record of his faith in the ability of print to structure the experiences of readers. The closet was not a particularly dangerous space for Mather because the Word of God could travel there.[41] Mather suggests that the reading of the closet would allow the reader to absorb the text, just by virtue of opening and perceiving the Bible: "Look . . . into the Bible that lies open before you, and Matter of Prayer will pour in upon you."[42]

Mather's expectation that the literal sense of the Bible was wholly accessible to believers was partly dependent on the Calvinist notion of free grace, which sug-gested that individuals were predestined to be saved or damned and that God's Holy Spirit would aid his chosen people in accessing biblical truth.[43] According to this view, believers could not misread the Bible because it was self-authenticating. The nonsaved also could not misread, since, metaphorically speaking, the bible was "closed" to them. Thomas Brooks likewise assumes that incorrect interpreta-tion is impossible, claiming that only the pious would be able to read God's word: "The Law of God to wicked men is a sealed book, that they cannot understand . . . 'Tis as blotted paper, that they cannot read. Look as a private letter to a friend contains secret matter that no man else may read, because it is sealed. So the Law of Grace is sealed up under the privy seal of Heaven, so that no man can open it or read it, but Christ's faithful friends, to whom 'tis sent."[44] Brooks' metaphor of God's word as "private letter" and "sealed book" suggests that readers are not in need of regulation because they are already regulated by the God's book of grace. Those who do not possess grace are not understood as bad readers but as illiterates.

Mather's confidence in the power of texts to govern the activities of the unseen closet can be seen in *The Pure Nazarite*, in which he confidently imagines the power of the written word to police individual behavior inside the closet's walls. The rest of the title is *Advice to a Young Man, Concerning an Impiety and Impurity (Not Easily to Be Spoken Of)*. The "impurity" that Mather is talking about is masturbation, which then, as now, was associated with teenage boys. Mather notes that God has declared it a shame to speak publicly about such topics, for fear of inspiring emulation. However, he creates a loophole in this divine command by asserting that texts can eradicate secret sexual acts. He says, "I am to *write* of those things, which it is a *shame* to *speak* of."[45]

Mather forges his theory of the printed word from a biblical notion of textual infallibility—hence writing gains a power that does not appear in speaking.[46] Mather demands that his readers "Think, *It is written*, that they who do such things as I am now Tempted unto, have the *Wrath of GOD* impending over them; Think, *It is written*, That they who do such things as I am now Tempted unto, *shall be shut out from the Kingdom of GOD*."[47] Mather has faith that what is written has a transcendent power not to be tainted by the sexual or interpretive propensities of readers. What is written has an unquestionable and broadly perceivable meaning—it is not open to interpretation. Mather further emphasizes the power of the written word by suggesting that if readers are tempted they should "immediately *read over again* the *letter*" which they have in their hands, as if text itself had the power to negate sinful thoughts.[48] Mather does not report back as to how well this worked. Though he bemoaned in his title that "sad occasions multiply" due to spoken communication about the topic, he does not seem to entertain the possibility that the written tract might have also introduced an idea to susceptible readers.

Though Mather's fetishization of print outstripped most of his contemporaries, *The Pure Nazarite* represents a common dynamic when it comes to Puritan attitudes toward children and their books. While there was an incredible amount of anxiety about children in the period, especially that they would die unconverted, there was not much anxiety about children as new readers or of print as a potentially dangerous medium. The *New England Primer*'s two alphabetic verses on reading, "My Book and Heart Shall Never Part" and "Thy Life to Mend, This Book Attend"—both referring to the Bible but also to the *Primer* itself—imagine reading as the solution to everlasting fire, not as the potential cause of a child's destruction.[49] Such confidence was in marked contrast to the anxieties about children's reading that were employed less than a century later. Indeed, although lots of Puritan young-sters died in children's literature, it was not until the late eighteenth century that young protagonists (such as Hannah Webster Foster's Eliza Wharton or William Hill Brown's Tommy Harrington) would die for being bad readers. In these later years, there was even considerable debate about giving the Bible to young children, as it was feared that they might not understand it—a sign that many people were not convinced of Mather's estimation of children's capacities.

In Puritan New England, literary manifestations of God's wrath are not usually directed at children who misread their books but rather at children who choose not to read at all. The naughty child who appears in the 1727 *Primer* piece, "Dialogue Between Christ, Youth, and the Devil," refuses to "mind thy book" and instead spends his time in "sports and plays."[50] In the eighteenth-century book, *The History of Little King Pippin* (British date unknown, first American edition 1786), a Puritan-esque scene unfolds with George Graceless and Neddy Never-Pray playing in a graveyard.[51] The hero, Peter Pippin, sits upon a tombstone reading religious lecture and tries to correct his unfortunately named friends by reading aloud from his book: "did you never read in your Bible, that WHOEVER CALLETH HIS BROTHER FOOL IS IN DANGER OF HELL FIRE; and don't you know, that one of the commandments says, THOU SHALT NOT TAKE THE NAME OF THE LORD THY GOD IN VAIN, FOR THE LORD WILL NOT HOLD HIM GUILTLESS THAT TAKETH HIS NAME IN VAIN?"[52]

Pippin reads "what is written" in capital letters, showing this book's fascination with print innovations, and assumes that if the other children had only read their Bible, they could not possibly act in the way they were doing. Alas, speaking the printed words does the bad boys no good, because it allows them to dismiss him: "Pooh, says little Graceless, don't tell me any of your nonsensical stuff about dying . . . do you mind your reading, and let me alone to my play."[53] Despite the nudging capital letters, Graceless refuses to read the word and therefore be saved—indeed it is unlikely it would have worked, since his name indicates his preordained lack of salvation. Later, as the naughty boys are eaten by wild beasts because they cannot think of a prayer, presumably never having read and learned one from a book, Pip-pin expresses his confidence in the power of another book, God's book of judgment: "There's not a sin that you commit, / Nor a wicked word you say, / But in God's dreadful book 'tis writ, / Against the judgment-day."[54] Even the boys' nonreading is subject to the dictates of a book.

Mather suggests that bad reading, if it was at all possible, was indistinguishable from nonreading. In addressing the Quakers, he did not criticize them for being bad readers but rather he incorrectly chastised them for being nonreaders of the Bible. In *Little Flocks Guarded against Grievous Wolves* (1691), he writes: "to withdraw men from the esteem and study of the *Scriptures*, has hitherto been the main Design of *Quakerism*."[55] He points out that the Quakers resemble an obscure Roman town that believed that "*no man who is able . . . to Read, shall be capable of any share in the Government.*" Mather is particularly affronted that the Quakers, as supposed non-readers, would dare spread their ideas in print: "They expressly reproach men for, *Doting on the Scriptures*; and at the same time [publish] their own silly Scribbles." He ridicules them for writing "whole books," sending "papers into the world," and for saying things "in print" when they have no respect for books.[56]

Of course, underlying Mather's vehement denial that Quakers did not read the Bible is the fact that they did read it and came to differing conclusions from those of Mather. Early Quaker George Keith answers Mather by quoting from a "printed book" by nonconformist preacher Richard Baxter and explaining how it supports him, not Mather.[57] It is perhaps because Mather did not believe that texts could be misread that his exchange with the Quakers was so provoking to him. In his mind, they were doing, with print, what was not supposed to be done. They made it thick with meanings, many of which did not support the status quo. He criticizes George Keith for "discoursing more ambiguously than ever any Daemon of *Delphes* did, and . . . imitat[ing] the *Cuttle-fish* by so darkening his Context with his *Ink*, that one can hardly find him without some evasion."[58] This "cuttle-fish" writing makes it so that the problem of misinterpretation is introduced: "let all unwary Readers know . . . if you swallow so much of the more specious and guilded *Quakerism*, you will soon find your selves entangled."[59]

Mather's claim that Keith is a "seducer" resembles later claims against novelists for luring their readership into false fantasies.[60] Mather expresses particular frustration that the Quakers lie in print, writing (we might imagine) in exasperation, "I did in print Admonish him of this *Lye*, because it was in Print he vented it; but he does in Print Reply upon me." Hoping to put an end to this supposed abuse of print, he refuses to "Transcribe the many other horrible passages, which continually fall from the Pens of the greatest *Rabbis* among the *Quakers*" (though he cannot help but transcribe some anyway). Mather does end up admitting that some interpretation might be at work in his claims about the Bible. Against Keith's claim that Mather has "falsified the Holy Scripture," he writes "I am deceived, if I have not the general-ity of Interpreters on my side."[61]

Given Mather's feelings about the Quakers, it would seem that other readers, especially unpracticed ones, might be in similar danger of misreading. Devotional practices that asked readers to pair readings of their lives with the Bible did in fact make for strange interpretations, which are found both in adults' and children's conversion narratives. In her description of her captivity, Mary Rowlandson uses the Bible to explain such seemingly unchristian acts as stealing a horse foot from a starving child's mouth.[62] If Cotton or his father Increase (who wrote the preface to Rowlandson's text) noticed these stretches of meaning, they did not comment on them. Rather, it seems that any repetition of the Bible was a good one. Mather has confidence in asking children to read autonomously, because he assumed that the texts would remain intact in their contact with readers—indeed, he assumes that their wisdom would, if anything, be repeated in their application to a larger number of situations. Mather emphasizes the widespread personal applicability of closet reading by comparing the Bible to an epistle. He claims that "the *Bible* is a *Letter from Heaven* as much unto *you*, as if your very name were in the subscription of it."[63] Mather authorizes readers to personalize their texts by marking places in the Bible that have to do with their own situations. Though these activities offered room for readers to interpret and adapt their books to personal ends, Mather's use of the letter metaphor does not encourage individual interpretation so much as it assumes that each child will engage in a dialogue with a relatively stable set of biblical meanings and will "write back" to God through their lives and prayers. For him, the meaning of the text became located in the reader only insofar as readers replicated biblical texts and proliferated them through holy actions.

Mather ultimately assumes that children's reading of the Bible would make them into living copies of the text. He writes, "Why should you not then take a Text, and think upon it, until you have your Minds into it; cast and fram'd into the lovely Mould of it?" The "form" into which children's identities were to be molded resembled the style of the catechism, as Mather encouraged them to adopt their cadences and language into their devotional practices. He likewise believed that texts such as the Bible could be employed to express readers' deepest beliefs. In his 1712 sermon for children, he also makes recommendations as to where closetgoers will get their prayers: "You can't be at any loss What you shall say. The CXIXth Psalm; the whole book of Psalms; all the whole Bible; the whole state of your Soul . . . will afford your materials for your supplication."[64] Mather insists that children conform their "*Affections* and *Practices*" to their catechism and other godly books, though his comment that parents must "contrive all the Charms imaginable, that [children's] *Hearts*, and *Lives* may be *Molded* into that *Form*" hints that this was a more difficult task than he admits.[65] Given Mather's faith in the power of texts, it is no longer surprising that he afforded young people with the power of religious choices. These choices were to be defined entirely by the texts they read.

"Relicks at Last . . . Faithfully Set Down for You and Yours in Writing from his Mouth"

As Mather believed that books were replicated in their readers, he imagined that telling stories of pious children would constitute another manifestation of the word of God. His faith in the sanctity of texts led to his near obsession with their replication and circulation. Child conversion narratives were perhaps especially appealing to Mather because they were often described as literally transforming the words of pious children into text. *The Compleat Scholler* (1666) purports to be "relicks at last . . . faithfully set down for you and yours in writing from his mouth."[66] Mather was instrumental in the spread of these narratives in the new world, publishing a version of Janeway's *Token* in 1700, with an appendix of stories about the children of New England. Mather's story about his brother Nathanael, who died at age nineteen, especially illustrates his notion that children could come to embody the word of God through reading. Cotton details Nathanael's division of the Bible into lists of passages that he could use to regulate the various parts of his life.[67] Mather cannot help but betray his fascination with the medium of texts as he explains that Nathanael's story in *Token* is a copy of the boy's own commonplace book, which Mather replicates and circulates in Janeway's narrative, but also has published in another book, *Early Piety Represented in the Life and Death of Nathanael Mather*—a redundancy that suggests his belief that the more copies available of biblical works, the more widespread the word of God. Throughout his version of *Token*, Mather traces not only each individual child's replication of the Bible but also the status of the child's story as a text that could be circulated. Many of his stories are reprinted from sermons, letters, and other printed narratives.

Yet the replication of biblical ideas in the minds of readers and in printed texts also raised the possibility that with each new repetition, the meaning could become further detached from religious orthodoxy. Indeed, New Englanders seem to have acted on Mather's suggestion in his New England version of *Token* that it would be "a very profitable thing" if the pious stories were multiplied in America. The sheer number of these accounts suggests parents' were eager to get in on the trend of recording their children's lives, which in addition to providing a means of mourning the losses of their children, granted them monetary and social capital. Some of these colonial titles include *A Legacy for Children: Being Some of the Last Expressions, and Dying Sayings of Hannah Hill* (1717) and *Early Piety Exemplified in Elizabeth Butcher of Boston* (1725). English titles were also popular. *A Token for Youth . . . Being the Life & Christian Experience of the Wonderful Workings of the Spirit of God on Cartaret Rede* (English publication date unknown) was in its twenty-fifth American edition by 1729.[68] These accounts were no doubt fictionalized to make the children into examples to follow, but birth records show that Butcher at least actually existed, making them important, though not unproblematic, historical archives of children's lives and reading practices from the period.[69]

Even if we cannot rely on the narratives to be unbiased accounts, they provide further evidence that the ideal model of childhood reading in the period was for children to read early and to read alone. Caleb Vernon, of *The Compleat Scholler*, learns to read at age four. In *Early Piety*—a good enough imitation of Mather's conversion narratives that it was once thought to have been written by him—Butcher begins learning to read at age two and a half. Memoirs written by adults also indicate that Puritan children learned to read astoundingly early; for instance, Joseph Sewall goes to a dame school, book in hand, at age two and eight months.[70] Children are frequently depicted reading by themselves in the closet or in corners. Butcher reads in bed: "It was her practice to carry her Catechism or some other good Book to Bed with her, and in the morning she would be sitting up in her Bed Reading before any of the Family were awake besides her."[71]

Other child characters, such as those in Janeway's *A Token for Children*, enter the closet at very young ages. One girl, age four, "was many a time, and often, in one hole or another, in tears upon her knees."[72] The authors of the child conversion narratives emphasize that the good children go to closet prayer as soon as they can "speak plain," or as White says, "nay sooner than [they] can speak plain."[73] The adult author-editors of these texts likely included these scenes of early piety and early reading to suggest that closet duties were instinctive and voluntary and, thus, that there was no distinction between a socially enforced practice of literacy and a natural expression of individual identity through closet reading. But a closer look at these texts suggests that the spread of print culture through children's reading, rather than unambiguously allowing biblical orthodoxy to cast a wider net of believers, created the potential for diverse meanings to be taken from texts. Children in several of these tales interpret their books in strikingly unorthodox ways, for a variety of ends, and get away with it. Even more strikingly, many of these children are girls, meaning that individuals who are doubly removed from the exercise of legal or patriarchal power, as well as from the higher levels of schooling, emerge as arbiters of interpretation and as central participants in an imagined religious community. The presentation of these stories by parents as examples of their children's piety suggest that the removal of biblical exegesis from the hands of clergymen created an increasingly flexible idea of what constituted pious reading and action, making this too a matter of interpretation.

These narratives include a surprising number of moments in which children use biblical language to criticize or manipulate their parents. Butcher, for instance, uses remarks about Christ to chastise her relatives for not giving her what she wants: "the Child being in great Pain and complaining of those about her for refusing to do some thing for her which she found relieved her, but they were fearful of overdoing, she said, *They do not pity me, but I hope Christ pities me, and will prepare a Place for me.*"[74] Butcher seems to be authentically pious in many respects, but this use of biblical language serves mainly to manipulate her relatives into answering her demands. It is only by appealing to piety that she is able to excuse such behavior—and it seems to work, as the adult author-editor of the book does not appear to notice that anything is amiss in Butcher's words.

Cartaret Rede also constantly excuses bad behavior with lip service to traditionally pious viewpoints. For instance, she cries because she can't have a special treat that she wants, presumably some sort of fruit or sweetmeat. Her mother thinks it will make her sick and asks her if she wants to die. The child answers that she does want to die so she can go to heaven. Cartaret's comment that she does not fear death and wants to go to God is a mark of the ideal Puritan, but the context reveals that she is also using her religion to manipulate her mother. In a similar scene, Cartaret's mother is having a nice outfit made for her. Cartaret comments that she would rather die than have it, because she does not want to be a sinner.[75] Again, the remark fits with Puritan theology, in that Cartaret is rejecting worldly dress in favor of spirituality. Nonetheless, it also provides an occasion for her to rebel against her mother. In still another passage, Cartaret rationalizes her bad behavior by making it part of God's plan. She has misbehaved while her mother is gone, and when her mother returns, she insists that she forgive her because "it is God's will." While it was conceivable and perhaps likely that a child's faith might have sometimes undermined parental authority, these moments seem outrageous in their clear appropriation of religious texts for personal ends and suggest some of the potentials for textual transmission to go awry through the child's (or potentially the parent-author's) interpretation of a text's meaning. If exceptionally learned and religious children and their parents might have sometimes used texts in unorthodox ways, it seems even more plausible that the less educated and pious youth who would have been the conversion narratives' targeted readers would have misread.

More subtly, conversion narratives encouraged children to participate in the creation of meaning by depicting them shaping their own stories and appearing as authoritative readers of other texts. Though the authors of these texts no doubt added to them, they often present themselves as mere documentary editors of what the children said and wrote, suggesting it is children who have the power to shape the meaning of their lives. The children's remarks about God, other members of the household, and books they read are taken down word for word. In *Token*, Janeway remarks that one child, Susannah Bicks, said many things that were "pass'd by without Committing to Paper, which deserved to have been written in Letters of Gold."[76] Besides attributing considerable significance to the words of a child, this passage makes it appear that the patriarchal author has limited control over his text. It is impossible to know whether Janeway is being genuine here, or even whether Susannah Bicks's story is true, but the power that he grants to his child characters is not unusual. The author of *The Compleat Scholler* similarly insists that Vernon's conversion narrative consists of direct testimony.[77] Cartaret Rede's conversion narrative begins with the author saying, "you have [the story] in its native simplicity, as it dropt from her mouth, without any variation as I know of."[78]

While some conversion narrative children merely shape the texts by their dying expressions, scrupulously transcribed by a relative or friend, others are granted an even more direct role in the creation of the text's meaning. At the end of Cartaret Rede's narrative, the author includes several letters that the child has written. It is not clear whether the letters are really written by the child; in this way, this part of the text prefigures the epistolary novels of the eighteenth century, in which authors presented themselves as mere editors of their fictional characters' letter collections. Regardless of whether Cartaret really wrote the letters, their inclusion implies that children's words are worth reading. In another text, *A Legacy for Children: Being Some of the Last Expressions, and Dying Sayings of Hannah Hill* (1717), the author (or possibly the printer) goes so far as to suggest that Hannah Hill is actually the author of the text; it is signed H.H., even though Hannah is dead by the time the text is published.[79] The effect of this for child readers is that the relationship between author and reader is cast as a relationship among relative equals rather than as an authority figure speaking to the child reader. It also suggests that meaning is located in the child character, and by extension the child reader, not the adult author-editor who has compiled the story.

Child characters are also consistently granted authoritative reader status in the stories. Cartaret Rede's reading choices, practices, and reactions are scrupulously documented. For example, one night she is "found in tears" while reading James Janeway's *Invisibles, Realities, Demonstrated in the Holy Life and Triumphant Death of Mr. John Janeway* (1690).[80] In *A Little Book for Little Children*, White includes eighty-four Bible passages in his text that a child has selected, taking up a considerable amount of space in his own narrative.[81] While it is not clear whether White is really publishing passages given to him by a child reader, he does not edit the passages in any obvious way or include any of his own commentary, a practice that grants the child's reading practices considerable autonomy. Although the boy's agency is necessarily limited by the fact that all of his passages come from the Bible, the most frequently recommended reading material for children, the child reader appears to take over authority from White for several pages.

Extant copies of the child conversion narratives also bear some evidence of children's attempts to claim actual and metaphorical ownership of their books. In a 1725 copy of Elizabeth Butcher's conversion narrative, there are three signatures at the back, all from young women also named Elizabeth: "Elizabeth Helyn her Book given to her by Mary Mather. Elizabeth Golty her Book given to her by Hannah Colegrove. Elizabeth Coxacre." The fact that the book was given to three children with the same name as the central character does not seem coincidental. As the buyer of the book, at least in the first two cases, was not the child herself, the book might have been purchased as a tribute to the recipient, suggesting she was like the pious child in the book. Or, possibly, the book might have been given as a not-so-subtle nudge for its child recipient to imitate Butcher's good behavior. But giving a child named Elizabeth a book about a girl named Elizabeth also somehow implies that the text is rightly hers to be read and interpreted by her alone. The signatures declare this, as each child signs that the text is "her book." Personalized in this way, the book seems to have inspired a readerly fantasy of identification, in which readers might have imagined getting attention in the manner of the book's central character. And, of course, the real Elizabeths could enjoy an even greater triumph than the textual one, as they could imagine all of the glory without having to die for it.

In *Token*, Janeway similarly imagines that readers will personalize their books, a goal that sometimes made for overly emotional responses. About a young woman named Mary A., he writes: "Her book was her delight and what she did read, she loved to make her own and cared not for passing over what she learned, without extraordinary observation and understanding; and many times she was so affected in the reading of the scriptures that she would burst out into tears and would hardly be pacified."[82]

Other children in the text are constantly found crying, moaning, and otherwise responding to what they read. For example, a "certain little child" between ages two and three, "quickly learned to read the scripture and with great Reverence, tenderness, and Groans, read till tears and sobs were ready to hinder him."[83] Though these moments were celebrated because the children were demonstrating great emotional affect, one might also imagine that it made the children difficult to control. In another incident, eight-year-old Sarah Howley, on being told by her father to have great cheer about her death because she was going to God, fell into a "great passion" and would not be calmed.[84] The sobs of these children seem to fall just short of the kinds of fits and tantrums that got a number of children into trouble for being possessed by witches during the Salem witch trials.

Other moments from these narratives, in their attempts to unconditionally celebrate children's closet reading, go so far as to tacitly license child readers to challenge parental authority through their interpretation of biblical texts. In a story of an unnamed five-year-old boy's death, Thomas White remarks that he took so much "delight in his Book that his Father and Mother have seen cause sometimes to hide [it] away from him."[85] Some stories like this also appear in *Token*. For instance, in a story by Janeway, a child named John Harvy gets sore eyes and is ordered to stop reading by his parents, but he is "so greedy of reading the scriptures . . . that he would scarce allow time to dress himself."[86] Janeway excuses Harvy's disobedience, saying that he never disobeyed his parents except when "he tho't they might cross the Command of God."[87] These moments not only excuse children's rebellion but also suggest that they should interpret texts themselves to judge when such defiance might be justified. While the idea that readers might follow the commands of God over those of their parents was not problematic from a religious perspective, the notion that the child could be the judge destabilized the transmission of patriarchal authority.

Because the pious child narratives cannot be seen as wholly transparent accounts but as representations of children's reading filtered through their eyes of parents, it is strange that these resistant moments made it into the narratives at all. Did parents love their dying children so much that they were blind to their manipulations? Were they so eager to capitalize on any repetition of religious language that they included even moments that seemed questionable? Did they exploit the more flexible interpretive potentials of the Bible to make their children seem even more pious in their minds and in those of others? Or were they, like Mather, so confident in the power of religious language that they believed only its replication paramount, notwithstanding its contextual meaning or use? Even if they rely on Mather's logic that any repetition of biblical ideas is a positive instance of the transmission of text, the writings of parent authors also suggest a more lax interpretation of piety than by clergymen such as Mather, made possible by the newfound potential for lay readers to weigh in on the range of meanings to which biblical texts might be put.

Though Mather sometimes mentions that not all children valued the Bible, he more often assumed that if they could just enter the closet and read its pages, they would be overcome by a devotion to God. As he puts it, the religion of the closet allows those inside to cry, "Abba, Father." He assumes that even those outside of the closet are characterized most strongly by their relationship to a patriarchal figure,

"But who then is the father of them that are Strangers to Secret Prayer? Alas, Who is their Father? What a Black Father have they!"[88] That Mather sees Satan as a father shows the extent to which he understood power as patriarchal. The great irony of Mather's assumption is that the closet placed greater authority into the hands of children, rather than fathers. This dispersal of authority is further demonstrated in the re-imagination of the closet in the mid-to late eighteenth century as the location for reading and writing novels and other entertaining books, the very texts that would be seen as threatening to the kinds of authority that Mather saw as inviolable. As authority over texts was removed from patriarchs, a new image of political and religious identity emerged, in which children and, indeed, all individuals imagined themselves as possessing the authority to make decisions and to govern themselves.

Awakening Revolutionary Children

The push toward independence—religious and political—has often been linked with unruly children.[89] By the time Mather died in 1728, many people claimed that New England's children had become wholly uncontrollable. Sereno E. Dwight's history of the Great Awakening claims that in Northampton, Massachusetts, at least, "the young became addicted to habits of dissipation and licentiousness; family government too generally failed; the Sabbath was extensively profaned; and the decorum of the sanctuary was not unfrequently disturbed."[90] This bad behavior became the occasion for another widespread attempt at gaining their religious loyalties, but one that would be controversial both in its methods, which heavily encouraged ecstatic emotion and imagination, and its positioning of mere children as central figures within a religious movement.

The Great Awakening, though a term that was not adopted until the nineteenth century, describes a vogue for revival-type preaching that began in the 1730s in New England and spread to many parts of the colonies. Though conversions happened among people of all ages, revivalism was usually portrayed as a trend affecting children and youth. Boston minister William Cooper claims that the conversions happened "mostly among the Young . . . And . . . some little Children."[91] Edwards estimates that, of the Northampton converts, "near thirty were . . . wrought upon between ten and fourteen years of age; two between nine and ten, and one of about four years of age," a young girl named Phebe Bartlet.[92] The emotionalism of the movement challenged restrictions on children's participation due to their supposed lack of mature reason. Many declared their religious affiliations through emotional and often physically expressive professions of faith, described pejoratively by Sunderland minister William Rand as "the *Groanings, Quakings, Foamings, Roarings* and *Faintings* . . . of [among other persons] *little, very little* Children."[93] Historian Robert Bremner argues that "revivalistic Calvinism created new forms of participation by children in religious life. As much as adults, they were capable of the faith and feeling which composed religious experience as revivalists understood and preached it."[94]

The children's participation was much celebrated by revivalist ministers, but established clergymen found the inclusion of young people threatening. Rand, writing in 1743, complained that "a vain *conceited* Temper prevails.—*Children* can teach their Parents and their Ministers."[95] Such reactions have caused Bremner to argue that the Awakening had a radical effect on children's political awareness, setting the stage for the American Revolution: "The Great Awakening prefigured both a recurring pattern of religious and social unrest and the prominent part henceforth to be taken by young people in the discovery and dramatization of moral and social truths."[96] In many ways, the direct connections to the Revolution and especially to a widespread empowerment of children are overstated. While Edwards often defended children's participation, he ultimately took conservative measures to prevent a democratization of society and religion, which included barring children under age fourteen from communion. Yet the revivals nonetheless brought the exclusion of children to the public attention and allowed children's participation to be discussed.[97] The Awakening made clear that, even if children were not full participants in government or religion, they were part of an imagined community. At the very least, the revivals pioneered ways in which these non-rights-bearing members could become imaginatively invested in the society of which they were a part.

A surprising amount of the vocal opposition to the Awakening centered on children's rational capacities, as well as the movement's emphasis on supposedly childlike and irrational qualities, such as emotion and imagination. Rand insists that children's religious feelings cannot be authentic because they cannot truly understand religion. He skeptically observes, "at a Time when there is a great deal of Talk about Religion, it is no wonder if some Children should speak now and then in a *religious* Strain . . . they understand not what they say, and speak *only by Rote*."[98] If they do somehow go beyond this parroting, Rand claims that their imaginations must be deluded, which he warns is a common occurrence in children. He accuses revivalist ministers of taking advantage of this quality and for not having more "Meekness and Gentleness" in their dealings with children: "Can it be wondered at, if *such* Persons, when they have had their *Passions* violently attacked by these Preachers . . . should cry out, and discover such *violent* Emotions of Affection." He concludes that children, and those who would make claims about their awakening, are "under the Power of an *ungovern'd Imagination*." Furthermore, voicing some of the concerns that are missing from the celebration of child conversion narratives, Rand further attacks the revivalists for being bad interpreters of texts. He complains that interpretation of the scripture has gone rampant and that people "have been led to a wild, extravagant, and mystical Interpretation of Scripture."[99] These imaginative responses to the Bible, far from personalizing it in the way of Mather, make the Scripture into "*a dead Letter*," a turn of phrase that means both "without spirit" and "a writ without force."[100]

Edwards's defense for including children, that they are not "innocent" but are "young vipers" in the sight of Christ, is often cited as a sign of the period's generally hard-hearted approach to child rearing.[101] However, Edwards was actually making an argument for children's capacities to understand complex religious issues and to hold autonomous religious meetings at a time when many people were highlighting their inabilities. Even more significant is Edwards's reason for defending children's religious capacities: "What is objected is Children's want of . . . Knowledge and Discretion . . . But it appears to me the Objection is not sufficient: Children, as they have the Nature of Men, are inclined to Society; and those of them that are capable of Society one with another, are capable of the Influences of the Spirit of GOD."[102]

Edwards here imagines children as participating members of society by nature. Though he did not go so far as to suggest that this capacity should grant children rights, he did see their religious inclusion as a matter of importance to the state, as he believed that New Englanders were in a war with Satan: "I make it my Rule to lay hold of Light and embrace it, where-ever I see it, tho' held forth by a Child or an Enemy."[103] George Whitefield, who came to Northampton in 1740, held a similar view that children must be allowed to participate fully in the revivals, though he was, characteristically, more brusque about it than Edwards was. As T. H. Breen and Timothy Hall recount, "Whitefield and his followers celebrated the predominance of young people among the converts, urging children whose parents remained unconverted to 'go to Heaven without them!' "[104]

While children's participation in the revivals was derided for being emotionally overblown rather that rational and measured, Edwards argued that it was not a problem if children's (or anyone's) participation should consist of imaginative flights or emotional displays. In doing so, he deconstructs the oppositions between affection and rational understanding, imagination and authenticity, that were emerging in the period and that were coming to structure divisions between children and adults. Rejecting the very notion that there is a rational deciding faculty that is protected from emotional sway, he claims that "The *Will*, and the *Affections* of the Soul, are not two Faculties. . . The Will never is in any Exercise any further than it is *affected*."[105] Edwards also rejects the idea that imagination is a sign of diminished understanding, fit only for children. While he claims that imagination can be a particularly effective tool for addressing ignorant people, who God sees "as Babes," he also protests, "I dare appeal to any Man . . . Whether or no he is able to fix his Thoughts on God or Christ, or the Things of another World, without imaginary Ideas, attending his Meditations?"[106] In this way, Edwards licenses readers to respond imaginatively to the Bible and suggests that imaginative responses can be a valid means and rationale for inclusion. The connections between affection and belonging, and affection and will, as we will see in chapter 2, became particularly important in the early republic, as politicians and educators considered how to teach children to be devoted and consenting citizens.

Later, though, Edwards tightened restrictions on church participation even over and above the rules of pre-revivalist ministers, making it clear that children's involvement was limited to imaginative participation and did not translate into arguments for rights or privileges. His predecessor at Northampton, Samuel Stoddard, had broken with the Halfway Covenant philosophy and had allowed all persons, including the unconverted, to participate in communion, but in 1749, Edwards caused a heated battle at his church by instituting new restrictions. Communion would be limited to those over fourteen who had signed a statement of conversion. In making these restrictions, Edwards contradicted some of his earlier positions about children's religious capacities, claiming that the "Scriptures were written for the sake of adult Persons."[107] He argued that baptism included children as "some Sort Members of the Christian Church," but did not "suppose them to be Members in Such Standing as to be the proper immediate Subjects of all . . . Privileges."[108] Children's diminished status not only formed the basis for their exclusion but also for the exclusion of anyone who could be compared to children in their understanding.

While these statements are in some ways unremarkable because they repeat the ruling of the Halfway Covenant and the official position of ministers like Mather, reactions to Edwards's new strictures show that the Awakening had by this time changed popular views of children. In his response to Edwards's new rules, Solomon Williams accuses Edwards of not dealing fully with infant baptism because it would overthrow his entire argument. He reasons: "a young Dove is as compleat a Dove as an old one, tho' it be not so large, nor has so many Feathers. So I am apt to conceive an Infant who is a Member of a Family, is as compleat a Member of that Family, and has as good a Right to all the Priviledges of it that he is capable to enjoy, as a Child who is grown up, tho' he be not so big."[109]

He then argues that baptism essentially makes children members of the church and accuses Edwards of kicking them out. While Edwards claimed that he was doing no such thing, but was only asking for a further profession in order to prevent church membership from losing its meaning, he ultimately lost this fight and was dismissed from Northampton.

Though it is impossible to know for sure why Edwards felt the need to rethink his position on children, it seems significant that the disagreement was exacerbated by another earlier dispute, specifically about children's reading. Dwight locates the origins of the conflict in a scandal involving the wealthiest of the town's youth:

> In the year 1744, about six years before the final separation, Mr. Edwards was in-
> formed, that some young persons in the town, who were members of the church,
> had licentious books in their possession, which they employed to promote lascivi-
> ous and obscene conversation, among the young people at home. Upon farther
> enquiry, a number of persons testified, that they had heard one and another of
> them, from time to time, talk obscenely; as what they were led to, by reading
> books of this gross character, which they had circulating among them.[110]

When Edwards went to punish the wrongdoers, the wealthy members of the town "declared . . . that their children should not be called to an account in such a way for such conduct." Dwight claims that "this was the occasion of weakening Mr. Edwards' hands in the work of the ministry; especially among the young people, with whom, by this means, he greatly lost his influence."[111] Did Edwards's objection to children being full church members proceed merely from his conscience, or was it also a response to the destabilizing effects of encouraging children to be members? How did the children's autonomy to behave as they pleased trump that of the town's most renowned patriarch? Though we cannot be sure of the answer to these questions, the incident suggests that, like Mather, Edwards was unable to ensure that child readers, when given free access to books, would remain faithful and obedient to his authority. While the aberrant children were not granted voting rights in the community, their contact with books undermined patriarchal rule and formed them into a constituency of readers with actual influence on political affairs.

By 1750, the year in which Edwards was removed from his church, children increasingly had the opportunity to choose what they read: religious works, but along with them novels, storybooks, and playbooks. At the forefront of the push for a more diverse literature of childhood was John Locke, whose *Some Thoughts Concerning Education* (1693) influenced John Newbery's decision to publish a series of little books to "amuse and instruct." The association between the foremost philosopher of modern consent theory and the first major children's book publisher was not co-incidental. The idea that children could read and interpret texts on their own was a logical extension of Locke's claim that they were not automatic subjects. At the same time, the educational texts that Locke envisioned became a powerful tool for limiting the radical potentials for children's interpretation and for teaching them to submit to legitimate authorities as a corollary to the love they had for their books.

In the early republic, reading was particularly important because political membership was no longer linked primarily to local religious culture, where individuals regularly encountered authority figures face-to-face (between their sessions in the closet). It was instead increasingly tied to a federal model of nationhood. Reading, as several scholars have argued, was a major way that individuals living in colonial America began to identify themselves as part of a nation. Because the new nation was thought to be composed of the people, not just adult male voters, children too needed to recognize these stories as their own.

The problem of interpretation and textual instability remained. Perhaps taking a cue from the Great Awakening's emphasis on children's emotional susceptibility, early republican children's books attempted to ensure their allegiance to the new nation and its narratives by soliciting their affection for various authority figures, including parents, authors, and the books themselves. This intimacy between the child reader and his (or often, her) book presents what eighteenth-century thinkers saw as an even more effective solution to the tensions between individual interpretation and textual authority discussed in this chapter; readers who obeyed their books out of voluntary love could be understood as independent and free-acting, at the same time that their affection worked as a powerful force to shape their interpretations and actions. The relationship between the people and nation came to be understood as not only shaped by rational consent, which was becoming less and less the purview of children, but also by affection. Filial love was constructed as the desired response both to national authority and book, creating a significant role for children and child figures in the emerging republic.

CHAPTER 2

Affectionate Citizenship
Educating Child Readers for a New Nation

> The unity of government, which constitutes you one people, is also
> now dear to you . . . you should cherish a cordial, habitual, and
> immovable attachment to it.
>
> *President George Washington,*
> *Farewell Address, 1796*

> In a word, public and private happiness; domestic and national
> prosperity; and what is more, the sum total of our hopes hereafter,
> as well as here, depend upon the education of the youth of the
> country. Alas! How little it is considered that liberty consists in
> restraint . . . Which then is best—to indulge misjudging child-
> hood in error—or to inure the mind when young to what it must
> submit to when old, and to make it so familiar with its duty, as not
> to reconcile them to, but make them love each other?
>
> Weekly Visitor; Or Ladies Miscellany, *1805*

In one of the first children's storybooks to be published in the colonies, *The Child's New Play-Thing* (1750), a child asks how he is to become a good man. The answer: he must learn to "love his book."[1] This lesson signaled a relatively new posture that child readers were asked to take, but by the end of the eighteenth century, "loving one's book"—referring sometimes to the Bible, but just as often to a primer or children's story—had become a pervasive idiom for all forms of moral wholesomeness. This rhetoric of affection permeated not only the relationship between reader and author but also a variety of hierarchical bonds, including those between children and parents, servants and masters, subjects and governors, and citizens and law.

Scholars have often linked this new emphasis on affection with the increased liberty of the child, the reader, and the citizen in general, an argument that coincides with the declaration of the citizen's freedom prior to and during the American Revolution.[2] In this chapter, I put forth the idea that the simultaneous rise of children's affectionate reading and the assertion that citizens were free was not coincidental. Like the child-centered rhetoric of patriarchal theory, the rhetoric of free citizenship that gained currency in the seventeenth and eighteenth centuries and contributed to the formation of the American nation was also intensely concerned with the status of children. Images of children as citizens frequently appeared in political theory, children's literature, and child-rearing texts, giving rise to a version of imaginary citizenship that I call *affectionate citizenship*, or the imagination that the citizen's allegiance to the state was freely given and based on love. This emphasis on affection was used to reconcile new notions of the citizen's freedom and independence with their necessary limitations, making the child an apt representation of the citizen, even though children were not afforded the legal rights of citizenship.

In particular, children were an integral part of John Locke's theories, which influenced the nation's founders politically and pedagogically.[3] In addition to including extensive analyses of childhood in his political works, Locke wrote a theory of the developing mind, *An Essay on Human Understanding* (1690), and an influential work on child governance, *Some Thoughts Concerning Education* (1693). But his viewpoint on childhood was fraught with contradictions, the most significant of which involved his conflicting representation of the relationship between children and citizens. He argued that parental power and political power were distinct and that the child was not a citizen, while simultaneously establishing the freedom of the child as the basis of the citizen's freedom. The contrast between Locke's account of children's free birth and his denial of their legal rights until adulthood created a tension that he was forced to address in his political and especially his pedagogical work. Although Locke is known for envisioning the independent rational free citizen, he also imagined the affectionate citizen, a subject whose political loyalty was not rational and independent but emotional and dependent. Affection, I argue, was a crucial supplement to the idea of a social contract: a means of motivating imaginative consent to the law in lieu of direct consent and of reconciling the tension inherent in citizenship between the freedom to make the law and the need for subjection to it.

Locke's underlying reliance on children's imaginary citizenship explains why Lockean liberalism has sometimes been associated with the creation of a passive and childlike citizenry, despite his denial of children's legal rights to act as citizens. A prominent account of the decline of American citizenship claims that citizens were once adults with public civic identities, but that they have, as a result of the increasing privatization of citizenship, become childlike. Michael Warner, for instance, argues that the early American republican model of active participation as the province of adult males degraded into a fictive, liberal "nationalist imaginary" that no longer distinguished between an active citizenry and a merely symbolic one.[4] Warner's "imaginary" resembles Lauren Berlant's recent theory of post-Reagan era citizenship as "infantile citizenship," in which "personal acts and values" have become "the primary activities of citizenship."[5] Berlant suggests that civic actions have been replaced with an understanding of citizenship as an intimate, private, and domestic practice. As a result, the child, who "paradoxically, cannot yet act as citizen" has come to represent true citizenship.[6]

I sympathize with these scholars' critiques regarding the passivity of many present-day citizens and agree that affectionate citizenship does to some degree encourage a passive identification with the law in place of participation, but I suggest that the recent use of the child to signify a degraded form of citizenship does not entirely account for the complex relationships between childhood and citizenship in the early United States. Children's imaginary citizenship is not separate from American citizenship in general and actually became important due to Americans' reliance on *both* the liberal ideal of free birth and the republican ideal of participation. The tension between these two political traditions posed difficulties in establishing the age requirements for citizenship. Classical republicanism cast the ideal citizen as an independent adult male with enough property to be truly disinterested enough to participate in the public sphere, but liberal thought, in emphasizing the free and equal birth of all individuals, made citizenship not as easy to circumscribe by age (or, differently, class or gender). Locke limited citizenship to rational adults, but his emphasis on the child's free birth raised questions about when and how children were to be recognized as citizens.

The issue of the child's role in politics was especially significant in the United States. Locke largely used consent as a hypothetical construct to hold the existing English government composed of aristocrats and a monarch accountable to citizens who were not directly involved in governing. Americans, however, were establishing a new republic in the context of revolution and wanted to actualize the citizen's consent, making it compatible with republican ideals of participation and action. This question of how younger citizens would enter into the nation in the future gave rise to impractical proposals, such as Thomas Jefferson's contention that the laws should renew so that each new generation could directly consent to them. Although these proposals failed to be passed into law, literary and educational texts from the period attempted to explain how the consent and participation of those who had not participated in the founding or government might be elicited.

As Warner has argued, early Americans attempted to manage the tensions between the ideal and the reality of how much citizens could participate in politics by viewing the imaginary transactions made possible by print as constituting political participation. In light of the size of the new nation and the impossibility of direct communication, print became a medium through which the impersonal and univocal expressions that constituted the people's participation could be represented. While Warner rightly states that republican print culture was based to some extent on the ideal of an abstract and objective textual public that required the prerequisites of masculinity and adulthood, the insistence that each new generation must consent to governance meant that the "We the People" in public texts such as the Constitution also referred to other kinds of citizens, especially children, who were the nation's inheritors. To ensure that the social contract would be actively embraced by people throughout the nation and would continue into the future, early American texts placed pressure on private relationships and public printed material to produce citizens who would consent imaginatively to that contract and would understand themselves as participating even when they could not do so directly. The concept that children were affectionate members of the republic, even though they played no role in its founding, helped to reconcile the notion of citizenship as public and active with the ways that it also had to be private and imaginary. Imaginary citizenship in this sense did promote a version of citizenship that was not primarily participatory, but it also did not preclude participation. Despite the fact that children did not have the power to actually vote or hold office, they were imagined as weighing in on matters related to political justice, and some children did indeed participate in this way.

While Warner has claimed that the "textual legitimacy" of the republic was based on "remov[ing] legitimacy from the hands of persons," what I would term the *emotional legitimacy* of the state also required that all citizens relate to this textual state as an object of affection and identification.[7] Because of the government's supposed root within the people, citizens needed to recognize laws as somehow derived from their families, friends, neighbors, and loved ones, as well as from themselves. Noah Webster, who helped popularize this idea in early American schoolbooks, remarked that every person in America "should *know* and *love* their laws" to maintain the liberty that is the foundation of all republican nations.[8]

Children's education was essential to their affectionate identification with the nation. According to Locke, children were initially subject only to the commands of their parents, while citizens' subjection was to law, an entity that was abstract, incorporeal, and textual. Children's books were a crucial way of transitioning both between these two kinds of authority and between a patriarchal system based on the image of the king as father to a mode of abstract but also personal, authority appropriate for a republic. Books written for young people frequently posed as "portable parents," working as an extension of parental power and translating parent into text, but these texts were not primarily about bolstering patriarchal governance in the nation or home. Rather, the culture was shifting from a patriarchal allegiance based on purportedly natural subjection to a national allegiance based on the idea that the people participated in government and that they should thereby identify with the nation and its laws. Children's books acted as an intermediary step in a chain of political associations, initiating citizens into affectionate relationships with the intangible entities of government, nation, and law. Benedict Anderson maintains that these institutions are largely "imagined" in terms of the citizen's daily experience of them and thus rely upon the associative bonds fostered by print culture.[9]

Publication records indicate that children's books were one of the primary ways through which Americans imagined a shared culture. As John Tebbel notes, at least 800 separate children's titles were published in the United States between 1682 and 1836, a number that far exceeded the approximately 100 novels produced in the same period.[10] Though literacy was not universal, one might imagine that these books would have been more accessible to non-fully literate readers than adult books.

The four children's books that appear in this chapter—*The History of Little Goody Two Shoes* (1765; first American edition 1775), *The Renowned History of Giles Gingerbread* (1764), Sarah Fielding's *The Governess* (1749; first American edition, 1786), and Hannah Webster Foster's *The Boarding School* (1798)—were part of a transatlantic culture of affective reading that influenced and helped bring affectionate citizenship into being in the new nation. *Goody Two Shoes* and *Giles Gingerbread*, which were first published by John Newbery and then adapted by Isaiah Thomas, replaced patriarchal theories of language with the idea that words were concrete, affectionate objects that could be played with and manipulated by readers, even as they could also be used to represent the law.

Building on these ideas of language as authoritative but also affectionate and personal, Fielding's children's novel constructs an imaginative version of the social contract in which child readers consent to increasingly representational and textual versions of their teacher's authority, mimicking the colonialist idea of a monarch as an affectionate governor. While the text to some extent supports a system of government that allows citizens to passively identify with government rather than actively engaging in politics, Fielding also departs from Locke's theories to envision a group of female children engaging in collective commentary, implying that imaginary citizens could try and fill in the gaps between the state's exercise of power and their own wishes by forming smaller communities to supplement the larger political community represented by the nation. Foster's version of the school story, which appears to derive its basic structure from Fielding's, adapts the idea of the people's affectionate governance for the American context, prompting readers to identify textual authority not just as the authority of a distant ruler but also as personal authority. Through texts such as Foster's, the law came to be seen as an affectionate representation of the will of the people. Though Foster's text dismantles some of the ways that the schoolgirls function as an acting community in Fielding's work by dispersing them throughout the nation, the ways of reading encouraged by the text might also be seen as allowing children to evaluate the state's representation of the voices of the people. The child's imagined political roles in literary texts therefore represent a spectrum of passivity and activity that perhaps encapsulates the way that many common citizens engaged with politics in the early nation.

Freedom without the Exercise of It

As I have noted, the patriarchal subject was both literally and metaphorically a child—a comparison that Locke and early American politicians in many ways rejected. Locke opens the first of his *Two Treatises of Government* (1690) with a critique of Sir Robert Filmer's *Patriarcha*. He rejects Filmer's theory because it allows for a conception of the citizen as a "slave" to government, while Locke prefers to think of the citizen as a "freeman."[11] The implied gender and age designations of citizenship are significant in that Locke is particularly interested in affording liberty to adult male property holders, whom he feels that Filmer has emasculated and infantilized by making subject to a divine sovereign. Locke flatly denies that children are citizens, asserting that they are under their "Father's Tuition and Authority, till . . . [the] Age of Discretion."[12]

The status of the child is nonetheless central to Locke's theory of citizenship, because Filmer's rationale for the citizen's subjection is precisely that "no Man is Born free" but is naturally subjugated to the patriarch who fathered him. For Filmer, children's submission to parental authority is not distinct from submission to political rulers, who have received their power in a direct line from Adam by virtue of being fathers. In order to contest this argument, Locke claims that children have a right to the "natural Freedom" that Filmer has denied, and thus he must begin, like Filmer, with the citizen's origin in the birth of the child. Despite Locke's assertion that children are under their father's authority, he maintains that individuals are "born . . . with a title to perfect freedom."[13] It is from Locke's account of the child's birth as a "freeman" with natural rights that the bonds between the child's and citizen's freedom begin to be forged, making the child an imaginative figure for the citizen.

Due to this inherent conflict in the text, the meanings and consequences of Locke's declaration that the child is "born free" have been by no means straightforward. Most frequently, his theories have been assumed to apply only to adult men, with the child's liberty a mere specter of the freedom to come. His argument that "a *child* is *free* by his father's title, by his father's understanding, which is to govern him till he hath it of his own" would seem to support this assumption.[14] Yet Locke's emphasis and syntax highlight the portion of the sentence that states that the "*child* is *free*," suggesting that he also wants to emphasize that freedom begins in childhood. Gillian Brown and Jay Fliegelman have argued that Locke granted children with freedom in order to make the bold claim that the powerlessness of youth was not incompatible with the right of self-determination. This logic captured the imagination of the American Revolutionaries, who frequently turned to metaphors of childhood to make their case for independence. Thomas Paine declares in *Common Sense* that "the infant state of the colonies" is "an argument in favor of independence."[15]

Nonetheless, Locke identifies the child's freedom as the root of the citizen's freedom in the context of a political theory that rests on the assertion that the child is not the same as a citizen. Locke's other emphasis—on children's rightful subjection—had important consequences in the colonies and the early American nation. Holly Brewer has shown that his theories caused many children to be denied activities of citizenship, such as voting and holding office.[16] In what Lesley Ginsberg has called an "undeclared war over the limits of citizenship," certain adults, such as women, slaves, and people of color, began to be compared to children and excluded from the full benefits of citizenship.[17] For instance, as Nancy Isenberg points out, while white women were sometimes understood as able to consent to government— for instance, they signed loyalty oaths during the American Revolution—the law often saw them as lacking the capacity for self-government, meaning that their political and legal status "never appeared to change from childhood to adulthood."[18] In this sense, childhood was understood as a marginal position.

Differing conclusions can be drawn from *Two Treatises* because children speak to the fundamental conflict that Locke's work addresses. To make his case for the citizen's freedom, Locke must make two contradictory statements regarding the status of children. On the one hand, he asserts that children are not like citizens because they have inherent incapacities that make them naturally subject to their parents. On the other, he argues that children are born free and that the "*Begetting of Children makes them not Slaves to their Fathers*," just as the citizen is not a slave to government.[19] Locke's conflicting claims about children are best summarized in a paradoxical statement: "*Children*, I confess are not born in [the] full state of *Equality*, though they are born to it." Locke goes on to explain that being "born to" equality, but not "in" it means that the child's subjection is temporary. When children attain reason, they will be no longer subject to the power of their parents and will become free citizens: "when he comes to the Estate that made his *Father a Freeman*, the *son is a Freeman* too."[20] In this sense, the child and citizen are necessary opposites: one is subjected, while the other is free. At the same time, the citizen's freedom is dependent on the status of the child at birth and on the child's education *into* the requirements of freedom. In this way, the child and citizen, and freedom and subjection, are not separate positions but continuous ones. This blurring between child and adult citizen is consistent with Locke's understanding of human development. While his political theories hinge on a sharp transition from childhood to adulthood, he argues in *An Essay Concerning Human Understanding* (1690, first American edition 1803) that "it is BY DEGREES" that children are furnished with knowledge.[21]

The confusion surrounding whether children are free or subjected, like citizens or distinct from them, can be explained by a problem that informs his concept of citizenship in general: even free citizens must be subjects of the law. As subsequent passages make clear, Locke's idea of freedom actually consists of subjection. He explains that the reason that children cannot be completely free is that they cannot understand the law sufficiently to follow it: "But whilst [the child] is in an Estate, wherein he has not Understanding of his own to direct his Will, he is not to have any Will of his own to follow: He that understands for him, must will for him too; he must prescribe to his Will and regulate his Actions."[22] Here, the child's subjection does not contrast with the citizen's freedom but anticipates restrictions on that freedom. The law replaces the parent by providing a new "understanding" that the citizen must follow.

This revelation that citizenship requires subjection can be no surprise to present-day critics, especially those who are well versed in arguments by Michel Foucault and others who argue that power simultaneously enables and constrains. Legal citizenship is, by definition, a form of constraint, since, as Brook Thomas points out, "citizens remain subjects of the state."[23] Yet the idea that citizens were not children and therefore not patriarchal subjects was a crucial part of the political rhetoric and legal reform of the period. To contest patriarchal theory, Locke must try to keep citizens and subjects separate. But, because the situation of the child gives rise to that of the citizen, Locke must insist on the natural freedom of children to make the case for the citizen's freedom, even as this makes for a logical paradox: "Thus, we are born free, as we are born Rational; not that we have actually the Exercise of either."[24] While Locke goes on to insist that the ability to exercise freedom and equality come with age, the need to follow an externally imposed law suggests that "freedom without the exercise of it" is a state that the child and citizen often share.

The actuality of constraint requires that freedom be elaborated through imaginary narratives, as much as through legal rights. Brown explains Locke's limitations on freedom by claiming that free consent always requires "augmentations" upon the present, which are most fully represented in "the suspended state before . . . the implementation of an act."[25] Freedom is not always realized, but is instead imaginative, located in mental processes that can be attained by all rational beings, even if they do not always have political power. Although Brown's location of consent in the imagination is accurate, reflected in the importance of fictional texts in inculcating citizenship, she identifies the child's ability to represent consenting citizenship only with the exercise of reason and not with the more irrational emotions of love and affection that were being associated with childhood and with imaginative reading in the period. These emotions were significant in contending with the gap between the citizen's freedom and the exercise of it, since rationally understanding the law could not guarantee that citizens would identify with it or see it as an extension of themselves.

Locke has been best known for his theories of rational citizenship, but he uses affection as much as reason to make his case for the liberty of the child and citizen. In the parental relationship, affection is a means to soften the fact of the child's subjection and to make that subjection consistent with freedom. He explains, "The Bonds of Subjection are like the Swaddling Cloths [children] are wrapt up in, and supported by, in the weakness of their Infancy."[26] Locke argues that because parents only subject their offspring to discipline out of love, the restrictions they place upon their children do not contradict their natural right to liberty.

Though Locke often rejects the parallel between childhood and citizenship and vehemently denies the patriarchal claim that father-like protection compels obedience, his argument posits that the law operates in a similar way as the parent, only imposing constraints that are for the citizen's protection. This rationale creates a messy formulation in which citizens give up their natural liberty in order to get a more limited form of liberty: "But though Men when they enter into Society, give up the Equality, Liberty, and Executive Power they had in the State of Nature . . . yet it being only with an intention in every one the better to preserve himself his Liberty and Property."[27]

The child within the family has little choice but to accept the parental protection given in place of liberty, but the citizen is understood as *consenting* to this uneven trade. While *Two Treatises* claims that the citizen consents judiciously to ensure the preservation of his property, Locke also relies on an irrational, hidden, and private force to carry out his model of citizenship: specifically, the citizen's imagination, inculcated in childhood, that the law is legitimate and even caring—and is thus a fair arbiter of property rights, as well as other kinds of justice.

Locke's anthropological account of the government claims that this affectionate feeling is how political societies began and what initially preserved them from
dissolving: "*a family* by degrees *grew into a commonwealth* . . . every one in his
Turn growing up under it, tacitly submitted to it, and the Easiness and Equality
of it not offending any one, every one acquiesced . . . without such nursing fathers
tender and careful of the public weal, all governments would have sunk under the
weakness and infirmities of their infancy."[28] Citizens were primed to accept the
governance of their fathers not by parental right, but by their consent, which was
motivated by affection. Locke suggests elsewhere that this consent was "tacit, and
scarce avoidable" since "they had been accustomed in their Childhood to follow his
Direction, and to refer their little Differences to him; and when they were Men,
who fitter to rule them? . . . Their little Properties . . . seldom afforded great Con-
troversies; and when they should arise, where could they have a fitter Umpire than
he, by whose Care they had been . . . sustained and brought up?"[29] Locke implies
that it was the citizen's belief in government's "tender" and legitimate "care" that
kept citizens from rising against the government even after the family gave way
to the commonwealth. Locke ultimately claims that the family is different from a
"politick society" and favors express consent over such tacit consent. However, his
theory of how governments emerged from families allows for an imagination of
citizenship and consent that is based not on the legal requirements of reason and
independence but rather on imaginative feelings and bonds. The citizen does not
surrender his liberty out of mere self-interest. Instead it evolves from the idea that
he is loved.

Affection's playing a major role in the formation of society was further elaborated by the Scottish "moral sense" school. Anthony Ashley-Cooper, third Earl of
Shaftesbury, who was educated using Locke's *Some Thoughts Concerning Education*,
maintained that civic virtue arose from benevolent feeling for others.[30] Francis
Hutcheson too claimed that humans had an innate "moral sense" and also a "public sense," in which they were pleased and pained by the situations of others.[31]
Hutcheson considered these senses as the primary basis for all action, including
political action. As David Shields argues, the frequent "identification of reason with
one's political affections" in the eighteenth century, "suggests that 'feeling' rather
than 'reason' more accurately names what was at work in [civic activity]."[32]

The expectation that the relationship between citizens and government would
be affectionate was one that was shared on both sides of the Atlantic and informed
much of the popular rhetoric during the Revolution. In *Common Sense* (1776),
Thomas Paine legitimizes America's rebellion by casting Britain as an unaffection-
ate parent: "But Britain is the parent country, say some. Then the more shame

Thomas Colley, "The Reconciliation between Britania and her Daughter America,"
1782. Loyalists to the crown showed the colonists as an Indian princess and Britain as a
loving mother asking her "good Girl" for a kiss. Courtesy of the Library of Congress.

upon her conduct. Even brutes do not devour their young, nor savages make war
upon their families."[33] A Loyalist political cartoon depicting mother England em-
bracing her rebellious American daughter (portrayed as an Indian princess) shows
a shared belief in the need for affection between governors and governed. In the
cartoon's fantasy of reconciliation, America says to England, "Dear Mama, say
no more about it," and England responds by asking for a kiss.[34] Though the conflict between Britain and its colonies could not always be reframed in affectionate
terms, and Paine denies the parent-child metaphor elsewhere in his work, Paine
suggests that Americans should nonetheless strive for affectionate citizenship in
creating a new nation. He declares that "as parents, we can have no joy, knowing
that this *government* is not sufficiently lasting to ensure anything which we may
bequeath to posterity" and contends that "the feelings and affections which nature
justifies" demand that America break with England and establish a government
that is more stable for American children.[35] Part of setting up this new government
meant ensuring that children did not have the same rationale for rebelling against
American leaders as they did against English ones.

    For Paine, as for Locke, the concept of affectionate citizenship complicates the
ideal age for citizenship to begin. Paine at first denies the image of the citizen as a

child, aligning himself with Locke's argument that children, while "born free" in a nominal sense, do not gain political power until maturity.[36] Drawing on Locke's claim that childhood is a time of subjection and adulthood a time of freedom, Paine accuses England of infantilizing America, stunting its growth as a mature nation: "We may as well assert that because a child has thrived upon milk that it is never to have meat, or that the first twenty years of our lives is to become a precedent for the next twenty."[37] It is the nation's maturity, only faintly prefigured by its birth, which grants it the power of self-determination. Yet Paine is ultimately unclear about whether the new nation is best represented by a "youth" on the verge of adulthood or an "infant," stages of life that seem at first to be differently positioned in Locke's story of political foundation, but that blur together both in Locke's work and in popular terminology. Consistent with the parlance of the times, Paine uses these terms interchangeably. He argues that that "the *infant* state of the Colonies" is "an argument in favour of independence" because "*youth* is the seed time of good habits, as well in nations as in individuals" and that "the intimacy which is contracted in *infancy* . . . [is] the most lasting and unalterable.[38] Diverging from his general assertion that freedom is the rightful province of adults, the passage equates infant and youth and ultimately associates neither with unqualified freedom, but instead with education *into* independence, which requires a foundation in "good habits." Society, instead of being formed by a free contract, is "contracted" through intimate relationships with fellow citizens. Rather than favoring a mature and rational citizenry, as he did in other parts of his work, Paine here suggests that children's citizenship is the best kind, because theirs is the most amenable to influence and mutual dependency.

Locke's *Some Thoughts Concerning Education* (1693), which Brown reports was even more popular in the early republic than his political work, offered a similar argument and provided Americans with a means for actualizing affectionate citizenship in the early republic. In this pedagogical work, Locke is quite transparent about the ways that affection manages the tensions between natural freedom and subjection to the law. His theory of child governance promises parents a way to introduce subjection without damaging the child's sense of natural liberty: "he that has found a way, how to keep a child's spirit, easy, active and free; and yet, at the same time, to restrain him from many things he has a mind to . . . he, I say, that knows how to reconcile these seeming contradictions, has, in my opinion, got the true secret of education."[39] As before, the "secret" turns out to be affection, which Locke describes as a specific means of creating docile behavior in adulthood, as in childhood: "Would you have your Son obedient to you when past a Child? . . . So shall you have him your obedient Subject . . . whilst he is a Child, and your affectionate Friend when he is a Man."[40]

Locke makes it clear that his affectionate adult citizen will believe himself to be free, but will still be constrained: "We would be thought Rational Creatures, and have our Freedom . . . If therefore a strict Hand be kept over Children *from the Beginning*, they will in that [adult] Age be tractable, and quietly submit to it, as never having known any other."[41] Here, unlike in *Two Treatises*, the parent's control of the child's affections is not considered fundamentally different from the governance of adult citizens but rather a necessary step in getting them to see lawful behavior in adulthood as free rather than constrained.

Locke does not explain how the authority of the law replaces the authority of the parent in the child's heart, but his work hints at some of the ways that this might happen. In particular, Locke claims that the relationship between child and book should mimic the power dynamic that he imagines between parent and child. Child readers, he argues, must be made subject to their books in a way that preserves their sense of liberty. To make reading "a Thing of Delight," he suggests that "Contrivances might be made *to teach Children to Read*, whilst they thought they were only Playing."[42] Locke is often credited with a shift in children's literature from books that were meant only to teach to those that were meant to gain the child's love.[43]

The pedagogy of affection had a profound effect on the ways in which child readers were encouraged to relate to their books on both sides of the Atlantic. The invention of entertaining children's books was not just an important innovation in the world of children's literature, but a crucial link underlying modern political theory, working to establish the deep associations between the child's affection and the citizen's freedom that would come to permeate national discourse. As both material objects and representations of ideas, children's books could act as a bridge between the present and absent, the immanent and representative, enacting the child reader's gradual initiation into love for things that existed primarily as abstract concepts, such as the law and the nation. By depicting the process in which the child graduates from parental control to textual governance and self-governance refracted through texts, children's books published in early America established a means through which children and citizens could love and obey the law by imagining that its power somehow *originated* in their own opinions and acts, further legitimizing Locke's and the founders' account of the citizen's consent to government. In this way, children's reading became a vital act of recognition—and misrecognition—of the state's foundation in the people.

Loving Language

No longer assuming that language is the province of fathers, eighteenth-century children's books go to great lengths to encourage readers to have affection for alphabetic characters and the books that contain them as personal and intimate objects. To this end, they often emphasize the materiality of letters, personifying them and giving them physical presence as material objects made of wood, metal, and gingerbread. As Seth Lerer summarizes, "Letters could be pasted onto dice or polygons; words could become toys; books themselves could become objects of delight."[44] In some sense, this makes language comparable to an affectionate parent, acting as a bridge between immanent and representative authority and allowing distant authority figures to function through language—a lesson fitting for a colony. But it also makes language a site of personal feeling, identification, and desire that can be possessed, preparing the child reader to understand the abstract entities of nation and law as personal. The transformation of the child in learning to read therefore mimics the larger cultural shifts that were happening during the American Revolution: the child transfers her affections from her parents to the law, and the nation replaces allegiance to a distant, but embodied, monarch with allegiance to the authority of the people represented through texts.

Illuminating examples of the new emphasis on book love occur in two of the most popular children's playbooks of the eighteenth century, *The History of Little Goody Two Shoes* and *The Renowned History of Giles Gingerbread*, both of which were published widely in the colonies and early nation. In *The History of Little Goody Two Shoes*, the alphabet is cast as both physical object and as legal apparatus. Fittingly, given the transfer of language from fathers to the people, the texts focuses on an orphan girl named Margery Meanwell, who is renamed "Goody Two Shoes" and begins to teach children herself. Referencing an educational innovation claimed to have been discovered by authors as diverse as Newbery and Samson Occum, Goody makes a set of wooden letters that the children can use as toys. Rousseau refers to this method of reading instruction as the "bureaux" method, the bureau being a "sort of case containing letters to be put together to form words."[45] In addition to giving readers a practical way to make reading a "game," as Locke suggests, the bureau makes letters into material objects that can be touched and held, making it easier for the child to understand them as personal. *Little Goody Two Shoes* suggests that the children's affection for the letters as physical objects prepares them to obey language when it is later presented as an abstract governing mechanism. Offering a basic version of the way that the law operates through language, Goody literally governs with the ABCs: whenever anyone is in a domestic dispute, she asks that the guilty parties say all of the letters of the alphabet before responding to each other.

Another striking embodiment of language in eighteenth-century children's literature comes in the form of what Patricia A. Crain has called "swallow letters," or letters that can eat or be eaten.[46] As an example of this motif, she cites the popular "A Apple Pye" rhyme that was found in children's reading texts of the period: "A Apple pye / B bit it / C cut it" and so on. Crain claims that this rhyme allows the alphabet to "contain and regulate the passions."[47] This curious tendency to make letters into food led to a number of descriptions of child readers as bibliophagi, a term that twentieth-century bibliophile Holbrook Jackson has used to describe readers who eat their books.[48] As a loving readerly activity, book eating sets the stage for understanding language as personal and for converting affection for one's book into love for abstract ideals, such as law. By way of the reader's stomach, the book itself disappears, but its authority remains as an invisible guide.

The most famous of the eighteenth-century bibliophagi was a Newbery child character by the name of Giles Gingerbread. Giles is taught by his father "Old" Gaffer Gingerbread, whose control of the language, shown by his skill at baking letters into gingerbread, is taken over by his child. As Giles's literacy attempts commence, it becomes clear that it is not enough for Giles simply to know his letters; he must have affection for books as personal, physical objects. Gaffer makes the entire alphabet of letters out of gingerbread so that Giles can learn to spell words with them—a method that was actually used to teach basic reading skills in the eighteenth century. In *Practical Education*, Richard and Maria Edgeworth claim that this is "usually" the method parents use, a tactic that they denounce as a "bribe."[49]

Despite this bribe, Giles is not very successful at his first attempt at ordering the letters correctly. When his father asks him to spell "goose," he spells it "guse." At this, Gaffer becomes angry at his son and says, "You Blockhead, is that your manner of spelling?"[50] Gaffer's anger seems misplaced given his playful presentation of the gingerbread letters, but it clues the reader in to the actual purpose of his gingerbread reading instruction. Gaffer explains to Giles that he does not sufficiently know the letters and their sounds. A reader of the text might argue that Giles actually does know the letters and their sounds very well for someone who is a beginner to reading, as he spells "goose" in a way that is phonetically correct. Gaffer's complaint reveals that what is at stake is not just basic literacy, but connection with language, and thereby, connection with a common, national culture. Gaffer makes Giles speak to the letters as if they were personal friends: "Mr. B, I should be a Blockhead if I did not know you / C, C, C, I shall know you Mr. C indeed, and so will every Boy that loves custard."[51] This activity suggests that the true goal of literacy instruction is affection, desire, and even longing, for language.

This moment in the text also reminds us that efforts to regularize spelling, which began in the Renaissance but were still active during the eighteenth century, were tied both to the rise of governmental institutions and to nationalism. Giles cannot individualize expression by spelling "goose" however he likes. Rather, he must make a personal connection with standard language, which was becoming a shared idiom appropriate for communicating governmental proclamations and laws. Only then could laws be seen as the language of the people. Of course, the commonality of the English language also became problematic during the American Revolution, leading Americans to differentiate their speech from that of their enemies. Webster claimed that his *American Spelling Book*, which used American spelling and pronunciation, was meant to "diffuse an uniformity and purity of language in America" and to "promote the interest of literature and harmony of the United States."[52] In sympathy with this effort, some American printers changed Giles's name to Tommy Gingerbread.

As a further means to entice Giles into seeing the letters as intimate objects, Gaffer makes him an entire book out of gingerbread. The gingerbread book gives Giles the possibility not only of devouring his book but also of destroying it, prefiguring the ways that seeing language and government as personal could lead to revolution against fathers' ways of doing things. The story makes the case that such change need not ultimately undermine lawful order—a lesson that would have been attractive on both sides of the Atlantic. Gaffer comes home one day to find that Giles has committed an even worse offense than misspelling "goose": he has eaten a corner of his book. But by reciting the part of the lesson he has eaten, Giles shows him that his eating of his book was not an unruly act but a ritual that allowed him more fully to internalize its authority. In doing so, Giles uses his intimate relationship to language to transfer his love to authority that exists only in the abstract and to see this authority as part of himself. This transformation is summarized by a rhyme found at the story's end: "See here's Little Giles / With his Gingerbread Book, / For which he doth long / And at which he doth look, / Till by longing and looking, / He got it by Heart, / And then eats it up / As we eat up a tart."[53] It is the connection between feeling an affectionate longing for one's book and the transfer of this affection to abstract lessons that allows the command "learn to love your book" to become inseparable from lawfulness and for the child to understand this lawfulness as freedom.

The Book as Governess

Books for older children such as Fielding's *The Governess* and Foster's *The Boarding School* also emphasized the affectionate authority of texts, but, instead of making language concrete and lovable, these texts made authority increasingly distant, abstract, and textual. The characters and narrators of these books are not often parents, but parent surrogates—usually brothers, friends, kindly aunts, or what Locke called "governors"—a motif that was part of a pervasive cultural attempt to gradually gain the child's affection for various modes of representative authority such as colonial governors, government representatives, texts, laws, and nations.[54]

The Governess is an extended meditation on governance, expressing in fiction many of the era's ideas about government. As the title suggests, Fielding's narrative takes as its ultimate expression of government the translation of the tutor into text, the physical body of the teacher made into a book.[55] The governess in question is Mrs. Teachum, who has nine female pupils. Through Teachum's increasingly mediated representation through a colonial representative named Jenny, through stories told orally, and finally through written language, the child reader learns to submit to increasingly representative and incorporeal forms of power. As such, *The Governess* can be seen as an ur-text of affectionate citizenship, through which imaginative links between the people and the law began to be established. While the book, as an English text, presents a singular governor, as in a monarchical system, it was written in an age of limits to the monarchy—in which the people were more fervently claiming representation in parliament—and in an age of empire, in which the monarch's power had to become representative and transferable to colonial agents. Through her account of a consenting community of affectionate readers, Fielding narrates the child reader's acceptance of the governess's authority as both a loving representation of the people's interests and as an abstract governing mechanism, forging the links between the personal and political that early American texts such as *The Boarding School* would further develop.

Basing the structure of *The Governess* on the social contract, Fielding employs key Lockean motifs such as the state of war and the notion of univocal consent to government. Rather than emphasizing reason as the motivation for entrance into the social contract, as is often done in interpretations of Locke, her interpretation highlights the role that emotion plays in consenting citizenship. Fielding further departs from Locke in that she makes it clear that affection is to be a motivator for dutiful citizenship even when the citizen has no property to protect. She is also less willing than Locke to alleviate the feelings of individual sacrifice and constraint that are associated with consent to the social contract. The affection that motivates consent is not immediately presented as a voluntary feeling but as a lofty moral virtue that must be learned and practiced to compel subjection and make it bearable. Even though the novel makes the case that consent is in the child's best interests, it does not focus primarily on freedom, as in Locke, but on happiness, which Fielding suggests is compatible with a fairly rigid government. But at the same time that the governess demands absolute obedience as textual monarch, Fielding also moves toward giving the children consciousness of their own feelings and powers, which lead both to their consent and to their emergence as a miniature community. The children (other than Jenny) do not participate in government. However, the society that the girls create alongside that government, while not entirely autonomous or free, can be seen as a consolation for the limitations of consent and affection in producing an entirely just society. Such imagined societies might provide a source for the child citizen if faced with political injustices.

This lesson would have been particularly important for Fielding's and Foster's primary audience, who were girls. Since these young women were doubly removed from participation rights by age and gender on both sides of the Atlantic and would not retain property rights after they were married, their claims to citizenship could not be predicated on ideas of equal representation in government or judicious protection of property. The fact that both *The Governess* and *The Boarding School* feature young women forming social contracts reminds us that women not having participation rights did not preclude them from being recognized as parties to the social contract. In fact, their lack of rights may have made it in some sense easier to manage their entrance into the contract, since it would not need to be backed up with actual participation in politics. Although girls did not always have equal access to schooling as boys, Mary Kelley has argued that girls at female academies, such as the ones portrayed in *The Governess* and *The Boarding School*, were encouraged to "envision themselves as historical actors who had claim to the rights and obligations of citizenship."[56]

Political education was uneven for children of different situations, but there is evidence, aside from the implicit lessons in these texts, that girls and boys alike were taught the rudiments of political knowledge, even though in most states only a relatively small percentage of boys would become voting citizens.[57] For instance, thirteen-year-old American girl Sally Ripley writes in her diary in 1799, "until the 4th July 1776 the present sixteen United States were British colonies, on that ever memorable day the representatives of the United States in Congress assembled made a solemn declaration of Independence."[58] Girls learned these lessons in part because they were meant to eventually teach their sons about politics. Girls were also part of the real and imagined social culture of politics, even if they were not allowed to vote when they grew up. Kelley shows that women attended political events and "modeled republican virtue in salons, informal gatherings, assemblies, and tea tables," instructing men in "the discursive and behavioral practices required for citizenship in the new nation."[59]

Girls could not expect to eventually gain the rights that (white, property-holding) boys would eventually attain, and so these social forms of citizenship were particularly crucial for them. At the same time, due to the practical limitations on any individual's ability to participate and contribute to government, boys too needed to be schooled in patriotic identification and emotional recognition of the law as a moral institution and a just representation of their values, even if they were not directly involved in its making. Girls' and boys' education into citizenship thus would have been similar in many respects despite the differences in their eventual rights. Significantly, by examining subscription lists in Britain, M. O. Grenby has found that the consumers of children's books were predominantly female, possibly because imaginary citizenship was so important for women.[60] But Grenby suggests that there was also significant sharing of books between the sexes, including *The Governess*, which was bought by at least two male tutors for use with their pupils.[61] Because civics textbooks were not in widespread use for either sex until the mid- to late nineteenth century in the United States (and even later in Britain), children's instruction in how to participate in citizenship activities would have relied on a motley curriculum pieced together from geography books, political treatises, elocution and spelling books, history books, and periodicals, as well as dialogues, novels, and children's stories such as the ones I discuss here.[62]

The Governess's political lesson begins prior to the girls' consent to Teachum's governance, in which they inhabit a state that resembles what Locke calls the state of nature, or human existence prior to the emergence of a social contract—though, since the girls are also pupils the whole time, it may also resemble a patriarchal view of a monarchical government in which the people have no role in consenting to government. However we understand the girls' pre-contract state, it quickly dissolves into a state of war or lawlessness. The first chapter provides "an account of a fray" in which the pupils of the school get into a violent, pigtail-pulling fight over who should have had the largest apple. The apple is an appropriate object of contention in this war because the fruit's status as a biblical symbol of individual knowledge and power contrasts with the authority to which the girls as citizens must affectionately consent: nominally the governess but metaphorically God and his representation in the king. The apple also anticipates the turn from the power of an embodied ruler to the textual power of the state, in that the apple was one of the first concrete objects that was first translated into text by children's rhymes such as "A is for Apple" and "A Apple Pye." As preparation for the girls' eventual progression to textual governance, Mrs. Teachum appears briefly to correct them herself, but from the moment of their consent to her control, her authority has already become representational. One of the girls, Jenny Peace, comes to stand in for Teachum, and it is she who oversees the children's submission to Teachum's rule, acting as what we might call her colonial representative among the girls. Jenny demonstrates by throwing the apple over the fence that fighting will not secure resources for any of them and hints that each could have better protected their property in the apple by letting Teachum divide it among them. Yet, complicating a reading of contract based on property alone, Jenny's action simultaneously writes property *out* as a reason for consenting to governance, demanding that the girls consent without any hope of gaining even part of the apple.

This initial moment of consent, parallel to Locke's in *Two Treatises*, instead emphasizes the role of affection in the citizen's peaceful surrender of freedom for the good of society. When Jenny first enters the scene, each child character is interested solely in her own natural freedom and right to the apple. Through an appeal to sisterly love, Jenny is able to convince the girls to confess that their unconstrained liberty is an obstacle to their mutual happiness and to tearfully accept obedience to Teachum: "Their Eyes, melting with Sorrow for their Faults, let fall some Drops, as Tokens of their Repentance: But, as soon as they could recover themselves to speak, they all with one Voice cried out, Indeed, Miss Jenny, we are Sorry for our Fault, and will follow your Advice."[63]

The consolidation of the girls' individual voices into one voice of consent to governance echoes the unanimous social compact imagined by Locke. The choice to enter into this decision is presented largely as a rational choice of society over individual desire. In spite of this, Fielding reveals the loss and restraint that the choice entails for the individual subject, hinting that reason and property is frequently not enough to justify sacrificing one's liberty for others—and certainly not for those who do not have property to begin with.

The Governess makes the argument that the sacrifice of individual liberty is an act that results from the child's outpouring of emotion and desire for happiness. Fielding writes in her preface, "love and affection . . . makes the happiness of all societies."[64] The outcome of this lesson is potentially twofold. On the one hand, the text speciously justifies constraints on the child's freedom by suggesting that they will make the child happy. While Teachum governs with affection, her rule is absolute and powerful. On the other, even if the girls are not totally free, they have each other. Their having formed a people of their own suggests a collective power

Frontispiece, *The Governess*, 1827 edition. In this book, young Jenny Peace comes to stand in for the authority figure and helps inculcate the children at a boarding school in the proper way to "love their book." Courtesy of the American Antiquarian Society.

that can make them a force for justice, even if this power is never used against their governess. Love and kindness also have the potential to offer alternative ways of interacting in society that supplement the overt rationality of the citizen in Locke's system and even complicate his quid pro quo model of civic engagement.

Just as the children of the story add their consent to the text's depiction of a loving social contract, the reader is meant to voice it as well; Fielding writes, "I depend on the Goodness of my little Readers, to acknowledge this to be true."[65] This address to the reader, found in the preface, attempts to assimilate the child into a community of readers, who represent a population that has unanimously consented to governance.[66] Many eighteenth-century children's books used dialogue as a way to incorporate the children's voices and dramatize their consent to textual authority. This idea of children and readers speaking in "one voice" as a response to authority is not unique to this text but is found in multiple educational texts of the period. Though these texts reflect the common practice in the period of having pupils read in unison in the classroom, the motif of children having "one voice" seems to go beyond a mere depiction of pedagogical strategy. This motif stems from the eighteenth-century's intense interest, explored by Locke and others, in the process by which the individual's "free" consent to governance and entrance into citizenship makes one voice out of many.[67] The children in *The Governess* hint at the difficulty of achieving this unanimity among the people, for instance when one girl says that she should not be punished because she "did not begin" the apple incident.[68] The text suggests that univocality can become habitual and tries to gain this uniformity by educating readers about how to read and respond to texts. At the same time, the text concedes that responses among readers vary and thus hints that readers can never be fully incorporated.

In the next section of *The Governess*, Jenny reinforces the children's decision to give up their liberties out of love for their society by telling a fairy tale called "The Story of the Cruel Giant Barbarico, and the Good Giant Benefico." This tale is a parable of governance in which Jenny reenvisions further envisions subjection to government as based on affection rather than on force or enslavement. In the story, two giant rulers have different approaches to governing. Barbarico, the cruel giant, governs through "Fear and Astonishment" so that "the whole Country . . . trembled" at the sound of his groans.[69] The other giant, Benefico, constantly carries out "acts of Goodness and Benevolence," which make everyone love and obey him. Over the course of the story, the savage Barbarico wreaks havoc on two citizens, Amata and Fidus. In the end, with the help of an enslaved dwarf named Mignon, the two bring the tyrant to justice and elect Benefico as leader.

As "their Governor, their Father, and their Kind Protector," Benefico demonstrates the ways in which affection can be used to legitimize various constraints on the citizen's freedom. Although Benefico's affectionate form of authority leads to a public proclamation of freedom, it is contingent on banishing the kinds of desires that Barbarico embodied: "Dissension, Discord, and Hatred were banished from this friendly Dwelling; and that Happiness, which is the natural consequence of Goodness, appeared in chearful Countenance throughout the Castle."[70] The story is meant to convince the children that such constraints can actually provide greater liberty, as long as they are founded on a principle of affection, reinforcing the lesson that they had lately learned about suppressing their desires for the good of their little society.

The tale also moves them to think about how to understand their power as citizens. Jenny suggests that one of the major points of the story is to suggest to the children that "whenever you have any Power, you must follow the example of Benefico, and do Good with it."[71] In part, the tale refers to the power that must be suppressed to become part of their happy society and to the power to consent to the social compact, as when the girls' transferred their natural authority to Teachum, who like Benefico is a just ruler. The story is followed by a confession by one of the girls that she used to mistreat people until Jenny taught her to stop fighting and join with the others. Yet the story also goes beyond the power to consent and suggests having the power to seek justice as part of a community. The girl's confession gives way to a short scene in which the girls observe another child being beaten next door. They protest this violence, and the child is released. The girls learn that the child was being beaten for lying and ultimately decide that they approve of this use of discipline. Their actions suggest that the community is not just one that is disciplined by their entrance into affectionate citizenship; the girls also form a coalition that can weigh in on matters related to social justice. Though this aspect of the text is a fiction—real children are not actually weighing in—it suggests that the people, including children, should have a voice in affairs such as the punishment of people who break societal laws. Historians of childhood have shown that children did emerge at times as historical actors, particularly within local communities.[72]

The frame surrounding the "Barbarico and Benefico" story also indicates that readers have a powerful role in interpreting and evaluating the narratives that make up the textual culture of a nation, especially since governing texts were supposed to be seen as a mirror of the power of the people. Though Teachum tries to control the ways that the story is read by telling Jenny what to emphasize for the girls, the children express several different viewpoints about the story, each valuing a different part of its plot. The parts that the children in the story like tend to be the most rebellious: for instance, Sukey Jennett likes the part where Benefico defeats Barbarico. Polly Suckling, the littlest girl, is most pleased by the dwarf Mignon and "the power of that little creature to conquer such a great monster."[73] There is some evidence to suggest that "Barbarico and Benefico" story was read differently by readers on either side of the revolutionary conflict and that American readers understood the text as promoting rebellion. Notably, this portion of *The Governess* was the first portion to attract an American printer. John Mein of Boston sold the story on its own in 1768, before the entire work appeared in 1791.

While Fielding's text seems to generally support English rule—a loyalty conveyed by Jenny as colonial figure—the date of the American printing of the fairy tale suggests that its contrast between free and corrupt governance spoke to Americans' growing concerns about colonial government. The idea that children had the power to consent also meant that they had the power to dissent and, as the Revolution would prove, one of the side effects of the theory of affectionate governance was that dissent could be seen as legitimate if government was cast as acting cruelly or betraying the citizen's love. At the same time, as Americans moved from breaking national bonds to building their own, they, like Benefico and Teachum, wanted to minimize dissent, requiring that they institute their own forms of affectionate governance. Affection for texts in this sense could also be understood as a way of encouraging children not to depart too much from the text's statements about its intended meaning—and *The Governess* has much to offer on this score. Teachum often coaches Jenny on how to interpret the tales for the girls, imposing her authority on and through texts.

Once the children have been convinced of the relative freedom that comes from affectionate obedience, they must consent to Teachum's governance at a greater level of abstraction. Jenny comes with another story to read and asks for their consent to hear it. The children voice their willingness in a way that echoes their first unanimous social compact, demonstrating that their consent is becoming trained and habitual: "It was the Custom now so much amongst them to assent to any Proposal that came from Miss Jenny, that they all with one voice desired her to read it."[74] Through this second social compact, the children's submission to Teachum's authority becomes a submission to narrative. While the tales are still somewhat embodied, as Jenny tells them orally, this is soon revealed to be an intermediary move that will prepare the children to love and obey governance that does not rely on physical presence.

The new story, "The Princess Hebe," places an even greater emphasis than did "Barbarico and Benefico" on obedience to authority figures, though it also suggests that children must remain vigilant against rulers that are not affectionate and moves toward a vision of the child acting as governor. Like the story of the giants, "The Princess Hebe" begins with a power struggle between two potential rulers. The king Abdallah is a benevolent ruler so "beloved in his Subjects" and "quiet in his Dominions" that his commands are always cheerfully obeyed and his force is rarely felt.[75] When Abdallah dies, his power-hungry and passionate sister-in-law Tropo designs for her husband Abdulham to take the throne, disinheriting the young Princess Hebe. The text's choice of names for the characters suggests more than a regime change between the two brothers. Abdallah and Abdulham are Arabic names and Tropo and Hebe are

Greek. In England and the United States, these languages would have been associated with stereotype versions of different political traditions: Arabic with despotism and Greek with democracy.[76] Although the text is ostensibly about monarchy, it also comments on these versions of government. It might be tempting to argue that author of the text wants to convey replacing the potentially tyrannical politics of Arab despotism with a new generation of neoclassical democrats capable of self-rule. However, both the good king and the bad king have Arabic names and the villainess and heroine have Greek names suggests that the text takes a more balanced approach to Arab and Greek political traditions and that even relatively free governments are not immune to the negative influence of passions.[77]

King Abdulham does not attempt to harm Hebe physically, as we might expect in a traditional fairy tale but is potentially even more dangerous by eighteenth-century standards: he threatens to take over her education. Princess Hebe and her mother, Queen Rousignon, escape to the house of a fairy named Sybella. The fairy, though occupying an enchanted forest seemingly removed from the domain of political governance, teaches Hebe more proper lessons about government than the usurping Abdulham can provide. Although Abdulham shows that authority can be suspect, Sybella's program of education, much like that of Jenny Peace, focuses on denying one's individual desires and submitting wholeheartedly to authority. Rousignon is the first to learn to suppress her passions, following a trajectory much like that of the children in *The Governess*. When she arrives at Sybella's house, the queen is overcome by her passionate desires for Hebe to have the throne, but Sybella suggests that Hebe will be happier if Rousignon dismisses these passionate urges for power in favor of quiet submission and resignation. Once she has come to this conclusion, Rousignon, like the girls at Mrs. Teachum's school, gets to hear a story about how Sybella's tyrannical mother tried to usurp power from her husband, in which Sybella highlights the dangers of both the passions and of misplaced power.

After Rousignon has conquered her "raging passions," Sybella tells her that she can offer Hebe any gift in her power. Rather than asking for Hebe's return to the throne, Rousignon asks that Hebe be given the gift of wisdom, which Sybella tellingly translates into obedience. She grants the wish, not by giving Hebe any power, but by telling her that she must obey her mother in every particular. In doing so, she reiterates that those being ruled, whether children, wives, sisters-in-law, or subjects, should submit themselves fully to authority, without trying to usurp control: "True Obedience . . . consists in Submission; and when we pretend to choose what Commands are proper and fit for us, we don't obey, but set up our own Wisdom in opposition to our Governors."[78] Significantly, the phrase "true Obedience . . . consists in Submission" is actually a play on a more common formulation in which freedom and submission are connected (see, for instance, the epigraph for this chapter, in which "liberty consists in restraint"). Like Locke's free citizen who must submit to the law, young Hebe learns that she can only be happy when she lays aside her own will, but Hebe's goal is not freedom, but rather doubled obedience.

At the same time, Hebe does eventually take the throne, allowing for another iteration of the idea that "power, if made a right use of, is indeed a very great blessing."[79] Although Teachum's pupils are not understood as ruling, but rather consenting to rule, this story imagines the possibility for children to eventually participate in ruling. In political terms, this power can only be imagined, as children and specifically girls did not get this chance, especially in the monarchical context in which the book was written—and readers likely understood that Hebe was a privileged character. But by emphasizing Hebe's education rather than simply her inheritance of power, the story also approaches the ideal of a government in which well-educated people could be understood as participating.

One of the ways that a government could imagine itself as a government of the people was by governing through laws and texts rather than corporeal governors. The remainder of *The Governess* further emphasizes the need for children to consent to the lessons of their books by suggesting that not only stories but also *texts* can act as governing mechanisms when authority figures are absent, making the way for this more radical step to be taken in other texts. At the end of the story, Jenny Peace has to leave school to live with her aunt (who notably just returned from the Americas), but her influence at the school remains in the form of her story: "All Quarrels and Contentions were banished . . . and if any such Thing was likely to arise, the Story of Miss Jenny Peace reconciling all her little Companions was told to them; so that Miss Jenny, tho' absent, still seemed . . . to be the Cement of Union and Harmony in this well-regulated Society."[80] Unlike in the storytelling scenes, where the girls' consent is accompanied by Jenny's physical presence, this final story, told in letters, entails a complete translation of Jenny's (and Teachum's) authority into text. From Jenny's letters, it does not take much to realize the method through which the child reader of *The Governess* has been governed all along. In addition to the governesses within the text, the book itself is governess.

Schooling for American Citizenship

While *The Governess* stops short of imagining that the girls (aside from Jenny) have any part in creating the texts that form this new kind of textual governance, the basic format of the text reappears and does take such a form in Foster's *The Boarding School*, a follow up to her best-selling novel *The Coquette* (1797). As the contrast between the singularity of "the governess" and the plurality of "the boarding school" suggests, Americans would ultimately consider affection an essential component of representative democracy and an illustration of their break from England. Print was a technology that could support both colonial and republican representation, making English children's texts adaptable by American writers to serve their own political ends. The premise of *The Boarding School,* slightly different from *The Governess,* is that the young pupils will be leaving the school and will no longer have their governess, Mrs. Williams, to govern them. Preparing for this dispersal of authority, Williams gives the students a final set of lessons to take away with them. The lessons are not simply rules for the children to follow but steps to transfer their obedience to abstract representations of authority. Like Teachum and Jenny, Williams trains her pupils to obey her authority in the form of oral narrative and, later, text. In addition to making her power incorporeal, Williams confers authority on the girls as the people, who will enact governance after the lessons are over. In this way, Foster imagines a more decentralized version of power than does Fielding, approximating the ways in which, in the democratic-republican United States, the government's power does not stem from the people's consent to a monarch but is expressed continually as the will of the people themselves.

Williams' pupils are not treated to explicit civics lesson in these final days with their teacher, but their letters indicate awareness of political ideas, suggesting that politics may have once made up part of their curriculum. One girl, Julia Greenfield, contrasts the "peace and good government" that they enjoy with other nations in Jedidiah Morse's *Universal Geography* (1797) and a patriotic poem by Harriot Henley is referenced, but not included. Williams' transfer of government to the girls itself provides a lesson in early American politics. While the American political system was founded on the notion of government by the people, for the people, *how* the people would be represented was a matter of much debate among politicians. Central to these discussions was a fundamental question: if the people could not all be literally represented in government, as in a true democracy, how would citizens recognize the state's power as their own? This question was more pressing for American authors than for English ones not only because Americans were trying to establish a republic rather than a monarchy but also because the moment of original consent to government, carried out by men claiming to represent the people, remained in living memory. While voting resolved the issue of the state's legitimacy for a limited number of male citizens, the vote was, for many, an insufficient assurance that the elected government would address their needs.

The emotional legitimacy of the state's claim to represent the people required that the people embrace the abstract language of political expression as personally motivated and shaped. Foster's text works to legitimize the notion that the people are the nation's governors by teaching children to read textual power as *personal*, stemming from their parents, from their friends, and ultimately from themselves. Previous readings of *The Boarding School* have focused on the girls as authors, arguing that they possess political agency, but the text lends children equal significance as *readers*, who recognize texts as representing their agency.[81] What results from this blurring of authorship of the law and readerly recognition is an even more seamless relationship between self-government and abstract political representation than found in *The Governess*.

The text begins, much like Fielding's, with Williams's attempts to make her authority incorporeal. Foster describes her strategies for governing at breakfast: "On these occasions, Mrs. Williams suspended the authority of the matron, that, by accustoming her pupils to familiarity in her presence they might be free from restraint . . . By this she had an opportunity of observing any indecorum of behaviour . . . which she kept in mind, till a proper time to mention."[82] This passage shows that Williams' child-rearing strategy is very similar to Locke's: the children feel that they are "free from restraint," while they are actually being monitored and directed. Williams's breakfast government creates a subtle distinction between her physical presence and her capacity as governing body. She acts as an extension of authority by personally remembering the children's faults, but Mrs. Williams simultaneously illustrates that authority can be separated from her person, so that her authority can appear later without her body to support it. This abstraction of authority is the text's most insistent lesson. Williams tells her pupils: "Think not . . . that your emancipation from schools, gives you the liberty to neglect the advantages which you have received from them."[83] The end of school replicates Locke's moment in which children become free from their guardians, but here, as in his system, their newfound freedom calls for a new form of constraint.

The Boarding School downplays this constraint to a greater degree than does *The Governess*. What was a "tearful" consent in Fielding's English text is, in America, a blithe, affectionate one: "With one voice, [the children] most affectionately assured Mrs. Williams, that it should be their daily study to profit by her lessons."[84] The contrast between this passage and the moment of consent in *The Governess* suggests that American children's books work harder to establish affectionate subjection as freedom. As a result, abstract political authority becomes even more closely associated with personal motivations, making it possible to imagine that the power of the state originates in common citizens and even children. The "one voice" not only declares the children's allegiance to Williams but also enacts their formation into a sovereign people, a mini-nation of citizens who will govern themselves. The girls, as the people, embody the ideal of representative citizenship. Though their governance is grounded in personal relationships, it is based on textual mediation rather than on face-to-face political exchanges. By reading and writing letters, the girls practice what Warner calls the "principle of negativity," in which government is "not an interaction between particularized persons, but among persons constituted by the negating abstraction of themselves."[85]

Although Warner claims that participating in creating such public textual representations was available only to adult men, *The Boarding School* represents girls abstracting themselves in print. The reason for this difference is perhaps that girl authors did not have the opportunities to appear in print that men had—and indeed, in the story the girls' letters form a private rather than a public forum and give rise to an alternative, miniature society similar to the one in *The Governess* rather than actual political interactions. Yet, from the point of view of the reader, the mode of representation is remarkably similar. By narrating the process by which the people's authority becomes textual, *The Boarding School* trains child readers to recognize and proclaim affection for abstract civic laws and constraints as the embodiment of their own opinions and desires, even when they played no role in making them or in evaluating them in public forums.

Williams prepares the girls to make personal authority abstract by using a technique similar to that of Jenny Peace: telling stories. This technique has two seemingly contrasting effects, which highlight the double requirement of American political action and expression to represent the people, but to represent them as non-particularized. First, the stories cast the authority of Williams's assertions as based not on her personal prejudices, rather, on textual authority. Second, they locate authority in the stories of dozens of other citizens. Alone, these tales are merely the tragedies of individuals. However, together they represent a veritable constitution of rules, rooted in the experiences and concerns of the people. For example, a story about a young woman named Camilla shows the need for people to regulate their tempers, a lesson that benefits society as a whole. For Williams, such rules of behavior function as laws: "Your behavior and conversation must be uniformly governed by the laws of politeness, discretion, and decorum."[86] The stories claim that such laws do not come from a particular person. Instead they come from a larger consensus of popular opinion that represents all citizens, including children.

The governess's directions for reading further substantiate this point. In her discussion of novels, she asserts that "those [books], which are sanctioned by the general voice of delicacy and refinement, may be allowed a reading."[87] In this passage, the "one voice" of citizenship returns. However, here the citizens are not consenting to be governed. They actually carry out the governing. As with the voice of consenting citizenship, the individual members of the community who make up the "general voice" have been absorbed. The voice appears to be coming not from particular persons, but from the abstract concepts of "delicacy and refinement." These distinctions are significant, because when the girls are formed into a people who will govern themselves, they must recognize abstract laws as their own governance.

The eventual distribution of authority into the children necessitates a further move from orality to textuality. Williams initiates this progression by emphasizing that the best authority is found in the textual representation rather than in any one person. For example, she lauds poetry because it "meliorate[s] the affections," books by "monitors" because they regulate conduct, and history because it helps to govern one's manners. Williams's lesson on books reminds us again of the mechanism through which the child reader of *The Boarding School* is already being governed. American children, in reading Foster's work, are already removed from Williams's presence and the authority therein is already abstract and representative. Later in the text, when Williams responds to an inquiry from one of the girls about marriage by suggesting that she read a book instead, she is insisting on textual expression as the best authority on even the most personal affairs.

These reading lessons prepare the children to recognize and embrace textual authority as originating in the experiences and beliefs of the people. Borrowing from *The Governess*, Foster demonstrates that an effective practice through which this recognition can be learned is correspondence, which, like many eighteenth-century children's books, relies on a fantasy of embodiment. After the girls return to their homes, they write letters to each other, a selection of which constitutes the remainder of the text. The text initially presents a community of children similar to the community in *The Governess*. The letters might also in some sense approximate an alternative community through which the girls can challenge authority (for instance, it has been remarked that the girls are not as harsh on fallen women as their teacher is). However, in this dispersal the girls in *The Boarding School* lose the collective power that Teachum's students wield. The individualized interactions in the letters do not allow the girls to organize themselves or even respond to similar events but give rise to isolated moments that cannot give rise to a unified narrative of resistance or collective action. Rather, providing a bridge between the presence and absence of their authors, the letters allow each child reader to accept popular authority in the distanced form in which it appears in American government and to obey it as if it were coming from a trusted friend and, ultimately, from herself. While the children's missives are personal in that they are ascribed to particular authors, they emphasize abstract lessons, making these moral laws appear to originate in the people.

Several of the children draw this connection in their letters, offering their own theories about how the presumably personal form of the letter can signify larger ideals. Critiquing letter collections by popular authors, the children argue that letters must engage the affections, but must go beyond personal musings to contain universal and abstract laws. Two of the child characters, Caroline and Cleora, discuss the Marie de Rabutin-Chantal de Sévigné's *Letters from the Marchioness De Sevigne to Her Daughter the Countess De Grignan* (1768). Caroline critiques de Sévigné's letters for not containing enough general principles, instead focusing on "local circumstances" and "family matters . . . many of which are of too trifling a nature." Because de Sévigné focuses on personal activities, her writing cannot be recognized as the authoritative language of the law. Later, Caroline enters into another exchange, this time with Sophia, in which the proper function of letters is defined. Sophia writes to Caroline about the Reverend John Bennett's *Letters to a Young Lady* (1791), which she claims "are the native language of affection: they can hardly fail to instill the love of virtue into every mind susceptible of its charms."[88] These letters differ from those of de Sévigné because, although they contain enough of the personal and concrete to engage the affections, they allow readers to transfer their love to an intangible concept: virtue. Thus, Bennett's letters are particularly appropriate to train the child citizen; Sophia recommends that Caroline read them at least twice. This rereading typifies the continuous work that must be done by the affectionate citizen in recognizing the values of the people embodied in text.

The girls' letters, on the whole, resemble Bennett's, yet Foster has further dispersed their authority by giving them multiple child authors instead of a unified parental voice. While, unlike many of the writers Warner studies, the girls do sign their letters and it is possible to distinguish some of the members of this letter-writing community by sketchily drawn personality traits—Maria Williams writes poetry in her letters, Harriot is sermon-esque in her moralizing, Caroline and Cleora take a particular interest in books—the child characters assume a voice of authority that is mostly disconnected from particular experience. The child authors cannot be easily distinguished, nor can their univocality be easily differentiated from the voice that Williams assumed in her lectures. In addition, there is no narrative semblance in the letters to establish the trajectories of the characters.

These features suggest that the ideal promoted by the text is a version of authority that is removed from particular persons, which the form of the letter makes appear to come from the children themselves. It is important to recognize that this is an imaginary ideal perpetuated by the text. Though the letters purport to represent the people's authority, they actually originate from the same source as Williams's lectures: Foster herself. This affectionate recognition through reading perhaps represents the ultimate equation of freedom and subjection: the child's willingness to love abstract authority as her own casts her subjection to this authority even as a kind of power. In this sense, the recognition of the state's power as representative always holds a degree of misrecognition. Yet affectionate citizenship also encourages citizens to seek a government that approaches the ideal of representation: one in which their voices are repeated back to them in text.

The importance of the child reader's affections in bolstering the often-celebrated notion of American political participation demonstrates the extent to which the child's and citizen's freedom are inextricably linked. The foremost significance of what I have termed affectionate citizenship is that these practices inaugurated an entire history of children's imaginary citizenship in America. The comparison between children and citizens henceforth became one of the primary anxieties about the American citizen. While children's books often concealed the citizen's childlike quality through appeals to the child's freedom, the child-citizen would come to be represented and challenged in novels such as William Hill Brown's *The Power of Sympathy* (1789), Foster's *The Coquette* (1797), and Tabitha Gilman Tenney's *Female Quixotism* (1801), which take the unstable and often impassable transition from childhood to adulthood as their central theme. Seen in this light, the political and pedagogical works of early America began one of the nation's most lasting preoccupations: the simultaneous fantasy and fear that American citizenship might be naïve, immature, and juvenile at its heart.

CHAPTER 3

Child Readers of the Novel

The Problem of Childish Citizenship

Let me advise you to consider this Turn of Life, to be as dangerous
as any you may survive, for most are apt to be so enamoured with
Freedom, that they forget the Dangers which accompany it, and
often by their Haste and Precipitation, lose the main Chance; and
to rid themselves of a gentle Submission, forfeit true Freedom, and
become perpetual Slaves of Penury and Wretchedness.

A Companion for the Young People
of North America, *1767*

Well may it be said that men are but children of a larger growth.
William Maclay on Congress, 1789

Because the affectionate citizenship of children was important in creating an entire
population of citizens who understood the law as representative of their power, the
child came to symbolize the (limited) liberty of citizens. Yet in Locke's *Two Treatises*
the child was also the foil to the citizen, necessary to mark his emancipation from
childish constraint. This argument too found its way into early American political
culture. As the nation sought to establish its own institutions, Americans developed
an ambivalent attitude toward the child, who came to represent both the ideal
citizen and the citizen's other. While the idea of a social contract simultaneously
excluded children from legal citizenship and gave way to imaginary ideals based on
children's citizenship, competing strains in literary and legal discourse in the post-
revolutionary era pushed back against both of these developments.

The early national government, controlled by Federalists, was much more apprehensive of the idea of natural freedom than Locke and Paine were, creating suspicion
about the child as an imaginary model of the citizen. Ironically, given that politicians such as George Washington were hailed as the patriarchs of the new nation,
Federalists used metaphors of childhood to describe perceived threats to citizen-

ship, which were often characterized as too literal readings of the notions of natural equality and popular sovereignty. John Adams argued that the equality of citizens should be limited by the so-called natural inequalities of property, class, gender, and ability, which justified the emergence of a "natural aristocracy" composed of privileged adult men.[1] To support this view meant stifling the voices of other groups that might imagine themselves as citizens and suggesting that imaginary citizenship was not legitimate. His famous letter to his wife denying her petition for women's rights specifically associates their broader bids for citizenship with the protests of children. When Abigail radically suggested that women would "not hold ourselves bound by any Laws in which we have no voice, or Representation," John lumped women's potential insurrection with childish rebellion: "We have been told that our struggle has loosened the bands of Government every where. That Children and Apprentices were disobedient and that schools and Colledges were grown turbulent . . . But your letter was the first intimation that another tribe, more numerous and powerful than all the rest, were grown discontented."[2] Though John goes on to teasingly suggest that men are really "subjects" of women, Abigail perceives that John insists on retaining an absolute power over wives despite the liberating language of the Revolution. The idea of the child citizen thus appears in the letter to infantilize the concepts of full equality and the right to dissent.

That dissent was childish had a particular role in stifling women's bids for a political voice. Under a patriarchal government, women were subject to male rule, but they were not thought to be more childish than anyone else. Infantilization as a form of domination affecting specific groups rather than all political subjects was tied to the emergence of childhood as a special category for persons who were unable to participate in their own governance. The contrast between the idea that all individuals must consent to be governed and men's desire to limit power on the basis of gender meant that women came to be seen as infantile even in their adulthood. The new politics assigned to childhood had a particular effect for women, but the association of further revolution with childhood also had an effect on the citizenship of all adults, since it could serve to stifle dissent. Such images of children peaked during the French Revolution. Using "childishness" as a pejorative, the Federalists attempted to differentiate their version of citizenship from what they saw as the puerile celebrations of natural equality and freedom developing elsewhere.

At the same time that *ideas* about childhood were used to limit citizenship to a group of privileged adult men, Federalists were more likely than their Republican opponents to return to legal understandings of citizenship based on inheritance and to therefore support decisions granting citizenship status to children, though these decisions were usually understood as conferring duties more than rights. As Rogers

Smith observes, "The Federalists became . . . the champions of almost unalterable hereditary allegiances" and "maintained that American citizenship was rightfully as much a matter of birth . . . as choice."[3] Many early American politicians rejected the patriarchal means of granting nationality by *jus sanguinis* (right of blood) and *jus soli* (right of soil), because they were associated with compelled deference to aristocratic landowners. However, they nonetheless based many of their laws on blood inheritance. One example was the U.S. Naturalization Act of 1790, which declared that the children of immigrants were to be considered citizens, as long as their parents were white and had become citizens themselves.

According to some legal decisions, the political bonds created in childhood were unalterable, even if they were not rationally chosen or supported by actual rights. In *United States v. Isaac Williams* (1799), Chief Justice Oliver Ellsworth argued that Williams could not renounce his citizenship upon coming of age, since his contract stemmed from birth and he could not break it without permission from the state.[4] Although the idea of an infant contract was not unheard of in contract theory—for instance, Thomas Hobbes asserted in *Leviathan* (1651) that babies imaginatively contract with their parents for care—Republicans denounced this decision as inconsistent with the freedom of the social contract.[5] A contributor to the *Aurora* responded to the Williams case by maintaining that "the adult only . . . can decide what country best suits his interest."[6] Nonetheless, the remnants of patriarchal theory and common law continued to influence legal decisions regarding political identity, meaning that the child was never fully distinguished from the citizen even in legal terms.

These two competing strands of discourse on children's citizenship created another divergence between legal and literary ideas of citizenship, which came to be recorded in the nation's earliest literature, particularly the early American novel. Children and youth are imaginatively represented in these texts as threats to the stability of the nation, who must be excluded because of their rebellious behavior. By emphasizing children's irrationality and their tendency to live in the world of the imagination rather than reality, many novels of the period present the more radical possibilities associated with children's citizenship, such as expectations for the full equality of all persons or affectionate identification with the law, as unrealistic. At the same time, these novels address readers as metaphorical children and attempt to introduce both characters and readers to their duties as good citizens. In this way, they bolster Federalist legal decisions that suggested that individuals should be quietly inculcated as dutiful citizens from birth.

Often, arguments against the child as an imaginary figure of the citizen specifically involved the child's status as a reader. Shrinking from the Revolution in France,

Federalists feared that children and other childish persons might misread the meaning of liberty, becoming seduced by what they considered radical ideas. This fear of bad reading culminated in the Alien and Sedition Acts of 1798, which prohibited writing against the government, as well as in panicked sermons and periodical articles about what women and children should read. Many early American novels, which flourished in the turbulent 1790s, can be also be read as attempts to regulate this volatile stage of life by depicting their heroes' and heroines' transition from childhood to adulthood, from bad reading to good reading, and from imaginary to realistic citizenship.

In making this argument, I provide a new assessment of the readership that emphasizes the blurring between adults' and children's literature of the period. Although many early American novels are now associated with an adult literary public, I take seriously the claim, made by authors from this period, that their works were dedicated to young readers and meant to be read by children. It would certainly be an oversimplification to argue that these novels were only children's books. Rather, many early novels were strongly invested in the meanings of childishness as they related to the young republic. Several suggest that the boundary between child and adult was unstable due to adults' failure to act like rational, law abiding citizens. By telling narratives of young characters on the verge of becoming adults, these novels attempt (and record their own failure) to stabilize the unclear boundary in the nascent republic between childhood and adulthood.

On the one hand, because childhood was deemed temporary, stories about young people allowed for both the expression and eradication of the citizen's otherness, which included both rebellious misreading of the rights of citizens and excessive subjection reminiscent of patriarchal subjecthood or even slavery. Many authors directed their text to "youths," or individuals who stood at the messy boundaries between dependence and independence, because they believed that novels could actively solidify these boundaries. Associating resistance with childhood and bad reading, many novels mark dissent as the result of immaturity and perchance for fantasy, associating non-rights-bearing citizens' expectations of power and equality with dependence, subjection, seduction, and civic illiteracy. In this way, both rebellion and subjection could be imaginatively eradicated in the name of adulthood and rational independence. A genre that was still in its own infancy, the novel therefore writes its own Bildungsroman as a genre, claiming to provide a vital civic service by narrating the coming of age of its characters and readers.

On the other hand, novels often associate various kinds of dependence with good citizenship, continually reintroducing the child as an image for the citizen. In some cases, even extreme acts of infantilization and subjugation, such as kidnapping the child reader and forcing her to read morally proper books, are deemed necessary for the establishing the citizen's habits and ultimate freedom. These acts resemble legal interventions that were established in the early nineteenth century to deal with delinquent children and that fall under the doctrine of *parens patriae,* or the notion that "the state is the father."[7] The increasing application of this patriarchal doctrine, which originally described the king's protection of all citizens, in legal cases involving children in the early nineteenth century was a sign that children and adults were becoming more separate under the law, but the courts' application of the doctrine also created new ties between children and citizens. Children's care was seen as necessary not just for their protection as domestic figures but also to ensure their obedience as citizens. The nation's incongruous investments in creating adult citizens and in keeping citizens as obedient children even in adulthood reveal themselves in the large number of novels with characters who appear as adult-children, exhibiting the characteristics of both stages.

Because they are not completely coherent or univocal texts, novels also include narrative strands that complicate their stories of children becoming adult citizens, suggesting that the others of citizenship cannot be so easily silenced.[8] Recording the failure of their own educational aims, many tell the histories of characters who either die before reaching adulthood or remain irrational even when they are adults. These bad outcomes suggest that these works also allowed for critiques of their own narratives of assimilation. Julia Stern points out that the gothic stories in many novels reveal that "the infant nation is erected on . . . a figurative grave" that represents the more radical possibilities promised by the American Revolution.[9] Because of the philosophical basis of America's government in the concept of natural independence, the reliance on education raised questions about how its influence might affect the individual's autonomy, particularly if that education was undertaken not by good authorities, but by rakes, hedonists, foreigners, and political subversives.

As a remedy for bad reading, education in the novel is fraught with problems, such as its tendency to infantilize the adult citizen and the possibility that corrupt persons might usurp the task of educating. Because novels were frequently written in epistolary form and represent multiple voices, it is often unclear how a person is supposed to read them. Were they meant to mourn the creation of a nation in which child characters cannot thrive or to see the novel's failed heroes and heroines as justly punished rogues from whom their own reading practices and political activities could differ? Either way, the boundaries between childhood and adulthood remained largely unstable. In the case of those mourning the limitations of citizenship, childhood and adulthood are revealed to be concepts with uneven application and unsure footing, hardly stable foundations for determining the competence of citizens. In the case of the just punishers, "childishness" (a word that perfectly signifies both the unruliness and vulnerability that the child came to embody) becomes an expansive term used to exclude even adults from citizenship and undermine their political activity by defining them as puerile and as bad readers.

"Oh my dear girls—for to such only am I writing"

While the novel has always been more than a children's book, a glance at the prefaces of several eighteenth-century novels demonstrates that they were frequently dedicated to young readers—often, but not always, girls. As Jay Fliegelman has shown, several English books came to the United States in abridged versions, but many were already dedicated to young readers in their original form, suggesting that abridgement was as much about broadening a book's audience to less literate readers as about explicitly creating children's versions. Samuel Richardson's *Pamela* (1740), for instance, announces that it is designed to "cultivate the principles of virtue and religion in the minds of the youth of both sexes."[10] American works were even more explicit in claiming the young as the central part of their readership. What many have called the first American novel, William Hill Brown's *The Power of Sympathy* (1789), is dedicated to "the young ladies of Columbia." *The History of Constantius and Pulchera* (1794) imagines that the "daughters of Columbia" will be responsible for circulating the work. Susanna Rowson's *Charlotte Temple* (1794) identifies "dear girls" as its true audience. *Monima; Or the Beggar Girl* (1802) is meant to inculcate "obedience, unbounded love, respect and veneration in the hearts of children toward their parents."[11]

These dedications are not surprising, given that nearly half of the population in 1776 was under age sixteen and that young people made up two-thirds of the population by the early decades of the nineteenth century. Yet the meaning of these addresses has been obscured by the indiscriminate meaning of the terms "young" and "youth" in the period, which referred to children beyond infancy, as well as to teens and recently married persons.[12] The *Oxford English Dictionary* entry for youth records this inconsistency, citing authors who refer to "youths" of age eight, eleven, fourteen, and twenty-four—the last of which is said to be a "young youth," even though another entry implies that youth ends by age twenty. Rodney Hessinger notices the difficulties of defining youth in this period:

> Early American society was less age-graded than our own, so fixing definitive ages
> for the category of youth is tricky . . . Rhetorically, it ended when one took on all

the responsibilities of adulthood, such as a marriage and an occupation . . . [But] if traditionally the life stage of youth ended when one was settled into a permanent station in life, in a bourgeois society, a world in which people are always striving to get ahead, most everyone could be said to be a youth.[13]

Despite the fluctuation and complications attached to the term *youth*, most scholars of the novel have proceeded under the assumption that novels were mainly the province of younger adults rather than teens or children. For instance, Cathy Davidson has noted that the advertisements included in early American novels indicate that they were "targeted specifically for children, women, or a new and relatively untutored readership" but does not spend much time discussing how novels may have been shaped by this audience, choosing rather to focus on republican mothers and other adults who might have needed to educate themselves through reading.[14]

This question of audience is important because it has the potential to complicate arguments about the novel's relation to citizenship, such as Davidson's landmark claim that the early American novel was a subversive genre designed to make the case for the inclusion of disempowered persons as citizens. Because of new theories of development in the eighteenth century, children could not be easily imagined as the kind of independently minded, dissident citizens that Davidson imagines reading novels, nor could the case be easily made for their immediate inclusion as autonomous participants in government, since they were being increasingly cast as a group with a strong need for further education and dependence. Accordingly, while novels were often represented (and thus have often appeared in criticism) as dangerously subversive texts that should not be read by volatile readers, nearly every work of this period explicitly understood itself as the exception to this rule, suggesting that the "bad novels" denounced by ministers and pundits were foreign ones from England and France.[15] American novels more frequently include overtly didactic aims that emphasize the child's status as an inadequate reader and citizen who is in need of the novel's supplementation before political recognition is possible. As Davidson herself notes, "Virtually *every* American novel written before 1820 (I can think of no exceptions) at some point includes . . . a discourse on the necessity of an improved education."[16] The question remains as to how young the imagined audiences might have been and what this educational posturing on the part of authors might mean for thinking about the novel as a genre.

The meaning of the dedications can be partially understood in terms of the genre's actual readership, which did in fact include children as well as teenagers and young adults.[17] Though textbooks and primers almost always outsold them, novels frequently found their way into children's reading repertoires. John Tebbel ranks *Pamela, Clarissa* (1748), *Tom Jones* (1749), *Charlotte Temple*, and *Vicar of Wakefield* (1766), among his list of early American best-sellers, noting that these were "devoured" by young men and women, as well as by "much younger children . . . if their parents permitted."[18] Firsthand accounts of children's novel reading suggest the young people were reading them at a younger age than is often assumed. Catharine Maria Sedgwick, who was born in the year of the first American novel, 1789, remembers reading them at age eleven.[19] From age twelve to sixteen, child diarist Sally Ripley records reading *Rassalas* (1759), *Evelina* (1778), *Emma Corbett* (1794), *Camilla* (1796), *Romance of the Forest* (1791), *Children of the Abbey* (1796), and *Fille de Chambre* (1792) alongside books more explicitly advertised as children's texts and schoolbooks, such as *The Children's Friend* (1789), *The Columbian Orator* (1797), and *The American Preceptor* (1797).[20] Other young diarists, such as Jenny Trumbell (age eleven), Julia Cowles (age fourteen), Ella Gertrude Thomas (age fourteen), and James Fiske (age sixteen) also discuss their opinions of popular novelistic works.[21] M. O. Grenby comments that, in Britain, "novel-reading was a particularly familiar feature of girls' autobiographical writing."[22] The characters are around the same age as these readers. Pamela is fifteen years old for the majority of her adventures; William Hill Brown's amorous brother and sister, Harrington and Harriot, are approximately sixteen; Pulchera is sixteen years old; and fifteen-year-old Charlotte Temple is constantly referred to as a "child" and "girl."[23]

From a twenty-first-century standpoint, these books contain multiple themes that would be considered by some to be inappropriate for young readers, such as incest, suicide, and sex. There were very few indications in the period that these topics were unsuitable for children or teens. Warnings abounded, but were usually predicated on moral rather than strictly developmental considerations. While children might be more susceptible to influence, they were not considered to be in special danger of being tainted by exposure to adult themes. The mature topics have perhaps led to some of the confusion regarding where young readers would have fallen on the continuum from childhood to adulthood. Many scholars largely treat "youth" and "adult" as synonymous, citing shorter life spans, earlier marriage ages, and, of course, the sordid material in most novels. Conversely, Ala Alryyes has argued that "youth" in fact meant something closer to child than adult in the period, mainly because the age difference between children and teens did not immediately "bring consent and freedom."[24] The *Political Class Book* (1830) confirms that the age of maturity was legally set at twenty-one years: "In the language of the law, all these persons [under twenty-one] are considered as being in a state of *infancy*. A youth of twenty years, and a child of twenty months, are *in law*, infants."[25]

This seemingly firm definition of childhood and adulthood in the law derived from political theory. Karen Sánchez-Eppler points out that Americans adopted Locke's definition of a child as a dependent and subjected person, with an adult being someone who had achieved independence and freedom.[26] The lack of precise developmental stages leading up to this coming of age made for a sharp boundary between the child and adult citizen, leaving both infants and youth on the side of childhood. But even though popular discourse was often in line with the legal definition of childhood ending at age twenty-one, definitions, practices, and sometimes even laws varied greatly, making the beginning point of adulthood, freedom, and citizenship unclear. The *Political Class Book* explains that, despite the legal age's being twenty-one, in many states males were taxable at age sixteen and could be enrolled in the militia at age eighteen. Males could also dispose of property by will at age fourteen. Both male and female children could be apprenticed until age fourteen without their consent or, if by a father, beyond age fourteen, but if the father was not living, a teenager's consent was required.[27] Nancy Isenberg claims that "legal adulthood had two stages: the age of consent (fourteen for men, twelve for women) and the age of twenty-one, when parental control over offspring ended. Significantly the age of consent implied the ability to use discretion and reason, while the arbitrary age of twenty-one presumed the acquisition of virtue derived from independence."[28]

Even Locke points out that the line between maturity and immaturity is not clear; it is "the age of one and twenty years, if not sooner."[29] Some prescriptions for children's reading reflected both a firm legal understanding of the boundaries of childhood as ending at twenty-one and potential blurriness for actual readers. Sarah Trimmer, who reviewed children's books in her magazine *The Guardian of Education* (1802–6), distinguished between readers younger than fourteen and over fourteen, but claimed that youth lasted until "at least twenty-one," leaving room for it to last longer.[30] According to Michael Grossberg, "the line between child and adult became the most critical legal boundary for young Americans. It has been, though, an uncertain marker because of the diversity of American children. Within the legal category of minors, children varied according to age, race, gender, capacity, and other critical factors and these variations complicated legal policies. Since the seventeenth century, the law dealt with this reality by devising particular policies for particular actions by particular groups of children."[31]

In effect, while America's claim to free citizenship was predicated on adulthood and childhood as having firm boundaries, popular and legal discourse had not yet settled on a definitive way of marking the difference. What's more, because of the sharp distinction between child and adult in philosophical writing, *partially* independent (and partially grown) individuals were left without a clear place in the social web. Isenberg writes, "The law presumed that adulthood conferred mental and moral capacities, but it had no method for testing actual intelligence, nor did the law distinguish between different grades of moral endowment."[32] As much as a description of the novel's young audiences, addresses to "youth" signal that authors were grappling with the unsolidified understandings of age categories that were emerging in the period. As one article about novel reading puts it, the books were for those who were "no longer children, and not yet quite women."[33]

Further complicating this category of not-yet-adult, "childishness" and "youth" in this context came not to refer immediately to developmental age, but to a particular location within the prerational, subjected phase of Locke's narrative of citizenship. For instance, despite the seeming difference that the above quotation makes between children and women, there was an especially blurry line between these two categories. On the one hand, children and women were distinct, since women were thought to have reached the age of reason, but on the other, women were lumped with children in legal terms. Rationales for this exclusion often had to be predicated on their supposed deficiencies. As Isenberg notes, "Women might reach the age of reason, [but] they were never understood to have achieved full independence or adulthood, because married women, like minors, had their rights circumscribed by the legal guidelines for capacity . . . Women's political status never appeared to change from childhood to adulthood."[34] Thus, "adult" and especially "child" became expansive categories that could be applied to individuals beyond current understandings of age differences. A child signified someone with a supposedly natural tendency toward relationships of subjection, as well as someone likely to be overcome with rebellious or selfish passions—someone in a deficient state of readership and citizenship. Women readers became especially associated with bad child readers because they were thought to share children's lack of self-sufficiency.

Perhaps out of a desire to disentangle women readers from children, critics have tended to understand these bad reader narratives, which often take the form of seduction novels, as being primarily about the potentials for sexual seduction facing the woman reader. The hysteria surrounding bad reading does not reflect only a cultural desire to preserve female virginity. It is also a discursive attempt to shore up national cultural and political legitimacy attempting to write away the potential for a seducible, childlike citizenry. Novels often use the trope of the bad reader as an attempt to regulate this unstable boundary between childhood and adulthood, drawing a line between the child and citizen. But liberation from the stage of childishness did not require that readers actually be children in the current sense of the word. The child became such a familiar symbol for subjected, seduced, and rebellious readership that even allegedly bad readers of an advanced age were depicted as puerile.

Two different types of novels addressed the problem of childishness in the early republic, the seduction novel and the Quixote novel, the latter often taking the form of a Bildungsroman. While both emphasize education, seduction novels tend to record the difficulty of emerging from childhood and the failures of educational attempts. Providing cautionary tales of what happens to bad readers, they also suggest that the production of young citizens has gone awry, littering their texts with children and youths who die early. Quixote novels, in contrast, suggest that education can counter the citizen's childishness, through it is often reinscribed by the very dependencies that education creates.

"A strange medley of contradiction"

It has often been remarked upon that the early American novel and nation emerged at the same point in history. William Hill Brown's "first American novel" was published in 1789 just as the U.S. Constitution was being ratified, George Washington was being inaugurated, and Congress was being seated for the first time.[35] A testament to the wide circulation of political language in the early republic, the text evokes many of the concepts that were foremost in the minds of the nation's political leaders—human nature, republicanism, democracy, sympathy, and slavery—without directly commenting on the political events that surrounded its creation. The title of the book, *The Power of Sympathy; or, the Triumph of Nature*, closely echoes Paine's declaration that the Revolutionary cause ought to motivate "every Man to whom Nature hath given the Power of feeling."[36] The reference to nature strongly evokes the political concepts of natural freedom and equality, which were tied to the child's status as birth.

Locke used both the concepts of children's natural freedom and their natural feelings of affection as the basis for free citizenship. But, while Paine uses nature and "the feelings and affections which [it] justifies" as synonyms for common sense, which, in his view, supports the Revolution, Brown associates nature and sympathy simultaneously with republican ideals and with a potentially incestuous bond between the text's central characters.[37] In doing so, he suggests that the consequences of nature, and an infant government founded on this concept, remained unclear. Was nature's "triumph" the necessary underpinning of democratic government, or was nature a passionate and lawless state antithetical to the restraint required by government? These questions applied equally to childhood and, as such, they were especially relevant as the nation moved from infancy to adulthood, signified both by a shift from British governance to American independence and from ungoverned nature to the social compact. That the shift was imagined in both of these terms reflects Americans' ambivalence about nature; while separating from Britain was considered a return to what nature had decreed, establishing a new state meant supplementing nature with law.

The Power of Sympathy opens with a description of "juvenile hero" Tommy Harrington that could apply equally to the nation as a whole.[38] Harrington describes his "constitution" as "a strange medley of contradiction" in which "grace and nature are at continual fistcuffs."[39] The tension between "nature," which refers to man's natural state of freedom, and "grace," which can be understood as the intervention of God, government, and manners, is further reflected in the text's overt theme of education, which requires individuals to negotiate between these two states. American politicians at their best were striving for balance—a political system that recognized and respected men's essential nature, while improving upon it through governance. Yet by continually asserting that young Harrington has fallen in love with his sister Harriot due to the "operation of NATURE—and the power of SYMPATHY," the book casts doubt on the usefulness of nature as a foundation for lawful government. Harrington's contradictory "constitution" echoes the Federalists' fear that human nature is not associated with a stable government, but with an overabundance of passion.

An often-overlooked feature of the first American novel is the fact that *The Power of Sympathy* is a bizarre rendition of a popular children's educational genre: letters written to children from their tutors. These texts, which included Lord Chesterfield's popular *Letters to his Son* (1774, first American edition 1775), John Gregory's *A Father's Legacy to His Daughters* (1773, first American edition 1775), and Hannah Chapone's *Letters on the Improvement of the Mind* (1777, first American edition 1783), were designed to aid the child's transition into adulthood.[40] The two main sets of correspondents in *The Power of Sympathy* are Harrington and twenty-one-year-old Jack Worthy, whom Harrington refers to as his "monitorial" correspondent, and Tommy's other sister, Myra, and her widowed friend Mrs. Holmes, who gives Myra "*Mentor*-like lessons of instruction."[41] These mentors recommend to Myra and Harrington several books that were intended for children and youth, including *Advice from a Lady of Quality to Her Children* (1784) and Noah Webster's *Grammatical Institute* (1783), though Harrington notably prefers the German romantic novel, *The Sorrows of Young Werther* (1774, first American edition 1784), to these educational tomes.[42] These books are meant to initiate the characters into a mature rationality, which, in the case of Harrington, is threatened by the influence of his natural passions.

Anxieties about the political consequences of man's natural state are specifically represented in a debate between Harrington and Worthy about the merits of childhood versus adulthood. At the most dramatic moment of the text, when Harrington realizes that his lover Harriot is the offspring of an affair his father had with another woman and, consequently, his sister, he remarks:

> If there are any happy they are those in thoughtless childhood . . . I THEN viewed the world at a distance in perspective. I thought mankind appeared happy in the midst of pleasures that flowed round them. I now find it a deception, and am tempted sometimes to wish myself a child again. Happy are the dreams of infancy, and happy their harmless pursuits . . . As I reflect on those scenes of infantine ignorance, I feel my heart interested, and become sensibly affected.[43]

Harrington's nostalgic lament presents childhood as an ignorant state, but for him this is an advantage, as it allows the natural passions to run free. Harrington rationalizes his potential seduction of Harriot from the vantage point of a presocial state of nature, "Shall we not . . . obey the dictates of nature, rather than confine ourselves to the forced and unnatural rules of [society]?" Worthy claims, on the contrary, that maturity affords the greatest happiness, for "love of life increases with age." When "reason is taken from the helm of life," he argues, "nature—lost to herself, and every social duty, splits upon the rocks of despair and suicide."[44] In effect, Worthy importunes Harrington to grow up by attaining reason. Harrington prefers to revel obstinately in his memory of childhood.

The children in the books I discussed in the previous chapter almost seamlessly become free citizens through the endeavors of their teacher-governors. This process is much more labored and treacherous in *The Power of Sympathy*. While the text makes many efforts to educate its characters and readers—for instance, Mrs. Holmes's didactic letters to Myra make up one-third of the book—education does not solve the major problem experienced by the characters: falling in love with one's sibling. Elizabeth Dillon observed that "the novel seems deeply contradictory insofar as it promotes a solution (deliberative judgment and republican virtue) that will not address the problem at hand (unwitting incest)."[45] Worthy and Mrs. Holmes are revealed to be quite inept as teachers; Mrs. Holmes fails to unfold her story of Harrington's and Harriot's kinship until the pair have fallen irrevocably in love and Worthy arrives too late to save Harrington from suicide, despite Harrington's many letters begging his assistance. It can be argued that it is because of their failings as teachers that Harriot dies while still in the bloom of youth and Harrington literally refuses to grow up, committing suicide at the age of sixteen. As the title of the novel suggests, nature (and childhood) triumphs. The gory scenes at the end of the book make moving beyond childhood seem all the more urgent, even as it is revealed to be unachievable for the main characters.

To further complicate matters, Harrington's romantic view of childhood (and even of incest) is not completely undermined. One of the most puzzling aspects of the text is that Harrington's excessive passions also give rise to republican feelings. Harrington's powerful declaration, "Am I a child that I should weep? . . . Curse on this tyrant custom that dooms such helpless children to oblivion," evokes the by-gone language of the Revolution.[46] It does not seem coincidental that much of the mischief in the text is done by Harrington's father, rather than the two incestuous lovers, echoing Paine's assertion that the English parent is a "monster."[47] The child-ish Harrington, after abandoning the aristocratic tone he wields early in the text when says he is not so much a "republican" as to marry beneath his class, becomes the most "republican" of all the characters, extending his affections not only to the poor ward Harriot, but to "mechanicks" and slaves. On a trip to the South, he sympathizes with the sufferings of a slave woman, remarking, "From thee! Author of Nature! from thee, thou inexhaustible spring of love supreme, floweth this tide of affection and SYMPATHY."[48]

This scene, however, is followed directly by Mrs. Holmes's revelation to Myra that Harriot is Harrington's sister, in which she exclaims, "GREAT God! . . . ad-mire, O my friend! The operation of NATURE—and the power of SYMPATHY!"[49] From this juxtaposition, Brown seems to be suggesting that the "natural" state of childhood gives rise equally to democratic feeling and to incest—and thus is not a legitimate basis for society.

More subtly, he may also be pointing to the inconsistent usage of these words in early American culture, which likewise presents difficulties for a political system purporting to stem from man's natural state. This attention to the instability of lan-guage recognizes the possibility for unorthodox interpretations of the terms impor-tant to citizenship. As Homi Bhabha has argued, "The problematic 'closure' of tex-tuality questions the "totalization" of national culture . . . The 'locality' of national culture is neither unified nor unitary in relation to itself [and] . . . generat[es] other sites of meaning and, inevitably, in the political process, produc[es] unmanned sites of political antagonism and unpredictable forces for political representation."[50] The novel seems at once aware of the difficulties of pinning down official meanings of these terms and anxious to close the gaps that language's instabilities produce by eradicating bad or childish reading. It seems no coincidence that Mrs. Holmes recommends that Myra read Webster's *Grammatical Institute*, an educational text widely known for attempting to create a uniform American language.

Despite the attractiveness of Harrington's compassionate stance on issues of class and race, his ultimate self-destruction with *Werther* by his side, his infantile dreams, and his disregard for even the most basic of human laws suggest that his understanding of the ideals of the Revolution and democracy are misguided, the product of bad reading. He is not a romantic child of nature, but childish. The text suggests that Harrington has misunderstood the fundamental meanings of nature, equality, and freedom by dwelling on their extreme applications. At the beginning of the book, he declares that he will not "be heard openly acknowledging for my bosom companion, any daughter of the democratick empire of virtue."[51] Foregrounding the issue of how to read and apply the language of democracy and republicanism circulating after the Revolution, he accuses his friend Worthy of committing a "solecism" (a grammatical mistake or nonstandard usage) by contesting him on this matter. Yet the text suggests that Harrington is guiltier than Worthy of misusing revolutionary language, for he fails to understand that, while democracy has complicated class as a way to determine virtue in the new republic, it does not necessarily advocate social leveling. Worthy makes this clear when Harrington decides to marry rather than seduce Harriot; he cautions that Harrington must first speak to his father for "a contrary step might terminate in the utter ruin of you both."[52]

Without taking this crucial step, Harrington not only decides that he is indeed enough of a republican to marry Harriot—who, it ironically turns out, is of the same class background as he—but also that he favors completely abandoning social inequalities. Witnessing the ridicule of a mechanic's daughter at a party, he declares, "I like a democratical better than any other kind of government; and were I a *Lycurgus* no distinction of rank should be found in my commonwealth."[53] While this populism was no doubt appealing to some readers, Harrington's attitude was also commonly denounced in the period as misperception of liberal political aims. Locke was clear that the equality of man did not erase other inequalities, saying "Though I have said above . . . *That all Men by Nature are equal,* I cannot be supposed to understand all sorts of *Equality; Age* or *Virtue* may give Men a just Precedency: *Excellency of Parts or Merit* may place others above the Common Level: *Birth* may subject some, and *Alliance* or *Benefits* others, to pay an Observance to those whom Nature, Gratitude or other Respects may have made it due."[54]

"Democratical government," rather than a celebrated American ideal, was a controversial system of governance, feared by many early American politicians as a sure way to the tyranny of the mob. Adams, for instance, opined that "democracy never lasts long. It soon wastes, exhausts and murders itself. There was never a democracy that did not commit suicide."[55] Carrying out this narrative of democracy's death,

Harrington persists in his bad reading until his own suicide, offering the perverse moral that he and Harriot will be united in heaven.

The text also suggests that youths can be seduced by bad reading because they are impressionable, an argument that casts further doubt on Harrington's ability to understand national politics. Beyond the incest plot, bad reading is easily the most persistent theme in the rest of the text, which directs its educational energies also to its female characters and young readers. Mrs. Holmes sends young Myra a lengthy record of a discussion at Belleview about what kinds of books are appropriate for young readers, and more specifically, for fourteen-year-old Miss Bourn. As part of this conversation, Worthy declares that because young women have little ability to resist the lessons of their books, their reading choices must be restricted: "Unless a proper selection is made, one would do better never to read at all." The Reverend Mr. Holmes, who as the father of Mrs. Holmes's late husband has particular authority as patriarch, goes on to argue that children represent all forms of impressionable readers: "Novels, not regulated on the chaste principles of true friendship, rational love, and connubial duty, appear to me totally unfit to form the minds of women, of friends, or of wives."[56] In this passage, childish readers are defined not only by age, but also by the degree to which they are shaped by their books.

In contrast to these readers, Mr. Holmes compares a presumably "adult" reader to a river whose bank has grown high enough to control the currents of text: "if books, which are the sources that feed this river, rush into it from every quarter, it will overflow its banks, and the plain will become inundated . . . a river properly restricted by high banks, is necessarily progressive." To come of age as a reader, the child must become a discriminating "lady" reader who is able to "discern with an eye of judgment, between . . . what may be merely amusing, and what may be useful."[57] While the "lady" in this passage is both young and female, qualities that would usually be associated with childishness, she is symbolically an adult reader due to her "eye of judgment." Significantly, *how* she reads is even more crucial to avoiding childish reading as *what* she reads, since even the "best books" may still hide evil intentions. Holmes claims that becoming a good reader is not contingent on being free of all influence but rather on learning to be influenced only by what is good.

By arguing that both childhood and bad reading can be transcended through education, *The Power of Sympathy* suggests that the state of deficient citizenship represented in the novel is potentially impermanent. To keep the child's limitations from spilling over into adult citizenship, the bad reader is expected to grow up to be a good reader. The novel's work is to attempt to narrate the end of childhood for its characters and readers. But even as bad readers mark the difference between children and adults, and the need for progression from one stage of life to the other, they simultaneously demonstrate the blurred and overlapping relationship between these two stages. The boundary between childhood and adulthood is unstable, a stage in which the production of good citizens might go awry. Seen in this second light, the application of child reader status even to readers who are not strictly children suggests that the novel troubles the boundary between adulthood and childhood, marking childhood's actual elasticity as a signifier of subjection, misreading, and rebellion. The novel is *about* the indistinct relationship between adult citizens and children. An obsession with the precarious transition from child to adult is constitutive of many early American novels, expressing itself most readily in the number of characters who remain childlike into adulthood or die without growing up.

Mr. Holmes makes it clear that the child's coming of age is not guaranteed; if the child reader is not able to build her riverbanks high enough, her love for reading will enslave her instead of leading to her freedom and acceptance of social norms. Though Miss Bourn protests that she never remembers what she reads anyway, Mr. Holmes suggests that bad reading can disrupt one's chances to become a free adult reader, keeping one a child well beyond the appropriate age. To illustrate this point, he mentions the tragedy of a famous bad reader: Elizabeth Whitman. Whitman, who also appears in Hannah Webster Foster's *The Coquette* (1797), notoriously met her downfall because she was a "great reader of novels and romances."[58]

Although Whitman was thirty-five by the time she died, Brown's portrayal of the famous bad reader casts her as an unsightly sort of adult-child, calling her a "young lady" and emphasizing her desire to play the youthful coquette despite the gradual "decay" of "the roses of youth."[59] Foster, in her version of Whitman's story, also depicts Eliza as childlike throughout the text, having just left her parents' home. We find out at the end of *The Coquette* that the heroine is upwards of thirty, a fact that surprises most readers. Whitman's childishness is not literal but figurative, signifying her supposed impressionability, as well as her subversive energy. Women's ability to be seduced was one reason that novels gave for their exclusion from citizenship despite universal claims about equality, but it was also because they were coming to be specifically linked with the noncitizenship of children.

In the end, Whitman does not choose to become a good adult reader and thus dies as a figural child, unable to grow up and be integrated into the progressive narrative of citizenship. Her death in *The Coquette* is notably accompanied by the deaths of several other children of the text, including Mrs. Richman's baby, Mrs. Sanford's baby, and her own child. Brown's text also ends with the deaths of its two juvenile characters, creating a pervasive symbolism of children who never grow up.

Both texts simultaneously bemoan the child's inability to mature and are subtly implicated in their continued immaturity; novels are simultaneously the books that correct bad reading and the books that bad readers read. As this paradox suggests, novels actually created an overlap between child and adult readers. While the process of training citizens must allow readers to transition between these two positions in order to avoid a seducible citizenry, it also seeks to create a continuation of childhood affection and obedience into adulthood. Readers *must* subject themselves to the governance of good authority figures. So, Brown cannot help but reveal that freedom and adulthood also demand submission to one's books. At an often-overlooked moment in the text, Mrs. Holmes sends a book to Myra entitled *Advice from a Lady of Quality to Her Children*. Mrs. Holmes explains that she does not "recommend it to you as a Novel, but as a work that speaks the language of the heart and inculcates the duty we owe to ourselves, to society, and the Deity."[60] This book title does not sound like a novel, but a children's pedagogical work that may or may not have used fiction as a device for gaining the child reader's attention. By labeling the work "not a novel," Mrs. Holmes protests perhaps a bit too much, actually drawing attention to the comparison between this supposedly good text and the bad novels that she and Mr. Holmes have denounced. Myra is clearly not supposed to shield herself from being impressed upon by the advice book but is expected to allow it to form her opinions and actions, similar to the ways in which Whitman uses her novels. The epigram to *The Power of Sympathy*, "Catch the warm Passions of the tender Youth / And win the Mind to Sentiment and Truth," emphasizes that it too attempts to gain the child reader's passionate allegiance.[61] As both works are addressed to young readers and even use similar conventions associated with advice literature, the reader is asked to take on the position of a child regardless of her actual age. Childish reading, in this case, is exactly what is necessary to create and maintain the citizen's obedience.

Seen in this light, the overlap between child and adult readers, and particularly between children and women readers, begins to take on an added significance. As members of society who would remain dependent even on reaching adulthood, young women such as Myra could be presented as ideal examples of obedient childlike citizens. Thus, the association with children did not only serve to restrict women's citizenship, as one might expect, but actually made women (or, more often, girls) key imaginary figures for citizens. By holding up Myra as an example, the novel encourages even readers who are not children to occupy imaginatively the position of good child reader. Novels' attempts to change child readers into adults and adult readers into children, even as their typically progressive and educative plots rely on a clear distinction between these categories, points to the continued instability of age distinctions in the novel's narrative of citizenship.

"Nurseries of Sedition"

The French Revolution amplified the cultural fear of childishness and bad reading. While the French Revolution was initially celebrated in the United States as an expansion of revolutionary ideals, the Federalist government did not look favorably on the actions of the French and attempted to curb popular enthusiasm for the cause, which included that of children. Records of celebrations throughout the country show that Republicans actively sought young people's support for the French cause. Organizers of rallies and holiday events used techniques associated with affectionate citizenship to teach children about France, such as offering them sweets inscribed with the ideals of the Revolution. At a December 24 celebration in Boston, "every child was presented with a civic cake bearing the words Liberty and Equality" to "impress on the tender minds of the rising generation the precepts of that glorious period."[62]

John R. Watson, then a boy in Philadelphia, remembers the mania among children of his acquaintance for anything French:

> With what joy we ran to the wharves at the report of the cannon to see the arrivals of French prizes; we were so pleased to see the British Union down! When we met French officers or marines in the streets we would cry Vive la république! Although most of us understood no French, we had caught many national airs, and the streets by day and night resounded with the songs of boys . . . All of us put on the national cockade . . . I remember several boyish processions, and on one occasion girls dressed in white, and in French tricolored ribbons, formed a procession, too. There was a great Liberty pole with a red cap at the top erected . . . and there I and a hundred others taking hold of hands and forming a ring round the same, made triumphant leapings, singing the national airs.[63]

Yet Watson's reflection ultimately echoes conservative critiques of the rebellion as childish. The French Revolution threatened to blur the boundary between foreign and native, young and old: "I hope never to see such an enthusiasm for any foreigners again. . . . It was a time when, as it now seems to me, Philadelphia boys had usurped the attributes of manhood; and men who should have chastened us had themselves become very puerile."[64]

Popular support for the French Revolution intensified in 1793 during the French Ambassador Citizen Genet's visit to the states to promote American support for the wars against England and Spain. Genet's visit gave rise to another round of elaborate celebrations, but additionally produced a specific language of puerility to describe the French and their U.S. supporters. The publisher of *Peter Porcupine's Gazette*, William Cobbett, described Genet's visit as "a variety of such nonsensical, stupid, unmeaning, childish entertainments as were never thought or heard of till Frenchmen took it into their heads to gabble about liberty."[65] Alexander Graydon reported, "[Genet's] being the first minister of the infant republic . . . was dwelt upon as a most endearing circumstance."[66] George Gibbs notes in his memoirs of George Washington's and John Adam's presidencies that the government saw the Republican societies that formed in the wake of Genet's visit as "nurseries of sedition."[67] Noah Webster, who had been a supporter of the French Revolution before Genet's visit, writes, "The convention in their zeal for equalizing men have . . . condescended to the puerilities of legislating even upon names . . . There is something in this part of the legislative proceedings that unites the littleness of boys with the barbarity of the Goths."[68] That Webster, who also dedicated much time to the importance of language, finds these matters "little," calls attention to the substance of his critique, which cannot be that matters of language are too trifling to be addressed, but that the particular reading of these words by the French was misguided in his view. Similar to Harrington, the French understood liberty and equality to mean the eradication of class inequalities as well as political ones.

Echoing these critiques of the French Revolution, Americans' general fears of the potential for social insurgency associated with democracy came to be signified by the figure of the rebellious child. In Royall Tyler's *The Algerine Captive* (1797), the narrator, Doctor Updike Underhill, becomes master of a country school, only to find that his pupils are engaged in constant attempts to thwart his authority. One child even goes so far as to sit in the schoolmaster's chair: "To have my throne usurped, in the face of the whole school, shook my government to the centre."[69] Rebecca, in Susanna Rowson's *The Fille de Chambre* (1795, notably, a French title), encounters an eight-year-old boy who has splashed paint on his brothers and sisters due to the overindulgence of his Mamma.[70] In Rowson's most famous work, Charlotte Temple rebels against her parents and runs away to America under the guidance of a governess who is, notably, French.

In addition to these fictional portraits, several writers expressed concern that the democratic equalizing aspects of French and American politics would lead to insubordinate children. Alexis de Tocqueville is famous for noting that American democracy created a situation in which "the bonds of filial obedience grow looser with each passing day."[71] As a response to the French Revolution, Hannah More, an English children's writer popular in America, memorably expressed her fears that too much freedom might lead to child revolt: "The next influx of that irradiation which our enligtheners are pouring in upon us, will illuminate the world of grave descants on the *rights of youth*, the *rights of children*, and the *rights of babies*."[72]

History gives some isolated cases in which postwar anxieties about children stemmed from real-life acts of child disobedience during and after the American Revolution. As Steven Mintz observes, some children challenged their parents' control by running away or forging papers to join the American army. Hessinger reports that student rebellions of the late eighteenth century also provided evidence that youth in America were becoming increasingly bold, to the worry of their elders.[73] But fears of child insurgence following the French Revolution particularly manifested themselves as anxieties surrounding children's reading habits. Richard and Maria Edgeworth, whose *Practical Education* (1801) was read in the United States, suggest that even mostly harmless books might incite rebellious behavior. They devote considerable attention to a line from Anna Laetitia Barbauld's *Lessons* in which a small child asks for his dinner. Barbauld's hungry child, they argue, could create societal breakdown through his rebellious employment of linguistic democracy, and this behavior might even lead to an inverted tyranny: "if [children] are permitted to assume the tone of command, the feelings of impatience and ill temper quickly follow, and children become the little tyrants of a family."[74] Because of the rebellious potentials in language, the Edgeworths recommend that parents censor books with scissors to take out the dangerous bits, a suggestion that invokes the similar actions that the American government took against seditious material.

While many attempts were made to address the child's reading through education, anxieties also arose that American readers were fundamentally childish. An 1801 column, "The Lay-Preacher," by Federalist and *Port-Folio* editor Joseph Dennie claims that the defining feature of early American and French culture were their tendency to childishness: "The world has, by the fancy of bards, or by the austerity of monks, been compared to a wilderness, a prison, and to a mad house. To me, its present aspect is a great nursery. . . . All are frivolously employed; and into whatever nook I cast my eyes, I see nothing but baby faces, and childish play."[75] According to Dennie, Americans' resemblance to children is most visible in their reading choices: "I am not at a loss in what class to rank an audience, who snore over the scenes of Shakespeare, and are broad awake to the mummery of pantomime." In literature, he concludes, "a childish taste prevails, and childish effusions are the vogue." In an image that anticipates a similar one in Nathaniel Hawthorne's later children's book, *Grandfather's Chair* (1840), he argues that American readers are "as aukward as my nephew Bobby, now riding across my study on a broomstick." Significantly, Dennie associates the childishness of these "full grown creatures" with an *illusion* of political freedom, power, and choice. Describing the French Revolution, he reports that "everything shows fantastic and puerile. Legislators with bits of motley ribbon in their caps; and compelled to wear this republican girth web, imagining themselves free."[76] Implied in Dennie's critique is that these readers not only misread Shakespeare but also do not understand the necessary qualifications to the citizen's freedom within a republic. Through the figure of the bad child reader, rebellion and dissent come to be represented as childish, resulting from poor reading skills rather than a legitimate political stance.

Kiddie Quixotism

Unlike the seduction tale, the Quixote story almost always allows the bad child reader to be reintegrated into a progressive narrative of free citizenship by becoming a good adult reader. Charlotte Lennox's *The Female Quixote* (1752) was perhaps the first text to attribute the affliction of elderly gentleman Don Quixote to young girl readers. Lennox's reimagination of children as the population most affected by the quixotic illness was significant in that it recast childish fantasy and misreading as a harmless stage that could be potentially grown out of.

Written by Tabitha Tenney, the wife of Federalist congressman Samuel Tenney, *Female Quixotism* (1801) tells a hyperbolic tale of reintegration, in which the main character, Dorcasina, is a caricature of all of the typical signs of the bad reader. She exhibits obsessive love for the wrong kind of books, theatrical speech and actions, ridiculous reliance on books to determine her behavior, and adamant refusal to accept the standards of proper conduct. Though this text is often (correctly) read as an attempt to enforce the rules of marriage for women, Dorcasina is not only a woman reader, but also a child reader, both literally and figuratively. The fact that Dorcasina is a young child when the text begins associates her with Tenney's most direct audience. It is the "younger part" of the female sex that Tenney addresses in her preface, which she begins "dear girls."[77] As citizens in formation, children would have been considered particularly in need of Tenney's satirical corrective on reading.

The ways that childhood and adulthood, especially womanhood, overlapped in the early republic is another overriding theme in this work. The child Dorcasina symbolizes both subjection and rebellion, making her the inverse of the citizen. The text attempts to show that Dorcasina's rebellion is a failed one and that her subjection ends when she resumes her proper education into a lawful adult citizen. *Female Quixotism* thus surpasses seduction novels such as *The Power of Sympathy* and *The Coquette* by providing a recuperative solution for the seduced reader. However, in the course of this process, the line between the child and adult female citizen is also blurred, an instability symbolized by Dorcasina's satirical status as a childish adult for most of the novel.

The text suggests that difficulties in creating adult citizens are to some extent inevitable, since bad readers are the product of the same process that trains good readers—and both are understood as childlike. Even more than Whitman, Dorcasina is strikingly similar to the loving readers described in chapter 2. The narrator begins by telling us that Dorcasina has lost her mother at a young age, a circumstance that she has in common with Goody Two Shoes and Jenny Peace. Much of children's literature treats such a loss of the parent as an advantage, as it allows children to become independent and transfer their love to more abstract objects such as books. Dorcasina, like those children, responds to the physical removal of her female parent by learning to love her book. Dorcasina's education also seems to be modeled after Locke's *Some Thoughts Concerning Education*. Mr. Sheldon always governs Dorcasina with affection rather than overt force and helps Dorcasina transfer her affection for him to books. While the text ultimately claims that this love goes wrong because it is applied to the *wrong* books, the process is all but identical to the training of the good child reader and citizen.

Dorcasina too applies her affection to increasingly abstract objects and develops a fierce identification with them. In the first few pages, she reads a letter from Lysander's father that convinces her that she will be in love with his son, even though she only knows him through text. This act of imagination is not so different from that required of good readers, who are asked to apply their love to distant authority figures and to other citizens and to identify with texts as a representation of their own wills. An even more striking instance of readerly affection comes later, after Dorcasina has met another one of her lovers, the Irish criminal O'Connor. Dorcasina has been separated from her lover but has collected a packet of his letters, textual representations that she loves as fervently as O'Connor himself. In a ritualistic manner, Dorcasina treats these texts as if they were stand-ins for her lover's body: "Taking the first in order, she kissed the seal, and the superscription; then, after opening it, and pressing the inside upon her heart, she read it three times over."[78] She even goes so far as to personify a handkerchief, kissing it and talking to it.

Dorcasina is cast as quite mad for carrying out this kind of affection for objects and texts. Her maid Betty is "surprised at scenes so new, and . . . foolish" and points out that the handkerchief cannot understand Dorcasina's meaning. Yet, when we consider Dorcasina's acts in the context of other children's narratives, we see that they are not at all "new" but are suggested by common commands that the reader should "love his book." Dorcasina talking to a handkerchief and kissing letters resembles Giles Gingerbread speaking to his ABCs and eating his books, though it takes on exaggerated and ridiculous form. Betty, of course, has a point in claiming that Dorcasina cannot really "talk back" to the handkerchief. What is cast as a loving and reciprocal relationship between reader and text, citizen and law, is often one-sided.

Despite her love for books and other texts, Dorcasina fails to become an ideal citizen. Instead she is depicted as a child with an overblown imagination. Taking the notion of affectionate citizenship a step further than the good readers of chapter 2, Dorcasina refuses to obey any authority that she does not love and uses her affection (or lack thereof) for texts as criteria for determining whether they have the right to exercise authority over her actions. Affection becomes the standard by which Dorcasina rejects many authorities, such as Lysander and Mr. W, whose letters are characterized by bland and uninspiring prose. Criminals such as O'Connor are better able to write what Dorcasina considers the language of love, and thus, she accepts the authority of all of their assertions. The myth that citizens need to love the law backfires when those representing the law are unable to compete with other more passionate lovers.

The rebellious implications of Dorcasina's readerly love become particularly evident in her rejection of Mr. W, the text's most abstract representation of positive authority. Mr. W is set off from the rest of the characters in the book in that he is represented purely as language, a member of the alphabet like Giles Gingerbread's Mr. B and Mr. C, while the other characters get full names that sound like the characters in Dorcasina's romance novels. As such, he is a near-representation of the law himself, of the state that is "made . . . of language."[79] Dorcasina initially seems to accept the authority of Mr. W, as she believes that he will support her in her rebellion against her father's plan to find a sensible lover by causing "another revolution, in the mind of her father."[80] While Tenney's language evokes the celebration of the rebel child in the American Revolution, the notion of a second revolution, following in the footsteps of the French Revolution, was precisely the fear of the governors of the early nation. Because Mr. W is aligned with the social standards that Dorcasina's love causes her to reject, no such "revolution" occurs in the mind of Mr. Sheldon. A bad reader both of books and of citizenship, Dorcasina resists Mr. W's law and refuses to credit his letter. This rebellious act, rather than offering a real challenge to the law, is made ridiculous by the fact that Mr. W is actually telling the truth; Dorcasina has been duped by both her books and O'Connor.

Any potentially subversive results of Dorcasina's rebellion are likewise made into scenes of satire. Committing what seems to be a dangerous symbolic act, Dorcasina allows several servants to take on her father's authority by wearing his clothes. Nonetheless, the potency of this act is undermined when the clothes lead their wearers into preposterous situations rather than into true positions of power. Betty, for instance, is forced to wear Mr. Sheldon's clothes but is made to look rather ridiculous when Dorcasina forces her to make romantic proclamations in the voice of O'Connor. Later, after Mr. Sheldon has died, Dorcasina orders another servant, prophetically named John Brown, to wear his clothes, as she believes he is a noble in disguise. As a result, Betty misrecognizes him as Mr. Sheldon's ghost, creating uproar in the house until the slave Scippio convinces everyone of the hilarity of the situation. A third image of a servant in masters' clothes occurs in the scenes where James takes on the identity of his master, Captain Barry. In this case, the joke is on Dorcasina, as she is made a fool by almost marrying a servant. While images of servants in their masters' clothes have the potential to emblematize the radical implications of revolutionary democracy, they appear in this text as no more harmful than a childish prank or game of dress-up.

Lest the reader miss the political import of such moments, Tenney reveals her position on rebellion by asserting that one of Dorcasina's other lovers, Mr. Seymore, is a bad man because he is "one of the new fangled sort, an atheist, a jacobite, and an illumbenator." Following the discovery of Mr. Seymore, Betty tells the story of a man named Mr. M (the inverse of Mr. W), who left his family "partly owing to a book that he is very fond of, writ by one Tom Paine, who I am sure deserves the gallows for leading men astray from their wives and families."[81] The book was almost certainly *The Age of Reason* (1794), which was considered scandalous in post-Revolutionary America for its exploration of revolutionary thought, and which *The Port-Folio* linked with childishness by calling "the second edition of Tom Thumb's Folio."[82] The notion that childish books could create rebels is central to the text's attempt to undermine rebelliousness.

Tenney suggests that the child's rebellion is a diminished thing that ultimately only hurts the child herself. By the end of the book, Dorcasina is withered, bruised, humiliated, and bald (a state common to old people and babies). While Dorcasina appears to exercise too much agency in her refusal of societal standards of behavior, the logic of the text also suggests that she is imprisoned by her foolish love of novels, which allows her to be forced into involuntary relationships with bad authority figures. We are led to believe that if she were truly free to think for herself, she would readily consent to the authority of rational figures such as Mr. W. The author's logic seems to suggest that Dorcasina's rebellious tendencies are not based on a mature adult decision to dissent but rather on being a childish victim. In this way, the text reproduces the reasoning of Locke's *Two Treatises* and *Some Thoughts Concerning Education*: when children are ignorant of how to follow the law, they are subjected to their parents and other authority figures; when they grow up, they will be both law-abiding and free. In Locke's terms, we must continue to see Dorcasina as a child, someone whose dependence and ignorance does not permit her to be an independent citizen.

Childhood, in this text as in the others I have described, is not simply a stage of life but a signifier of the dependency that keeps children from being full citizens. Because she is considered to be a deficient citizen, Dorcasina is continually presented as a child rather than an adult woman, even after she has moved beyond her childhood years. When she goes to visit O'Connor in the inn, Tenney writes, "This was one of the most extravagant [schemes] that had ever yet entered the romantic imagination of a love-sick girl, and such as no lady, in her sense, would have attempted to execute."[83] The clash between Dorcasina's age and her childlike behavior is often the material for jokes in the text. She once tries to appear young by concealing her white hair with powder (a joke that is on Dorcasina since powder is also white). As we saw with *The Coquette*, heroines who are older than they seem are common to early American literature. This feature of the novel suggests that Americans of this period had difficulty accounting for the ambiguous political position of adult women and therefore reduced them to being represented as children.

The implication seems to be that Dorcasina will grow up only when she gains reason and respect for the standards of society. In the end, Dorcasina substantiates this narrative of citizenship when she writes to her friend Harriot of her conversion from a young and inexperienced girl to an adult woman. But Tenney's staging of Dorcasina's transformation from a seduced and subjected child to a free citizen also reveals the continuities between her child and adult selves. Instead of becoming independent as a result of her education, Dorcasina transfers her affections back to her father and finally to a more lawful form of book love. These actions come as a result of seductive tactics that resemble those used by the unseemly characters that Dorcasina is being taught to reject. Mr. Sheldon frequently uses affectionate language in a way that resembles that of O'Connor and the other seducers in the text, managing temporarily to manipulate his daughter's affections: "Regard for her lover was for the moment swallowed up in love for her father."[84]

Rather than representing a graduation from childishness to adult wisdom, Dorcasina's growth at the end of the text can be read as a transfer of obedience from her lovers back to an abstracted version of her father. The book ends with Dorcasina recognizing her obligations to her proxy father, Mr. Stanly, who has rescued her from ignorance. In demanding Dorcasina's allegiance to this abstract father, the author anticipates American judges' increasing reliance on the common law doctrine of *parens patriae*, or the idea that the state "has the responsibility" to take on the role of parent and "care for those who are legally incapable of caring for themselves."[85]

Grossberg describes this legal turn as producing a "new doctrine that would dominate legal debates about children into the twenty-first century: *the best interests of the child* . . . The legal doctrine contained the assumption that children had their own needs . . . and when [parents] failed, judges or other suitable public or private officials such as the overseers of the poor, must determine them."[86]

Though Mr. Stanly is a neighbor rather than a government representative, his assumption of Dorcasina's care after her father's death anticipates the ways that this doctrine would be applied to delinquent children in the nineteenth century whose parents have failed to control their behavior. Grossberg continues, "Beginning in New York in 1824, houses of refuge were constructed throughout the country to provide wayward or neglected youngsters with special treatment aimed at making them grow into responsible adults."[87] As one example, in 1838, the Pennsylvania Supreme Court decision *Ex parte Crouse* dictated that young Mary Ann Crouse could be placed in a house of refuge for her "vicious conduct" against her will because "the basic right of children is not to liberty but to custody."[88] Such decisions were part of a legal trend of denying children's rights on the basis of their noncitizenship, though they notably corresponded with the Federalist interest in nominally granting children national citizenship, suggesting that laws were beginning to define the child as a special kind of national legal subject (if not a citizen) without the right to freedom. The idea was that children under such care would transition into free, rational adult citizens with the help of the state, but subjection was needed to ensure that this would happen.

The text's version of *parens patriae* overtly distinguishes between protective education, which supposedly liberates children and allows them to transition into adult citizens, and forceful subjugation, which threatens their freedom and growth, but also reveals the ways that these types of restrictions overlap. In the name of Dorcasina's protection, Mr. Stanly carries out a seduction scheme that rivals that of any ne'er-do-well. Echoing Richardson's seduction scenes in *Pamela*, the kidnapping scene in Rowson's *Charlotte Temple*, and an earlier abduction in *Female Quixotism*, Mr. Stanly forces Dorcasina into a coach and takes her to an isolated house in the country where she no longer has access to any of her books.[89] Pamela is forced to read dirty propositions from her seducer, but Dorcasina is compelled to read books about history, which were frequently recommended by pedagogues to train children to be respectful citizens. On the one hand, any appearance of subjugation in this kidnapping is given the aura of legitimacy by positing it as the result of Dorcasina's childish behavior. Even though Mr. Stanly's actions require deception and seduction, the text suggests that he is actually protecting Dorcasina from her own false beliefs and helping her grow up.

On the other hand, anxieties about invasions of the child's and citizen's liberty seem to underlie the novel. *Female Quixotism* seems to give the understanding that individuals are not just susceptible to seduction by bad authorities; they also can and must be seduced through education into following a moral code of behavior and political system that values obedience over resistance. As Elizabeth Barnes has noted, while the trope of seduction "ostensibly [represents] the perversion of republican virtue," it actually signifies the methods by which citizenship often operates.[90] By removing children from the direct context of the family in order to carry out this education, *parens patriae* gave them a more direct relationship to the state as child-citizens, but it is unclear whether this change makes them more effective citizens, or makes citizenship more childish. By treating her as a political nonentity until she accepts fatherly care, Dorcasina's maturation into an adult citizen is shown as contingent on her voluntary acceptance of continued nonage. Seen in this light, Dorcasina's status as an adult child does not mark her difference from the grown-up citizen; rather, it reveals the citizen's crucial childishness. The fact that adult citizens were expected to be obedient is also reflected in the fact that Dorcasina is subject to Mr. Stanly's protective care not as a child, but as an adult woman. While *Ex parte Crouse* is often seen as a sign that children and adults were coming to be more firmly separated under the law, Tenney's application of the doctrine of *parens patriae* blurs child and adult. As Isenberg has argued, the logic of proxy parenthood was extended in the nineteenth century to legitimize constraints on adults—especially women— who were not thought to be capable of rational behavior.

The connection between education and seductive subjugation finds anxious expression in Tenney's depiction of Dorcasina's seducers, Philander and Mr. Seymore, who are also schoolmasters. Though the first of the two is described as "an excellent scholar," his name, Philander, associates him with a rake rather than a tutor.[91] The second, Mr. Seymore, is an even darker figure, who has "squandered all of his time and money in gaming houses and brothels" and who has actually succeeded in molesting a schoolgirl.[92] The literal merging of schoolmaster and seducer implies again that education is not in opposition to seduction, but, as Karen Sánchez-Eppler has also suggested in her analysis of nineteenth-century temperance narratives, has seductive potential that can result in coercion, manipulation, and even abuse.[93] One strain of the text argues that good authority differs substantially from bad authority and that obeying good authority makes one a free, adult citizen. However, the trope of schoolmasters who are indistinguishable from rakes—and of fathers who gain obedience through seductive language and kidnapping—also inculcates that education into citizenship might entail a degree of coercion.

Tenney's preface further demonstrates the similarity between good authority figures and rakes by using seductive language to describe her own intent. She says that her book "courts" her young readers' attention and that she hopes that they will be "induced to read it."[94] The balancing act of *Female Quixotism* requires that readers buy into a narrative in which novels are potentially dangerous, while simultaneously agreeing to the authority of Tenney's text. Of course, Tenney would not need to court her reader if a resistant reading of her own book was not also a possibility. Whether she is successful or not depends on how good a reader the child is, but this readership is in question from the beginning. Tenney in fact dedicates her book to the very readers that she is attempting to eradicate: "All Columbian Young Ladies Who Read Novels and Romances."[95] The uncertainty surrounding the child reader's reaction returns us to a major problem that the bad reader narratives address: the inability to ensure what kind of character we are dealing with in a world in which relationships of power have become abstract. To the extent that authority had become abstract and representational, child readers had also become difficult for the would-be pedagogue to fully pin down. They existed, not only within the closet and the local schoolhouse but also across an entire nation.

"Stories for Children by a Baby Six Feet High"

Two decades after the publication of *Female Quixotism*, the figure of the bad child reader gained new significance with the appearance of Washington Irving's *The Sketch Book of Geoffrey Crayon, Gent.* (1819), a book that was famous for its depiction of another quixotic reader: Ichabod Crane. Ichabod would become well known throughout the nineteenth century as a portrait of a country schoolteacher. But Ichabod was also a reader, whose obsession with Cotton Mather's "History of New England Witchcraft" inspired his irrational fear of the Headless Horseman. Irving's work is significantly different from that of the early American novelists, perhaps in part due to his insistence on writing sketches—or short stories—rather than novels. As Aman Garcha has pointed out, while the narrative plots of novels create an "illusion of progressiveness," sketches create "the consolations of stasis . . . in which truly meaningful progression is impossible."[96] Similar to this interpretation of the sketch in general, the most frequent argument made about Irving's text is that it asserts the stability of patriarchal systems, resisting the revolutionary energy of the new republic.[97] Irving dwells on the absence of a revolution in the realities of the everyday citizen, most famously in "Rip Van Winkle," where the portrait over the tavern door is relabeled from King George to George Washington with no significant alteration. In addition, Irving casts Americans as grown-up children, an oxymoron that, in the context of a revolution that was founded on a narrative of the child's coming of age, threatened to undermine the concept of the free and rational American citizen.

At face value, "The Legend of Sleepy Hollow" follows a similar logic to that of *Female Quixotism*, relying on Locke's narrative of progressive education in which the subjected child grows up to be a lawful, but free, adult citizen. Irving's bad reader tale makes a compelling case for the citizen's childishness, not least because the child reader in the story does not turn out to be a pupil of the country school-house. He is its teacher. Ichabod Crane is frequently considered to be a feminized reader, evidenced by his affinity with the "old wives" of Sleepy Hollow. He is just as strongly marked as childlike, the "companion and playmate of the larger boys" in the schoolhouse.[98] Like Dorcasina, his books seduce him because he is unable to relate to them in a rational manner. His belief in the outmoded authority Cotton Mather causes him to have night terrors, a disorder that is generally associated with small children. The fact that Ichabod is a male character who is described as a child reminds us that women were not the only citizens whose obedience was required in the new nation. While having some participation rights was not unimportant, even adult men faced limits on their liberties and had to view themselves as free despite the fact that they could not always participate in their own governance. "Sleepy Hollow" is an indictment of the ways in which early American culture did and did not encourage its citizens to grow up.

Early illustrations of *The Sketch Book* support this characterization of Ichabod as childish. Although Irving described the schoolteacher as tall and skinny, the popular depiction by Felix O.C. Darley shows him in a diminutive light: perched upon a high stool, surrounded by children, with his feet unable to touch the ground. As the picture hints, Ichabod is not interested in the old wives because he identifies with them, but because he desires their food, to be cared for as if he were a small child. Ichabod's propensity to love the wrong books is linked with this childlike fixation on food. Irving writes: "His appetite for the marvelous, and his powers of digesting it, were equally extraordinary . . . No tale was too gross or monstrous for his capricious swallow."[99]

As we have seen, swallowing one's books was a well-known trope of the child's internalization of social lessons. Giles Gingerbread learns to read by eating books made of gingerbread. On the flipside, anxieties about children's exposure to bad books were also expressed through concerns about what a child might swallow. Mary Wollstonecraft stated that women should breastfeed their own children because those "who are left to the care of ignorant nurses, have their stomachs overloaded with improper food, which turns acid."[100] Servant's tales were considered as poisonous as their tainted milk. Wollstonecraft warns that servants tell stories of "bugbears," which threaten children's development into rational adults. The association of bad tales with servants demonstrates the political stakes of correct reading choices: the oral and written culture of these classes complicated the equation of literacy and morality that was so central to the American definition of freedom. Children also threatened to dismantle this equation because they were believed to have a natural attraction for these fantasy stories—a problem that, in this case, caused the influence of the parent to be pitted against that of the governess and storyteller.

There is evidence that early readers read Ichabod's character, and Irving's work in general, with similar anxieties in mind. Ghost stories, such as "The Legend of Sleepy Hollow," were associated with childish tastes rather than with adult reason, freedom, and self-sufficiency. A New York reviewer claimed that Sleepy Hollow brought to mind "the dim, floating impressions of the nursery days . . . the . . . appalling stories of Jack O'Lantern and Whip-poor-Will, of dough-faces, of winding sheets."[101] Irving's "Tales from a Traveler," which contained more ghost stories, attracted virulent comments from a Philadelphia reviewer who scorned its childish appeal. He writes, it is inappropriate for an American author "to speculate on the most *weak, infantile,* and *degrading* of all the fears that make man a wretched victim to his distempered fancy," especially in an age that has abandoned "all the vulgar errors and prejudices that formerly fettered the reason."[102] He recommends that "Mr. Washington Irving's [work] would sell more rapidly if the Booksellers would alter the Title, and call it 'Stories for Children' by a *Baby Six Feet High.*"[103] This reviewer finds the idea of an American author bound to the impressionable reading habits of childhood particularly offensive because it challenges the notion of an educated citizenry that has come of age. Read through this cultural lens, Ichabod will only grow up when he is able to wield reason and become free from his childish attachment to his books.[104] If not, he will be like the reviewer's caricature of Irving, a grown-up baby.

Irving remains unclear about whether Ichabod is able to grow up, instead choosing to offer two alternatives: one told by a farmer and the other told by the old wives of Sleepy Hollow. In the farmer's version, Ichabod leaves the town after his encounter with the Headless Horseman and becomes an adult citizen, turning his attention from his ghost stories to the law. Ichabod's reorientation is typical of an early American story of a bad reader's reeducation. His ride with the headless horseman is even somewhat tame compared with Dorcasina's kidnapping in *Female Quixotism.* After Ichabod has been awakened to the foolishness of his childish reading practices, he becomes (according to the farmer) a model citizen. We learn that he has "been admitted to the bar, turned politician, electioneered, written for the newspapers, and finally been made a justice of the Ten Pound Court."[105] The fact that Ichabod is able to participate in this wide array of citizenly duties by learning to read the law lends credence to the nation's most hallowed political narrative in which education secures the child's development into a free adult.

But despite the old farmer's ending for Ichabod, Irving does not seem to believe that education can or should create this kind of rational, participatory, and socially mobile adult citizenship. After all, he casts doubt on the old farmer's story by locating it in the realm of mere hearsay. Even if Ichabod grows up to become a politician, he only does so by being duped—a detail that suggests that both irrational books and American political narratives rely on the citizen's "swallowing" of spectral fantasies. It is thus no coincidence that the cause of Ichabod's bad behavior is a history book written by the Puritan forefather Cotton Mather—the kind of book that was supposed to cure bad reading. By making the foolish Ichabod a politician and judge, Irving hints that one must have quixotic tendencies to have confidence in the law. In doing so, he recalls a passage from his earlier *Salmagundi* (1807), in which foreign visitor Mustapha Rub-a-Dub Keli Khan compares the U.S. government to a "mighty windmill" composed of hot air and words that have no effect on the average citizen.[106] Mustapha also balks at a handbill written by the "ghost of George Washington" and observes the "fatal . . . despotism" that "empty names and ideal phantoms exercise . . . over the human mind."[107] Political propaganda, it seems, is not so distinct from ghost stories.

In this light, the narrative of Ichabod's transition into a free adult citizen becomes not a triumphant celebration of the effectiveness of rational education but a joke. The punch line comes from the "old wives." In their version of the story, which Irving suggests is "better," Ichabod is not transformed into a free citizen. He becomes a ghost who haunts the local schoolhouse.[108] Thus, Ichabod remains a perpetual child, forever located in an infantile space and never reaching adult status. The postscript of "Sleepy Hollow" casts further doubt on the farmer's progressive narrative by reducing it to an absurd syllogism: "For a country schoolmaster to be refused the hand of a Dutch heiress is a certain step to high preferment in the state."[109] The postscript also pokes fun at the pedagogical assumption that books enact the reader's education: the listener receives this nonsensical logic when he asks what the "moral" of the story is supposed to be.

In an ironic twist of fate—or perhaps a self-fulfilling prophecy, *The Sketch Book* later came to be imagined as a book for children. The two most famous stories "Rip Van Winkle" and "The Legend of Sleepy Hollow" are now best known as classics of children's literature. This appropriation for child readers was not the work of twentieth-century readers, as one might suspect, but of Irving's contemporaries. The text's transformation into a children's book can be traced to its first readers, many of whom disregarded pedagogues' warnings about the dangers of ghost stories and read "Sleepy Hollow" at family gatherings. Henry Longfellow, who claimed the *The Sketch Book* was his "first book" when he was a schoolboy, likely encountered the text this way.[110] As early reviews that claimed that his work was infantile gave way to Irving's heroic institution as the founding father of American literature, children became an even more central part of his readership. Surprisingly, given the text's derision of the very principle of educational literature, *The Sketch Book* was adapted as a children's reading textbook, though discerning pedagogues suggested that readers skip the postscript. Along the way, Irving's pointed critique of the childish American reader and citizen was increasingly lost, as Americans embraced the figure of the (often happily submissive) child citizen.

The first textbook based on Irving's work, *The Crayon Reading Book* (named after sketchbook narrator Geoffrey Crayon), appeared in 1849, an event that more than one reviewer cited as the height of Irving's literary career. This celebratory attitude, praising child readers as Irving's ideal audience, could hardly represent a more drastic shift from the early reviewer who berated Irving for writing ghost stories. The change in the public estimation of child readers suggests that the fear of bad readership had in some ways subsided as the nation itself matured, dulling Irving's critique of the childish citizen and reader. Yet the association of ideal readership with schoolchildren highlights the ways in which childish impressionability remained a desirable feature of citizenship. *The Crayon Reading Book* reasserts the ties between literacy, seduction, and perceived freedom. One reviewer claims that the text was particularly adept at *enticing* "the youthful mind along the pathway of knowledge."[111]

Other pedagogues followed suit, declaring that Irving's work would aid in the project of creating dutiful American citizens through reading. One nineteenth-century schoolbook by Homer Sprague, headmaster of a Boston high school for girls, built an entire curriculum around *The Sketch Book*.[112] An advertisement in the back of Sprague's edition argues that love for good books creates moral readers, acting as an antidote to bad or rebellious readership: "Young people whose tastes are trained to the enjoyment of Scott's Ivanhoe or Irving's Sketch Book will not become infatuated with sensational literature. . . . When we are able to provide our boys and girls with wholesome reading, we guard them from the evil in books."[113]

This advertisement uses a logic similar to Tenney's *Female Quixotism*: the child who loves bad books is "infatuated" with or subjected to her books, while the child who loves good books is free to have "gratification" and "pleasure."It is interesting that the advertisement also includes the phrase, "A Revolution in School Reading," demonstrating the co-optation of revolutionary language to describe children's limited freedom in reading and to sell socially acceptable books.

Books intended to introduce children to Irving in the less institutionalized space of the home, such as Amanda B. Harris's *American Authors for Young Folks* (1887), also demonstrate an effort to preserve social norms through reading.[114] Harris evokes an affectionate approach to readership, suggesting that it is not enough to "have a page of two of Rip Van Winkle" because it is unlikely that such indifferent readers "really know Rip, and his dog Wolf." Truly an advocate of the command to "love one's book," she suggests that readers must understand what makes Irving "our Irving." Harris claims that this love for books will encourage morality and essentially eliminate bad readers: "as you grow up with a love of books . . . you will know how to choose the sweet kernels of truth, and learn to loathe the evil, and to distrust everything which confuses the border lines between right and wrong."[115] Irving's text seems to be interested precisely in confusing border lines: between good readers and bad readers, between freedom and subjection. To reestablish these lines, pedagogues often had to engage in what seems to be willful misreading of the book. A critic for the *American Whig Review* claims that "Sleepy Hollow" is a celebratory tale of the common citizen's rise to political power. He writes"[it] is a fact well authenticated that genuine country schools have been the nurseries of the most exalted intellects that have shed renown on our history."[116] As true or false as this may be, Irving's story belies this very conclusion. Ichabod's pupils never graduate from the schoolhouse, but abandon it, reasoning that if literacy leads to behavior like Ichabod's, it is best not to read at all.

The abandonment of the schoolhouse in "Sleepy Hollow" hints that one strategy for disentangling freedom and submission is to abandon education altogether. The Irving of *The Sketch Book* seems somehow unsatisfied with this solution. Revealing his ambivalence about the citizen's childishness, he claimed that Americans should try to address their juvenile status by taking their "examples and models . . . from the existing nations of Europe."[117] This attitude is complicated by sketches that depict Britain's books as stale and irrelevant to modern readers. In "Roscoe," he depicts an impoverished British poet, who is forced to auction his library to cover his financial losses. Irving compares the buyers, a group of barely literate commoners, to "Pigmies rummaging the armory of a giant, and contending for weapons which they could not wield."[118] The "pigmy" (or small, childlike being) would have been familiar to Irving's audience as a trope for Americans' stunted intellectual and political development. Crayon claims early in *The Sketch Book* that he went to

England to see the giants from which his race had diminished. Still, while American readers and citizens lack the skills that Roscoe possesses, Irving hints that the kind of patriarchal and hyper-learned adulthood that Roscoe represents is outdated, in need of reinventing.

Irving explores this vision more implicitly in his treatment of child readers. In "The Mutability of Literature," Irving employs unruly children to create a different possibility for American citizenship and literary enterprise. In this sketch, as in "Roscoe," Britain becomes a place of archaic books that are not of use to the present-day reader. Exploring the Westminster library, Crayon meets with an old book that talks and expresses a desire to be rustled through by rowdy child readers. The dusty tome says, "Books were written to give pleasure and to be enjoyed . . . let [the dean] once in a while turn loose the whole School of Westminster among us" so that we may have an airing.[119] The book's proposition shocks the bookish Crayon, who has gone there to escape the "madcap" schoolboys. Yet the sketch celebrates the potential for the child reader to make things new. Irving hints that young Americans must ultimately reject the dusty reading of Britain altogether, allowing for a new generation of genius. "Rip Van Winkle" likewise celebrates childishness as a valuable feature of American literary culture. Rip is the playmate of the village children and, though not explicitly a reader, he is a teller of superstitious tales. While he was punished as a member of the British colonies, the new American nation honors Rip as a valuable member of the community, whose fantastic story is known by all of the "rising generation."[120]

Irving wryly suggests that the nation's power rests not in coming of age but rather in harnessing the imaginative capacities of childishness for literary and social purposes. It is no coincidence that Crayon's pen name would come to evoke the child's broad imaginative strokes rather than Roscoe's black-letter poetics.[121] Recalling Ichabod's propensity to swallow every book he reads, Crayon was himself described as a child reader who devoured books of voyages and travels. The description of Crayon as a "book-eater" became part of the mythology surrounding Irving himself in children's culture. Harris claims that he was " 'a dawdler in routine studies,' but boy-like, fond of *Pilgrim's Progress, Robinson Crusoe, Sinbad* [and] *Orlando Furioso.*"[122] Like Ichabod's "swallowing" of superstitious tales, this type of bibliophagia was considered dangerous by pedagogues. If romances were considered to be the most treacherous books for girls (and country schoolmasters), adventure books were the equivalents for boys. Maria and Richard Edgeworth warn that, whereas girls will soon perceive "the impossibility of their rambling about the world in quest of adventures," boys will not be stopped by the difficulties in indulging their tastes for rebellion.[123] Indeed, the child Crayon does not accept the "impossibility" of such literary adventuring but instead gives free rein to his imagination. He writes: "How wistfully would I wander about the pier-heads in fine weather, and watch the parting ships . . . and waft myself in imagination to the ends of the earth!"[124] Moments like this anticipate a paradigm shift in the very definition of childhood. Locke associated childishness with subjection and adult rationality with freedom. The nineteenth century's romantic and sentimental redefinition of childhood would often reverse these terms.

Thus, while one strain of *The Sketch Book*'s literary afterlife envisions the book as a means through which to create wholesome citizens and readers, its other legacy is its representation of childhood as a potential space of imaginative freedom.[125] Though many nineteenth-century Americans remained suspicious of childhood as a model for citizenship and nationhood, these two possibilities both suggest that childhood was coming to be less differentiated from adulthood in this regard. In the next two chapters, I trace the ways in which idealistic notions of children's citizenship helped Americans contend with major changes in the political, economic, and geographical landscape of the nation. In the early years of the nineteenth century, the idea of a sentimental child citizen helped integrate the republican politics of self-sacrifice with the acquisitive goals of economic expansion by casting children as the keepers of national "goods" such as education, morality, and feeling. After the Civil War, Americans attempted to return to the notion of children's natural citizenship in order to remedy the challenges to citizenship represented by slavery. As a result, children gained more legal representation as citizens, most notably in the Fourteenth Amendment's declaration that all who are born in the nation are citizens, though the difficulties in interpreting this legal understanding of citizenship have often reintroduced the imaginary politics of childhood that were so important and threatening to early Americans.

CHAPTER 4

Reading for Social Profit
Economic Citizenship as Children's Citizenship

> Every father . . . should provide himself with a library of entertain-
> ing and instructive books, taking care to add to it from day to
> day according to his means, such new productions as are really of
> value. A few dollars thus laid out . . . will bring him a better inter-
> est, if he can look for it in the advancement of his offspring, than if
> invested in the most gainful of stocks.
>
> Common School Assistant, *1836*

> Imagination was bestowed upon us by the Great Giver of all
> things, and unquestionably was intended to be cultivated in a fair
> proportion to the other powers of the mind. Excess of imagination
> has, I know, done incalculable mischief; but that is no argument
> against a moderate cultivation of it.
>
> *Lydia Maria Child,* The Mother's Book, *1831*

In *The Exhibition of Tom Thumb* (1775, first American edition 1787), the proprietor
of an imaginary collection of curiosities describes a "conjuring box" that transforms
any object into "the very thing that it ought to have been."[1] The first object put
into the box is a children's book, probably *The Exhibition* itself, as the American
editions of both of the books are published by "Mr. [Isaiah] Thomas." On opening the box, the book has been "changed into a swinging folio, very magnificently
gilt and lettered; and at the bottom of the title page [is] printed in large capitals,
'PRICE THREE GUINEAS.'"[2] With its shrewd emphasis on economics, *The Exhibition* contrasts with other eighteenth-century books that encouraged children to
sacrifice their interests for the good of the commonwealth. The fact that Thomas,
a canny businessman, decided to adapt this Newbery book "for the instruction
and amusement of American youth" in the same year that the Constitution was
being adopted reminds us that self-interested motives also influenced citizens in

the young nation.[3] Beyond wanting to protect their property, many of the nation's early inhabitants were seeking a way that they might actively profit from the social compact. For Thomas, this meant pirating English books and insisting that truly *American* youngsters needed to buy his new, minimally altered versions. Passing on this economic worldview to readers, the thought experiment represented by the magic box encourages children to think of reading in terms of how they might profit from it.

Though the desire for profit in America dates from the early days of transatlantic trade, profit became associated even more with ideas of citizenship and nationhood as the new country expanded its national trade networks in the beginning of the nineteenth century. David Paul Nord describes this "market revolution" this way: "Propelled by both westward expansion and eastern urbanization, trade, agriculture, and small-scale manufacturing flowed everywhere and drew ordinary Americans— artisans and farmers—to regional markets and commercial relationships."[4] Thus, although profit had long been a metaphor used to describe the end result of education—for instance, in seventeenth-century Protestant religious language—profit as a motivation for reading gained new life as the U.S. book market grew and transformed as the result of innovations in manufacturing, transportation, and distribution.[5] By teaching children to consider the economic value of their books, *The Exhibition of Tom Thumb* acted as a precursor to the nineteenth-century children's books that I discuss in this chapter, many of which take the form of miscellanies. These compilations of various genres represent the proliferation of reading materials on the nineteenth-century book market. They frequently incorporated economic language, presenting themselves as "budgets" (another word for miscellany), "premium" books, and "lottery books." As miniature markets of ideas, miscellanies provided young readers with an occasion for thinking about the economy of reading: how to determine which materials are the most worthy and how to maximize their moral and monetary profit by circulating, saving, and gambling with bits of knowledge.

The economic orientation of these nineteenth-century children's books might seem surprising for several reasons. For many years, the scholarly paradigm regarding the nineteenth century suggested that the sphere of childhood was becoming separated from both the political sphere and the world of exchange. Anne Scott Macleod suggests that "to enter the juvenile fiction of antebellum America is to enter a twilight world, a world that seems at first almost wholly sheltered from the robust life around it."[6] Although scholars have long criticized this paradigm as overly simplistic, since children were involved even in public aspects of economic exchange, the idea of separation corresponds with certain legal notions of children's economic status in the period.[7] Children's ability to enter into economic contracts was becoming curtailed around the same time as their ability to enter into political contracts was. As Holly Brewer argues, most children in earlier eras could enter into economic arrangements relatively freely, but "by the early nineteenth century . . . virtually all children had custodians to make decisions for them during a custody that usually ended at a standard age of twenty-one."[8] Many children worked, but they were not usually legally responsible for making or even fulfilling the contracts that licensed them to do so. As Michael Grossberg notes, these changes gave way to a large-scale redefinition of childhood as a special legal category of individuals who required protection from the state rather than liberty: "The intent, if not the full result, of changes like these was to use the law to increase children's dependence on adults and to remove the young from the adult spheres of the marketplace and the civic community."[9]

Macleod claims that this separation of children from the world of exchange had the effect of zoning morality into the domestic sphere. She suggests that it was easier for children's writers "to separate intellectually . . . contradictory sets of values than to reconcile them," so they created a literary sphere of domesticity in which virtue thrived, untouched by the greed of the economic world.[10] Yet Macleod's formulation does not explain the ways that Americans did try to reconcile economic exchange and morality and the ways that economic values came to be associated with moral and social values. Such an explanation can be found in the economic orientation of many children's books of this era. The ideal economic member of society was an imaginary citizen whose economic participation was also imaginary: the child.

I suggest that imaginary versions of children's economic participation, such as those found in fictional stories and in miniature imaginary economies such as the Sunday school ticket system, helped to address the changes to civic life that resulted from economic expansion. As in Macleod's argument, histories of citizenship also tell a story of separation between virtue and economic participation, though these qualities are usually positioned slightly differently vis-à-vis childhood, as well as the public and private spheres. One typical story of the evolution of U.S. citizenship posits that Americans were more fully transitioning in the early nineteenth century from a civic-minded republican model to a liberal economic one, in which the law was seen less as an instrument for achieving common good and more as a set of protections designed to allow private individuals to maximize their own profit.[11] For instance, Andrew Jackson, elected president in 1828, embraced a laissez-faire economic policy, decreased federal power over the economy by dismantling the federal bank, and championed westward expansion as a means of increasing national and individual wealth.

In spite of these events, economic development was an unsettling change for many Americans, since economic individualism was often understood as contrasting with traditional ideas of civic virtue and common happiness. As J. G. A. Pocock has claimed, the clash between the coarse realities of economic life and traditional notions of virtuous citizenship was related to the transatlantic shift from a property-based to a commerce-based economy that began in the late seventeenth century:

> The universe of real property and personal autonomy now seemed to belong to a historic past; new and dynamic forces presented a universe which was effectively superseding the old but condemned the individual to inhabit a realm of fantasy, passion, and *amour-propre* . . . He could identify and pursue the goals proposed to him by his fantasies and passions, but he could not explain himself by locating himself as a real and rational being within it . . . The dominant paradigm for the individual inhabiting the world of value was that of civic man; but the dominant paradigm for the individual as engaged in historic actuality was that of economic and inter-subjective man, and it was peculiarly hard to bring the two together.[12]

Although those inhabiting the American continent were involved in commercial endeavors throughout the seventeenth and eighteenth centuries, the economic changes that Pocock describes most strongly affected citizenship after the War of 1812, as this is when states began to ease property requirements for suffrage. Changes to the laws regarding citizenship meant that citizens had more exposure to the fluctuations of the economy than ever before. Jackson further depicted the ideal citizen not as a property owner rendered independent and disinterested by his wealth but as a "common man" whose ingenuity allowed him to exploit the unstable world of commerce to his advantage. The change from a citizenry composed of property holders to a citizenry composed of capitalists and workers complicated the ideal of citizenship as only available to rational, independent individuals, because, as Pocock points out, the ideal of autonomous and disinterested participation depends on "a reality" based in property.[13] Commercial exchange, conversely made "the foundations of personality . . . imaginary," since "the individual could exist . . . only at the fluctuating value imposed upon him by his fellows." Instead of rational and disinterested, economic players had to be self-interested and speculative, traits that were considered to be childish in comparison to the autonomous personality traits held by property owners in a republican system.[14]

Pocock tells a slightly different story than Macleod does, but his narrative resembles hers in suggesting that the clash between citizenship and capitalist exchange produced a separation between economic participation and morality that was organized around childhood. According to Macleod's theory, moral value persisted in the private worlds of children rather than in the lives of adults. Pocock, unlike Macleod, associates corruption with the private sphere—and metaphorically, with childhood—while claiming that virtue remained ideally connected with the public sphere and adulthood. He saw that the separation between the economic and civic virtue was much more fraught: while Macleod suggests that the domestic sphere worked largely successfully as a cultural placeholder for morality, Pocock believes that individuals could not maintain divisions between economic and civic life. This inability to separate the spheres was magnified by a blurring between childhood and adulthood, as well as an intrusion of imagination into public decisionmaking. Although Pocock does not discuss the role of the child in Locke's work, his account of the ties between childishness and economic liberalism potentially offer a new rationale for children's importance in Locke's theories. For better or worse, childhood and imagination were encroaching on the terrain of the citizen.

In this book so far, I too have suggested that the imagined divisions between children and adults were not fully distinct in modern forms of citizenship. These divisions were becoming even less solid as economic expansion further complicated the republican ideal of disinterested political participation with a (more Lockean) world increasingly oriented toward the private interests of individuals. The association of childhood with economically motivated forms of citizenship was largely more imaginary than literal, since most children did not have substantial property and were still losing political rights (even Locke, who claims that children have a right to inheritance of property, does not give them a natural right to economic participation in the same way that they have the right to freedom). Yet, because the tumultuous economy of the early nineteenth century threatened to make dependence a perpetual, rather than transitional, state, Americans were forced to reconsider the political assumptions attached to childhood and other forms of dependence. While economic growth theoretically offered the possibility for any person to grow out of dependency, the instabilities associated with the economy also threatened to return any person to a position of dependence. During the panics of 1819 and 1837, many individuals were reduced to being paupers. Particularly in the latter crisis, formerly rational men were understood as possessed by childlike irrational passions that caused them to engage in rampant land speculation. The imaginary register of the market created particular anxiety, as currency was not always backed by specie and credit could not always be trusted. Because the volatile world of the market made rational independence a difficult position to achieve and maintain, the new citizen looked to some commentators dangerously like a child. Benjamin R. Barber's current theory of the "infantilized" citizen, "consumed" and "swallowed whole" by the market, has its roots in this era of U.S. economic expansion.[15]

Pocock suggests that for commerce to be understood as a basis for political identity with social benefits, it had to be linked with "the exchange of real goods and the perception of real values."[16] Accordingly, political ideas popular in England in the late eighteenth and early nineteenth centuries emphasized the real in their justification for industrial expansion; for instance, Jeremy Bentham and John Stuart Mill rejected the "legal fictions" of natural law and the social contract and suggested that laws should be weighed for their present utility and contribution to human happiness, personal and corporate.[17] Yet, as I show, in the United States the perception that the economy could circulate social values often required that imaginary ideas of citizenship and economic activity be privileged over legally sanctioned ones. Specifically, Americans returned to models of children's imaginary citizenship as they tried to legitimize economic participation and reconcile it with political ideals of social responsibility.

Nineteenth-century children's literature was instrumental in these attempts to resolve the tensions between civic and economic life. Imaginary versions of children's economic participation helped Americans to claim that social goods could result from economic growth. Some of these "goods" included literacy, knowledge, sentiment, human connection, and the educated child, who was an investment in the nation's future from which all citizens could presumably profit. The perception that the market could generate the interests of society provided a political ideology to accompany economic expansion: a model of capitalist citizenship in which the multiple interests of citizens could be combined to create greater individual and social returns.

Of course, images of children's imaginary citizenship were necessarily being transformed along with the expansion of the economy. The tension that Pocock notices between civic and economic values complicated the ideals of the independent adult citizen and the affectionate child citizen alike. Despite the prevalence of affectionate education well into the nineteenth century, economic competition frequently undermined the ideal of an affectionate national community. The supposedly natural unequal relationships between children and parents or teachers, which were used to teach love for the law, markedly contrasted with the disparities between creditors and debtors and the changes associated with economic development meant that citizens would be shaped by forces *other* than affection. The children's books that I discuss in this chapter deal with the problem of how to reconcile economic actions with good citizenship.

There was considerable debate about how social benefits could derive from the market even in imaginary versions of the economy for, as the conjuring box implies, exchange value frequently diverges from social and personal use value. Adam Smith famously claimed that the seemingly illogical and immoral calculation of economic value was based on the work of an "invisible hand," which transcended individual participants in the market and created the common good of economic prosperity: "By pursuing his own interest [the capitalist] frequently promotes that of the society more effectually than when he really intends to promote it. I have never known much good done by those who affected to trade for the public good. It is an affectation, indeed, not very common among merchants, and very few words need be employed in dissuading them from it."[18]

Smith's economic truism places little importance on social goods—including activities like reading and learning—with intangible moral and sentimental value, implying rather that social values will result when economic players pursue their own interests. While some children's texts, such as "lottery" books, seemed to rely on mysterious and random forces similar to the "invisible hand" in their promotion of learning, this concept was not yet commonly accepted, especially among educators and proponents of popular religion. Sentimental children's authors differently argued that if citizens were to be dependent and tied to the machinations of the market—if they were to be like irrational children—they must use this mutual vulnerability, dependence, and inequality to consciously generate social benefits.

The perception that the economy could generate real social values was considered vital to the preservation of free citizenship precisely because the market threatened to produce negative effects, among them inequality and social stratification. Sentimental authors do not maintain only that moral goods can come of capitalist exchange. They also believe that the inequalities generated by the market create opportunities for citizens to support, nourish, and educate each other. While these points of view frequently offered an alternative set of values that complicated some of the acquisitive goals of capitalism—for instance, locating riches in the mind and in heaven rather than just on earth—they also made it possible for many skeptical people to embrace capitalist exchange, creating support for further expansion. As children were imagined as participating in the market with moral values as their guide, they made its transactions seem patriotic, virtuous, and emotionally moving.

The child's economic citizenship was, at its heart, imaginary. However, this alliance between commerce, morality, and citizenship required the myth, summarized by Pocock, that individuals are "free . . . to recreate the world in accordance with [their] fantasies."[19] This justification of market values was not always successful and the vagaries of the market frequently created tensions between monetary and sentimental profit and national and individual interest. The social values that educators insisted that children factor into the exchange gradually came to be construed as natural results of the market. Simultaneously, individual gain and monetary profit began to be considered as having social values in themselves. The function of government could thus become the negotiation and protection of the multiple interests generated by the market, which could stand in for the government's role in encouraging the virtue of its citizens. The freedom to participate in government could be re-imagined as the freedom to participate in the market.

Some nineteenth-century Americans registered this shift in the origin and location of value from citizens to the market itself and would come to see capitalism's effects as depersonifying, dehumanizing, and alienating. Children, who came to be associated both with rampant consumerism and with the most exploited form of industrial labor, were thought to be particularly susceptible to this dehumanization. Thus, child readers also continued to signify the childishness that had come to haunt American citizenship.

Books, Citizens, and Other "Artificialities"

As Pocock and other scholars have noted, the ideal of a national union that benefitted all citizens relied on the idea of an ever-moving frontier, including the development of imperialist interests. But, in addition to the supposedly common goal of expansion beyond existing borders, many Americans believed that all citizens could benefit from the improvement of individuals through education, which would shore up the nation's future through the ingenuity of its child-citizens. For instance, as cited in the epigraph, one 1836 commentator remarked that books bought for children would bring "a better interest than if invested in the most gainful of stocks."[20] In this way, the expansion of the country relied on creating new generations of citizens as much as it did on pushing the physical frontiers.

An even more practical reason for using childhood as a frontier for economic expansion was that the debts incurred in the formation of the nation required the prosperity of a future public to shoulder the costs. Individual and national prosperity were specifically intertwined in the notion of public credit, which, as Patrick Brantlinger has argued, relies on "the faith a society or 'public' has in itself to prosper or in the future—presumably eternal—power and glory of a given nation state."[21] Because the debts and deficiencies of the present "can only possibly be repaid by forging ahead hopefully, expansively, into the future," the future generation of child citizens was not only a desirable but also a necessary national investment. According to Brantlinger, public debt is "even more fundamental to the fictional or ideological creation and maintenance of the imagined communities of modern nation-states than are more explicitly nationalistic cultural forms."[22]

Yet, figuring out how to invest in the nation's children was difficult because economic transactions were traditionally thought to have a detrimental effect on citizens, preventing them from exercising reason or compassion. As Cathy D. Matson and Peter S. Onuf explain:

> Relations based on credit were irrational and fitful, and the merchant who followed an interest defined in such insubstantial terms could hardly be master of his own economic behavior. Rational as his daily choices might be, the dangers to which he exposed his character by relying on the vagaries of credit and the ploys and subterfuges of competitors seemed to preclude the emergence of a permanent substantial commercial interest that could support and advance the general welfare.[23]

Politicians feared that, if economic interest encroached on citizenship, people would rank their own interests over those of the nation. For example, merchants might trade national staples to foreign nations for goods with only "artificial" market value (labeled by critics as "artificialities"). This dependence on such foreign goods might undermine citizens' independence and judgment. A writer for the *Virginia Journal* wrote in 1785, "For an independent nation to depend wholly on the supply of others . . . such a people may please themselves with sounds of their independence like a child's rattle."[24]

The "artificial" makeup of the economy contributed to concerns about the "artificiality" of citizens, who might also act based on self-interest rather than reason or virtue. Benjamin Franklin, famously comfortable with artificiality, exploited this possibility in his *Autobiography* when he claimed to have left his lamp on all night to give the impression he was working. In *Advice to a Young Tradesman* (1748), he invited young apprentices to carry out similar ploys to increase their credit.[25] The literary form of the miscellany, which Franklin perfected in *Poor Richard's Almanac*, supported this strategy by allowing readers to quickly gain small bits of knowledge that would increase their reputation without requiring intensive study.

Concerns that children who approached learning in this way would not gain the knowledge needed to be truly virtuous citizens troubled educators. An 1818 columnist for the *Academician* complains that many readers rely on the false "credit of great reading" while remaining "very little improved in their intellectual faculties."[26] The nineteenth-century book market threatened to produce such stunted readers because of the increasing number of materials available to young people, which made possible extensive as well as intensive reading.[27] As one 1826 commentator remarked, "the market is overstocked with such books as children and youth would read."[28] Educators worried that reading a large number of poorly chosen books—or worse, books that compiled of bits of knowledge from unknown sources, such as almanacs and pocket libraries—created the illusion of a well-rounded education. While extensive reading had the immediate effect of allowing individuals to display their cultural capital, critics argued that it devalued real education by flooding the market with nonsense. One columnist complains, "a great deal of reading does by no means imply a great stock of valuable knowledge . . . None [is] more vain, or more intolerable, than those who having learnt by rote a multitude of maxims and facts, deal them out by the gross."[29]

To prevent the crisis that they feared might result from a republic of well-read but ignorant citizens, Americans needed to link both economic participation and extensive reading to the development of positive character traits. Pedagogues theorized that children's books, as a special kind of educational commodity, could counter the tendency toward artificiality in the market. When read with an eye to moral and educational profit, children's books, even miscellanies, represented the possibility that knowledge could be a national storehouse of wealth in which all citizens were interested.

Thomas's American publication of *The Exhibition of Tom Thumb* in 1787 capitalized on the imperative to secure a moral basis for economic citizenship, suggesting that the many imaginative possibilities of the market could be transformed into social value when collected, performed, and personified by the child reader. *The Exhibition*, with its large number of "valuable curiosities," resembles museums created by Charles Willson Peale and Daniel Bowen in Philadelphia and Boston in the 1780s.[30] By compiling descriptions and stories of fictional objects, *The Exhibition* comprises what Jared Gardner has called a "literary museum."[31] Other "literary museums" of the period include magazines, such as *The American Museum* and *The Massachusetts Magazine; Or Monthly Museum*, which contained "anthologies of a range of excerpted pamphlets, books, reviews, and letters."[32] These texts represent the propagation of texts and goods in the capitalist marketplace—the contents of museums, after all, frequently resulted from the travels necessitated by international commerce. Peale's museum was a model of what *The Exhibition* sought to do in print. Peale specialized in the "collection and careful preservation of individual subjects," rendering items "valuable in a collective view" that are "otherwise lost to the publick, and of little value to their possessors."[33] As Peale's methodology suggests, the museum provided a way to manage the sheer number of materials on the market, attributing "collective value" to items that, by themselves, have ephemeral or fleeting market value. With respect to child readers, this means "curating" all of the lessons from their extensive reading to create a stable value in the self, which can be seen as a collectively profitable national asset: the learned and virtuous citizen.

By Thumb's calculation, readers will benefit from being shrewd about what materials they choose to read. After putting the book in the conjuring box, Thumb explains that it "might possibly contain more useful instruction, and more real good sense, and be of three times greater value than many a swaggering and unwieldy folio."[34] In this context, the swaggering "folio" evokes "portfolio." In addition to being the miscellaneous contents of a literary magazine—one of the most famous early American periodicals was Joseph Dennie's *The Port-Folio*—this word was coming to mean the collection of various investments to create the largest profit.[35] In Thumb's economic model, the child reader needs to avoid an "unwieldy" number of investments, instead consolidating "useful instruction" into manageable collections. This consolidation of knowledge by the reader is implied by the emergence of the "gilt book" from the machine, the description of which evokes special editions that were created especially for book collectors.

Thumb uses this description metaphorically; he does not want children to literally seek out collectors' versions of books. Book collecting, which became a rage in the early decades of the nineteenth century, was, according to Phillip Connell, "a historical episode in which . . . the arbitrariness of economic value threatened to destabilize the more legitimate criteria implied by the notions of 'learning' and 'taste.' "[36] The conjuring box instead suggests that all that is required to make *The Exhibition* a gilt book is the reader's imaginative participation, which makes the child's mind into "gilt book" that contains her collection of useful information. Thumb hints at the importance of children's participation by calling the book a "little performance," suggesting that the collection of knowledge requires the actualization of the book's contents in the person of the reader.[37] Children must activate the book's social value by learning and reciting its lessons.

The premise of *The Exhibition* hinges on the reader's performance. Thumb explains that the curator of his exhibit will not allow the children to enter until they "bow to him in the most respectable manner." They must "be able, not only to tell their letters, but to read any part of this little book with great fluency and exactness."[38] Through this gambit, the reader learns that education yields a profit in the self that can preserved and exchanged, like money. The performance is indeed better than money—that worthless paper stuff that is fantastically endowed with value—because money is *not* accepted for entrance into the exhibition. Only the reader's improvement will pay the price of admission.

This imagined social profit from reading lends credibility to the imaginary register of credit. Thumb explains that the readers who can perform the book will be able to produce "some Gentleman or Lady of reputation, who can honestly recommend them for their good behavior."[39] Credit was understood as resting on flimsier grounds than the virtues associated with property. However, *The Exhibition* suggests that credit can signify both economic viability *and* the moral properties of individual personality, both of which, in the book's estimation, are achieved through reading. Credit creates new foundations for citizenship, what Jacqueline Reiner has called a move from "virtue" to "character." While virtue relies on the sacrifice of one's passions and interests for the good of the commonwealth, character relies on attaining an individual reputation, often to support self-interested activities. Children's books such as *The Exhibition* attempt to counteract the dangerous effects of the market on children's characters by linking credit with moral values, including the "self-restraint appropriate for an economy of developing capitalism."[40]

The imperative to collect knowledge could be seen as inviting selfishness. Thumb curbs this potential selfishness by forcing children to refine their manners and self-regulate their desires in order to continue profiting from the exhibit. He notes that admission includes access to a large supply of oranges and sweetmeats. A child seeking immediate profit would presumably hoard these rare treasures, but Thumb warns that if any child takes too many, he risks getting thrown out of the exhibit (not to mention that an overabundance of oranges would eventually spoil, ruining the investment). Despite Thumb's attention to moderation and even frugality, the child's mannerly performance is not seen as contrary to the economic world of passions and interests. The child learns that greater profit will result from staying and collecting the entire educational exhibit than from acting rudely and getting expelled. It is thus through the contact with the book as both an educational tool *and* as a profitable commodity that children learn the virtuous manners needed to yield the largest gains in both moral value and profit. The French called these civilizing effects of trade *doux-commerce*, which, as Jane Thompson reminds us, refers to the "exchange of information, of money, and of sentiments."[41]

The concept of *doux-commerce* (literally "sweet" commerce) implies that even a self-interested approach to the market can lead to social cooperation. Jennifer Jordan Baker has put forward the idea that trading in the market requires trusting other individuals to continue valuing one's currency, whether money, a collection of rare materials, or a recitation of one's book. She writes, "Far from encouraging unchecked economic liberalism, [credit] invests market transactions with moral consequences . . . The individual who had assets on paper relied upon the rest of the exchange community for the maintenance of that fortune."[42] This was Locke's argument too: he claimed that paper money was a sign of the rise of consensual political societies.[43] The child's preservation of knowledge requires cooperation with others to ensure that they too recognize the value of this project. In this way, the interests of the individual child, as well as the interests of the market, could be seen as compatible with the moral interests of society. The collection of comprehensive knowledge, unlike the collection of random facts, was considered in the nineteenth century to be a universally valued task. According to Connell, book collectors were thought to make "a valuable contribution to the preservation of literature and learning for the benefit of society as a whole" introducing "a notional permeability between private . . . wealth and an evolving sense of public literary heritage."[44]

Of course, as the word "performance" also implies, the economic registers of use value and exchange value might also diverge, so that the performances of knowledge that garner social capital might not require true learning. Children's collections of knowledge, like collections of rare books, might constitute only a "show of learning and cultivation rather than productive scholarly labor on the part of the owner."[45] Book collectors were accused of only liking to *look* at their books rather than being able to understand their contents. Beyond this, even a performance of literacy can be faked—as anyone knows who has read a book to a young child long enough for the child to pretend to "read" the words. For educators, counterfeit performances endangered the social value of learning, devaluing real knowledge.

A child's knowledge also risked losing currency if not valued by the market. As Connell and James Bunn have claimed about book collections, the "exotic" items contained within might have value only in references to the "arbitrary" will of the owner.[46] In *The Exhibition*, it is unclear whether knowledge ever truly has a going market rate. After all, Thumb's scene of sweetmeat eating happens in the reader's imagination. The exhibition, located "at the upper end of *Education-Road*" does not really exist, and the reader's performance, which will supposedly allow admittance, *is* the only true exhibition. The reader is asked to join in the fun of imagining that reading can be traded for admission to a museum, but it is understood that it cannot. The fictiveness of the book's premise makes the case that reading should and does accumulate profit that can be exchanged like money, while simultaneously foregrounding the fact that reading does not work exactly in this way. The "little book" published by Mr. Thomas is not, finally, made of gilt paper and worth three guineas but is made of cheap Dutch paper and sold for a few pence.

Premium Books

In *The Exhibition of Tom Thumb*, children's ability to procure admission through reading rests on a fictional construct, a wink and a nod to readers that rests on the mutual recognition that the exhibition is make-believe. The nineteenth-century in-stitution of the Sunday school, conversely, attempted to make the imaginary profits of reading literally exchangeable as currency. In doing so, Sunday schools made an even stronger attempt to reconcile economic participation with traits befitting moral citizens, though this attempt was ultimately complicated by the numerous incompatibilities between religious and secular ideas of economy.

With 710 schools in seventeen U.S. states by midcentury, Sunday schools were instrumental to the growing mass circulation of children's reading materials.[47] As Stephen Rachman reports, "Between 1800 and 1880 the nation was flooded with streams of tracts, pamphlets, hymnbooks, devotional books, journals, magazines, and newspapers. By 1830, the American Tract Society (equipped with a steam-driven press) was producing more than six million tracts per year."[48] Sunday school tracts, like "literary museums," brought together the multiple kinds of knowledge that children might encounter in the expanding book market, including general history, voyages of discovery, philosophy, astronomy, natural history, biography, and moral tales in addition to religious works.[49] Tract societies also produced compilations of stories and organized them into "bookshelves" of 50–150 books that could be bought for between $5 and $70. These encyclopedic book libraries, which accompanied the creation of some of the first physical libraries explicitly for children, took the extensive reading materials that were available in this period and organized them into manageable volumes that could be profitably read by child readers.[50]

Further integrating economic ideas with moral development, the Sunday schools instituted programs in which children could earn tickets and "premium" certificates as payments for reading.[51] One such certificate reads, "A premium presented, as the reward of merit, by D. Jaudon, to his amiable young friend and pupil, Miss Rebecca Irvine, Union Hall, A.D. 1808." Premium means a "prize," which here refers to the pretty pictures, scripts, and borders that adorn the certificate and which were rare enough in the nineteenth century to be considered precious among child readers. But, according to the *Oxford English Dictionary*, premium also means "a sum added to an ordinary price or charge" or "worth more than usual." This added value, one might imagine, did not refer just to the worth of the prize, but to the child, who had appreciated in value as a result of reading.

The profits of reading came to be even more precisely quantified through the popular Sunday school ticket reward system, in which learning could be traded for commodities with moral value, such as books. In one frequently used scheme a "blue ticket was given to a child for the recitation of a hymn, or a certain number of verses from the Bible, for punctuality or regularity of attendance, good behavior, &c. Five, ten or twenty of these blue tickets were made equivalent to one red one, and two or more red tickets entitled the holder to a two, five, ten or twenty cent book, which became the child's own property."[52] One effect of this endeavor

Premium certificate, 1808. Children earned these certificates, greatly prized for their ornate decorations, when they read and memorized Bible verses in Sunday school. Courtesy of the American Antiquarian Society.

was an increase in the number of children who could afford to have books in their homes. In 1827 alone, the American Sunday School Union printed a staggering 484,000 premium books, which they proudly quantified for the subscribers to their annual report.[53]

Sunday schools had reason to assimilate capitalist understandings of incentives, as they were initially aimed at child workers in England. In addition to giving the poor children who went to these schools a sense that their efforts in learning would be paid, the notion that Sunday school children could *work* toward their charitable rewards reflects transformations in philanthropic practices that began in the mid-eighteenth century. Under a patriarchal system, charity had been considered an act of benevolence given from the ruling class to their inferiors and did not necessarily require effort on the part of the recipients. However, later philanthropists developed institutions in which the so-called deserving poor traded labor for aid. The notion that economic participation would create virtue in the poor was significant to capitalist expansion in both England and America. Hanway explicitly connected the work of the poor to the increased wealth of the English nation: "our care of the poor is the instrument of rendering ourselves rich . . . the wealth of the country relies on the industry and frugality of the poor."[54] The American Sunday school movement, which broadened its audience to middle-class as well as lower-class children, dropped most of the more tangible charity items given by Sunday schools (such as combs and shoes) but preserved the idea that national wealth could be embodied in children's moral economic participation.

The argument that economic participation could potentially yield collective national wealth was particularly urgent during the early years of the nineteenth century, because the poor state of the U.S. economy had given rise to doubts in the market's capacity to generate real values, both figurative and literal. There had been ongoing debates, beginning with the Revolution, about whether the paper money issued by banks had to be backed by specie.[55] Against the economic theories of Benjamin Franklin and Adam Smith, which asserted that too much specie in the bank was "dead money," early Americans such as John Adams, James Madison, and Noah Webster argued that the money issued should represent the exact quantity of the gold and silver available in bank vaults. Yet, amidst two short-lived attempts at establishing a national bank in 1792 and 1816, independent "wildcat" banks were left largely unregulated and printed their own currency, which frequently was not backed by gold and silver. Loans in this unstable currency led to defaults, bank runs, and failures in 1819 and 1837. These economic downturns created panics about the nation's role in managing money and value, as well as about the imaginary basis of money and the benefits of the economy to citizens.

Sunday schools attempted to counter these fears by printing their own currency in the premiums, which would be backed by the riches of salvation, as well as by the child's morals, character, and knowledge. The certificates resembled paper money and stock certificates in their size, shape, and engraving, but with the important addition of the child's name, to signify that their value merely stood in for the moral value that resided in the child. In addition to the children's names, the premiums were also adorned with woodcuts of children reading, working, and giving charity, pointing to the civic actions that would underwrite their worth. In adopting these prize systems, Sunday schools worked to counteract the randomness associated with the nineteenth-century speculative economy, as well as with other prize economies such as the lottery, which gave participants an equal shot of winning rather than rewarding merit.

Moral value and exchange value nonetheless remained incommensurate even within the Sunday school's imaginary economy. The tickets appeared famously in Mark Twain's *Tom Sawyer* (1876). This Tom, naughtier than his thumb-sized ancestor, trades his profits from whitewashing to win a Bible without memorizing any verses. Twain's comedy hints at the ongoing difficulties of aligning social and monetary profit, showing that market value is determined by what others in marketplace deem most valuable. Tom can take advantage of the system because he has acquired objects that are worth more, in the minds of children, than the plain, forty-cent Bible—including licorice and a fishhook. Tom, who has not memorized two thousand verses, profits only economically, gaining both the Bible and undeserved credit.

Tom seeks the Bible in the hopes of gaining his own premium, a glory that will lead to the elevation of his worth in the minds of the other children, especially Becky Thatcher. Tom's case more precisely represents the meaning of a premium than does the Sunday school award system. In economic terms, an investment "worth more than usual" implies a change in market price, which may *not* be accompanied by a change in inherent worth. Since Tom is his same naughty self, his unusually high performance is soon undercut when he claims in front of the entire church that the first two disciples were David and Goliath. Tom's foray into the Sunday school economy demonstrates the importance of artificial values in the workings of the market, which are not necessarily based upon moral or social worth.

The premium certificates too became tokens of exchange, suggesting their value was not indefinitely tied to children's stock of learning. Children exchanged colorful pictures, such as those found on the certificates, in an unofficial barter economy, like traders of baseball cards in more recent times. The pictures, perfectly shaped for pasting into books, were prime material for the practice of scrapbooking, which was popular in the nineteenth century. In some ways, scrapbooks mimicked the logic of the literary museum by assembling pictures, poems, and other memorabilia. A Sunday School Union publication in 1839 suggests that "scrap-book" originally referred to an anthological compilation of pieces arranged under the head of biography, philosophy, anecdotes, poetry, and miscellany.[56] But frequently they had a more whimsical composition, assembling found or traded objects alongside earned ones. Keepers of scrapbooks also collected a new class of premiums that one did not have to learn anything to get: advertising premiums. Reinventing the reward premiums, advertisers created colorful lithographed cards, puzzles, books, mirrors, miniature banks, and other toys, which were included in product packaging. These premiums sometimes had educational content, such as the ABCs or birds of the world, or were based on children's books such as *Aesop's Fables* and *The Cries of London* (all of these examples were found on cigarette premiums). But these lessons serve to lampoon the idea of educational or moral value rather than to teach moral values. Collecting knowledge was secondary to buying the products—which, as the example of cigarettes demonstrates, were not especially linked to social good.

Sunday school ticket programs, it was eventually decided, were too close to the vagaries of the market to carry out the spiritual imperative of cultivating moral value. A dialogue written to entice well-off children to go to the Sunday schools suggests that moral values were a difficult commodity to quantify and sell:

MARY. The instructors will pay you for all you learn.

EMMA. Mama tells me I shall be very rich, and that I shall not want: why then need I go and get money from learning this dry book?

MARY. They do not give you money. They give you blue and pink tickets . . . but do not think you will be rich; for all things are uncertain. You may read in the Bible, "for riches certainly make themselves wings, they fly away as an eagle towards heaven." Think not about such things, but think about heavenly things.

EMMA. I don't want any of their books, for I had rather play.[57]

Another frequently reprinted story tells of a (reportedly real) little girl who balked at the idea that she should earn tickets to purchase a large Bible, instead remarking that her little Bible contained everything in the larger one.[58] Facing even more hostile objections, a Sunday school teacher reports that the tickets caused "much uneasiness among the scholars; an uneasiness which often grew into a dislike of the school and sometimes a desertion of it."[59]

In response to such problems, many Sunday schools abandoned the prizes altogether and instituted the less costly alternative of Sunday school libraries, with library privileges granted for good behavior. Many of the books included in the libraries were the products of massive publishing efforts undertaken by religious institutions, which often presented their endeavors in baldly numerical terms. The second annual report for the auxiliary New York Tract Society, published in 1827, notes that they have published 2,693,100 tracts in English, with 36,114,500 pages, 24,768,232 of which were circulated. In the next year, the American Sunday School Union published 156,000 copies of *Youth's Friend Magazine*, 18,000 tracts, 22,000 spelling books, 51,5000 catechisms, and 13,500 alphabet cards, along with large amounts of premium books and tickets.[60] Though these numbers made the annual reports read like business ledgers or stockholders reports, the difference was that the societies did not seek to profit from their efforts. Rather, as David Paul Nord has argued, these were "noncommercial" endeavors, driven by donations rather than sales: "religious entrepreneurs inverted the strategy of a private business. They proposed to deliver a product to everyone, regardless of their ability or even desire to buy."[61] The tract societies insisted that their numbers represented spiritual, not economic, value.

The tract societies ultimately caused a decline in the price of reading materials by purposefully glutting the market with the cheap tracts, the prices of which were kept low by the funding of wealthy donors.[62] Founders argued that the goals of public education required that books be given away or sold cheaply, in contrast with the high value that they were hoping to set on their contents.[63] As one Sunday School Union report opines, "The popular effort is to bring a good education within the reach of every child, and to this end every thing about it must be cheap."[64] Another brags, "No books are found in the market at so low a price as those we publish."[65]

The tract society reports show that the distribution rate was considerable, but there is some evidence that the perception that the materials were cheap and plentiful led them to be devalued, creating another rift between exchange value and moral value. Among their intended audience of new settlers and the poor, many of the tracts were given away for free to the captive audiences at Sunday schools, while others were sold nearly at cost to auxiliary societies or bartered for farm goods.[66] Some subscribers, who purchased tracts in bundles to send to unsettled parts of the country such as Maine, Kentucky, and Tennessee, considered their purchases as one-time charitable donations and did not bother to circulate the materials. The tract societies were often in debt. James Eastburn, in the second annual report of the New York Tract Society, noted that subscriptions had already fallen short of what was first promised.[67] In the third annual report, the organizers lament that there has "rarely been funds enough in the Treasury to meet the current expenses of two weeks."[68]

Authors, who often battled the Sunday school societies for distributing and revising their books without permission, maintained that the low estimation of the price of knowledge could only hurt the nation. Some felt that readers actually devalued the property of the author rather than giving it worth.[69] At a dinner celebrating the American publishing industry and its authors, Judge John Irving complained that "the noblest efforts of the mind . . . should be considered as common property, and appropriated often to the use of those who not only have not the power to invent, but often not the capacity to appreciate them."[70] Because readers cannot appreciate their books as much as their authors, Irving argues, the intellectual value of books is degraded through reading. If readers *could* manage to profit from their books, Irving accuses them of seeking only private gain, profiting intellectually, but not serving the interests of authors or society at large.

Readers of tracts seemed to be particularly offending in devaluing their books. While, according to the society publications, the tracts were "eagerly read" by multiple readers, not all readers seem to have been as enthusiastic as they claimed. James Lawrence Whittier, for instance, checks out a copy of *Cousin Elizabeth* from the library only to note that two or three copies of the tract were languishing at home.[71] Another annual report of the New York society tells of an infidel who encountered a torn tract floating in a lake and was saved as a result, suggesting the underlying story that someone else ripped it up and threw it in the tarn.[72] Other stories tell of the tracts being burnt, trampled, or discarded on their way to more grateful readers. Because they could not trust readers to take on the moral values in the books, the tract societies sometimes personified the books themselves and further distanced them from economic value. One report rhapsodizes that the books "preach without pay."[73]

Sunday school proponents also increasingly complained that secular books tampered with the careful economy of reading that the librarians had created. One writer bemoans, "I have seen [books] on the Christian character . . . standing week after week untouched . . . but . . . the most valueless book upon the shelves, that contained a story, was much called for and much read."[74] Such complaints suggest that proponents thought that the Sunday school libraries had taken on too many qualities of the market at large, creating collections that were *excessively* miscellaneous. Some librarians argued that the book market, which rewarded money for literary productions, inhibited children from profiting educationally because the sheer number of books could not be systematically read or organized: "The very fact, that books are generally written and published to make money, without regard to their moral effect, has multiplied their number and increased their size on every subject on which books are written. There can be no doubt but that comparatively few volumes would contain all the solid, authentic, and useful information on all subjects, now scattered through many hundred volumes."[75]

Expressing his dissatisfaction in economic metaphors, another writer states that "Sunday-school libraries are crammed with moral chaff, where it requires all powers of mature wisdom to find the few grains of truth concealed . . . The little particle of gold is hammered and beaten out into a leaf inconceivably thin, too delicate for any one to grasp."[76] These two images reflect the double effects of the economy on reading. On the one hand, the larger number of secular books obscured the few items that are really valuable, a situation that might have inspired readers to become the workers who sort through the chaff and make grain of it. But, on the other hand, the market "pounded" real values into small, superficial, and easily marketable bits that could not be profitably reassembled—meaning that seekers of true religion could not turn to the economy for salvation.

The Lottery Approach to Reading

Unlike the Sunday school's imaginary version of the economy, the nineteenth-century economy frequently rewarded entrepreneurs who abandoned moral values in favor of turning a profit. A further evolution of the Tom Thumb character in America was the emergence of the child star, General Tom Thumb, in P. T. Barnum's 1843 travelling show. At only five years old and twenty-five inches high, Charles Stratton ("General Thumb") brought in huge sums that a newspaper commentator said made him "worth his weight in gold."[77] Born in 1810, Barnum might have grown up reading Tom Thumb stories. His American Museum, which was famous for hoaxes such as the "Fegee Mermaid" and "Cardiff Giant," resembled Thumb's *Exhibition*, but eradicated the educational content. Barnum often used deceptive advertising for greater sales, profiting from the gap between social and exchange value. He particularly understood that the latter could be increased by the manipulation of consumers' imaginations, which he exploited in his promotion of Thumb. Though Thumb learned how to sing, dance, and do impersonations, at least one commentator argued that his deformity was "the only thing about him" and wondered whether he was worth the extravagant sums that he and Barnum flaunted.[78]

In addition to inflating Thumb's social and economic worth, Barnum concocted his own premiums for children at his famous New York City baby shows. With winners chosen from a hundred babies, the premiums were based solely on appearance, rarity, and random drawing, not educational performance. Dramatically outdoing the Sunday school premiums, Barnum offered $100 for the finest baby, $50 each for twins, $70 for triplets, $250 for quaterns, and $50 for the fattest baby. He noted that if parents did not want paper money, he could pay in "gold or silver plate," mixing the appearance of worth with the reality of a less worthy (probably copper) center.

Though Barnum's calculated dismissals of social values in favor of quick, easy profit actually required creativity and strong mathematical skills on his part, his business model thwarted the attempts of educators to make the market generate sustained moral and civic virtue. Barnum's schemes required that he divide his energies and skills into multiple ventures, rather than working hard to master any one area of knowledge. When applied to reading, this division of attention resembles what disapproving educators labeled the "lottery approach" to education. Among his other ventures, Barnum ran a book auction and state lottery in Connecticut. Though it is unclear whether Barnum saw the two enterprises as related, many nineteenth-century bookstores printed and advertised lottery tickets.[79] Perhaps as a result of this shared machinery and juxtaposition in the minds of consumers, books containing bits of knowledge came to be known as lottery books.

Like the Sunday school premiums, children's lottery books taught literacy using rewards, but more clearly reflected the irrational fluctuations of the market. J. Horner's *The Silver Penny; or New Lottery Book for Children*, which went through at least six editions between 1805 and 1816, contains no silver and no penny, but an alphabet illustrated with a picture for each letter. On the first page, the child reader finds "The Apple with its rosy cheek / Doth first begin this pretty toy; / How sweet the taste! And oft is made / The prize of each good natur'd boy."[80] This passage suggests that learning the letter *A* provides increased credit, which can be traded for the apple. The adjoining pictures, which are bordered with a fancy design resembling the paper money of the period, cast each letter as a token that the reader can earn and presumably cash in for the large variety of objects pictured. The reader's increased worth also presumably activates the value of the book itself, which is figured as a silver penny that the reader can spend. The significance of this worth, as in *The Exhibition*, is potentially twofold. By learning to read from cheap paper books, children could endow the market with educational benefits, while at the same time becoming softened by the literary prerequisites of engaging in the book's version of trade.

Yet, also like the Sunday school premiums, the value of this alphabet lottery money did not have a market exchange rate. Learning had to be cast as a prize in itself. An earlier lottery book published by Thomas, *A Little Lottery Book* (1788), recommends that children play for "apples, oranges, almonds, raisins, gingerbread, or nuts," echoing the affectionate instructional methods of Gaffer Gingerbread. But in *The Silver Penny*, the child does not really gain an apple, but a picture of one—and that for being "good natur'd" as much as for learning to read. Though the picture is made lucid by the reader's literacy, education yields only counterfeit dollars. The rhymes for the letters *N* ("Here is a nag, and harness too, / Which ev'ry little boy may gain, / If they will strive to mind their books, / And afterwards prove honest men.") and *S* ("Here is the Squirrel cracking nuts, / Pears, plumbs, and apples it devours; / O what a play-thing 'tis, / And may perhaps in time be yours") clarify that the child's prize is the picture and the ability to "read" it, rather than a voucher for the object it depicts.[81] Even if a nag could *eventually* be purchased through the credit incurred from learning, a live squirrel has never been a common object of trade, a reality that is hinted by the text's refusal to name a price (educational or otherwise) that the child must pay in order to get it. The child's ability to get the squirrel is instead mysteriously uttered in the manner of a fortuneteller; it "may perhaps in time be yours."

The mystification surrounding the acquisition of the squirrel also reminds readers that this alphabet book, which purports to pay money for learning the letters, is actually a lottery book. Though it does not provide instructions as to how it can be used to play the lottery, the process is presumably similarly to other lottery games with pictures, such as the Mexican lotería, which derived from a game played in

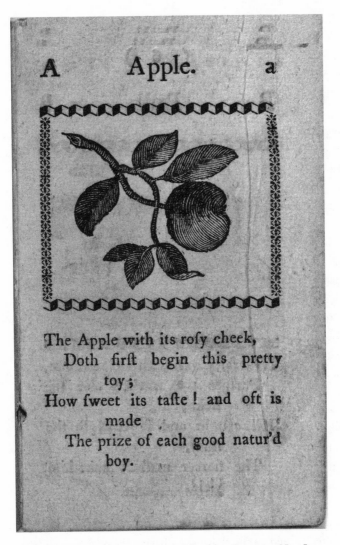

A   Apple.   a

The Apple with its rofy cheek,
  Doth firſt begin this pretty
     toy;
How ſweet its taſte! and oft is
    made
The prize of each good natur'd
    boy.

Page for the letter *A* in J. Horner's *The Silver Penny; or New Lottery Book for Children,* which went through at least six editions between 1805 and 1816. The book contains no silver and no penny. Instead the pictures for each letter were "the prize of each good natur'd boy." Courtesy of the American Antiquarian Society.

fifteenth-century Italy. Typically in these games, each picture is assigned a number and players try to win a prize by collecting a row of pictures. *A Silver Penny* may have represented a simplified version of this game, in which the reader pretended to win the pictured prize by shuffling the pages or turning to a particular numbered page. Thus, instead of being paid for learning, the child is subject to the whims of fortune, which may or may not reward learning. Instead of gaining the squirrel through hard work or the resulting credit, the child must dip into the book at random until the squirrel appears. The picture for U, a county fair ride called the "Up and Down," evokes this fantastical and fortune-based view of the market and provides a fitting description of the nineteenth-century American economy, which was frequently erratic.

An understanding of the economy as random and irrational had potentially devastating implications for citizenship. If readers could not rationally determine what kinds of reading would be most valuable, they were forced to speculate or, just as dangerously for many pedagogues, to diversify in their quests for knowledge. Viewing themselves as subject to the uncontrollable whims of the market, children learned to invest their attentions superficially in multiple texts. Educators feared that this "lottery" mind-set was detrimental to readers' education, causing them to venture into various books for little facts, rather than reading for long-term educational or moral value. This approach to reading was prevalent enough by 1816 that a columnist for *The Panoplist, and Missionary Magazine* could decry reading the Bible as if it were a lottery book: "Many professing people make a sort of lottery-book of the Bible. They open it at random and think the first passage they cast their eyes upon to be designed of God for them."[82] Though this method of reading the Bible had been employed by devout figures in history, such as St. Augustine and Mary Rowlandson, it became suspicious in light of the incursions of the economy on literary value.

Educators may have had a similar response to *The Silver Penny*, which was designed to teach children the alphabet by having them "win" each letter randomly rather than by a slow and steady affectionate familiarization with all of the letters. Pedagogues criticized children for memorizing isolated facts at random rather than learning to understand the overall arc of literature and history. Maria and Richard Edgeworth warn that "in accumulating facts, as in amassing riches, people often begin by believing that they value wealth only for the use they shall make of it, but it often happens that during the course of their labours they learn habitually to set upon the coin itself, and they grow avaricious of that which they are sensible has little intrinsic value."[83] This passage suggests that reading for profit is not necessarily problematic in itself. The problem emerges when readers focus on the monetary values set by the market, rather than on the social values only *signified* by money. The Edgeworths suggest that profit-based reading can easily lead to this problem, because perceived wealth might accompany actual moral bankruptcy. If the Edgeworths' denunciation of this behavior is any indication, child readers quickly learned how to exploit the social capital of a learned reputation.

Other writers feared that the imaginative speculation created by the lottery approach would distract children from useful activities, teaching them to live in a fantasy world. "A Letter from a Lottery Adventurer" in *The Evening Fire-Side, or Literary Miscellany* (1805) tells the story of a young apprentice who ruins himself and his store by dreaming feverishly of the returns that a lottery might bring him.[84] He "heats" his passions by using secret thought experiments—not wholly unlike a conjuring box—to convince himself of his luck and, in the process, distances himself from hard work.

But not everyone believed that the lottery and its "heating of the imagination" had such damaging effects. S. S., an 1821 contributor to *The New Monthly Magazine and Literary Journal*, argues that the imaginative activities of lottery players could actually contribute to the creation of good citizens and readers. In a variation on the phrase, "nothing ventured, nothing gained," S. S. insists that gambling builds character, largely because it encourages people to try to re-create reality in accordance with their dreams. By turning children's attentions from the actual to the possible, the lottery generates creative thinking. Lottery players "build castles on earth and in the air"—an imaginative practice that writers such as Ralph Waldo Emerson and Henry David Thoreau would later celebrate.[85]

S. S. also believes that fantasies about winning the lottery, even if irrational, enlarge and enhance children's minds, allowing them to imagine a better world and even better reading materials: "The sober student . . . calculates the accession his library will receive, if . . . fortune should smile upon him. Having studied mathematics . . . he is not sufficiently confident of success to involve himself beforehand; though upon his pillow, at night, he contemplates sundry fine editions of learned authors coming into his possession, and dreams of purchasing rare manuscripts from a collector of his acquaintance."[86] As the mathematician's refusal to engage his fantasies in the daytime suggests, such imaginative activities were becoming increasingly correlated with children and childishness, an association that persisted in later understandings of childhood and imagination. Jean-Paul Sartre claimed much later that in the imagination there is "always . . . something of the imperious and the infantile, a refusal to take account of distance and difficulties."[87] Nonetheless, Sartre claims that imagination's reconstruction of the world actually works on some level: "The very young child, from his bed, acts upon the world by orders and prayers. Objects obey these orders of consciousness: they appear."[88] S. S. likewise claims that the enhanced hours of life that these dreams provide must be "admitted toward balancing pecuniary losses" just like real money.[89] They can even be imagined as beneficial to citizenship; S. S. tells of an apothecary who imagines himself governing as "Speaker of the House." While the apothecary sometimes makes decoctions "unknown in the art of compounding," suggesting that his dreams are perhaps unrealistic, these imaginative moments provide him with a high office to try and reach.[90]

Sentimental Budgeting

Authors of sentimental literature made a similar argument, suggesting that, if educational gambling and imaginative speculation could not be curtailed, they could be cultivated in a limited way to yield moral profit for oneself and for society. *The Silver Penny* mostly creates a erratic view of the market by encouraging the child to randomly amass ephemeral paper pictures, but one alphabetic character, the letter *G*, claims that children can circulate moral value through a re-imagination of the market: "Gold when to virtuous hands 'tis given, / It blesses like the dew of Heaven: / Like Heav'n then hear the Orphans cries, / And wipe the tears from Widow's eyes."[91] Gold, unlike paper money, implies real worth, which the rhyme associates with moral instrumentality. If the child gains this precious prize, even if through the seemingly random machinations of the economy, she must infuse it with moral meaning by using its power to relieve the suffering of those less fortunate. The figurative language of the passage recasts children as godlike distributors of capital. By employing their "virtuous hands," they can nudge the "invisible hand" of the market to bring profit to the deserving.

Real gold was difficult to come by in the nineteenth-century economy, but it was a frequent metaphor for social value and the power of the imagination. In one of many nineteenth-century sentimental stories that personified money, "History of a Gold Dollar," a little girl uses her gold dollar to buy a magazine. The dollar is eventually dropped on the ground, but the gold dollar undauntedly boasts: "Then see my power over mankind! . . . You may take the veriest dunce in creation, and let me show off my powers on him, and men will reverence him as a Socrates, or a Solomon. I make ministers, lawyers, doctors, mechanics, and farmers. And who but I seats the President in the White House, and collects the Legislative and Congressional bodies together! . . . I can relieve the distress of the poor, and brighten the heavy eye."[92] In this vision, gold has the power to animate the government and benefit society for the better. Yet, as these dreams fade and the dollar is covered with dust, he mourns that replaced by the false value of "paper dollars," and concludes his story, "Yours, if you can get me."[93] Through the sad tale of the dollar's personification and demise, the story suggests that the child must bring money back to life; it is only through the continued imaginative association of money with moral instrumentality that the economy can truly benefit all Americans.

Author Lydia Sigourney, who wrote a number of children's books and parental manuals during the nineteenth century, claimed that profit-oriented reading could bring children a real visionary power, also signified most powerfully by gold. While she bemoans that the age of "miscellaneous reading" has left readers in "leading-strings," unable to fully master any one area of knowledge, she suggests that extensive reading can lead to individual *and* social profit if done correctly. By reading diverse materials carefully, each reader "render[s] herself an entertaining and instructive fireside companion, by daily replenishing her treasury, with that gold which the hand of the robber may not waste, nor the rust of time corrode."[94] The gold of knowledge, unlike other commodities on the market, does not easily alter in value.

Like Washington Irving, Sigourney was an innovator of the sketchbook, which resembles a lottery book with its short, entertaining pieces. A more approving economic name that was used to describe such books was a "budget." Stemming from the word's original meaning as "the contents of a bag or wallet," "budget" was used in the nineteenth century to describe letters, journals, and miscellanies that were "stocked to the brim with news and stories."[95] A children's budget that used the word in its multiple meanings was John Aiken's and Anna Barbauld's *Evenings at Home; Or the Juvenile Budget Opened* (1792–96), which provided a model for Lydia Maria Child's American version called *Evenings in New England* (1824). The books contained slightly longer pieces than the lottery books, including fables, dialogues, and lessons on geography, history, and economy. The word "budget," unlike the "lottery book," implies that children are capable of storing the diverse contents of books in pieces small enough to be retained, but large enough to contain real moral value, and of dispensing this wisdom judiciously. Aiken and Barbauld's version contains a frame story, in which the children of the Fairborne household keep the stories in a box until the whole family is home for the holidays, thus avoiding the price of more expensive amusements and ensuring that the most educational profit is garnered by its spending. The children's careful collection and preservation of the diverse materials affords them continual returns in knowledge, as well as a good reputation among their neighbors.[96]

Nineteenth-century periodicals, which often had titles with the words "cabinet," "museum," and "miscellany," also structured their contents as budgets, or diverse bits of knowledge that could be saved and spent at the right moments. An 1824 piece from the children's magazine, *The Guardian,* claims that the magazine includes "many little thoughts" that are each worth at least twenty-five cents.[97] Though these thoughts do not encompass the intensive knowledge that the Edgeworths recommend, the author of the periodical piece claims that "enough of such little things will make any man great" and explains how readers can budget the thoughts contained in the magazine to get large returns: "A thought obtained in youth is worth more than in old age . . . A good thought is like a sum of money upon interest; it begets more." This means not spending the thought too early, as "a thought is worse than none, if it is but half ripe . . . A single thought may, if well delivered, open the purse of your friend."[98]

Urging both creativity and caution in response to the economics of reading, Sigourney claims that readers can budget by considering intuitively which reading materials will be the most valuable, calming the irrational fluctuations of the market by giving these materials an embodied reality. She does not deny that the accumulation of both personal and economic worth requires speculation on the part of the individual and, in fact, claims that young female readers are better at this than adult men: "Men go abroad into the busy current of life, and throw aside their chagrins and disappointments, and lose the narrowness of personal speculation, in its ever fluctuating tide. Home, the woman's province, admits of less variety. She should therefore, diversify it by an acquaintance with the world of intellect, and shed over it the freshness derived from the exhaustless fountains of knowledge."[99]

Sigourney believed that, as men were attempting to negotiate a vast sea of economic interests, they were not always able to attune themselves to what would be most valuable. Female children were less distracted by others' interests and could thus focus on their own, which led to the greater social benefit. When undertaken systematically, reading was a good social investment because it allowed the individual reader to tap into a potentially limitless and "diversified" market of knowledge, morals, and sentiment. Precisely because female readers would use these diverse investments to build their personalities, rather than throwing aside their personal "chagrins and disappointments," their wealth would remain secure from the fluctuations surrounding other goods. This diversification was necessary because of the changes to citizenship that happened due to economic growth: "the nature of our government admits of unexpected changes in the condition of men, and reverses for which there could have been little or no preparation."[100]

Sigourney insists that her seemingly self-interested preservation of knowledge will ultimately serve society's interests more broadly, observing that "the strength of nations" begins with the child's ability to pursue her educational interests. The final act of reading, she claims, is "social, rendering her treasures available to the good of others." Sigourney again believes that female children can be trusted to achieve this social benefit more than men or boys can: "Man may have more knowledge, and yet hoard it up in his cabinet, or imbody it in expensive tomes, or confine it to the professions through which he receives sustenance, or attains distinction . . . But woman, like earth, the sweet mother, gives freely what has been intrusted to her; the corn ripening for the harvest, the flower blushing in the sunbeam, the rich grass which covers the dark brown mould with unconscious beauty." Sigourney sees learning as a common property, a social "good" in which all citizens can have a shared interest. Quoting Lord Bacon, she implies that the political and economic interests of all can be safeguarded by the child's education, as "the most barbarous and unlearned times have been the most subject to tumults, seditions, and changes."[101]

Children often emerged in nineteenth century texts as the ideal imaginary citizens for a turbulent economic world, providing a model for adult citizens to follow. Writing about the increasing number of American men who defaulted on loans in the nineteenth century, David Anthony claims that such men were forced to inhabit "a radical state of disempowerment and dependency"—a state that more closely resembled childhood than rational adulthood.[102] Partly in response to this economic shift the literary and cultural tropes of the nineteenth century reimagined childhood as a state that was ideal not in spite of but because of its deficiency. Hannah More, a British author whose works were imported as American Sunday School books, explains: "The very frame and being of societies, whether great or small, public or private, is joined and glued together by dependence. These attachments which arise from and are compacted by a sense of mutual wants, mutual affection, mutual benefit, and natural obligation are the cement which secure the union of the family as well as the state."[103] Working from a similar idea, Anthony suggests that debt was ultimately "far from . . . [a] crisis that renders . . . an excessive threat to the social order" and was rather "productive, because it places the debtor male in possession of a highly emotional, feeling body."[104] Children, particularly girls, had long been the models of how such persons with such feeling bodies could be understood as citizens. It is partly for this reason that sentimental books featuring child protagonists became so important to America's self-image in the nineteenth century and came to be read by children and adults alike as models of social engagement.

Sales figures for sentimental novels rivaled and often exceeded those of early children's textbooks and novels; Maria Cummins's *The Lamplighter* (1854), for instance, sold more than 40,000 copies in its first two months (to compare, *The Scarlet Letter* sold fewer than 10,000 in Hawthorne's lifetime).[105] The social models portrayed in sentimental texts were often opposed to the law's division between supposedly independent and dependent economic players and portrayed children engaging in their own economic affairs rather than accepting the custodial guardianship of less than ideal adult citizens. As Karen Sánchez-Eppler has argued, sentimentalism was defined by what reformers called "moral suasion," which assumed that obedience to the current law was no longer sufficient to inspire morality and that children could be the bringers of a new moral society.[106] The most frequent plot of sentimental fiction, according to Nina Baym, was the dilemma caused by "mistreatment, unfairness, disadvantage, and powerlessness, recurrent injustices occasioned by [the heroine's] status as female and child."[107] Through enduring economic and other hardships, the sentimental child came to act as a privileged figure in American culture, beckoning others citizens to help end economic suffering by following her example.

A classic instance of a sentimental child's attempts to establish her own economic and moral identity appears in Susan Warner's wildly popular *The Wide, Wide World* (1850).[108] The text begins with the rigid presence of the law. Ellen's father's loss of a lawsuit sets the text's events in motion. Ellen is quickly separated from this world dictated by legal versions of gains and losses, as she is sent to live at her Aunt Fortune's farm. Despite the affluence implied by her name, Fortune turns out not to be a particularly generous guardian. In a chapter called "Mother Earth rather than Aunt Fortune," the name of which evokes Sigourney's image of the freely giving mother, Ellen wanders the mountains near her new home and meets another young woman, Alice, who meets this description. Along Ellen does not participate in an actual economy and is indeed very embarrassed when she gets a banknote for Christmas from a family friend, the young people weigh in on the economy by critiquing the unchristian habits of the rich, who thrive on pleasure and exploit the poor. Together they seek to remedy social injustices by spreading Christian morals.[109]

This sentimental approach to the economy required the collection and preservation of knowledge and moral values and their continued circulation, which created relationships between self and others. Catharine Sedgwick's 1836 *The Poor Rich Man and the Rich Poor Man* argues persuasively that the wealth of knowledge and virtue cannot simply be personified in the individual child but must be used to create mutual obligations and dependencies among all citizens. The premise of Sedgwick's book is that the inequality and interdependence of the U.S. economic system can inspire Americans to be generous and nurturing of others, rather than selfish and corrupt. Sedgwick sees children as central to this patriotic fantasy: "There is no telling what a nation, with our institutions, might become . . . if children were brought up from their cradles to be temperate and true, industrious and frugal,—if every opportunity were seized for improving them in knowledge, and in the practice of soul-preserving virtues."[110]

The national import of the text's ideology is even more apparent when Catharine's children's tale is read in conjunction with her brother Theodore's book, *Public and Private Economy*, which was published by the same press as Catharine's book in the same year. Theodore, who was involved in state politics, maintains that private commerce is essential to social benefits because it represents "the power to do good."[111] Theodore suggests that individuals, especially children, must both gain and *spend* the profits of their reading and education, so that profit is a means of usefulness, never an end unto itself. He writes, "To do good . . . with the property which we have gained or saved by our honesty, economy, temperance, and industry . . . should be the first lesson of all education."[112] Though this perspective represents some hopeful naïveté—and to some extent represents a retreat into the imagination since children actually were losing economic autonomy—the argument that the economy could generate sentimental feeling resulted from the harsh realities of the nineteenth-century market. With the increasing visibility of the poor, particularly in cities, Americans could see the inequality that capitalist self-interest could produce and wanted a practical way to counteract this suffering.

The Rich Poor Man teaches children to see books specifically as tradable objects with social value that must eventually be recirculated. The book opens with three children, Harry, Charlotte, and Susan, admiring the books they have won at a local Sunday school. The soon-to-be "Rich Poor Man," Harry, has won a "little Bible, bound in red morocco" and clearly understands the social and moral values that the book represents. His ability to calculate the worth of this object is attributed partly to his good nature, but Sedgwick suggests that those who are economically or physically dependent are also more likely to appreciate their books. Charlotte, who is not only poor but also chronically ill, remarks, "it seems to me that those who are well, and strong, and at ease, can never value that book as those do who are always sick and suffering pain."[113]

The children's musings are interrupted by the arrival of "The Poor Rich Man," Morris Finch, who tells them that his friend Paulina has traded her book for a fancy handkerchief. Morris announces that he also will be selling his prize, *Bewick's History of British Birds*. *Bewick's* demonstrates the complexities in calculating a book's moral and monetary profit. With its two volumes and multiple engravings, it was a more expensive book than Harry's Sunday school Bible, but with less moral value, even though its author, Thomas Bewick, saw the book as implanting "Religion and Morality" into the hearts of readers through their understanding of nature. Unlike Harry, who attributes a "priceless" moral value to his Bible, Morris calculates only the book's exchange value, pointing out that his book "cost twice as much" as Harry's. Morris even goes so far as to conflate his book with money, saying, "If you could reckon interest and compound interest as well as I can, Miss Susan, I guess you would not like to have your money lying idle on a book shelf." In his vision of the economy, money is an end in itself; therefore, he claims that it "should work" constantly to make more money. Eager to trade his book rather than using it to structure and build his personality—even though his name, "Finch," suggests that a bird book might be appropriate for doing so—Morris reflects the market's emphasis on superficial wealth. He does not personify value, so much as being dehumanized by the market. His face becomes "an account book, written over with dollars and cents, as if he had coined his soul into them."[114]

For Sedgwick's good child characters, it is a great folly to view money—or even the educational wealth represented by books—as having value in itself. Instead, as Sedgwick has Harry explain, "Money is representative of power—the means of extended usefulness." Money and wealth are meant to "work," but in an entirely different sense of the word than Morris's use of it. Riches have value only so far as they facilitate interdependence, cooperation, and the exchange of sentiment and charity between human beings. Harry will not cash out his property in the book for a quick profit. Susan points out that this alone makes it worth *more* than Morris's book, because its lessons are given life by Harry's good behavior and sentimental attachment to it. But Sedgwick makes clear that this wealth must reenter the market, which will bring the children into contact with others. Susan points out that they hardly despise money, as long as it is used to forge sentimental relationships and create social benefits: "I would do anything in the world to get enough [money] to take Lottie to that wonderful New-York doctor."[115]After hearing this, Harry decides that he will sell his Bible, gaining a dollar that he can contribute to Charlotte's physician's fees.

Sedgwick states that circulating wealth does not dissipate it. Instead it makes the riches available to everyone. Harry insists that riches "perish not in the using" but make returns to one's heart and soul that are more valuable than the money spent. Only in the service of this greater social good are the children willing to engage in the contrivances of the market: Harry thinks of what he might get for his possessions, which include a dog and "two squirrels he had tamed with infinite pains."[116] As in *The Silver Penny*, the squirrels, which can only become a commodity with "infinite pains," call attention to the imaginative aspect of children's literature's version of the economy. Even these unlikely commodities get endowed with social value, the ability to trade for moral instrumentality.

The most important lesson of Sedgwick's text is that child readers must not simply collect profits but must learn to translate social value into monetary value and vice versa, so that intangible values can be factored into the capitalist exchange.

Books, such as those in the opening scene, provide a metaphor for this exchange. As Melissa Homestead has argued, Sedgwick explicitly wrote *The Poor Rich Man* as a sentimental object that could yet be traded, saying that the book resembled food or cloth produced by U.S. textile mills from American-grown cotton. It was "like bread-stuff, or like satinets and negro-cloths, to be a little more modest in my comparison, suited to the market, the thing wanted."[117]As commodities, books are an example of the good that can come of economic exchange. In contrast to Judge Irving, Sedgwick emphasizes that books represent the *shared* property of authors and readers: "Is [a book] not a cabinet which contains the most interesting creation of God, the mind of a human being, a portion of the Divine Mind? . . . But here it has come to your home, to dwell with you, to impart to you its best thoughts, to communicate to you its observations."[118] Books mediate between human beings, filling the lack that each person has without the other.

This interdependence is meant to provide the occasion for circulating wealth and to increase the social values of community and charity, metaphorically turning "lead to gold."[119] To perform this alchemical transformation, making the poor man "rich" and the rich man "poor," Sedgwick requires a redefinition of the market in the mind of readers. In saying that Harry is richer than his money-loving friend Morris, Sedgwick is not simply privileging moral and social value over material value but is also asking her child readers to bring about an economic system in which moral value equals monetary value, in which Harry would literally be richer than Morris. At the end of Sedgwick's book, the Aiken family receives a discount on their home as a reward for offering charity to others. Now an adult, Harry tells his own children, "So you see, that virtue, and good habits and manners . . . are not only in the highest sense treasures, they are *money* to you."[120] Sedgwick argues that the only way in which social values can gain a larger hold in the economic system is for children to assign them actual monetary worth and to circulate them accordingly.

For this to happen, children must learn a keen sense of estimating value, so they can gain the largest profit in happiness for their money. This is a difficult lesson, which Sedgwick's text suggests is only possible with ample knowledge of money management. In opposition to the lottery mind-set, children cannot simply allow good things to happen randomly. They must actively invest their money in moral actions. Sedgwick's text gives an example of a problematic do-gooder in the character of Uncle Phil, Susan and Charlotte's adult guardian. When a neighbor causes the death of his horse, Phil believes that he is being generous because he does not ask for a replacement. Yet, because Phil does not actively donate the horse, the neighbor does not realize that Phil forgoes its replacement out of caring and concern and, thus, does not return any gratitude to Phil. Furthermore, Phil only gives the horse once it is dead and no longer useful to anyone. His charitable investment perishes along with his horse. Phil's inability to manage his household is embodied by the tragic death of one of his daughters and the illness of another.

Miraculously, given Phil's bad management, Susan and Charlotte are able to make up for his poverty by sensitively managing the family finances. Sedgwick remarks that Phil never dreams he is a poor man because Susan and Charlotte run his house so well. The children also actively carry out charitable acts in their daily lives. When Susan sees their neighbors' daughter wearing tattered clothes and taking care of her drunken mother, she insists that she come to live with them. As a result of this kind act, the Aiken family becomes acquainted with Mr. Beckwith, a rich property owner who later helps them buy an affordable home. In this way, children actively invest in good deeds and bring about charitable actions on a larger scale.

By redefining the value that can result from exchange, Sedgwick infuses economic participation with sentiment and virtue. Because of the happy profits money can produce, it becomes endowed with sentimental value for her characters. On her way to buy a "ribband" for her sister, Susan tells her money, "I suppose you will seem to other folks just like any other quarter and they will pass you from hand to hand, without thinking at all about you." While those who value wealth for its own sake participate mechanically in the market, buying and selling acquire an almost sacred quality for Sedgwick's good children because of their power to create happiness in others. By the end of her text, Sedgwick has endowed money with an almost magical, miraculous power. The extent of her optimistic view of American economic potential is so great that she extends the power of benevolent exchange to correct even natural disabilities like blindness and deafness. She writes, "If the rights of the poor *of all classes* were universally acknowledged, if intellectual and moral education were what they should be, the deaf would hear and the blind would see."[121]

But Sedgwick's text also points to a flaw in the heart-filled ideology of children's books, and foreshadows its failure to fully reconcile economic and social value. Both the market and sentimental narratives ultimately require inequality to persist. Within a few lines of her miraculous claims about the American economic system, Sedgwick writes, "If there were a perfect community of goods, where would be the opportunity for the exercise of virtues, of justice and mercy, humility, fidelity, and gratitude?" Harry reiterates this position at the end of the book when he says, "If there were none of these hateful rich people, Ruth, who, think you, would build hospitals and provide asylums for orphans, and for the deaf and dumb, and blind?"[122] The return of the deaf and blind children here, despite Sedgwick's earlier claim, symbolizes the limitations of using a virtuous market to remedy the corruption associated with economic participation. Sentiment, which was supposed to eliminate inequality from the market, is the very reason that, for Sedgwick, inequality must continue to exist. Without inequality, she reasons, there is no sentimental story to inspire children to moral action.

Child Workers

The complications of Sedgwick's narrative return to a question important to the intersection between economics and citizenship: does profit, whether monetary, moral, or educational, have to be at someone else's expense, undermining the national sense of community? And, similarly, does the sentimental economic model require that some individuals will remain forever dependent? Sedgwick seems to give two answers: no, because all participants are using their vulnerability to nourish others and yes, because the perpetuation of inequality is necessary for this to happen. This continued inequality is particularly obvious for children. The requirements of the capitalist marketplace meant that young people were valued not just for their sentimental instrumentality but also for their ability to labor outside of the home as apprentices, servants, factory workers, and farm laborers.[123]

Female factory workers in Lowell, Massachusetts, some as young as age ten but ranging from teenage girls to women in their early thirties, used their renowned miscellany, *The Lowell Offering* (1840–45), to show that the proliferation of goods on the market was often underwritten by the disenfranchisement of certain economic participants. The editors of the magazine claim that Lowell is "quite a book market" and a "reading community" that is approximated by the *Offering* itself.[124] One of the major topics of the publication was to teach workers how to best budget their earnings in order to amass knowledge and reading materials, such as mini-libraries. They nonetheless argue that one unfortunate side effect of the market and the miscellany form is that the reader's improvement can create the impoverishment of another worker, the author:

> There are loads of little Pocket Companions and Daily Foods sold here, besides countless copies of The Young Lady's Guide, The Young Lady's Friend, The Young Lady's Assistant, The Young Woman's Companion, Letters to a Young Lady, &c. . . . We do not so highly approve of many of these compilations . . . In compilations there is . . . frequently injustice done to the author. Why not buy the Writings of Hannah More, with her own name attached to them, instead of anonymous selections?[125]

Through this commentary, the Lowell editors convey a truth they likely knew well, which is that the profit of one individual often results in the exploitation of another.

The names of the miscellanies suggest a simultaneous depersonalization of the author and the reader, who is reduced to the general name of "a young lady," or sometimes a "girl." Oddly, given their frustration with other miscellanies for removing the authors' names (the *Offering* insisted that names be appended to submissions), the editors frequently had to strip the stories of their authors' names before printing them, substituting initials or a pseudonym. This practice suggests that the workers were to some extent resigned to the depersonalization of the market, perhaps a result of the relative anonymity of being a worker in the Mills. The anonymity may also have offered them protection for criticizing some of the more unpleasant aspects of factory life.

The Lowell workers vehemently resisted narratives of their own victimization, expressing annoyance that politicians used sentimental tales of their inequality to make political capital. The *Offering* takes care to demonstrate the collective wealth and rich knowledge of their creative community. They point out that working at the factory gives them access to various "schools, lectures, and meetings of every description, for moral and intellectual improvement."[126] But they nonetheless assert that effects of commerce provide a real danger to their ability to use their reading to construct coherent and valuable personalities: "We know that there are light, worthless, and injurious books, papers, &c. which are partly supported by the factory girls . . . Some may say, the short intervals, which alone these girls can devote to reading, render it impossible that they should read long works, or those which require close attention, and consecutive thought."[127] The miscellany form not only approximates the number of materials on the capitalist market, but also, through its anonymity and fragmentation, supports the depersonalization of knowledge and skills that accompanies the turn to industrial labor. Many materials may be good for the market and for sales but "worthless" and even "injurious" to readers. The difficulty of "consecutive thought" references the very real problems that economic expansion posed for the development of personality, especially for line workers in factories. To the extent that readers are able to piece together and embody various kinds of knowledge, as the Lowell workers tried to do, they counteract this process by granting the diverse bits of information on the market a stable whole. But if they fail to integrate these pieces, their personalities have the potential to be impoverished and fragmented, a vulnerability that is difficult to overcome and use as a starting point for fostering charitable relationships.[128]

The Lowell Offering problematizes the idea that economics can create benefits for all citizens. In the following chapter, I show that a growing number of mid-nineteenth-century Americans also did not believe that an economic model of reading was the solution to the potential dependencies and inequalities inherent in American citizenship, especially when considering the atrocities associated with slavery. More and more pedagogues rejected the market and its textual corollaries, choosing instead to champion what they called a "natural" form of reading. These educators feared that, despite attempts to link economy and socially engaged character, the economic aspects of reading had the opposite effect of turning children into automatons, who could recite the narratives of citizenship without consent or understanding. The solution put forth by some pedagogues proposed that reading should no longer be taught by miscellaneous reading books, such as spellers, but by "the book of nature" and its textual incarnation, the natural history book.

The turn to natural history books as the best reading books accompanied a turn natural or inherent citizenship as a way of understanding children's citizenship, which was ultimately enshrined in the Fourteenth Amendment's claim that all individuals are born citizens. The amendment attempts to turn imaginary citizens into real, legal citizens, making the child a more obvious image for the citizen than ever before. Yet, the history of natural citizenship as an alternative way of understanding childhood, which includes thinkers such as Jean-Jacques Rousseau, Ralph Waldo Emerson, Nathaniel Hawthorne, and Frederick Douglass, shows that natural citizenship is notoriously hard to separate from imaginary citizenship, anticipating the amendment's failure to resolve the issue of children's citizenship or citizenship in general.

CHAPTER 5

Natural Citizenship
Children, Slaves, and the Book of Nature

> I think I would like to go to school so to have a school room
> confined by no limits, with the clear blue sky above, smiling upon
> us with the sweet birds singing music into us with the little flowers
> springing up at our feet, and looking up at us, as if they would beg
> us to learn the lesson contained under their leaves, and penciled
> on their petals. Of course, we cannot, in this country of "wailing
> winds" go to school in groves, but we can all learn a lesson from
> the lilies of the field, and the birds of the air—we can learn many
> lesson which will be of great use of us, as well as a great source of
> happiness.
>
> *Mary Allen Ware, School Journal, 1838*

The debates about citizenship following the Civil War demonstrate the extent to which children's citizenship—and citizenship in general—was still an unsettled issue in mid-nineteenth-century America. When the Fourteenth Amendment was being drafted, the committee argued that the first section of the amendment, the citizenship clause, should not be included because "the word *citizen* had no exact meaning in the United States."[1] In its place, a similar phrase declared the intention of Congress to protect the rights of all "persons" within its jurisdiction. As the citizenship clause was reintroduced in Congress, politicians continued to express puzzlement over the concept. Senator Frank Cowan mused, "I am really desirous to have a legal definition of 'citizenship of the United States.' What does it mean? What is its length and breadth?. . . Now, I should like to know, because really I have been puzzled for a long while and have been unable to determine exactly . . . the lines and boundaries which circumscribe that phrase, 'citizen of the United States.' What is it?"[2]

Since the Fourteenth Amendment was preceded by a few months by the Civil Rights Act of 1866, which also contained a definition of citizenship, Cowan's questions were partially rhetorical. Yet Cowan foregrounds the ways that both pieces of legislation offered a potentially radical change in definitions of citizenship. Cowan's uncertainties result from the status of children and other nonlegally enfranchised citizens; he points out that "it is perfectly clear that the mere fact that a man is born in the country has not heretofore entitled him to the right to exercise political power."[3] By the end of these debates, however, the U.S. Constitution declared the citizenship of all by declaring the citizenship of children. The citizenship clause in the Fourteenth Amendment would come to read, "All persons born or naturalized in the United States . . . are citizens of the United States."

While the Fourteenth Amendment was easily the most important legislation regarding citizenship in the nineteenth century, proponents of the amendment argued that it merely reinforced the laws of nature. Senator Jacob Howard claimed that it was "simply declaratory of what I regard as the law of the land already, that every person born within the limits of the United States . . . is by virtue of natural law and national law a citizen." Howard's claim that the citizenship clause is based on "natural law" downplays the change in citizenship law represented by the Reconstruction Acts and the ways that these laws interpreted nature. The Fourteenth Amendment and Civil Rights Act represented a major change in legal understandings of children's citizenship by using the concept of *jus soli* ("right of soil") instead of the more limited notion of *jus sanguinis* ("right of blood") that had informed earlier naturalization laws; it was their birth on U.S. soil—not parentage, race, affection, or any other standard—that these new laws claimed made people into citizens. Although the ideal of the social contract was not replaced by these laws, they also represented a move away from this political fiction by suggesting that citizenship was a natural and automatic status. Likely aware of this change despite his claim that it was merely recapitulating "natural law," Howard declared that the Fourteenth Amendment would settle "the great question of citizenship" that "has long been a great desideratum in the jurisprudence and legislation of the country."[4] In forging a definition of citizenship that began in childhood, the Fourteenth Amendment used the child to redefine citizenship, and at the same time to deny doing so, suggesting that citizenship was a natural, a priori condition, a feature of birth.

The radical declaration that children were, by nature, citizens may have gone largely unexamined because the Reconstruction Acts declared that children were natural citizens as part of the goal of granting citizenship to someone else: former slaves. Even though the Fourteenth Amendment was not applied to children until much later, it made sense for children and slaves to be aligned in the amendment from the beginning, since political theorists had often rejected slave and child as two individuals who could not be citizens. In the patriarchal institution of slavery, childhood and slavery came to be intertwined, as slaveholders used concepts of children's noncitizenship and what I have called imaginary citizenship to rationalize restrictions on slaves' liberties. Several scholars have noted that apologists categorized slaves as children to "prove" that slaves' exclusion from basic rights was the result of their inability to rationally exercise these rights.[5] As I show in the first part of this chapter, they also used fictional stories of faithful slaves to reconcile slavery with free choice, suggesting that slaves could be imaginary citizens at the same time that they were enslaved. Given this alignment of slaves and children, it does not seem coincidental that establishing former slaves' citizenship meant an explicit declaration and redefinition of children's citizenship. To make former slaves into citizens meant establishing citizenship as a feature of one's birth rather than an outcome of a reasoned contractual agreement or an imagined status. It also meant attempting to turn imaginary citizens into natural citizens and constructing more extensive legal channels for defining and protecting that citizenship.

Despite Howard's optimistic declaration that the Fourteenth Amendment would settle the great question of citizenship, the law has suffered from its shortcomings. Although the amendment helped to end chattel slavery in the United States, making its passage a watershed moment for human rights, it did not outline a procedure for ensuring equal political participation. As a result, rather than making imaginary citizens parties to the social contract, it changed the terms through which citizenship was understood while leaving many of the restrictions in play. More directly related to the issue of children's citizenship, the law challenged Locke's declaration that the child is born the subject of no government but did not fundamentally change the limits on children's rights or even offer a way that children should be understood as citizens in lieu of direct participation. The law stated that voting was to be the province of males over age twenty-one, but notably did not guarantee even this freedom, but only threatened to punish states that would deny suffrage to any adult men. Ever since its ratification in 1868, the law has been subject to debates over its meaning. My analysis of the politics of natural citizenship does not focus on the recent question of whether immigrant children should be included in the Fourteenth Amendment's declaration of citizenship, as it seems clear that the original debates about the amendment and subsequent legal cases have decided this issue in favor of inclusion. Rather, I make the larger argument that the amendment does not settle what citizenship means and how it is to function, particularly for children, but ultimately for all citizens.

To explain why the law has failed to settle the question of citizenship even by declaring that it is a natural birthright, I trace the history of ideas about children's natural citizenship, beginning with the origin of this concept in the work of eighteenth-century thinker Jean-Jacques Rousseau and leading to a rich culture of debate that emerged in antebellum America among authors Ralph Waldo Emerson, Nathaniel Hawthorne, Samuel Goodrich, and Frederick Douglass. Children's natural citizenship has a long history as an alternative to imaginary citizenship and as a proposed means of social transformation. Although Lockean theory rested on the idea that the best citizen was a rational adult who could understand the laws of society, Romantic thinkers such as Rousseau and Emerson argued that society was corrupt and proposed new ideals of citizenship that took the child as their explicit model—though, as we will see, Rousseau was ultimately more skeptical about his hypothetical child citizen than Emerson was. The proposal that children might be the best citizens addressed several problems that were inherent in Lockean contract theory. If children were capable of becoming political beings without the need for imaginary narratives or for legal constraints, no moment of consent or subjection to the existing system would be required and society could be transformed. Furthermore, they could be included as children, without the need for an imaginary citizenship to fill in the gaps between freedom and the exercise of it.

Even so, these authors did construct imaginary narratives of how natural children could be integrated into society and function as citizens. A major reason why the Fourteenth Amendment has failed to resolve the issue of citizenship is that natural citizenship cannot be fully separated from imaginary citizenship. In the case of Rousseau and Emerson, the possibilities for natural citizenship specifically depend on fantasies about the relationship between social and natural law—the very registers that Howard tries to collapse—as well as about nature as having a transparent language that could be read. Both authors reveal that to blend these two laws is not possible without the manipulations of imagination.

To further demonstrate that the concept of children's natural citizenship requires imaginary narratives, I show that that the idea of citizenship as an instinctual impulse also appeared in children's books of the nineteenth century—especially children's natural histories, which were becoming more popular in the mid-nineteenth century as instruments for reading instruction. An 1828 columnist in the *American Annals of Education* expresses a fear, common among pedagogues, that children had lost their connection with the real world as a result of the new diversity of reading materials. He further suggests that, to restore the "delicate and tender sentiments" that come from the direct perception of this world, children should learn to read using stories about natural objects.[6] Such arguments accompanied a marked shift in children's reading materials. R. R. Robinson reports that stories about nature increased dramatically in school readers from an average of one or two stories between 1775 and 1825, to eight to eighteen stories after 1825, ultimately making up more than one-fourth of all school lessons.[7] Many of these stories make the case for children's natural citizenship by suggesting that civic virtues already exist in the plant and animal kingdoms. In their extreme attempts to connect nature with citizenship, however, these books also anticipate some of difficulties that other writers had with the idea that citizenship was inherent: namely, that nature could be chaotic and that it required major imaginative leaps to see how a citizenship inhering in the child's birth and bolstered by children's education about nature could lead to a unified population of citizens who could follow the law and who had the skills necessary to participate in the political life of the nation.

In this court, writers such as Goodrich and Hawthorne recognized children's importance as citizens but emphasized the need to secure their allegiance to avoid the social chaos that they believed might result from their automatic inclusion. Others, such as Douglass, knew that nature was not enough to ensure free citizens. In these authors' minds, with allegiance also came the responsibility to provide children's education and secure their consent, something that wasn't taken for granted or easily imagined. This type of thinking led both to patriotic attempts to educate children about the nation and to the resurgence of recitation and other mechanistic modes of training children to be citizens (particularly the children of immigrants and former slaves), even after the Fourteenth Amendment declared all native born individuals to be natural citizens by birth. In the absence of children's actual enfranchisement, many of the practices associated with imaginary citizenship have been kept alive.

Enslaved Citizens

As Caroline Levander and Lesley Ginsberg have shown, metaphors of childhood were used in the nineteenth century to create an expansive category of persons ineligible for active citizenship, which included free blacks, women, Indians, and slaves.[8] While scholars have discussed how comparisons with children were used to deny citizenship to slaves, they have overlooked the ways that these comparisons also made it possible to think of slaves as imaginary citizens. On the one hand, slaves used imaginary citizenship to protest their legal exclusion. For instance, in "What to a Slave Is the Fourth of July?" Douglass addresses himself to his "fellow-citizens" to highlight the ways that the liberty guaranteed by the Constitution was denied to slaves.[9]

But, on the other, imaginary citizenship could be a way of legitimizing slavery and reconciling it with the ideal of freedom without freeing slaves from bondage. Showing this logic at its perverse extreme, stories for children about faithful slaves made the case that citizenship could be compatible with slavery, as long as slaves exercised what the stories considered choice in their enslavement. Literacy provided the means for expression of that choice, thus acting as a supposed instrument of freedom but also revealing the ways that imagination was an insufficient solution to the limitations of citizenship for slaves and children alike. More disturbing, because Americans also used stories of imaginary citizenship to legitimize limitations on everyone's rights, faithful slave stories had the potential to expose the ways in which citizens were not entirely distinct from slaves—a problem that, as we will see, also preoccupied Rousseau and Emerson.

It is not surprising that faithful slave stories are commonly read as blatant apologies for white supremacy—for instance, Jessica Enoch offers such a reading of a Lydia Maria Child story in which a black boy decides to sacrifice himself to save white children.[10] But these stories also represented a paradoxical thought experiment that attributed slaves with the very quality that they were supposedly denied: the ability to make a rational choice. In this way, the stories resembled other texts that elicited children's imaginary consent and showed how their affection could be used to legitimize unequal social arrangements. The logic went that, if slaves were given the choice, they would choose to be "faithful"—that is, enslaved. Rather than presenting this as a bad choice that demonstrated slaves' irrationality, the stories insisted that this choice was a proof of slaves' disinterestedness, the very capacity for citizenship that they were not supposed to possess. This insistence on the slave's ability to imaginatively consent to their own subjection made slaves similar to citizens rather than distinct from them. Thus, the stories opened up the possibility that slaves could claim citizenship and exercise choice, perhaps in ways unanticipated by the stories. But simultaneously the stories represented a stark reminder of the ways that literary extensions of citizenship to excluded persons did not in themselves lead to a legitimate or compassionate society, especially when the rights of those concerned were not recognized by law. The stories also hinted that even rights were not enough to ensure a free society, since citizens were integrated into a political world with a limited number of existing choices.

The faithful slave motif was particularly prevalent in children's literature, reflecting children's similar encounters with the limited agency of imaginary citizenship, as well as the ways that slaves and children were aligned in nineteenth-century culture. An illuminating version appeared in Mary Pilkington's children's miscellany, which was published in London and Philadelphia in 1800. Pilkington's version of the faithful slave narrative seems at first to be a depiction of a slave child's education, but finally highlights the role of literacy in maintaining his subservient position. In the story, a white child named Julius meets a slave boy named Yanko and asks his father, Mr. Godfrey, to buy the child. Godfrey at first pretends not to have heard of the condition of chattel slavery, an odd affectation given that slaves remained a presence in England and the North after slavery was abolished. This denial sets the tone for the story, which offers both a departure from slavery and a reinstitution of it. Julius succeeds in establishing Yanko as a family servant, though it is unclear whether Yanko is paid. The ambiguity surrounding Yanko's status in the Godfrey family is conveyed by the title of the story, "The Faithful Slave; Or the Little Negro Boy"—conditions that can either be understood as opposites or equivalents. Being seen as a boy in some sense categorizes Yanko as a noncitizen, the same as when he was a slave, but it also establishes freedom as his birthright. At the same time, his continued description as a "faithful slave" suggests that the difference between slavery and the imaginary citizenship of children is only slight: one requires forced subjection and the other allows an imaginary subjection that can be understood as equivalent to freedom. By blurring the two statuses, the story foregrounds the ways in which children and slaves are both encouraged to imagine themselves into citizenship from positions that are politically powerless.

As with many slave stories, reading instruction figures prominently in the tale. Godfrey resolves to instruct Yanko to read partially to teach his son Julius that "nature has been as bounteous to [slaves] as to any other of her children, and they are equally capable of becoming great, noble, and disinterested."[11] The argument that Yanko can be disinterested is striking, as this was a major requirement for citizenship. Godfrey is making a claim that many abolitionists and former slaves found useful—the claim that slaves could be citizens if they were allowed to gain an education.

It is unclear how much Godfrey succeeds in teaching the boy, since Yanko continues to speak in broken dialect throughout the story. However, Yanko does acquire the requisite literacy to engage in imaginary citizenship. He sings the following verses about his condition while cleaning Godfrey's coats:

Yanko happy—Yanko bright—Like de stars dat gild denight;
Yanko's bosom ever seem
Like de Niger's silver stream. Ever flowing, ever free,
Ever full of joy and glee,
Yanko love his massa dear,
Love, because he can no fear,
When no cat-o-nine tails' near.[12]

This poem suggests that Yanko believes that he is not a slave, but a freeman. Yet Yanko's poem also reveals deeply rooted connections between subjection and freedom in the discourse surrounding slavery and citizenship. The freedom stirring within his bosom is not only compatible with his love for his master but also *results* from this love. The story makes the case that this affectionate subjection is different from the condition of slavery, not because Yanko's life is significantly different, but because Godfrey provides Yanko with protection. What makes these qualifications different from slavery's version of patriarchalism is that Yanko *chooses* his relationship of subjection by casting Godfrey as a surrogate parent rather than being forced to serve a slave master. He is not an enslaved subject, but an enslaved citizen.

The poem, which attributes the highest freedom to cleaning his master's coats, is also highly ironic. The fact that the slave boy punctuates each new stanza of his poem with the pounding of dust out of the coats lends an especially vivid image of the connection between perceived freedom and continued subjugation as it relates to both child citizens and to enslaved Africans.[13] While the story emphasizes Yanko's voluntary submission, it also records the limited choices with which Yanko is presented. Yanko is not offered the choice of running away or insisting on pay. Rather he is given an either/or choice of serving Godfrey or a slave master. The difference between these two was not unimportant, but it reveals the limited choices that were frequently available to former slaves and to citizens in choosing their own subjection.

The ties between slavery, childhood, and citizenship are particularly evident in the ending of the story, in which Yanko substantiates his ability to understand citizenly virtue through his heroic rescue of his "massa" from a murder plotted by the other servants. This dramatic motif, which recurs often in accounts of faithful slaves, demonstrates that Yanko holds an ambiguous position in relation to both slavery and childhood. In one sense, Yanko proves that he has escaped from slavery when he declines a new set of clothes as a reward for his heroism. This act repudiates the patriarchal justification for slavery, in which slave masters claimed to provide their childlike slaves with clothes in return for labor.[14] By refusing to participate in this culturally resonant performance of slave deference, Yanko asserts himself as an independent citizen who does not require Godfrey's paternalism, choosing instead to serve him as an equal. His rationale, that he will not accept a reward for doing right, positions him as an educated man who possesses the moral and rational prerequisites for political decisionmaking.

Yanko also refuses money, an act that links him to paternalist notions of childhood and slavery that viewed the child and slave as separate from the world of exchange. As the tale ends, Yanko continues to provide the most rhetorical force as a child rather than an adult citizen. Mr. Godfrey explains slavery to Julius's friend Charles by pointing out that both Yanko and Charles's slave, Peter, have been forcibly snatched from their African parents. By asking Charles to imagine what it would be like if did not have parents to take care of him, Godfrey implies that Yanko and Peter are still in need of this care, which they must now establish through relationships of affection with surrogate parents. In the end, Yanko cannot transition from child to rational being, illiterate to literate, subjected to free, slave to paid laborer, subject to citizen, but rather exists in all of these categories simultaneously, demonstrating the precarious position of the imaginary citizen.

Children's Natural Citizenship and the Book of Nature

One way that political thinkers and abolitionists attempted to reframe the issue of citizenship was to argue that all individuals were natural citizens from birth—a claim that disrupted dominant understandings of children's political capacities but followed certain legal precedents. As I have discussed in chapter 3, birthright citizenship represented a competing strain in American political discourse because of the residual influences of English common law. Even as early Americans rejected patriarchal theories of subjecthood, they struggled with the ways in which certain aspects of the legal tradition they inherited from England maintained that children were natural subjects. Extending this tradition, many children were naturalized as citizens based on the Naturalization Act of 1790, which granted citizenship to children of free white immigrants with good moral character. A series of naturalization bills between 1841 and 1854 further iterated that children born abroad were to be considered citizens based on parentage.

In spite of these laws, children's natural citizenship, in the eyes of critics, constituted a slave contract: an unequal agreement made without full knowledge. One early commentator bemoaned that attempts to designate children's citizenship from birth meant that "the chains of slavery are fastened upon [the child] while he is incapable of resisting."[15] This passage insists that the voluntary bonds of citizenship are separate from the involuntary chains of slavery, and should be inaccessible to children and slaves for this reason. It also suggests Americans believed that "slavery" was a possible outcome of citizenship if introduced too early—the irony, of course, being that actual slaves were not legal citizens. Underlying such claims was the assumption that runs throughout this book: that children were unable to understand or engage meaningfully in politics because they did not yet possess the ability to make rational decisions.[16] More subtly, comparisons between child citizens and slaves suggest the ways in which citizenship (even of adults) could overlap with coercive bonds, a problem that Rousseau and Emerson both attempted to solve.

Contesting the citizen's metaphorical slavery and, later, actual slavery meant changing ideas about childhood. Certain thinkers—many who have come to be associated with Romanticism—argued that children's natural impulses were at least as valuable as adult reason. These thinkers were not against educating children but felt that they primarily needed help in resisting the corruptions of society. Although some Romantics reached the conclusion that individuals must remain unencumbered by the expectations of society and citizenship in order to maintain their original condition of integrity, others tried (in Rousseau's words) to integrate the natural "man"—who was aligned with the child—and the "citizen."[17] Since Rousseau was the first major political philosopher to consider the child's natural citizenship outside of patriarchal theory, my account of natural citizenship begins with him.

Rousseau's famous assertion in *The Social Contract* (1762) that "man was born free; and he is everywhere in chains" addresses the potentially slippery connections between childhood, citizenship, and slavery and calls for a form of citizenship that was free of slavish constraints.[18] As this passage suggests, Rousseau believed, as Locke did, that humans were naturally free. He also agreed with Locke, in contrast to Hugo Grotius, that slave contracts were not legitimate and could not coexist with a free society. But Rousseau differed from Locke in his assessment of society; rather than claiming that government had to be imposed to offer protection, he claims that warlike attitudes must have come from society and that the government formed by passionate men was inevitably corrupt. As a result, Rousseau placed more emphasis on the potential of society to enslave and the value of natural man, who was closely aligned to "savages"—literally people of the forests—and children. While Rousseau sees natural men and children as imperfect because they are not fully rational and do not understand social virtues, they are naturally compassionate and value freedom. Though he claims that humans cannot go back to a state of nature, as passions have destroyed their original simplicity, he seeks to understand how governments might respect man's basic goodness and desire for liberty.

Because no return to the state of nature was possible, his major theory of citizenship in *The Social Contract* has no pretensions about making citizenship natural, claiming rather that he is interested in making social constraints legitimate through the imaginary apparatus of the social contract. About the transition from free birth to social constraint, Rousseau writes: "How did this transformation come about? I do not know. How can it be made legitimate? That question I believe I can answer."[19] Still the child remained a problem for him, since it was unclear how young people's participation in the social contract was to be ensured without imposing coercive restraints. Furthermore, Rousseau claimed that educating a child to be free and independent, befitting the modern world, did not make him a good citizen. As he puts it in *Émile, Or An Education* (1762): "The natural man lives for himself; he is the unit, the whole, dependent only on himself and on his like. The citizen is but the numerator of a fraction, whose value depends on the community. Good social institutions are those best fitted to make a man unnatural, to exchange his independence for dependence, to merge the unit with the group, so that he no longer regards himself as one, but as part of the whole."[20] The problem of how the child would become a citizen was troublesome, because Rousseau's fantasy state based on the collective will of its members did not yet exist, meaning that he needed future citizens to bring it about.

Carol A. Mossman points out that Rousseau's theories shaped the celebratory language surrounding childhood in the French Revolution: "the figure of the child assumed enormous symbolic importance as the very embodiment of the future."[21] Ala Alryyes also claims that Rousseau's "emphasis on children as national raw material" created a new model of nationalist politics in which "the citizen was to be a child of nature and a child of the state."[22] Yet, Rousseau's representation of the child citizen is as anxious of the child as it is hopeful, attempting to manage a number of paradoxes related to citizenship, society, and language. By considering how the child could be a citizen, Rousseau offered a vision of natural citizenship meant to free all individuals from unnatural subjection, while also raising a set of problems that complicated any such vision. As we will see, the idea of children's natural citizenship was met with equal measures of celebration and trepidation by literary authors in the United States.

Although Rousseau stops short of exploring the transformation from birth to citizenship in *The Social Contract*, his pedagogical work does attempt to understand how the transformation comes about and to more fully mend the gap between the natural man and the citizen. But although he declared *Émile* the "best and most important of all my writings," scholars have disagreed about its argument regarding citizenship.[23] Some critics maintain that *Émile* is not really about citizenship at all. Robert Wokler points out that the text never "recasts [Émile's] character, or prepares him for a new identity as part of a whole greater than himself, in the manner stipulated in Rousseau's account of popular sovereignty in *The Social Contract*."[24] Wokler suggests that "for Rousseau's plan of a civic education, readers must turn elsewhere," particularly to his *Discourse on Political Economy* and *Consideration on the Government of Poland,* which both present authoritarian means of educating children to love their country that are incompatible with the freedom of the social contract.[25] Gerraint Perry also contends that *Émile* "is not the place to find an account of citizen education."[26] Instead, Émile's education is "intended to arm [him] against a corrupting society rather than assist him in contributing to a just one."[27]

Tzvetan Todorov concurs: "the moral individual [represented by Émile] is not the citizen . . . He is not indifferent to the institutions of the country in which he lives, but . . . it is up to him alone to win his liberty."[28] Judith N. Shklar points out that Rousseau's *The Social Contract* and *Émile* present two utopias that cannot be reconciled: "For there is no compromise to be worked out between self-repression and self-expression."[29]

Rousseau, however, insisted that his political and pedagogical works "together form a complete whole" and that *The Social Contract* was "a sort of appendix" to *Émile,* suggesting that his proposal for political reorganization was tied to his plan for educating children.[30] Mossman argues that *Émile* addresses what Rousseau saw as the timeline problem associated with the social contract. For a social contract to emerge as the will of the people, Rousseau claimed, the "effect would have to become the cause; the social spirit which must be the product of social institutions would have to preside over the setting up of those institutions; men would have to have already become before the advent of law that which they become as a result of the law."[31] In other words, for individuals to enter into such a contract, the society that the contract means to create would have to already exist and to mobilize itself in producing the citizens that created it. Earlier political philosophers dealt with this problem by constructing imaginary narratives about the past and by pulling children into the current contract. Rousseau refuses to tell such a narrative, arguing that these stories speciously endow nature with the features of society. Neither do they inspire change, as the individual identifies with existing systems rather than bringing about a shift in government. Thus, he differently seeks to consider whether the child could become a social being prior to contact with the law. From there, he considers whether it is possible to forge a citizen who retains the qualities of this natural man: a natural citizen.

Because of the timeline problem, Rousseau's child citizen cannot be an imaginary citizen, constructed to identify with the existing state through reading. Mossman asserts that Rousseau's remedy for corrupt politics "can be conceived only in terms of birth . . . States ineluctably issue forth from the matrix of history."[32] It is no coincidence, she notes, that Émile's wife, Sophy, is pregnant as the text ends: "giving birth to a new body politic, producing a new citizen capable of reproducing the new order: these urgent enterprises were swaddled in a rhetoric of reproduction."[33] The underlying theme of birth nonetheless points to a central tension in Rousseau's work between the natural and the educated citizen, a citizen who is born and one who has to be made (a tension that, as we will see, forms two poles of nineteenth-century American thought about the child citizen, represented in this chapter by Emerson and by Goodrich and Hawthorne, respectively).

Rousseau, contrary to popular belief, does not romanticize the child. He emphasizes even more than Locke does that the child is not rational or moral, but, unlike Locke, suggests that education harms rather than helps. He attempts to manage this tension by offering a plan of "negative education": a paradoxical means of educating while claiming to leave the pupil untouched. The fact that Sophy is pregnant at the end of the book reintroduces the problem by raising the question of whether it is Émile or his unborn child that is to be the ideal citizen (Sophy is never a candidate). If, as some scholars argue, it is not Émile himself because he still lives in a corrupt society, it is unclear whether this ideal citizen can exist, since Émile's tutor works with the most perfect conditions available when starting from the current system and Émile's child presumably faces the same problems. But if *Émile* fails to produce the citizen of the social contract, it is not because Émile is not meant to be a citizen; rather, Rousseau is wrestling with the difficulties of realizing his own philosophy, refusing to fully disguise the gaps between his imagined political system and the child's practical entrance into it.

For Rousseau, the possibilities and failures of the child's natural citizenship are closely tied to the possibilities and failures associated with language. Rousseau makes clear that language and society are bound up together, each requiring the other. Thus, it is difficult to see how language can play a role in transforming existing systems. He denounces the abstractions that I have claimed are necessary to citizenship as unnatural, declaring that "he who concocts imaginary relations, which have no real existence, is a madman."[34] He links society's corruption to children's learning of language from books, famously declaring that his young charge, Émile, shall read nothing except Daniel Defoe's *Robinson Crusoe* (1719). But he is not ready to give up on language altogether. He initially suggests that Émile can avoid taking on the constraints of imaginary citizenship by learning "no book but the world"—a passage that casts the world as a text.[35]

For his image of the world as book, Rousseau draws on the pervasive image of the "book of nature," which dates from at least the early Christian era and which thrived in the Middle Ages and Renaissance. While the phrase "book of nature" may seem like an oxymoron, religious thinkers of these periods understood word and world as signs of God, whose dual authorship of both books forged a natural link between language and objects, as well as between human society and animal creation. Such a book, they argued, could not be misread—and it revealed God's plan for human society. Sir Thomas Browne, for instance, writes, "what Reason may not go to school to the Wisdom of Bees, Ants, and Spiders? . . . the civility of these little Citizens more neatly sets forth the Wisdom of their Maker."[36]As these examples suggest, multiple ideas were attached to the concept of nature: human nature, physical nature, and nature as a past or primitive state of society that continued to inform human government, but ideally these were supposed to be reflective of each other, bearing witness to the involvement of God in all things.

The belief in the legibility and morality of nature was perhaps one of the major influences upon political philosophy's attempt to locate the origin of society in a state of nature. It is also no coincidence that Locke recommended *Aesop's Fables* as the primary reading material for children. The anthropomorphic fables depict animals' knowledge of a natural code of ethics, as well as their transgressions of that code, suggesting both the innate morality and freedom of the natural state and the need for augmentations to it. Locke's approach to the fables reminds us that, while Lockean contract theory had attempted to ground the free citizenship guaranteed by government in the natural and free birth of the child, it also cast government as necessary to activate the rights that were supposedly inherent in the natural state. Government institutions came to be understood as replacing natural rhythms with more predictable ones into which the child must be artificially trained. Rousseau rejected such educational systems and doubted the idea that the governments described by Locke and others were actually based on natural law. Rousseau agreed that governments should recognize man's natural freedom, but he argued in *Discourse on Inequality* that most did not.

Rousseau nonetheless presents the book of nature as a potential basis for society's reconciliation with the freedom of the state of nature. Rousseau explains that his tutor will keep the child "dependent on things only," so that he will believe that he is free as far as his strength allows and is not subject to unnatural constraints. While this "dependence on things . . . does no injury to liberty and begets no vices," "dependence on men . . . gives rise to every kind of vice, and through this master and slave become mutually depraved." Rousseau suggests that in the ideal society, the general will would be as powerful as nature, so that it could not be contradicted: "If the laws of nations, like the laws of nature, could never be broken by any human power, dependence on men would become dependence on things; all the advantages of a state of nature would be combined with all the advantages of social life in the commonwealth."[37] In this way, the citizen becomes indistinguishable from natural man: both are limited only by their own powers.

At the same time that Rousseau presents the book of nature as one solution to the tension between the man and the citizen, the paradoxical nature of the image also draws attention to the flaws in this project of reconciliation.[38] Much of *Émile* suggests that he actually saw book and world, society and nature, as irreconcilable opposites. Rousseau expresses particular ire against social fables about nature. He distrusts these fables because they blur the difference between "the conventional fox" and the "the actual fox."[39] Since social conventions and natural objects are not easily convertible into one another, it is not clear how conventions such as laws can function in the same way as natural prohibitions.

Furthermore, *Émile* reveals that even dependence on things relies on a particular fantasy of language: the image of the world as book suggests that objects are language and that no interpretation is needed to transform them into a governing force. Because Rousseau saw nature as largely unlawful and society as unnatural, this fantasy does not hold. Émile notably cannot read the book of nature on his own. He needs the tutor to shape the natural world into law. In one particularly poignant scene, Émile learns to garden, an apt metaphor for the ways in which Rousseau's nature must be coaxed into providing the right lessons. The scene purports to be a simple lesson in natural consequences—one plants seeds and then they grow—but the tutor contrives to calm Émile's acquisitive passions by having the gardener pluck up his beans. This punishment is not a natural consequence for any misbehavior on Émile's part, since the tutor is the one who has suggested the garden, and it is not a natural occurrence, or "law of things," since the tutor has told the gardener to do it. If there were not so many contrivances about it, the scene might be read as a way of declaring that the cultivation of nature can be used in service of creating human relationships, but this lesson is diluted by the layers of manipulation and artificiality that the tutor introduces to the situation (denounced later by William Godwin as "hypocrisy and lying").[40] Émile is dependent not on things, but on the tutor's translation of them into lessons. Nature is not an open book and the soil is, literally, not enough to make him into a good citizen.

This situation is not so much a contradiction in Rousseau's theory as an indication of his awareness that nature and society cannot be fully reconciled without artificial narratives. Later, when Rousseau suggests that Émile will learn to read only *Robinson Crusoe*, as this book teaches a natural relationship with things rather than with words alone, artificiality and imagination are at once required, as the child gains a natural relationship with the world by reading a book. Émile does not just learn to build things. He also pretends that he is Robinson Crusoe on an island building them. It is only as a pretend "solitary man" that Émile can "judge all things as they would be judged by such a man in relation to their own utility."[41]

Rather than baldly declaring that citizenship is not a natural thing as he does in *The Social Contract*, Rousseau tries in *Émile* to manage the tensions between society and nature. Applying the timeline problem to Émile means that to be a natural citizen, the child must be, without being taught or introduced to the law, what he can only become through education and adherence to laws. The book of nature allows Rousseau to temporarily manage this problem, since it offers Émile a code for behavior that is apparently natural and inherent, instead of the result of socialization or legal enforcement. But, despite the tutor's efforts at making Émile dependent on things alone, Rousseau suggests that entrance into an existing society and adherence its laws is practically necessary. He also suggests that the preexistence of society has made retaining one's natural state impossible, since "no one can remain in a state of nature in spite of his fellow creatures, and to try to remain in it when it is no longer practicable, would really be to leave it, for self-preservation is nature's first law."[42] This passage suggests that Rousseau's natural child is also, by necessity, an unnatural one. Appropriately, when Émile enters society, Rousseau reintroduces the fables.

Although it is clear from these circumstances that *Émile* is not a text that gives rise to the ideal of the social contract, Rousseau still considers whether Émile can reimagine society. He claims that Émile must learn political principles, since "he who would judge wisely in matters of actual government . . . must know what ought to be in order to judge what is." At first, he suggests that Émile must simply find a place where he will not be bothered by laws, supporting critics' claims that the text is not meant to create a citizen. He also notes that "if Emile returns from his travels . . . without a full knowledge of questions of government, public morality, and political philosophy of every kind, we are greatly lacking." He encourages his hypothetical child to answer two questions regarding the government: "How does it concern me; and what can I do?" This passage, while not often discussed, momentarily places Émile in the role of citizen-activist, suggesting that he is to have a role in social transformation. At the same time, Rousseau and his child character largely leave the questions open-ended and unanswered. Rousseau further suggests that reimagining society is difficult because children are inevitably biased by "the partiality of authors, who are always talking about truth, though they care very little about it."[43]

Émile's political decisions suggest Rousseau's ambivalence about government. After learning about the ideal of the social contract, Émile comments on its fictiveness: "One would think we were building our edifice of wood and not of men; we are putting everything so exactly in its place!" Ultimately Émile and his tutor do not become activists, choosing instead to go off on a journey to see existing governments. After this trip, Émile declares that he will not be bound to one nation or law but only to the laws of necessity: "What decision have I come to? I have decided to be what you made me; of my own free will I will add no fetters to those imposed upon me by nature and the laws. The more I study the works of men in their institutions, the more clearly I see that, in their efforts after independence, they become slaves." The tutor concurs: "In vain do we seek freedom under the power of the laws . . . For the wise man [the laws of nature] take the place of positive law."

Yet he encourages Émile to be an affectionate citizen even though the social contract does not exist in ideal form: "What matter though the social contract has not been observed . . . Your fellow-countrymen protected you in childhood; you should love them in your manhood."[44]

Ultimately, Émile is to be "a natural man living in society . . . a savage who has to live in the town."[45] Rousseau clarifies that this means Émile must be in society, but not of it (an interesting corollary to Locke's claim that the child is born "to" equality but not "in" it). This compromise does not force Émile to give up all of his natural freedoms—as Rousseau points out later, his charge will not be carried away by society's hankering after fashionable baubles—but it also means that Émile will have to accept artificial constraint if he wants to avoid social obscurity. As such, he lives happily, but only until the tragic sequel, in which Rousseau undoes the boy's transition from man to citizen. The adult Émile abandons the affective chains that bind him to his wife and children and, ceasing to be a citizen, reenters his life as a man.

The continued tension between the natural man and citizen in Rousseau's work is to some extent a foregone conclusion; Rousseau admits in his preface that "he who would preserve the supremacy of natural feelings in social life knows not what he asks. Ever at war with himself, hesitating between his wishes and his duties, he will be neither a man nor a citizen."[46] As Troy Boone points out, Rousseau's refusal to fully resolve this issue calls into question the entire premise of the work, suggesting that he intends the text "to be read not as a practical guide to raising children, but as a philosophical exploration of an intractable problem."[47]

Though *Émile* presents itself as a coming-of-age story (indeed, many scholars have called it a novel), it is perhaps best read as a circular narrative, rather than a linear tale or practical guide. Paradoxically, one of the words that Rousseau uses for the "natural child" who must live in society is an "automaton" (in French, *automate*). He writes, "Where shall we find a place for our child so as to bring him up as a senseless being, an automaton?"[48] Rousseau was perhaps thinking of the original Greek root, *automatos*, or "acting of one's own will," but this word choice is still immediately odd for its connotations of involuntary and unnatural movement. An automaton seems to move of its own will, but it is really a fabrication, wound by its inventor—an apt description for the tutor's treatment of Émile.[49]

Rousseau's use of the word "automaton" is all the more striking given an earlier use of the same word in the text, referring to the kind of education that Rousseau is denouncing: "such a child-man would be a perfect idiot, an automaton, a statue without motion and almost without feeling."[50] It is true that Rousseau often claimed that he used words in contradictory ways and that the French language was not large enough to convey all of his ideas. However, the repetition of this word to describe both the kind of child that Rousseau wants to create and the kind that he does not reveals the circularity of the problem that Rousseau has identified and the difficulties of reimagining citizenship through the child. A number of educators in Europe, such as Johann Pestalozzi and Thomas Day, tried to institute natural education, but they missed Rousseau's essential point: the natural child cannot help but become an automaton, a subject who must be moved through a narrative of social incorporation.

American Automata

Rousseau's image of the child as automaton anticipated the trajectory of children's education in post-Revolutionary America, which set the stage for new conversations regarding the alternative possibility of children's natural citizenship. Visions of mechanical children first emerged when classical methods of affectionate education began to be rivaled by educational institutions based on the rhythms of the factory. Benjamin Rush, arguing for the establishment of public schools in Pennsylvania, famously envisioned transforming children into "republican machines." The metaphor of the government machine was quite deliberate: Rush knew that the social contract would require automatic habits as well as voluntary choices in order for it to work.[51]

Continuing Rush's legacy in the nineteenth century, Americans imported cheap systems of public education that were pioneered in Europe and its colonies. For instance, beginning in 1807, Americans imported the Lancaster or "monitorial" system, developed by British philanthropists for training the poor.[52] Monitorial schools resembled factories of learning, using peer monitors to lead children in drills assembly-line style so that one teacher could instruct hundreds of students at once. While these schools were celebrated as a way to spread learning to the masses and, in fact, offered children some agency by having them act as teachers of their peers, they also made compromises in order to promote fast learning. Children in Lancaster schools learned to read "without any attention to the sense," reserving knowledge of meanings for advanced study.[53] This approach, known as the "spelling book method," became the typical method of reading instruction in the early nineteenth century. As an 1818 article put it wearily, "Spelling, spelling is the cry."[54] Though standardized spelling had only recently been introduced—and pedagogues complained that it had not produced the univocal American public that pioneers such as Noah Webster had envisioned—it nonetheless had a major influence on printed materials for children. As fictional children's reading materials traveled slowly to the less populated parts of the country, spellers took up residence in most American homes. *The United States Spelling Book* (1809) was the first book printed to the west of the Allegheny Mountains.[55] When missionaries associated with the American Tract Society went west to spread their reading materials, they noted that nearly all households had two books: the Bible and a spelling book, and some households made do without the Bible.[56]

Critics of this new, more standardized, system feared that the rage for spelling was turning children—and therefore citizens—into trained animals or automatons. Daniel Adams, author of *The Understanding Reader* (1804), claimed that child readers had come to resemble a popular carnival act, the Learned Pig, because they understood "nothing . . . of those subjects, which they read."[57] In an equally poignant image of uncomprehending performance, children were compared to machines. Reports of wooden dials for teaching reading abound in periodicals of the period, often linked with quack inventors seeking easy money.[58] In addition to a catch-all term for this newfangled teaching machinery, "spelling machine" became a slang term for describing child readers. William M'George, of the Dutchess County Academy in Poughkeepsie, boasted that he had styled a "self-spelling machine" composed of the children in his classroom.[59] Some pedagogues clearly marveled at the achievements of their students, but others worried that "reading without intelligence" might have the negative consequence of injuring "the brain and stomach mechanically."[60] A contributor to the *Ladies Port-Folio* in 1820 reacts to the "daily improvements" in the "mechanic arts" of reading:"I am apprehensive that human ingenuity may be indulged too far . . . When this takes place, the material world will be rapidly changing into wheels, axles, &c . . . the human race will be annihilated."[61]

Throughout the antebellum period, a surprisingly large number of American pedagogues echoed the *Ladies* contributor by questioning whether children's reading was sufficiently "natural." Did children sound natural when they were reading aloud?[62] Did they realize that the words that they were reading had referents in the real world? For the *Ladies* contributor, these critiques went beyond children's reading to tackle questions related to citizenship. Envisioning a negative version of Rush's "republican machines," she sarcastically suggests that a trend for mechanical reading has created citizens who can "outdo Washington and Franklin" and stall political assemblies by reciting "for hours and hours upon a subject of little or no importance."[63] The transcendentalists drew from this culture of educational critique in making their arguments about American culture. Emerson also uses an image of Americans as "children who repeat by rote the sentences of granddames and tutors" to suggest that they had become detached from nature, rendering their language and their government, "misrepresentative."[64] Henry David Thoreau used a similar image of Americans "forever repeating our a b abs . . . sitting on the lowest and foremost form all our lives," a practice associated with reciting from spelling books.[65]

Such critiques resonated with the public because school performances made children's reading a more visible civic activity in this era than with any previous generation. Schools conducted public examinations in which pupils spelled words, read aloud, and sang poetry in chorus. Often located in political spaces such as town halls, these examinations were a form of civic exhibition, through which the education of child citizens could be performed for the rest of the nation. Yet young people's comments about the examinations reflect their awareness that some observers considered the performances empty of meaning. For instance, recording the criticism of her teacher, fifteen-year-old Sally Ripley writes in her diary that she "observed that though many of us pronounced our words well . . . we did not read intelligibly."[66] For some, the mechanical training of schoolchildren was cause for revolution. Sara Willis Payson, writing under her penname Fanny Fern, vowed that in order to save the "little automatons," she would "throw down the gauntlet for children's rights."[67]

The notion that children were not learning was bad enough, but when read through Rousseau's image of the automaton, the concern that children would be transformed into machines lays bare one of the major assumptions of American political representation: that acting on one's own will is ultimately inseparable from acting on the will of another. While affectionate citizenship had imagined that the nation's laws could be recognizable as the results of one's own actions, the automaton image suggested conversely that one's own actions could be manipulated, so that it was impossible to distinguish one's natural behavior from that which was prescribed by society.

In protesting automated reading, commentators revived the comparisons between children, citizens, and slaves that had appeared in earlier texts. At the same time that slaveholders were casting slavery as a great patriarchal institution in which slave masters took care of their affectionate children, images of child citizens as automatons forged a different connection between child and slave for, as William Lloyd Garrison points out in his introduction to Douglass's slave narrative, slavery reduces the human being "to the condition of a thing."[68] Slavery often appeared as a metaphor for children's education. One writer remarks, "Of all the youths crowded into a public school, how few are there to whom learning is not rendered a more irksome and detested slavery."[69] Another asks, "How comes it to pass, that the process of education is marked by mental slavery?"[70] Though such "mental slavery" was clearly distinct from the abuses of chattel slavery, natural citizenship was posed as an answer to both forms of enslavement.

The problem of maintaining one's natural freedom in a world of unnatural restrictions was central to the work of the transcendentalists, especially the preeminent American theorist of nature, Emerson. Though the child never takes center stage in Emerson's work, several of his texts might be understood as an extended reconsideration of some of the problems raised in *Émile*.[71] For Emerson, children's natural citizenship becomes a more hopeful prospect than for Rousseau, in part because the social contract is less of an ideal for him. Writing in a nation founded on such a contract that was becoming divided by civil disagreements, he returns to a notion of citizenship as natural and available to even the youngest members of society, but he notably distances this citizenship from government. While Rousseau's natural citizen has to become an imaginary citizen, Emerson's natural citizen appears to remain natural by operating outside of existing institutions. Still, if nature was to be harnessed for political purposes, it had to reenter the realm of the imaginary.

At first, Emerson's political work seems to reject the child as a model for the citizen. In "Politics" (1844), he writes, "Society is an illusion to the young citizen. It lies before him in rigid repose, with certain names, men, institutions, rooted like oak-trees to the centre . . . But the old statesman knows that society is fluid; there are no such roots and centres."[72] The young citizen's perception that laws are "rooted" in nature makes him susceptible to bad government. Emerson complains, "Republics abound in young civilians, who believe that the laws make the city . . . and that any measure, though it were absurd, may be imposed on a people."[73] The old statesman, conversely, knows that government does not have a fixed natural basis. As the "fluidity" of society in the eyes of the statesman suggests, Emerson preferred airy and watery metaphors for natural citizenship, distinguishing it from the supposed fixity of government.

Emerson's argument that it is primarily young people who falsely perceive government as natural suggests that his critique of American politics is a critique of typical forms of children's education. Using the prevalent book as food metaphors that circulated in early children's books, he writes, "We are shut up in schools . . . for ten or fifteen years and come out at last with a belly full of words and do not know a thing."[74] Unlike in chapter 3, where people were concerned that children might "swallow" the wrong kinds of books, this passage suggests that no books can nourish children or teach them "a thing" since words are separate from the objects they signify. Emerson also bemoans the affectionate tutor motif associated with the eighteenth-century school story as a misleading ploy to gain the reader's trust for textual governance. Evoking the many moral guidebooks written under the guise of a governess or family member, Emerson writes, "when we mistake books for divinity and genius, they become 'nonsense' and the guide is a tyrant. We sought a brother, and lo, a governor."[75] Citizenship, as I have argued throughout the book, relied on such a logic of replacement: books could be governors, liberty could be resigned through the linguistic act of consent, and the nation could be constructed out of words.

If government were to be understood as unnatural and illusory, Emerson claimed that citizenship operated beyond the limits of government and therefore *could be* understood as natural. To illustrate how the natural man can be a citizen in spite of unnatural government, Emerson revisits Rousseau's law of things: "Things have their laws, as well as men; and things refuse to be trifled with . . . They exert their power, as steadily as matter its attraction."[76] Unlike Rousseau, who implies that the laws of society cannot operate like the laws of things, Emerson claims that the natural law is always the hidden basis of human relations. Though most members of political parties can "give no account of their position," they "mark some real and lasting relation. We might as wisely reprove the east wind, or the frost, as a political party."[77] These passages suggest that reconnecting society and nature is possible since nature's influence can never be denied. Elsewhere, Emerson states that there really is no conflict between society and nature: "We talk of deviations from natural life, as if artificial life were not also natural . . . Nature, who made the mason, made the house."[78]

Nonetheless, Emerson maintains that, as long as people remain unconscious of the fact that nature has built the nation, they will still attempt to create stifling laws: "There is not . . . a sufficient belief in the unity of things to persuade [people] that society can be maintained without artificial restraints, as well as the solar system."[79] As a remedy to this problem, Emerson believes that individuals must learn to read natural phenomena. Though nature's "code is seen to be brute and stammering" and it "speaks not articulately," it "must be made to."[80] While "Politics" does not explain how this will happen, Emerson provided a thorough discussion of how to read nature in texts such as "Nature" (1836) and "Self-Reliance" (1841). In the first of these essays, Emerson expresses the hope that "by degrees we may come to know the primitive sense of the permanent objects of nature, so that the world will be to us an open book."[81]

Despite his critique of young citizens in "Politics," Emerson suggests that young people have the best ability to read nature in its full meaning: "The sun illuminates only the eye of the man, but shines into the eye and the heart of the child."[82] In "Self-Reliance," Emerson famously claims that "the nonchalance of boys . . . is the healthy attitude of human nature."[83] Children's ability to read nature meant that they were, in Judith Plotz's words, "obedient to the deepest natural law that rolls through all things."[84]

Emerson's early work did not immediately relate the question of children's natural citizenship to the problem of African slavery, but his work does evoke notions of race and class in the period: "The idiot, the Indian, the child and unschooled farmer's boy stand nearer to the light by which nature is to be read."[85] Emerson's association of Native Americans and children sought to revise ideas that were circulating at the time. Because of the politics of westward expansion, Andrew Jackson portrayed Native Americans as "natural children."[86] In contrast, Emerson's work is striking for its notion that childhood did not necessarily mean social exclusion. The claim that children were natural citizens would ultimately coincide with attempts to include people of color within the space of the nation, though it is important to note that, in the case of Native Americans, these efforts were initially unsuccessful. For many years, the children of Indians, unlike children of foreigners or slaves, were not allowed to be naturalized.

Emerson forges his more inclusive notion of natural citizenship by making clear that his natural children are not "savages" but citizens. Rather than attempting to separate his nonchalant little boy from politics, Emerson imagines him in the role of a citizen. The main activity of such a boy is meting out his own system of justice: "looking out from his corner on such people and facts as pass by, he tries and sentences them on their merits, in the swift, summary way of boys."[87] The boy's judgment is important because Emerson claims that "self-reliance" is not "mere antinomianism."[88] He insinuates that by learning to read the world as children do, individuals will spontaneously form moral character and live together in a state of natural freedom. Elsewhere Emerson assumes that this natural reading will prevent disunion, as nature is a "discipline" that provides moral accord consistent with the citizen's natural liberty: "Space, time, society, labor, climate, food, locomotion, the animals, the mechanical forces give us the sincerest lessons, day by day."[89]

The development of individual character through the reading of nature was meant to make the state and its books "unnecessary."[90] Echoing Rousseau without Rousseau's ambivalence, Emerson writes, "the wise man is the state . . . He needs no library, for he has not done thinking . . . no statute book, for he has the lawgiver."[91] Though Emerson's claim that natural citizenship will be the providence of a "wise man" shows some distrust of the child, "Self-Reliance" suggests that nonchalant little boys were more likely to carry out this model of autonomous statehood than adults, who were "clapped into jail by [their] consciousness."[92] Emerson implicitly trusts children to read nature without heavy instruction. The nonchalant little boys seem not to have met Rousseau's tutor, and no one stands between them and their reading of nature. One thing that does seem significant is that they are boys; both Emerson's and Rousseau's images of children as natural citizens presuppose a male child. The same would be true for the natural citizenship established by the Fourteenth Amendment. Women's initially unsuccessful attempts to gain participation rights under the Fourteenth Amendment suggest that it was more difficult for lawmakers and jurists to imagine girls as active citizens, even as citizenship was becoming nominally universal.

One reason why Emerson does not need a tutor is that his theory of natural language is simpler than Rousseau's. Emerson expressed confidence that the book of nature would yield one unmistakable understanding of the world. In "Self-Reliance," Emerson speaks of the inevitable "resolution of all into the ever blessed ONE," an image that he would often revisit in his writing.[93] While the tutor in *Émile* seemed to worry that the book of nature could not produce a lesson without heavy manipulation, this "resolution" happens naturally for Emerson because the individual does not just read the law of things but *is* a thing: "The soul, is not diverse from things, from space, from light, from time, from man, but one with them. . . If I see a trait, my children will see it after me, and in course of time, all mankind."[94] This transcendental perception of nature had political meaning for Emerson, as a similar passage from "Politics" makes clear: "If I put myself in the place of my child, and we stand in one thought, and see that things are thus or thus, that perception is *law* for him and me."[95]

Emerson's rendering of the child and citizen as "things" recalls the automaton image from Rousseau, raising the question of whether the natural citizen's will comes from external forces or from himself. Ultimately, Emerson collapses these categories. By disregarding the question of how to distinguish individual agency from the will of nature, Emerson can ascribe social power even to the infant, who has no agency: "Infancy conforms to nobody; all conform to it."[96] For Emerson, infants are self-reliant not because they are completely independent, but because they are reliant on things, not artificial laws. Plotz argues that "the [Romantic] link to nature makes for a paradoxical and consolatory association of childhood with power, a way of ignoring actual social powerlessness."[97] Emerson projects this powerlessness on those surrounding the infant, reintroducing the problem of conformity. This conformity is not problematic in Emerson's view because it is conformity with nature mediated by the baby. By reframing conformity, Emerson is able to create the illusion that no submission is required to create a unified citizenship. As Elizabeth Hewitt points out, "there is ultimately no distinction between the interests of the one and the interests of the many."[98] If all are aligned with nature, "the citizens find [themselves] in perfect agreement."[99]

This imagination that children could perceive an absolute law of things in nature informed transcendentalist educational projects. A. Bronson Alcott used his perception of nature to create what Elizabeth Peabody calls a "very autocratic" method of governance at his Temple School.[100] She explains that his strictness evolved through a careful study of "the voice of nature": "And is not this a legitimate autocracy, in the moral sense of the word? Are not the laws of human nature sufficiently intelligible, to enable sensibility, and observation, and years of experience, to construct a system, whose general principles need not be reviewed?" In addition to consulting the "laws of nature" in punishing his students, Alcott consults the students themselves, whose agreement substantiates the "intelligibleness" of nature's authority, as well as their status as natural child readers who have the capacity to understand nature's truths. Peabody notes that the children never fail to consent.[101] Notably, students who seem to have been genuinely inspired by the idea of the book of nature seem to have had more consciousness of the difficulties associated with reading laws in nature. Margaret Fuller's pupil, eighteen-year-old Mary Allen Ware, muses in her journal, "[God] has written many beautiful things, which all to whom He has given sight, can see . . . He has written, but His children will not read . . . Shall we not *try* to read?"[102]

Although the law of nature was supposed to be obvious to all who bothered to read it, even Emerson's version of natural citizenship betrays a need to arrange nature to give it a social meaning and political potential. Emerson's first use of the "book of nature" image after visiting the Jardin des Plantes in Paris relies heavily on the arrangement of nature for instructional purposes. By viewing the exhibits of the "Cabinet of Natural History," Emerson saw that nature could be organized into legible displays that were wordlike in their ability to communicate. In his lecture on "The Uses of Natural History" (1833), which is usually read as the inspiration for "Nature," Emerson explains how the cabinets of the museum drew his attention to the "grammar of botany" and the "green and yellow and crimson dictionary, on which the sun shines, and the winds blow."[103] Emerson's dictionary and grammar images suggest that he understands nature as an ordered, alphabetized text. To make nature into such a text was a task that was taken up by many children's books of the nineteenth century. These texts suggest that for the child to be a natural citizen required more than just innate perception; it required the interventions of education. Ultimately, it would also require the interventions of law, reintroducing the problem of how natural citizenship can be recognized by the institutions of existing government.

Paper Birds

In light of Emerson's arguments that children must learn to read the book of nature to be self-reliant citizens, the vogue for children's natural history books in antebellum America takes on a political significance.[104] While children's natural histories were written by authors with a variety of educational and religious motivations, many of the nineteenth-century reforms were influenced directly by political theories, as was the case with Alcott and other reformers such as Robert Dale Owen. Educators echoed Emerson by claiming that natural reading could make children into free citizens rather than slavish automatons. A writer for *The North American Review* opines, "Let this man have been educated, not in the technical, artificial way, which too much prevails, but . . . let something of the science and mystery of nature have been opened to him . . . If our people swerve from this . . . it matters little whether, in name and in form, they are freemen or slaves."[105]

But educators often diverged from philosophers in that they explicitly advocated for printed texts as a part of children's natural education. The Swiss reformer Johann Pestalozzi, who had a major impact on American schoolbooks, cast aside Rousseau's restrictions on reading materials, instead advocating for a "mother's book," which would transform the book of nature into a text with illustrations.[106] Perhaps recognizing the hidden work of Rousseau's tutor, Pestalozzi claimed that direct experience of nature was not useful on its own because, "Neither trees nor plants here come before [the child's] eyes in such a manner as . . . to make him observe their nature and relationships" and suggests that nature must be condensed to its essential characteristics."[107] As an image of this process, he tells the story of a peasant woman from the Appenzell region of Switzerland who places a colored paper bird above her child's cradle so that "Art [can] begin to bring the objects of Nature firmly to the child's clear consciousness."[108] The paper bird is evocative of a live bird, so that the representation is connected to the object it represents, and an amalgamation of the various birds that exist into a man-made image and medium of communication. The translation of nature into "paper birds" is the work of many children's books of the nineteenth century, which confront the tension between nature and language and attempt to repair it by imaginative means.

One of the most common ways that pedagogues attempted to encourage natural reading was to create alphabet books about animals. The *Illustrated Alphabet of Birds* (1851) combines animals with letters, as the building blocks of language.[109] As the letters progress, the difficult marriage of nature and language becomes clear. The text begins with the seemingly easy conjunctions of the letter *A* with "Auk" and the letter *B* with "Blue Bird," but it ends with the observation that "Z stands for none / Of the feathered race" and concludes that the letter therefore "must serve as a roost, / Or lose the last place."[110] (Impressively, the text does manage to find a bird for X by using the Latin name, "Xanthoronus," for the "Baltimore Bird.")[111] Though none of the letters can really stand for a bird, the forced pairing of Z and roost foregrounds the fact that nature is a non-ordered, non-communicative space. To keep the order of the alphabet intact, the book insists, the letter must claim its position as a man-made roost, reining nature into language—even as it does this, however, it faces potential obscuration by nature, as the *Z* in the picture is beginning to be covered over with birds. The child learning to read this book is not a transcendental reader who can perceive the laws of nature without instruction. Rather, the child is asked to try and fit nature into language, as it is only in these contexts that nature can become a basis for social order.

Other children's books of the period combine multiple narrative forms (fictional stories, naturalist accounts, descriptive portraits), representing a multilateral strategy of trying to render nature legible and useful to humans. *The Aviary; Or the Child's Book of Birds* (undated) uses a strategy similar to that of the alphabet books, attempting to enclose the birds in text. The description of the "bartailed humming-bird" compares the bird's tail to a legible human sign: "it consists of two parts, standing out at an angle to each other like the letter V."[112] But at the same time that the book transforms the bird's tail into a letter, it is forced to concede that it cannot be read as a letter with meaning; the author points out that "we are not very well informed with regard to the manners of many of the family" and concludes weakly that the V-shape is likely "capable of some corresponding action which is essential to the welfare of the bird."[113] Another bird, the carrier pigeon, seems to offer a more likely source for human meaning, given that it has "from very remote ages" been used by humans for communicating messages. The picture of the pigeon is fittingly sharp and codelike, but the text suggests that despite the bird's adeptness in carrying messages, its behavior can only be explained by "unaccountable instinct."[114]

Unlike Emerson, who suggests that nature *is* political, these representations of blank nature come close to forcing citizens to confront the extrapolitical, the excess that cannot be governed. This extrapolitical nature points to an ungoverned part of the citizen, which was also symbolized by the figure of the feral child. At the same time, by imagining a connection between animals and language, the text attempts to deny nature's blankness and to make it compatible with social modes of interaction.

In an even bolder attempt to appropriate nature for human purposes, many books transform natural objects into national symbols. The letter *E* in *The Illustrated Alphabet* yields the rhyme "a Bald Eagle, / So bold and so free; / On the flag of our country / He spans land and sea."[115] This verse uses the image of the eagle to suggest that human institutions such as the nation can be natural even as they replace natural objects with artificial symbols and laws; the flying of the bird seamlessly becomes the flying of the flag. *The Anti-Slavery Alphabet* (1847) goes even further in that it endows language itself with the natural qualities of the eagle.

The letter *E* does not just stand for, but "*is* the Eagle, soaring high," "An emblem of the free."[116] Yet, the book also foregrounds society's failure to align with nature: "while we chain our brother man, / *Our* type he cannot be."[117] The national eagle becomes a paper bird, reduced to being a letter and an emblem only, without its natural meaning of freedom. The solution, frequently offered by abolitionists in other contexts, seems to be to reshape society so that its language and symbols are compatible with nature.

A few pedagogues directly admitted that fictional narratives were necessary to give nature human meanings. An *American Annals* columnist insists that children need stories about nature to perceive a close connection between citizenship and nature's instinctive operations: "A bee, an ant, or a beaver, endowed with free will, (as a child's imagination will easily be led to believe), may serve as mediums of moral instruction to children,—being members of a community."[118] The columnist makes it clear through the parenthetical remarks that it is only through artificial manipulations of the "child's imagination" that animals are granted the free will necessary to be seen as citizens.

Perhaps the most extended comparison between animal and civil society appears in *Natural History, or Uncle Philip's Conversations with the Children about Tools and Trades among the Inferior Animals* (1835), with chapters that include "The Politician Bird," "Ants that . . . build Cities," and "Ants that go to War . . . and have Slaves." In these stories, Philip relies on scientific coincidences to portray nature as inherently social. His animals fight wars, follow leaders, devise systems of labor, and build cities—making them "citizens" in the oldest sense of the word. The animals also approximate political consciousness. The "politician bird," so called because it uses pieces of newspaper to build its nest, gives Philip the opportunity to raise the importance of political awareness for human citizens: "No good government, my boys, will ever be afraid to let the people have newspapers."[119] The implied fantasy of the politician bird "reading" the newspaper makes the case that the activities of informed citizenship are not inconsistent with the natural state of animals or humans. Of course, underlying this account of the politician bird is a sense that citizenship is not entirely natural, since the bird needs a human invention to become a political being. And, because children cannot read newspapers without instruction (and birds can't really read them at all), there is a sense that some intervention is necessary for individuals to become citizens. This moment reminds us that Philip's book, too, is a step removed from the book of nature, implying that children need an adult interpreter to learn the lessons of the animal citizens.

In Philip's text as in *The Anti-Slavery Alphabet*, chattel slavery is the institution that especially reveals the difficulties of granting citizenship a natural basis, even

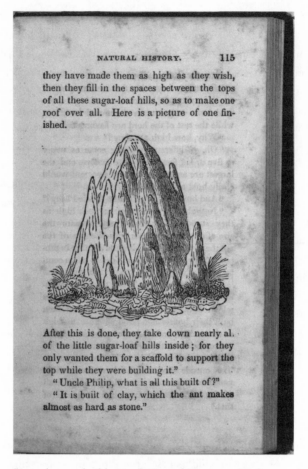

"Ants that . . . build cities," *Natural History, or Uncle
Philip's Conversations with the Children about Tools and
Trades among the Inferior Animals,* 1835. During and after
the Civil War, natural history was seen as the way to train
children to be good citizens by giving them examples from
the animal "kingdom." Courtesy of the American Antiquarian
Society.

though Philip tries to argue that slavery represents good citizenship. Reiterating
arguments in the period that slavery was "natural," Philip tells the story of "ants who
own slaves." The slave-owning ants are predictably "white ants," while black ants or
as Philip calls them "negro ants" are enslaved. Philip argues that this animal slavery
equals good citizenly behavior: "Nothing can be more faithful and affectionate than
these poor slaves are . . . I expect that in some things the legionary [ant] does for

the negro ant what it could not do for itself. God has made them necessary to each other, and this is the reason they live together so kindly."[120]

As historian Eugene D. Genovese has pointed out, slaveholders often talked about their relationship with slaves as one of reciprocal duty, in which slaves gave their labor in return for parental guidance.[121] Levander has further shown that Americans tried to ground racial distinctions in notions of childhood and nature. Anglo-Saxons were represented as free citizens by virtue of the natural traits with which they were born.[122] An irony that we learn via the pictures in the book is that "white ants" are termites, a species of bug that, while good at building cities of its own, is very destructive to other creatures, especially humans. Though this was likely an unintended irony, since Philip's defense of slavery seems earnest, slavery provides an occasion to unravel Philip's argument that nature yields good citizens.

No Man Can "Be Born a Government-Maker"

In response to the inscrutability of nature and its tendency to support unjust actions, other authors contested the idea of natural citizenship, preferring to assert the necessity of artificial laws and the necessity of children's allegiance to them. Despite Goodrich's frequent use of natural history in his magazines, much of his work focuses on the dangers of using nature as a model for citizenship. In "The Story of Philip Brusque," published serially in *Robert Merry's Museum* in 1841, the author (probably Goodrich himself) uses the story of French revolutionaries wrecked on a desert island to argue that nature does not constitute a viable model for society. By setting his story during the French Revolution, Goodrich associates natural law with disorder. The villain of the story, Rogere, is an amateur naturalist and manic transcendentalist who claims that the people should be ruled by the government already established by the "God of nature."[123] He supports this view by "reading" nature, but what he finds in nature is not social harmony, but violent force and megalomania: "Look around, and everywhere you see that in the dynasty of nature all is regulated by force. There is a power of gravitation, which controls matter, and bids the earth roll round in its orbit. Even matter, then, the very soil, the inanimate clod, the senseless stones, obey the law of force. And it is so with the animal tribes: among birds, the eagle is master of the raven; with quadrupeds, the lion is lord of the forest; with fishes, the whale is monarch of the deep."[124] Rogere argues that animals are not brutes but "legislators" who know to "leave things to their natural course."[125] Yet he uses the power granted by nature to forcefully subordinate the heroine of the story, Emilie, to his sexual proclivities and to enslave his followers. The hero, Philip Brusque, is a repentant revolutionary, who protests that "if we follow animals, we must adopt their modes of life . . . If you allow the strong to take what they can grasp, we go back at once to the savage state."[126] Goodrich's civic textbook, *The Young American*, made a similar point using a natural history plate of wolves eating a deer with the caption: "Natural Liberty. Might is Right."[127]

Such statements would have had strong public resonance in the context of the debates over nature as a foundation for citizenship and education. Brusque, in fact, aligns the two, bemoaning that if nature is seen as the foundation of human activities, "man is to be the pupil of the bird; the brute is to be the lawgiver of human beings!"[128] It is no coincidence that many of Goodrich's nature stories feature domesticated dogs; they are the only animals that, in his view, can really be good citizens. *The Young American* too makes it clear that children need more than the lessons of nature to become citizens. They need instruction in human activities: "A man can no more be born a government-maker, than he can be born a house-maker, or a watch-maker; he needs to learn his trade as much as in one case as the other."[129]

Nathaniel Hawthorne's stories for children differently use the figure of the natural child to explore the need for children's education and, additionally, their consent. Though Hawthorne questions the viability of social institutions such as schools, he suggests that Emerson's model of natural citizenship fails to account for the irregularity of children's tastes, as well as the chaotic forces within human nature. He concludes that the artificial ordering mechanisms of the law are necessary to prevent the destabilization of society. His children's literature imagines what would happen in a world of Pearls, and reminds us that even Hester Prynne's illegal child has to fashion her eel-grass into a scarlet letter.[130]

Hawthorne's hesitancy regarding the transcendentalist project is well documented, but he also shared with the transcendentalists many of the criticisms of education that abounded in the period. He begins his children's book, *A Wonder Book for Boys and Girls* (1851),with an observation reminiscent of Emerson's arguments against the American schoolhouse reader. He describes his young storyteller, Eustace Bright, as a scholar whose eyes have become bad because of too much reading: "A trouble in his eyesight (such as many students think it is necessary to have, nowadays, in order to prove their diligence at their books) had kept him from college a week or two after the beginning of the term."[131] Eustace is a primary example of American education gone wrong, his blurry eyes demonstrating the ways in which education has led not to liberty but to debilitation. Hawthorne emphasizes the child's ability to resist this bad education by remarking "for my part, I have seldom met with a pair of eyes that looked as if they could see farther or better than those of Eustace Bright." In this second claim, Hawthorne suggests that even though school has blinded Eustace, he has retained the powers inherent

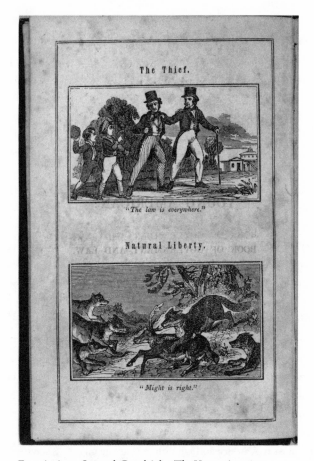

Frontispiece, Samuel Goodrich, *The Young American,*
1842. In this civics textbook, Goodrich shows that allowing humans to revert to their natural state, rather than
following the civilizing force of society, will make them
savage, as shown by a pack of wolves eating a deer with the
caption "Might is right." Courtesy of the American Antiquarian Society.

within the child's natural vision of the world. He insists that Eustace, even at age
twenty, "was just as much a boy as when you became first acquainted with him."[132]
His child listeners are likewise unspoiled, taking their names from nature, such as
Primrose and Cowslip.

But reflecting his ambivalence about transcendentalism, Hawthorne's idealized
portraits of children are often accompanied by skepticism about the natural child's
ability to produce a moral society without the force of textual and legal discipline.

"The Paradise of Children," for instance, hints that the transcendentalist vision of a nation composed of natural children unleashes social evils similar to the corruptions described by Rousseau in his *Discourse on Inequality*. The story is a retelling of Pandora's box, but casts all of its characters as children. The paradisiacal society in which the children live approximates the world that might result from a population consisting of Emerson's nonchalant little boys sure of a dinner: "Then, everybody was a child. There needed no fathers and mothers to take care of the children . . . and there was plenty to eat and drink. Whenever a child wanted his dinner, he found it growing on a tree."[133]

The children do not seem at first to need a social compact in order to be free; they are able to coexist peacefully without the intervention of law: "What was the most wonderful of all, the children never quarreled among themselves; neither had they any crying fits."[134] Ultimately, though, Hawthorne's problematizes this social model by suggesting that natural children are not immune to the influence of selfishness and greed. Children, Hawthorne suggests, may be even more susceptible to these passions than adults are—the story claims that it is a child who unleashes the negative influences of passion on the world. Pandora and her friend Epimetheus are not self-reliant citizens, but "naughty" children, a term that Hawthorne also uses to describe Eustace's child listeners.

Recognizing that children had strong wills of their own, for Hawthorne, meant that their education and consent would be necessary to secure their allegiance. In another of his children's books, *Grandfather's Chair* (1840), the potential child citizen is represented by Charley, who gallops away on a broomstick during his grandfather's tales of early America and who interrupts the tales to voice his disagreement with his grandfather. He reacts to his grandfather's tragic depiction of the burning of Tory homes in the Revolution by saying that he would rather celebrate with the rebels than mourn the losses of the enemy—something that makes him a good American, perhaps, but not a particularly empathetic member of society. Charley's outbursts and inattention endanger the model of social cohesion promoted by both the tales and the story's frame narrative. Hawthorne notes that the grandfather would not have continued the story had it not been for his more amiable listeners. Eventually, the grandfather manages to assimilate Charley into the national community that the grandfather's historical tales establish—a process that we know is complete when Charley decides to name his sled "grandfather's chair"—but this unification is, for Hawthorne, a difficult and lengthy process, not what he would have seen as the naïve natural unification that Emerson envisions.[135] Hawthorne understands that children can and do protest—and this ability would need to be respected if they were to ultimately participate in society.

The frame story of *A Wonder Book* links Hawthorne's concerns about the antinomian potentials of natural citizenship to anxieties about children's reading. "The Paradise of Children" is framed as a disciplinary tale, told in response to the bad reading of Primrose, one of Eustace's child listeners. Primrose undermines the model of a natural citizenship established through reading nature by demonstrating that the interpretations of so-called natural children are not homogenous but are frequently incompatible or even hostile to each other. She often provides negative commentary and rejects Eustace's conclusions in favor of her own. Though her objections to Eustace lead to humorous exchanges, she represents a threat to the community that is being created in the text through the children's shared explorations of nature. Her attempts to interrupt the stories and assert her own ideas endanger the telling, as when Eustace threatens to "bite the story short off between my teeth, and swallow the untold part" at the slightest interruption.[136] "The Paradise of Children" wreaks poetic justice on Primrose, and by extension, any child who dares to be a resistant reader; Eustace remarks that the story will show how paradise was destroyed "by the naughtiness of just such as little imp as Primrose here."[137] On the one hand, Hawthorne seems to be having fun with his child readers, but, on the other, through the disciplining of Primrose, he suggests that a model of society based on children's natural reading would be disastrous.

Hawthorne contends that child readers, particularly flighty ones such as Primrose, cannot be trusted to read correctly or uniformly without intervention. The frame story surrounding "The Paradise of Children" provides an example of how this acquiescence might happen through books, as it is this tale that begins Primrose's gradual surrender to the authority of Eustace and his stories. While *A Wonder Book* begins with Primrose threatening to fall asleep when Eustace tells a tale, she is soon requesting the tales herself, albeit in a way that attempts to disguise her true investment in them. In the end, it is Primrose who encourages Eustace to tell his final tale on the top of bald summit, claiming that "now that we are up among the clouds, we can believe anything."[138] As the cloaking of Primrose's submission in language that seems to manifest her independence suggests, Hawthorne remains invested in the ideal of self-reliant childhood. Yet his text asserts what Emerson's does not: children's natural citizenship and reading requires some unnatural manipulation to make nature readable and thereby secure their allegiance.

The problem of how to read nature was especially crucial when it came to the child's role in the social reforms of the nineteenth century, the most important of which was the abolition of slavery. If natural citizenship were meant to be an antidote to actual slavery as well as metaphorical slavery, Americans would have to agree on what the natural order was. Was slavery an aberration that was found nowhere in nature? Or was it found in the most natural of relationships? Though Uncle Philip claimed the latter, abolitionists just as often used appeals to natural citizenship. Exploiting the notion that children were closer to nature, abolitionists used stories about natural history to draw young people to the cause. As Ginsberg and Deborah De Rosa have both shown, one of the primary motifs in children's antislavery periodicals of the period depicted animals in cages as slaves, making the powerful rhetorical argument that slavery was unnatural.[139] For instance, a poem by abolitionist Ann Preston includes a little boy's realization that slavery is wrong through a natural history lesson about a squirrel: "Howard thought he should not like / A little slave to be; / And God had made the nimble squirrel, / To run, and climb the tree."[140] Eliza Lee Cabot Follen told similar stories about a squirrel and a rabbit proclaiming their "Liberty" after a short time as pets.

Abolitionists further suggested that slaves, like natural children, could read nature, signaling their right to be freemen. The abolitionist novel, *Blake: or, the Huts of America* (1859–62), claims that the natural impulse for freedom was "so simple that the most stupid among the slaves will understand it as well as if he had been instructed for a year. . . . So simple is it that the trees of the forest or an orchard can illustrate it; flocks of birds or domestic cattle, fields of corn, hemp, or sugar cane; tobacco, rice, or cotton, the whistling of the wind, rustling of leaves, flashes of lightning, roaring of thunder, and running of streams all keep it constantly before their eyes."[141]

Douglass's slave narrative contains a similar instance of natural reading. Douglass recalls, after learning to read at age twelve, "Freedom . . . was seen in every thing . . . It looked from every star, it smiled in every calm, breathed in every wind, and moved in every storm."[142] Yet Douglass understood these readings of nature as no less imaginative than Philip's. He knew that the natural world did not necessarily signify freedom, because he had no knowledge of these meanings prior to learning about his enslavement. His further musings suggest that nature might symbolize blissfully unconscious subjection as well as freedom. Slaves, for instance, had long been associated with enslaved animals: "In moments of agony, I envied my fellow-slaves for their stupidity. I have often wished myself a beast. I preferred the condition of the meanest reptile to my own."[143] Knowing that nature provides no answers, Douglass seeks momentary comfort in nature's ability to evade human meaning.

Douglass's efforts to obtain literacy as a child are focused on gaining control and mastery of abstract language, rather than relying on natural objects. When learning to read, Douglass focuses just as much on the letters as on their ability to signify. He learns the letters *S, L, F,* and *A* on the timber from ships. While these do have concrete meaning in the directions on the ship, they are important to Douglass because he can use their abstract shapes to trick white boys into teaching him to write more letters. Douglass further highlights the importance of language by declaring, "Mistress, in teaching me the alphabet, had given me the INCH, and no precaution could prevent me from taking the ELL"—an ironic variation on the racist saying "If you give a nigger an inch, he will take an ell."[144] By transforming the "ell," which is a concrete measure of distance, into the letter *L*, Douglass's pun suggests that it is the letter as much as the distance that leads to his liberation. *The Anti-Slavery Alphabet*, aside from the passage about the eagle, also centers on giving slaves and reformers the language to contest slavery. For instance, "A is an Abolitionist—/ A man who wants to free / The wretched slave—and give to all / An equal liberty."[145] Its verses are combined with large letters on every page. Douglass's similar discussion of the word, "ABOLITION," also shows that it is important to possess the abstract word as well as the thing it signifies.[146] Though Douglass's frustration with the diction-ary definition of the word, "one who abolishes," shows that concrete meanings are important (and not easily gained by reading more language), it is the word itself that draws him to any conversation pertaining to the anti-slavery movement, allow-ing him to work toward realizing its meaning. Learning that abolition referred to the abolition of laws pertaining to slavery, Douglass understood that to control the meaning of nature, and who got to be a natural citizen, one had to simultaneously master language and the law.

Natural Citizenship as Imaginary Citizenship

Paradoxically, it finally took a law to make citizenship natural. One might argue that the Fourteenth Amendment remedied the problems associated with children's citizenship and the citizenship of former slaves by affirming their rights as citizens. The citizenship granted by the amendment did not challenge the fundamental logic underlying existing limitations on participation rights, because it was based neither on extending this adult activity to children nor on declaring that former slaves were not children but adults. According to Anna Mae Duane, one common argument made by abolitionists was that "enslaved people . . . like children, could move out of a state of dependency and into the role of consenting adults," but the amend-ment notably did not use this definition of citizenship.[147] As we will see further in the conclusion to this book, the law kept potential comparisons between slaves and citizens intact. It did not directly link the citizenship it was granting with suffrage. The very inclusion of children in the amendment reveals that it was working from a different notion of citizenship than social contract theory and therefore could not entirely address the limitations on political rights under that system. But it also did not offer anything new: the Fourteenth Amendment, while potentially transformative, neither offered a major reassessment of children's ability to be acting citizens nor a procedure for how children could become such citizens. Instead, the Fourteenth Amendment made it clear that natural citizenship *is* imaginary citizenship. While the amendment purported to narrow the gap between imaginary and legal citizenship, it did so not just by making imaginary citizens into legal citizens but also by making legal citizenship dependent on imagination.

In the face of the Fourteenth Amendment's lack of a clear procedure for creating active citizens, imaginary narratives and models of education were still needed to explain how the natural citizenship of the amendment would function and how children and former slaves would enter into citizenship. In some sense, this imaginary citizenship is unavoidable, since there is no way to easily grant children, as natural citizens, with the legal right to vote even if former slaves could be granted this right. The imaginary narratives that have been offered have not been very creative or transformative but have frequently distracted from a meaningful notion of children's citizenship.

Speaking more directly to the concerns of authors in this chapter, the lack of a meaningful way of connecting natural citizens to actual government has remained a particularly significant issue because the Fourteenth Amendment to a large extent affirms the power of government. Consequently, it leaves unresolved many of the problems that Rousseau and Emerson were trying to remedy, such as children's unnatural subjection to the imaginary ideas of their books and the citizen's unnatural subjection to the law. On the one hand, the amendment addressed actual slavery and attempted to mend the gap between the right to natural freedom and the constraints set up by certain laws. It dramatically lessened the states' rights to make laws "which shall abridge the privileges or immunities of citizens of the United States." But, on the other hand, the amendment was a major exertion of legal force, a compelling demonstration of the power of artificial law to grant citizenship to whomever it chooses. Deak Nabers argues that Reconstruction actually led to a change in American popular opinion away from natural rights and toward the enshrining of the law as the guarantor of freedom: "What it means to be free, from the perspective of the Reconstruction amendments, is to be subject to the law *rather* than a human master. The Thirteenth Amendment, for instance, does not eliminate slavery altogether; it instead subordinates slavery to a legal procedure, prohibiting it, 'except as a punishment for crime whereof the party shall have been duly convicted.' "[148]

The Fourteenth Amendment works similarly. By making natural citizenship into a legal right, it suggests that nature is insufficient without the intervention of the law. What it means to be a natural citizen is, therefore, to be a citizen under the law—as the term "naturalization" makes abundantly clear in the case of immigrants. It thus becomes very important exactly how the law understands the relationship between government and citizens. Although the amendment resulted in a major change in laws regarding children's citizenship, it does not address the problems of how the citizen's natural rights should be adequately represented in law or language or how natural law should be read and respected. Instead it assumes that natural rights are self-evident. The amendment, therefore, has not eradicated the transformation through which "man is born free; and he is everywhere in chains." Making this transformation legitimate, as Rousseau knew, means accepting that this tension cannot be easily resolved and yet continuing to engage in the ongoing attempt to understand the political engagements of the child.

The Legacy of the Fourteenth Amendment

Limited Thinking on Children's Citizenship

A recent political cartoon by Pulitzer Prize–winning cartoonist Nick Anderson brings the historical periods that begin and end this book into the present day. The cartoon depicts a pilgrim family carrying an infant, and hiding in the bushes are two Native Americans in stereotypical dress, commenting "[expletive] Anchor babies!" The humor of this cartoon is easy to decode, but it is anachronistic in more ways than one, because children's citizenship prior to the Fourteenth Amendment was uncertain. The child in this image would likely have understood himself or herself as the subject of the English king, but, unlike the children to whom the derogatory term refers, this child would not have been firmly recognized as a citizen. This is partially because citizenship was not yet the colonists' primary way of understanding themselves, but it is also because the Fourteenth Amendment's argument that all individuals were citizens by birth had not yet been made.

By transporting the debates about "anchor babies" from the twenty-first century to the seventeenth, the cartoon leaves out the ways in which the interim period was a transformational with respect to children's citizenship—and perhaps easily so, since anachronism has characterized understandings of the amendment from the beginning. Those who supported the amendment declared that children were already citizens by nature as part of their goal of allowing former slaves to become citizens. While children's citizenship had never been more legally significant, the amendment largely tabled the issue of children's citizenship and deflected away from questions regarding children's political rights and responsibilities. Indeed, the declaration of children's natural citizenship has actually kept Americans from thinking about what the amendment—and citizenship—means for children, even when commentators are talking about "anchor babies." While questions surrounding children's citizenship have resurfaced in the current debates surrounding the Fourteenth Amendment and its conferral of citizenship on immigrant children, these debates tend to take children's citizenship for granted and to sideline actual children. The limited ways that citizenship is understood mask ongoing restrictions on children's rights, ignoring the rich potentials that their active citizenship might bring.

Natural Citizens as Child Citizens

The Fourteenth Amendment puts the child at the center of its definition of citizenship, seeming to offer a new understanding of both children's citizenship and citizenship in general. But, although the amendment is a compelling piece of legislation that has been applied in many important ways, its intervention into the political situation of children turns out to be much less radical than it appears at first glance. The logic of the amendment remarkably resembles the logic that informed imaginary citizenship from the beginning. Children are symbolically significant, but they remain marginalized. The amendment's declaration of children's citizenship by birth did not fundamentally change children's participation rights or even the participation rights of other excluded citizens.

The foremost significance of the law when it was passed was not the redefinition of citizenship through childhood. Instead it was the extension of citizenship to former slaves. Yet the citizen's new alignment with the child affected the way that this citizenship was understood. Though the amendment protected certain rights and proposed restrictions on representation for states that did not grant blacks the power of suffrage, it notably did not make consent through suffrage an official feature of citizenship. The primary part of the law emphasized the citizen's protection. Even though this was not insubstantial— especially because the law provides a due process for citizens that protects them from abuse of the law—this major feature did not immediately distinguish the law from patriarchal ideas of protection. Indeed, the law institutionalized an idea of citizenship that did not immediately entail the citizen's participation in government. This omission required the separate intervention of the Fifteenth Amendment, which was not fully enforced until the Civil Rights Act of 1964.

Protective rights were an improvement for former slaves, but the amendment arguably did not dramatically change the popular understanding of free blacks' political capacities. An article in the *New Englander and Yale Review* (1847), written prior to the Fourteenth Amendment, states that"in most of our states . . . [free blacks] *are recognized as citizens*, and protected in person, property, and reputation."[1] Even after the Fourteenth Amendment, the citizenship of African Americans continued to be understood in markedly childish and protective rather than participatory terms. When the Fifteenth Amendment granting suffrage was passed, it remained easy for many states to create ways of denying blacks the rights of citizenship based on their comparison with uneducated children or as individuals lacking the sufficient resources to have true independence.

The limitations of citizenship for former slaves and other free blacks were not lost on Congress or the American public. Senator John B. Henderson pointed out that arguments against suffrage for former slaves were based on the same comparisons with children that had enslaved them in the first place: "Until the child is twenty-one years of age the father has the power of correction and enjoys the fruits of his labor . . . Slavery proceeds from the same argument."[2] Henderson suggested that if blacks were granted suffrage, there would be no need to protect their rights in the Fourteenth Amendment, as they could protect their rights themselves. In reaction to the amendment's failure to include suffrage, another observer decried that "the black man is dealed citizenship, and kept in the dust," but he might as easily have complained that the amendment kept him in metaphorical childhood.[3] By choosing a common law notion of citizenship via *jus soli* over a consensual version of citizenship for former slaves, the amendment left potential comparisons between children and African Americans intact, even as it declared the citizenship of both for the first official time in U.S. history.

A literary version of the Fourteenth Amendment's combination of symbolic power with actual ineffectiveness can be found in Mark Twain's *The Adventures of Huckleberry Finn* (1885), which also ties together the former slave and child, suggesting that Jim and Huck have a common right to both humanity and citizenship. The clear villain, Huck's Pap, goes on a diatribe about blacks being able to vote, suggesting that the author to some extent sympathizes with voting rights for blacks.[4] Furthermore, the text casts the child Huck as an ideal citizen in the sense that he understands that slavery is morally wrong before the adults do.

Yet, as many critics have pointed out, the pairing of Jim and Huck is not necessarily good for the former slave, as it causes him to divert from the plan of crossing the Mississippi into a Illinois, instead sending him South deeper into slave territory.[5] At the end of the book, another child, Tom Sawyer, puts Jim through an elaborate play escape plan, failing to tell him that it is entirely imaginary and that he had been freed two months prior. The fact that *Huck Finn* was actually written after slavery ended also suggests that the imaginary narrative at the center of the text—escaping from slavery—is distanced from the reality of considering how former slaves can be citizens. Twain ends with Huck lighting out for the Western territories, meaning that the text can also avoid the question of how to address the fact that the child is a better citizen than the adults. Rather than failing at resolving these issues, I suspect that Twain was aware of the limitations of his book, reflecting the limitations of the culture's treatment of these issues in general.

Women also tested the limitations of the Fourteenth Amendment by using the citizenship clause to make the case that they should be allowed the vote. In the years preceding the amendment, women had used ideas about nature and natural law to argue for their equal citizenship. Like abolitionists, women also used images of natural freedom in their bids for suffrage; as Nancy Isenberg explains, "activists looked to the sky, mountains, and forests" and Elizabeth Cady Stanton even advocated walking in nature to challenge the division between the political sphere and the home.[6] But the Fourteenth Amendment's notion of natural citizenship was not initially compatible with women's arguments for enfranchisement. In fact, as Isenberg notes, "It was the first time the federal constitution explicitly associated the words 'suffrage' and 'citizenship' with 'male.'"[7] In the case of Virginia Minor, a St. Louis woman who tried to vote and was turned away from the polls, the Supreme Court declared that women were indeed natural citizens under the Fourteenth Amendment but that the "privileges and immunities" of this citizenship did not include voting.

Arguably, the amendment did ultimately contribute to women's cause, but the initial interpreters of the law made it clear that the citizenship established by the amendment did not include direct participation or recognition as citizens beyond basic protections. To gain participation rights, feminists have often had to separate themselves from children. As Mary Celeste Kerney has written about the emergent field of girl studies, "feminists have a lengthy tradition of uneasy identification, and sometimes disidentification with girls, which unfortunately has led many woman activists to believe, albeit unconsciously, that girls are irrelevant to feminist politics and scholarship."[8] Feminist ethics, which usefully emphasizes the insufficiency of rational independence as a model for citizenship, tends to focus more on thoughtful parenting than on children's own involvement.

For children, the struggle to be meaningfully recognized as citizens through legal recognition and participation rights is ongoing and will likely remain so due to children's need for dependence. As Peggy Cooper Davis has shown, the Fourteenth Amendment has been frequently interpreted by courts as giving parents the right to raise their children how they choose, not as giving children participation rights.[9] Beyond a short-lived campaign for such rights in the 1970s, the American public has been reluctant to fully embrace the idea that children might participate in government, choosing rather to focus on the worthy but limited goal of protecting children from harm. Michael Grossberg writes:

> Devising rights for children proved difficult because the existing concept of rights was designed only for adults who could assert their own claims directly against the state. Children could not do this, nor did reformers want them to. Instead

they fashioned an idea of paternalistic rights that defined children's rights in special age-bound terms of needs and parental failure instead of the individual autonomy associated with adult legal rights. Reformers did so by recasting education, socialization, nurture, and other fundamental needs of children as rights. In this way children's rights acquired a restrictive meaning.[10]

Provisions such as the UN Convention on the Rights of the Child have to some extent eroded the association of children's rights with dependence and participation rights with independence by declaring that dependent persons have a positive right to a nationality, free speech, and free assembly. Yet even the convention does not suggest that children should have any sort of direct role in politics. Furthermore, the United States is one of only two nations that have not ratified the UN Convention.

These circumstances suggest that, rather than setting the stage for a meaningful notion of children's citizenship, the Fourteenth Amendment, by making children nominal citizens without requiring their enfranchisement or any kind of involvement, in many ways disguises the remaining limitations on their ability to be represented beyond token means of inclusion. Barbara Bennett Woodhouse tells the story of a young boy named Tony who, on being taken against his will into state custody, pointedly questioned the usefulness of the Fourteenth Amendment in even protecting the rights of children, much less thoughtfully eliciting their participation: " 'Look here,' he said, pointing to the text of a pocket size U.S. Constitution I had given him. 'It says here "all persons born in the United States are citizens." And it says "nor shall any State deprive any person of life, liberty, or property." Ain't I a person? . . . Ain't I got rights?' "[11] The recent debates on "anchor babies" ironically derive from children's continued lack of political weight, as they emphasize immigrant children's role in getting their parents rights upon reaching adulthood, not their own status or rights as citizens. This assumption that children, while birthright citizens, are politically insignificant affects all children, not just immigrant children—and it is arguably reflected in the low turnout among young voters (still only 18 percent in the last presidential election).

The current claim by some conservatives that birth is not enough and that citizenship should legally require allegiance differently underestimates the child citizen.[12] By assuming that political affiliation is an issue involving only immigrants and not all children, commentators take children's citizenship for granted and take no opportunity to illicit their real consent or allegiance. Such arguments began with the debates surrounding the amendment as it was being debated in Congress, as critics immediately turned to discussing parents and casting children's citizenship as an issue specifically affecting certain segments of the population. Most dramatically, Senator Cowan, who had argued that citizenship was still a blurry term under the amendment, questioned the proposed rights of immigrant children: "Is the child of the Chinese immigrant in California a citizen? Is the child of a Gypsy born in Pennsylvania a citizen? If so, what rights have they?"[13] Cowan declared that he would see the inclusion of gypsy children as particularly "mischievous," since adult gypsies had no intention of entering the social contract, leaving little basis for their meaningful or productive citizenship.[14] Since the amendment was designed to address racial inconsistencies in citizenship, Cowan's viewpoint did not ultimately have a major impact on the bill. The children of Chinese immigrants (and presumably gypsies too) were included in the amendment's declaration of citizenship via *jus soli*, as would be made clear by a later court case, *United States v. Wong Kim Ark* (1898).[15] This case established that Ark, the American-born son of Chinese immigrants, was a citizen under the Fourteenth Amendment and could not be excluded based on the claim that nonnaturalized immigrants were not in the jurisdiction of the United States.

While Cowan's questions were clouded by his racial prejudices, the issue that he raised points to a larger question regarding children's political identity. Although he did not apply his argument that children should consent to white or African American children, he might just as easily have wondered how their investment in the nation and their ability to be good citizens would be elicited or measured, since the amendment provided no standard of knowledge, reason, or education in order to be a citizen. While such standards are in place for naturalization, the inclusion of such a standard for all children is likely unadvisable (one only has to be reminded of the literacy tests presented to former slaves to see the potential for abuse). Yet Americans have been left without a unified way of determining children's readiness for citizenship or preparing them to exercise it—things that could potentially lead to a greater access to politics for children who are ready for social engagement. The result has been that children's citizenship still resides in the gap between natural freedom and the exercise of it.

The Fourteenth Amendment and Civic Education

Because the Fourteenth Amendment's definition of citizenship was not based primarily on consent, the problem of how to secure citizens' loyalties persisted for children, as well as for former slaves and immigrants. Like Cowan, many nineteenth-century Americans feared that U.S. citizenship was wasted on these individuals because they were not sufficiently committed to American ideals, an argument that is currently being revived by some conservatives. Although the Fourteenth Amendment grants these groups citizenship anyway, lawmakers continued to use some of the same rationales for limiting minority citizens' rights as were used for limiting those of children. For instance, as Peter Schmidt has observed, politicians in the Jim Crow era sometimes argued that the citizenship rights guaranteed by the Fourteenth Amendment were not immediately available and "[could] only be given at an unnamed future date," after the individuals in question were sufficiently schooled in American language, politics, and values.[16]

Though some forms of civic education have been progressive in nature, emphasizing community awareness and involvement, others have emphasized discipline and loyalty. Methods of training new citizens have often overlapped with educational methods for training children, which quickly took a turn back toward the so-called unnatural modes that were popular in the early nineteenth century. Educators involved in postslavery literacy efforts frequently recommended the very books that were considered unsuitable by Rousseau and Emerson as the perfect material for former slaves. For instance, the spelling book returned with a vengeance in the late nineteenth century.

The emphasis on spelling books was due in part to slaves' own positive feelings about them. Douglass learned to read from such children's books as the *The Columbian Orator* and Webster's *American Spelling Book*, which were cast off by his master's son. Later, when teaching slaves in a Sabbath school on the Covey plantation, Douglass also uses "old spelling-books."[17] Though the young Auld boy presumably cast off his books because he has simply outgrown them, it is possible that spelling books were so often recommended (and available) for educating former slaves because they were out of fashion for white children by the 1850s. For Douglass these books were important because attaining literacy was largely a practical matter; he did not just want blacks to be natural citizens but to be citizens with an actual claim to rights—and this meant returning to arguments for their citizenship based on their ability to be rational and consenting citizens, a possibility that he associated with literacy. Emerson, when speaking to a group of African American orphans at an 1864 fair in Concord, painted a similarly powerful image of blacks using spelling books to gain political power: "American genius finds its true type—if I dare tell you—in the poor negro solider lying in the trenches by the Potomac, with his spelling book in one hand and his musket in the other."[18]

It is true that spelling books were considered as tools for attaining a free and literate citizenship. However, the fact that slaves were reading the very books that some antebellum educators associated with the unnatural subjection of all students suggests that literacy efforts for former slaves kept alive notions of the "republican machine" even as citizenship was being established as a natural thing and a right of birth. In this sense, it is not surprising that, as Lynn A. Casmier-Paz has found, literacy did not always fulfill its promise of providing slaves with freedom but instead reintroduced the problems of subjection to one's books that had long haunted American citizenship.[19] For many former slaves, being educated with spelling books was highly preferable to exclusion from literacy, and I would imagine that this remains true for minorities living in impoverished school districts. It has nonetheless meant, as Saidya Hartman has put forward, that arguments for black political inclusion have been frequently compatible with, and indeed dependent on, arguments for their subjection and assimilation—a claim that has in many ways remained true for children in general.[20]

It was not long before spelling books again became a fixture of all children's education. Critiques of the spelling book method in the late nineteenth century were largely limited to how to make it more effective and universal, rather than how to establish a more natural approach to training citizens. Signifying a change in public sentiment from the 1820s, Francis A. March wrote in 1880 that spelling was "part of the machinery of civilization and progress; and the amendment of it is seen to be like the improvement of other labor-saving machinery. It is doutful whether the invention of the steam-engin or the telegraf contributes as much to the welfare of man as would the invention and introduction of a good fonetic system of spelling."[21] (Since March was advocating for a new phonetic system of spelling that never took, his essay on spelling has several words misspelled.) The author of an 1881 article similarly hopes that "the time is coming when the ricketty old spelling-machine will be 'smashed,' and a beautiful reconstruction come into existence."[22] Though "reconstruction" is here referring to the author's dreamlike vision of a shiny new spelling machine based on a universal, rather than "whimsical," orthography, the nation's Reconstruction was similarly based on claims that children (especially minority children) needed to be uniformly trained as readers of language. These pedagogues' obsession with uniform spelling quickly found new expression in the argument that immigrants should know Standard English as a precondition for citizenship.

Though efforts to institute this requirement as law, as with spelling reform, have failed, childhood remains a battleground for ways of defining citizenship beyond the law. These debates have the potential to open up meaningful questions about how to encourage children's active consent and citizenship. Yet, all too often questions relating to national allegiance and political participation have been satisfied by rituals of empty patriotism rather than meaningful instruction or respect for children's actual wishes. While Julia Mickenberg has shown that progressive educators did (and still) advocate active and even radical civic education for children, the children's text that has arguably influenced current children's citizenship the most is the children's magazine *The Youth's Companion,* which put together a uniform program for children to learn and recite for the first national celebration of Columbus Day and simultaneously led a campaign to put American flags in every schoolhouse.[23] The most famous portion of the Columbus Day celebration is still recited by children today: the Pledge of Allegiance. The *Companion's* report on the event boasted, "The flag over the schoolhouses . . . impressed powerfully upon the youth that we are a nation. As the millions of pupils, with upturned faces and outstretched arms, saluted the nation's emblem in the same words,—'I pledge allegiance to my Flag, and to the Republic for which it stands: one Nation indivisible, with liberty and justice for all,' a lesson of thoughtful patriotism was taught which will never be forgotten."[24] The pledge's emphasis on univocality and indivisibility suggests a different form of children's citizenship than Emerson imagined, a common understanding of nation that is enforced not through identifying natural impulses for community, but through drilling. The pledge sounds like another answer to the problem of consent, giving children a chance to imaginatively agree to the government that has long been in place. However, its institution *after* the passage of the Fourteenth Amendment suggests that it is actually a form in which natural and imaginary citizenship come together through a basic lesson of language: the child, who is already a natural citizen, nonetheless pledges his allegiance to the imaginary symbols of nationhood and thereby perpetuates the fantasy that nature and nation are compatible, that the flag and the language of the pledge itself can actually stand for the natural entities of community and citizen. Despite the magazine's emphasis on what it called "thoughtful patriotism," discourse surrounding the pledge rarely considers exactly how the rights it mentions apply to children, and anyone who has heard children droning the pledge will likely observe that its pedagogical function does not encourage thinking.

Reimagining Children's Citizenship

Although children's citizenship remains a problem that was not solved even by an explicit declaration of their natural right to be citizens, this does not mean that children's citizenship should be dismissed as an impossible topic. In fact, one of the most important aspects of the Fourteenth Amendment is its admission that citizenship and childhood are not finally incompatible categories. Rather than seeing dependence, imagination, and inadequacy as external to citizenship, it is important to see these features as always internal to the problem of citizenship and to consider how they might be incorporated into responsible forms of citizenship. This is not a question with an easy answer and, instead of providing such answers, the significant work of this book has been to reframe the questions that can be asked regarding citizenship.[25] If we assume, like Locke, that citizens are free and rational, there is no opportunity to address the very real limits on citizenship. Likewise, if we either assume that children are and have always been citizens, but don't address their rights, or assume that they cannot be citizens, there is no chance of forging a meaningful understanding of citizenship that takes dependence and limitations into account. It is perhaps only by taking an honest look at citizenship's limits that its true potentials can be understood.

Some ideas toward alternate possibilities can be found in the history of debate surrounding children's citizenship. For instance, work by the English radical Thomas Spence, *The Rights of Infants; Or, the Imprescriptable Right of Mothers to such a Share of the Elements as is sufficient to enable them to suckle and bring up their Young* (1797), shows that the notion of children's imaginary citizenship had the potential to redefine ideas of social justice from around the time that it emerged. In this treatise, Spence stages a dialogue between a mother and a member of the aristocracy, in which the mother proposes a radical redistribution of wealth. The mother declares powerfully: "Ask the she-bears . . . and they will tell you what the rights of every species of young are.—They will tell you, in resolute language and actions too, that their rights extend to a full participation of the fruits of the earth . . . And seeing this, shall we be asked what the Rights of Infants are? As if they had no rights? As if they were excrescences and abortions of nature? As if they had not a right to the milk of our breasts?"[26]

Even though the rights of infants were not recognized legally in this period, except for a vague notion that the king protected them, they are used here to suggest legal changes that go beyond protection, nutrition, and nurturing to self-actualization and "full participation of the fruits of the earth." Spence goes on to propose that rents be distributed equally among the members of society, based on the number of children that they have, for their subsistence and their education. Notably, Spence was also involved in creating a phonetic form of spelling to help people learn to read, suggesting that he continued to see the ability to engage in imaginary forms of citizenship as a way to enact social reforms. For instance, he contended that if people of various classes could read and pronounce words similarly, they might be open to other forms of legal equality. Although Spence's proposed reforms were well before their time and did not become law, they represent the potential to change minds and perhaps ultimately change experiences, anticipating work by recent scholars such as Amartya Sen and Martha Nussbaum that seek to create a fuller notion of political rights.[27]

Building on these redefinitions of citizenship, it might be worth further considering how children, not just parents, can contribute to a model of politics based on mutual dependence and care. The foundations for alternative understandings of children's participation in activities related to citizenship can also be found in historical images of children as imaginary citizens, even as these images sought to bolster notions of adult agency and consent. For instance, in depicting children consenting to government and participating in the economy, the female authors and characters that I discuss in chapters 2 and 4 might be seen as advocating for a political society and economy based on love and compassion as much as on consent and self-interest, though they often presented these ideas as harnessed together. The argument that not only children but also citizens have a right to love and care—indeed, a right to dependence— disentangles the usual link between rights and independence and therefore has the potential to eradicate the reasons for distinguishing between legal and imaginary citizenship. The effect of this disentangling is that imagined claims to citizenship can become the basis for arguments for political change.

Ultimately, the group that stands to benefit the most from alternative ideas of citizenship is young people themselves. Notably, one of the major ways in which rational, consensual models of citizenship have failed is in inspiring the civic habits and practices of young people, who when finally given the chance to vote, do not largely choose to exercise this right. Although young voters aged eighteen to twenty-four have had better turnout in recent years than in the past, still only about 18 percent of eligible young voters voted in the presidential election in 2008.[28] It is perhaps because of the limitations of independent consent and participation in describing their experiences of citizenship that young people are so reluctant to trust civic opportunities when they arise. For instance, as James W. Loewen argues in *Lies My Teacher Told Me*, the uninspiring way in which history textbooks characterize citizenship has a negative effect on how young people interact (or rather, don't interact) in the political sphere: "Evidence suggests that history textbooks and courses make little impact in increasing trust in the United States or inducing good citizenship, however these are measured. Voting is one form of citizenship that the textbooks push, yet voting in America is way down, especially among recent high school graduates."[29]

Historically and currently, when children and young people have been involved in civic activities outside of voting, their actions have been particularly powerful.[30] A richer understanding of and respect for the imaginary dimensions of children's citizenship has the potential not only to invigorate their participation when they reach adulthood but also to revitalize and transform citizenship, offering a wider range of entry points for meaningful civic action and identification. An honest discussion of children's citizenship has the potential to make imaginary citizens realize that they are also real ones.

Introduction • From Subjects to Citizens

1. Samuel Goodrich, *The Tales of Peter Parley about America* (Philadelphia: Thomas, Cowpertwait, and Co., 1845), iii.

2. Ibid., 131.

3. See Daniel Roselle, *Samuel Griswold Goodrich, Creator of Peter Parley: A Study of His Life and Work* (Albany: State University of New York Press, 1968), vii.

4. "Merry's Monthly Chat with his Friends; Answers, Questions, Enigmas, Charades, etc. Hieroglyphical Rebus," *Merry's Museum and Parley's Magazine* (1856): 122. Lest anyone think these comments are entirely tongue in cheek, the magazine provided a forum for readers to tackle serious issues of political inequality; for instance, a letter by Alice B. Corner caused a stir when she implied that she (or any other young lady) would be a better president than Franklin Pierce.

5. Caroline F. Levander and Carol J. Singley, *The American Child: A Cultural Studies Reader* (New Brunswick: Rutgers University Press, 2003), 4.

6. Lauren Berlant, *The Queen of America Goes to Washington City: Essays on Sex and Citizenship* (Durham: Duke University Press, 2002), 23.

7. Barack Obama, "Full-Text Inauguration Speech," *MSNBC online.* www.msnbc.msn .com/id/28751183/.

8. For instance, while many politicians boasted about the possibilities of the "infant nation," one early commentator complained that President John Adams had tried to "hold her in safe leading-strings," stifling the development of a democratic government. E. M. Cunningham, *Correspondence between the Hon. John Adams, Late President of the United States, and the late William Cunningham, Esq.* (Boston: Published by E.M. Cunningham, 1823), vi.

9. Jay Fliegelman, *Prodigals and Pilgrims: The American Revolution against Patriarchal Authority, 1750–1800* (Cambridge: Cambridge University Press, 1985).

10. Gillian Brown, *The Consent of the Governed: The Lockean Legacy in Early American Culture* (Cambridge, MA: Harvard University Press, 2001).

11. Steven Mintz, *Huck's Raft: A History of American Childhood* (Cambridge, MA: Belknap Press of Harvard University Press, 2006); Caroline Cox, "Boy Soldiers of the American Revolution: The Effect of War on Society," in *Children and Youth in a New Nation,* edited by James Marten (New York: New York University Press, 2009), 13–28; and Vincent DiGiromalo, "In Franklin's Footsteps: News Carriers and Postboys in the Revolution and

Early Republic," in *Children and Youth in a New Nation*, edited by James Marten (New York: New York University Press, 2009), 48–66.

12. John Locke, *Two Treatises of Government*, edited by Peter Laslett (Cambridge: Cambridge University Press, 1988), 347.

13. Holly Brewer, *By Birth or Consent: Children, Law and the Anglo-American Revolution in Authority* (Chapel Hill: University of North Carolina Press, 2005). Brewer's work challenges essentialisms about children by suggesting that laws regarding their inability to engage in political activities such as voting and holding office by virtue of age were introduced only in the late seventeenth century.

14. See Rogers Smith, *Civic Ideals: Conflicting Visions of Citizenship in U.S. History* (New Haven: Yale University Press, 1997), for a detailed account of court cases and debates surrounding birthright citizenship in the early republic.

15. As Paul S. Boyer notes in his preface to *Children and Youth in a New Nation*, 2, "The median age in 1820 was 16.7 years: fully half of all citizens were under seventeen years of age. In 1860, the median age was still only 19.4. (In 2004, it stood at thirty-six.) In terms of numbers alone, to neglect the historical experience of children and youth in these years is to ignore 50 percent of the population."

16. Quoted in Hugh Amory. "Printing and Bookselling in New England, 1638–1713," in *The History of the Book in America*, vol. 1, *The Colonial Book in the Atlantic World*, edited by Hugh Amory and David D. Hall (Cambridge: Cambridge University Press, 2000), 51.

17. Sally Ripley, Manuscript Diary, August 9, 1800, and May 25, 1801; Edmund Quincy Sewall Jr., Manuscript Diary, April 14, 1838. Courtesy of American Antiquarian Society.

18. F. L. Mott, *A History of American Magazines*. vol. 3, *1865–1885* (Cambridge, MA: Harvard University Press, 1939), 6.

19. Cathy N. Davidson, *Revolution and the Word: The Rise of the Novel in America*, expanded ed. (Oxford: Oxford University Press, 2004), 24.

20. See "Conventions; The Convention Organized," *Merry's Museum and Parley's Magazine* (1856): 176–81.

21. See Nathan Tierney, *Imagination and Ethical Ideals: Prospects for a Unified Philosophical and Psychological Understanding* (Albany: State University of New York Press, 1994), 43.

22. I do not discuss the work of Jacques Lacan as it relates to theories of the imaginary here. However, the idea that literary images of citizenship encourage children to identify with a fuller and more powerful representation of themselves than they are able to actually achieve in their disempowered state bears some resemblance to Lacan's description of the mirror stage as an infant's way of coping with its fragmented and helpless body. Lacan's contention that the infant identifies with the image in the mirror as a way of gaining mastery might explain why the child reader is so eager to identify with imaginary depictions of citizens. See Jacques Lacan, *Écrits: The First Complete Edition in English*, translated by Bruce Fink (New York: Norton, 2006).

23. Michael Warner, *Letters of the Republic: Publication and the Public Sphere in Eighteenth-Century America* (Cambridge, MA: Harvard University Press, 1990), 173.

24. Benedict Anderson, *Imagined Communities: Reflections on the Origin and Spread of Nationalism* (London: Verso, 1983), 6.

25. Thomas Paine, *Common Sense* (Printed for the Perusal of the Inhabitants of the Thirteen United Colonies, 1776), 30.

26. Early work in the field of early American studies made the case for the importance of Puritanism in the development of American politics. See, for instance, Sacvan Bercovitch, *The Puritan Origins of the American Self* (New Haven: Yale University Press, 1975). Yet, recent work has broadened its understanding of how American politics developed, focusing on cultural variations according to region and ethnic descent.

27. Thomas Jefferson, "Letter to James Madison," quoted in *Jeffersonian Legacies*, edited by Peter S. Onuf (Charlottesville: University of Virginia Press, 1993), 283.

28. For an extensive discussion of how concerns about childhood indexed national anxieties, see Anna Mae Duane, *Suffering Childhood in Early America: Violence, Race, and the Making of the Child Victim* (Athens: University of Georgia Press, 2010).

29. See, for instance, *The Child's New Play-Thing: Being a Spelling-Book Intended to Make the Learning to Read a Diversion instead of a Task* (Boston: Printed by J. Draper, for J. Edwards in Cornhill, 1750). 73.

30. Berlant, *Queen of America*, 52.

31. Philippe Ariès, *Centuries of Childhood: A Social History of Family Life*, translated by Robert Baldick (New York: Vintage, 1962).

32. See Linda Pollock, *Forgotten Children: Parent-Child Relations from 1500 to 1900* (Cambridge: Cambridge University Press, 1983), as well as recent work on the children's culture of the medieval and Renaissance periods, including Daniel Kline, ed., *Medieval Literature for Children* (New York: Routledge, 2003), and Andrea Immel and Michael Whitmore, eds., *Childhood and Children's Books in Early Modern Europe, 1550–1800* (New York: Routledge, 2006).

33. While it is beyond the scope of this introduction to elaborate on how the concept of childhood emerged in Europe, I would suggest that a more extensive discourse of childhood was tied to the emergence of modern theories of citizenship in places other than England and the United States. As I discuss in chapter 3, American representations of the French revolutionaries associated their vision of citizenship with childishness. And, as I discuss in chapter 5, French political philosopher Jean-Jacques Rousseau was intensely concerned with how the child comes to be a citizen. Ariès also implies that a connection exists between citizenship and childhood in France; he opens *Centuries of Childhood* with a discussion of how modern ideas of "civil status" require that individuals know exactly how old they are. Ariès, *Centuries of Childhood*, 15.

34. Brewer, *By Birth or Consent*, 2.

35. See ibid., 48.

36. Sir Robert Filmer, *Patriarcha and Other Writings*, edited by P. Sommerville (Cambridge: Cambridge University Press, 1991), 10.

37. The argument that children are miniature adults derives from Ariès's analysis of sixteenth- and seventeenth-century children's portraits and continues to be repeated by writers of textbooks about child psychology and the sociology of the family. See, for instance, David M. Newman and Liz Grauerholz, *Sociology of Families* (London: Sage Publications, 2002), 364, and H. Rudolph Schaffer, *Introducing Child Psychology* (Oxford: Blackwell Publishing Ltd., 2004), 21.

38. Smith, *Civic Ideals*, 45.

39. Locke, *Two Treatises*, 349.

40. Ibid., 349.

41. Richard Baxter, *A Christian Directory* (London: Printed by Robert White for Nevill Simmons, 1673), 19.

42. Brewer, *By Birth or Consent*, 2.

43. Ibid., 27.

44. Ibid., 348.

45. John Locke, *Some Thoughts Concerning Education*, edited by Ruth W. Grant and Nathan Tarcov (Indianapolis: Hackett Publishing, 1996).

46. Duane, *Suffering Childhood*, 128.

47. Elisa New, "'Both Great and Small': Adult Proportion and Divine Scale in Edward Taylor's 'Preface' and *The New England Primer*," *Early American Literature* 28 (1993): 121.

48. New, "Both Great and Small," 122. Of course, this was a status that could be to some extent chosen by adults, where children were forced to be understood as dependent.

49. Étienne Balibar, "Citizen-Subject," in *Who Comes after the Subject?* edited by Eduardo Cadava, Peter Connor, and Jean-Luc Nancy (New York: Routledge, 1991), 42. In this work, Balibar explains that the connection between God and king in absolute monarchy produces a split loyalty among the people, giving rise to dissent: "Absolute monarchy in particular develops a contradiction that can be seen as the culmination of the conflict between the temporal power and the spiritual power . . . the person (the 'body') of the king must be divided: into divine person and human person. And obedience correlatively."

50. John Bunyan, *Divine Emblems: or, Temporal Things Spiritualized* (Philadelphia: Printed by James Carey for Matthew Carey, 1794), iii.

51. Ibid., iv. Notably, the *Oxford English Dictionary* traces the contemptuous use of "child" and "baby" to describe a foolish person to the late sixteenth and seventeenth centuries, though child to describe an immature person was used much earlier.

52. Locke, *Some Thoughts Concerning Education*, 117.

53. Benjamin Keach, *Instructions for Children: or, The Child's & Youth's Delight* (New York: Printed and sold by Will. Bradford at the Bible in New-York, 1695), 1.

54. Keach, *Instructions for Children*, 9. The child's reflection echoes First Corinthians 13:11 in the King James version of the Bible, "When I was a child, I spake as a child, I understood as a child, I thought as a child: but when I became a man, I put away childish things."

55. David D. Hall, *Cultures of Print: Essays in the History of the Book* (Amherst: University of Massachusetts Press, 1996), 57. These books appeared regularly in booksellers' advertisements and inventories. There is also evidence that the circulation of children's books was likely even larger than booksellers' lists indicate, as people took it for granted that they would be available.

56. Benjamin Rush, *A Plan for the Establishment of Public Schools and the Diffusion of Knowledge in Pennsylvania* (Philadelphia: Printed for Thomas Dobson, 1786), 3.

57. Susanna Rowson, *Charlotte: A Tale of Truth* (Philadelphia: Printed for Matthew Carey, 1794), 36, and Catharine Maria Sedgwick, *Hope Leslie, or Early Times in Massachusetts* (Piscataway: Rutgers University Press, 1987), 348.

58. Quoted in George Eliot, *Middlemarch*, edited by Karen Chase (Cambridge: Cambridge University Press, 1991), 92.

59. See Beverly Lyon Clark, *Kiddie Lit: The Cultural Construction of Children's Literature in America* (Baltimore: Johns Hopkins University Press, 2005).

60. Quoted in Nina Baym, *Novels, Readers, and Reviewers' Responses to Fiction in Antebellum America* (Ithaca: Cornell University Press, 1984), 49.

61. Balibar, "Citizen-Subject," 39.

62. Ibid., 45, 49.

63. Ibid., 44–45.

64. Caroline Levander, *Cradle of Liberty: Race, the Child, and National Belonging from Thomas Jefferson to W. E. B. Du Bois* (Durham: Duke University Press, 2006), 4.

65. Étienne Balibar, "The Nation Form: History and Ideology," in *Race, Nation, Class: Ambiguous Identities*, edited by Étienne Balibar and Immanuel Wallerstein (London: Verso, 1991), 93.

66. Warner, *Letters of the Republic.*

67. Noah Webster, "On the Education of Youth in America," in *Essays on Education in the Early Republic*, edited by Frederick Rudolph (Cambridge, MA: Belknap Press of Harvard University Press, 1965), 65.

68. Berlant, *Queen of America*, 27–28.

69. Louis Althusser, "Ideology and Ideological State Apparatuses," in *Literary Theory: An Anthology*, edited by Julie Rivkin and Michael Ryan (Malden, MA: Blackwell Publishers, 1998).

70. Brook Thomas, *Civic Myths: A Law-and-Literature Approach to Citizenship* (Chapel Hill: University of North Carolina Press, 2007), 9.

71. Althusser, "Ideology and Ideological State Apparatuses," 300, 303.

72. Thomas, *Civic Myths*, 9.

73. Ibid.,10.

74. Marah Gubar, "Peter Pan (1904) as Children's Theater: The Issue of Audience," in *The Oxford Handbook of Children's Literature*, edited by Julia L. Mickenberg and Lynne Vallone (Oxford: Oxford University Press, 2011), 478.

75. M. O. Grenby, *The Child Reader: 1700–1840* (Cambridge: Cambridge University Press, 2011), 10.

76. Ibid.

77. Ibid. The introduction to Grenby's book provides valuable insight about how to conduct further research on this topic.

78. Pat Pflieger, "An 'Online Community' of the Nineteenth Century," *Nineteenth-Century Children and What They Read.* www.merrycoz.org/papers/online/online.htm.

79. *Merry's Museum, Parley's Magazine, Woodworth's Cabinet and the Schoolfellow*, vols.35–36 (New York: J. N. Sterns and Company, 1858), 127.

80. *Merry's Museum*, vols. 35–36, 59. For a transcription of all of the letters to Merry's Museum, see Pat Pflieger, *Letters from Nineteenth-Century American Children to* Robert Merry's Museum Magazine (Lewiston, NY: Mellen Press, 2001).

81. David Clapp, Manuscript Diary, July 1823. Courtesy of the American Antiquarian Society.

82. Edmund Quincy Sewall Jr., Manuscript Diary, April 4, 1838. Courtesy of the American Antiquarian Society.

83. *Merry's Museum*, vols.35–36, 61.

84. Ibid.

85. Locke considered madness a disorder of the imagination. See John Locke, "Memory—Imagination—Madness," in Lord King, *The Life of John Locke with Extracts from His Correspondence, Journals, and Common-Place Books* (London: Henry Colburn, 1829), 326–29.

86. Davidson, *Revolution and the Word.*

87. Lorinda B. Cohoon, *Serialized Citizenships: Periodicals, Books, and American Boys 1840–1911* (Lanham, MD: Scarecrow Press, 2006). Cohoon's work perhaps shows the per-

vasiveness and influence of children's imaginary citizenship by the 1840s, a period in which children's citizenship actually became more of a mainstream concept and mode of citizenship. As we will see in later chapters, gender does seem to have also shaped the concept of imaginary citizenship; since girls were doubly excluded from rights and in special need of alternative representation in the social body, many of the foremost representations of imaginary citizens are girls. Yet, it is important to note that boys' citizenship also operated in the realm of the imaginary—a point that previous work on children's citizenship has tended to obscure. While their gender may have given them special privileges related to schooling, mobility, and public speaking, boys also faced limits on their liberties. Frederick Douglass, in fact, pointed out that boyhood resembled slavery, only with a potentially more satisfying end date: he observed to a group of boy workers in the shipyards, "You will be free, as soon as you are twenty-one, *but I am a slave for life!*" See Frederick Douglass, *Narrative in the Life of Frederick Douglass, An American Slave, Written by Himself,* in Douglass, *Autobiographies,* edited by Henry Louis Gates (New York: Library of America, 1994), 41.

88. Berlant, *Queen of America,* 48.

89. Karen Sánchez-Eppler, *Dependent States: The Child's Part in Nineteenth-Century American Culture* (Chicago: University of Chicago Press, 2005). Many of the essays in Monika Elbert's recent anthology, *Enterprising Youth: Social Values and Acculturation in Nineteenth-Century American Children's Literature* (New York: Routledge, 2008), make similar claims.

90. Locke, *Two Treatises,* 308.

91. Alison Gopnik, *The Philosophical Baby: What Children's Minds Tell Us about Truth, Love, and the Meaning of Life* (New York: Picador, 2010).

92. Ruth Lister, "Unpacking Children's Citizenship," in *Children and Citizenship,* edited by Antonella Invernizzi and Jane Williams (London: Sage Publications, 2008), 15.

93. Annette C. Baier, *Moral Prejudices: Essays on Ethics* (Cambridge, MA: Harvard University Press, 1995).

94. Ibid., 30.

Chapter 1 • Youth as a Time of Choice

Epigraph. Solomon Williams, *The True State of the Question Concerning the Qualifications Necessary to Lawful Communion in the Christian Sacraments. Being an Answer to the Reverend Mr. Jonathan Edwards* (Boston: Printed and sold by S. Kneeland, 1751), 3.

1. See *Children in Colonial America,* edited by James Marten (New York: New York University Press, 2007), 235–37, for a critical history of scholarship on Puritan attitudes toward their children.

2. The literacy law gave the selectmen of each village the power to inspect households to make sure that children were being taught to read, to catechize them, and to set up schools. See Edmund S. Morgan, *The Puritan Family* (New York: Harper and Row, 1966), 88.

3. Kenneth Lockridge, *Literacy in Colonial New England; An Enquiry into the Social Context of Literacy in the Early Modern West* (New York: Norton, 1975). E. Jennifer Monaghan has argued that signatures do not provide a full picture of literacy in America, because people were generally taught to read before they were taught to write. Monaghan does not discuss the chance that some of those who could sign might have been functionally illiterate. See Monaghan, "Literary Instruction and Gender in Colonial New England," in *The Book*

History Reader, edited by David Finkelstein and Alastair McCleery (New York: Routledge, 2002).

4. See Holly Brewer, *By Birth or Consent: Children, Law, and the Anglo-American Revolution in Authority* (Chapel Hill: University of North Carolina Press), 49. As she explains, "The meaning of consent was worked out first in religious writings, particularly those about baptism and about conscience. . . . Many argued that only through understanding could a person exercise the choice necessary for conversion and faith."

5. Brewer, *By Birth or Consent,* 343.

6. Similar restrictions governed African slaves living in the colonies; Cotton Mather may have been thinking about the Halfway Covenant when he declared in *The Negro Christianized* (Boston B. Green, 1706) that baptism did not equal liberty and therefore was no threat to owners' rights.

7. In this way, white children had a much higher position than other supposedly nonrational persons. Mather actually suggests that white children could be employed by busy masters to teach their slaves. Children thus enjoyed some sense of symbolic and even privileged membership, even if they did not have the ability to weigh in on the matters most important to the community. As Dana Nelson notes in *The Word in Black and White: Reading "Race" in American Literature, 1638–1867* (Oxford: Oxford University Press, 1994), Mather's diaries suggest that his children successfully catechized the family's slave, Onesimus.

8. *The New England Primer Enlarged for the True Reading of English. To Which is Added, Milk for Babes* (Boston: Printed by S. Kneeland & T. Green, 1727), 68.

9. Brewer, *By Birth or Consent,* 79.

10. Jean-François Gilmont, "Protestant Reformation and Reading," in *A History of Reading in the West,* edited by Guguelmo Cavallo and Roger Chartier (Amherst: University of Massachusetts Press, 2003), 220.

11. See Ibid., 236.

12. Ian Green, *The Christian's ABC* (Oxford: Clarendon Press, 1996), 104.

13. Robert Filmer, *Patriarcha and Other Writings,* edited by P. Somerville (Cambridge: Cambridge University Press, 1991), 8.

14. Ibid., 41, 57.

15. Ibid., 2, 37, 39.

16. Brewer, *By Birth or Consent,* 20–21.

17. Ibid., 20.

18. At the same time, as Patricia A. Crain has argued, the letters can only attempt to pin down the range of interpretations and uses to which language might be put. The whims, innovations, and limitations of early printers often meant that religious meanings like the ones implied in the Adam couplet might be complicated by printers' inclusion of aberrant images, such as those associated with tavern signs (such as the Cat with the Fiddle). See Crain, *The Story of A: The Alphabetization of America from the* New England Primer *to* The Scarlet Letter (Stanford: Stanford University Press, 2000), 48–49. See also Courtney Weikle-Mills, "'My Book and Heart Shall Never Part': Reading, Printing, and Circulation in the *New England Primer,*" in *The Oxford Handbook to Children's Literature,* edited by Julia Mickenberg and Lynne Vallone (Oxford: Oxford University Press, 2011). The role of printers in creating these texts might itself be seen as a sign that language was not entirely controlled by fathers. Brown too points out that the pictures and the text might not mix, subtly giving children the opportunity to consider an interpretation of their meaning together. Brown argues that texts such

as the *Primer* therefore led to the notion that the people, including children, were capable of perceiving God and the law apart from the rule of the king. See Gillian Brown, *The Consent of the Governed: The Lockean Legacy in Early American Culture* (Cambridge, MA: Harvard University Press, 2001), 37–39.

19. See Lawrence A. Cremin, *American Education: The Colonial Experience 1607–1783* (New York: Harper and Row, 1970), 156.

20. See Sargent Bush, Jr., *The Correspondence of John Cotton* (Chapel Hill: University of North Carolina Press, 2001), 458.

21. For their part, later Puritans, such as Increase and Cotton Mather, were more likely to support the king, since the original charter had by that point been revoked and the king's support was needed to protect the Puritans from interference, but their goal remained religious sovereignty, even if they had no hope of political sovereignty. See Bruce Tucker, "The Reinvention of New England, 1691–1770," *The New England Quarterly* 59.3 (1986): 315–40. Though Cotton's catechism was included in one of the earliest extant editions of the *New England Primer* (1727), the king does appear in the *Primer*'s alphabetic couplet, "Our King the Good / No Man of Blood." Later, however, it was replaced by "Kings Should Be Good / Not Men of Blood" in the 1779 *Newest American Primer* (Philadelphia: Printed by Styner and Cist, 1779) and "The British King / Lost States Thirteen" in the 1788 New York edition (New York: Printed by S. Loudon, 1788).

22. Jay Fliegelman, *Prodigals and Pilgrims: The American Revolution against Patriarchal Authority, 1750–1800* (Cambridge: Cambridge University Press, 1985); and Brown, *The Consent of the Governed*.

23. Cotton Mather, *Cares about the Nurseries* (Boston: Printed by T. Green for Benjamin Eliot, 1702), 18. Mather might seem overly optimistic about children's access to printed books, especially in light of David D. Hall's caution that paper was expensive in colonial America and only the affluent were able to afford large libraries. However, Hall's evidence on book ownership suggests that the majority of families did come into contact with certain books. His research on Middlesex County, Massachusetts, suggests that two-thirds of homes owned the Bible and 60 percent had a few other books, including a catechism and primer. See David D. Hall, "Readers and Writers in Early New England," in *A History of the Colonial Book in America: The Colonial Book in the Atlantic World*, edited by Hugh Amory and Hall (Chapel Hill: University of North Carolina Press, 2007), 124. See also, Hall, *Cultures of Print: Essays in the History of the Book* (Amherst: University of Massachusetts Press, 1996), 57. "Most persons," Hall argues, "had the use of, or owned, a Bible, psalmbook, primer and catechism." Hall's list reveals a particular emphasis on children's piety, since the latter two books were often explicitly addressed to child readers. Matthew P. Brown's *The Pilgrim and the Bee: Reading Rituals in Early New England* (Philadelphia: University of Pennsylvania Press, 2007) has also shown that New England preachers assumed that their congregations had access to religious books and encouraged them to engage in text-based rituals on their own.

24. Cotton Mather, *The Religion of the Closet* (Printed by T. Fleet, & T. Crump, for Samuel Gerrish, 1715).

25. The term *closet* was used as early as the sixteenth century in this context; see, for example, in Angel Day's comment in the *The English Secretorie* (London: Printed by Peter Short for C. Burbie, 1599) that "We doe call the most secret place in the house appropriate unto our owne private studies . . . a Closet." Historians have documented that, as the seventeenth

century progressed, there was increasing division of the home into private and individualized spaces: "Closets for prayer, private chapels for private masses, cabinets for reading and storing collectibles and oddities." See Cecile M. Jagodzinski, *Privacy and Print: Reading and Writing in Seventeenth-Century England* (Charlottesville: University Press of Virginia. 1999), 13.

26. Cotton Mather, *The Young Man Spoken To* (Boston: Printed by T. Green for Samuel Gerrish, 1712), 42.

27. Cotton Mather, *Early Religion* (Boston: Printed by Benjamin Harris for Michael Perry, 1694), 48.

28. Although many books would have been read by entire families, often in group settings or family worship, references in the literature of the period suggest that children were beginning to read and own some books individually. See Mather, *The Young Man Spoken To*, 9, where he claims that parents who do not provide individual Bibles for their children are "worse than sea-monsters." See also James Janeway and Cotton Mather, *A Token for Children. To Which is Added, A Token for the Children of New England* (Boston: Printed for Nicholas Boone, 1700), 66. In *Token*, several dying children bequeath their books as legacies to other children in the family. For example, Tabitha Alder leaves her Bible and a few other books to her mother and little sister. The period also gave rise to specialized children's books such as *Token* and Thomas White's *A Little Book for Little Children* (Boston: Reprinted, by T. Green, for Benjamin Eliot, 1702), which may have been more widely available than many books for adults. For instance, even though Hall cautions that books were scarce, he admits that he may underestimate ownership of certain types of books, such as those written for children, because he relies on largely on probate inventories. Cheaper, unbound books, such almanacs, schoolbooks, and catechisms, may not have been considered valuable enough to be listed (additionally, as probate inventories were conducted after the owner had died, books owned as a child were often long gone or destroyed). Thus, the circulation of these books may be even larger than indicated in the inventories. One might easily imagine a situation in which this would be the case: American printers were forbidden to print Bibles by law, so orders for children's books, such as catechisms and primers, would have been a crucial part of overall revenue in the colonies. The wide circulation of books for children suggests that they may have provided booksellers with a consistent source of income in an otherwise risky business, and, in fact, made it possible for printing and bookselling to thrive. According to Hall, when Boston bookseller Michael Perry died in 1700, schoolbooks constituted one-fifth of his total stock, about 1,200 copies. See Hall, "Readers and Writers in Early New England," 125. Such large figures suggest that the profits from children's books probably even helped to fund orders for less popular books.

29. Mather, *Early Religion*, 40.

30. Mather, *The Wonders of the Invisible World* (Boston: Printed by Benjamin Harris for Sam Phillips, 1693), 66.

31. Mather, *Early Religion*, 21.

32. Ibid., 40. See also Cotton Mather, *The Best Ornaments of Youth* (Boston: Printed and sold by Timothy Green, 1707), 6. Notably, Mather specifically equates the phrase "young man" with "child": "A Young Man, I call him; and I will tell you Why. He was not an Infant: For there was Notice taken of what was in him. He was not of Full Age: For he is called, A Child. He must then be a Young Man."

33. Mather, *Early Religion*, 71. Mather may have based his opinion of such children's capacities on his own life: he was reading fifteen chapters of the Bible by age seven or eight

and he entered Harvard at age twelve. See David Levin, *Cotton Mather* (Cambridge, MA: Harvard University Press, 1978), 11.

34. Janeway and Mather, *A Token for Children*, no page number.

35. Ibid., no page number.

36. Monaghan, "Family Literacy in Early 18th-Century Boston: Cotton Mather and His Children," *Reading Research Quarterly* 26.4 (1991): 355.

37. Mather, *The Religion of the Closet*, 20. Only White expresses doubt over the question of children's closet reading, suggesting that children not "take a Book" into the closet—but he explains that this is only because he wants children into the closet even faster: "I by no means forbid you, but would have Children use to go alone to Pray before they could either read or speak plain." See White, *A Little Book for Little Children*, 17.

38. Quoted in Thomas M. Davis, "The Exegetical Traditions of Puritan Typology," 29.

39. White, *A Little Book for Little Children*, 19.

40. Monaghan, "Family Literacy," 350. There is evidence that readers treasured these books and saw them as personal property; many of the copies owned by the American Antiquarian Society are signed with the names of their owners. Some of Mather's books, such as his reading instructional text, *Good Lessons for Children*, have not survived to the present day, suggesting that they were read to tatters.

41. A broadside of George Burder's *The Closet Companion* (Boston: Printed and sold by Manning & Loring, 1798), which was meant to be "fixed up in the Christian's usual place of retirement," made this image into a literal reality—though it perhaps shows that, by the late eighteenth century, authors placed a little less trust in readers to structure their private reveries around the texts themselves. The broadside emphasizes more than Mather that its "dear readers" must use the evidence contained in the scripture as a stable measure against their own behavior—that they must be interpreted in light of the text, not the text in light of them.

42. Mather, *The Religion of the Closet*, 20.

43. Though Mather's concept of the power of the texts was also based on the emergence of developmental science. Theories of the mind in this period, such as those proposed by John Locke, understood the child's mind as a blank page that could be inscribed through exposure to various experiences and texts. See Locke, *Essay Concerning Human Understanding* (Boston: Printed by David Carlisle for Thomas & Andrews, 1803).

44. Thomas Brooks, *The Privie Key to Heaven; Or Twenty Arguments for Closet Prayer* (London: Printed for John Hancock, 1665), 81.

45. Cotton Mather, *The Pure Nazarite: Advice to a Young Man, Concerning an Impiety and Impurity (Not Easily Spoken Of) Which Many Young Men Are to Their Perpetual Sorrow, Too Easily Drawn Into* (Boston: Printed by T. Fleet for John Phillips, 1723), 3.

46. Although William J. Gilmore argues that many New Englanders did not distinguish between oral and print communication at first and saw both as controlled by religious authorities, Mather's work demonstrates an attempt to separate these two arenas. See Gilmore, *Reading Becomes a Necessity of Life: Material & Cultural Life in Rural New England, 1780–1835* (Knoxville: University of Tennessee Press, 1989), 36. See also Mather, *Early Religion*, 3–6. Many of Mather's books were printed versions of his sermons; he often calls attention to the printed medium, as if to educate people about how to see print as a separate genre. For instance, in Mather, *Things that Young People Should Think Upon* (Boston, in N. E. Printed by B. Green, & J. Allen, 1700), 7–8, originally given to a "young Auditory," he calls attention to print arrangement by reflecting on one of the "greatest Paragraphs in the BIBLE" and

capitalizing phrases such as "BOOK" and "WORD." Mather also frequently used metaphors related to the alphabet, printing, and grammar, showing that he viewed his sermons for children as reading lessons as well as religious lessons. In the same sermon he contrasts the inevitability of death with the mutability of printed language: "What one says of the Grammarian, may be said of every Child of Adam, That being able to Decline all other Nouns in every Case, he can Decline Death in no Case at all."

47. Mather, *The Pure Nazarite*, 5.

48. Ibid., 15.

49. Others, especially Baptists, who had a vested interest in proving children's ineptitude since they wanted to deny baptism to children, may have been more concerned about children's poor interpretations. For instance, a prominent exchange in Benjamin Keach, *Instructions for Children: or, The Child's & Youth's Delight* (New York: Printed and sold by Will. Bradford at the Bible in New-York, 1695), 9, goes as follows:

> FA. What hast thou learned, or dost thou know of God?
> CH. I am a Child, and know but a little; I understand as a Child, and think as a Child.
> FA. Does thou not understand my Question?
> CH. I fear I do not . . .
> FA. Who is God?
> CH. I do not know very well; is it not an old Man?

Though the child's claim that God is an "old man" is in many ways a fitting answer given the patriarchal comparison between God and all fathers, it is also blasphemy and a sign that the child is not yet capable of understanding.

50. *The New-England Primer Enlarged*, 62.

51. Sometimes attributed to Thomas Bewick, *Little King Pippin* was published in at least nine editions in early America between 1786 and 1800.

52. *The History of Little King Pippin; with an Account of the Melancholy Death of Four Naughty Boys, who were Devoured by Wild Beasts* (Philadelphia: Printed and sold by Young, Stewart, and M'Culloch, 1786), 24–25.

53. Ibid.

54. Ibid., 26.

55. Cotton Mather, *Little Flocks Guarded against Grievous Wolves* (Boston: Printed by Benjamin Harris, & John Allen, 1691), no page number.

56. Ibid., 13–14, 5, 12, 14.

57. George Keith, *A Serious Appeal to All the More Sober, Impartial & Judicious people in New-England to whose Hands this May Come, whether Cotton Mather in his Late Address, &c. Hath Not Extreamly Failed in Proving the People Call'd Quakers Guilty of Manifold Heresies, Blasphemies and Strong Delusions* (Philadelphia: Printed and sold by William Bradford, 1692), 1.

58. Mather, *Little Flocks*, 17.

59. Ibid.

60. Ibid., no page number.

61. Ibid., 26, 6, 32.

62. Mary Rowlandson, *The Soveraignty & Goodness of God; Being a Narrative of the Captivity and Restauration of Mrs. Mary Rowlandson* (Cambridge, MA: Printed by Samuel Green, 1682), 46.

63. Mather, *The Young Man Spoken To,* 9.

64. Mather, *The Religion of the Closet,* 34, and *The Young Man Spoken To,* 39.

65. Mather, *Cares about the Nurseries,* 24–25.

66. *The Compleat Scholler, or Relation of the Life, and Latter-End Especially, of Caleb Vernon* (London: Printed for J.W. and W.S., 1666), no page number.

67. Janeway and Mather, *A Token for Children,* 17.

68. Later versions of this text, likely erroneously, attribute it to Janeway. Early versions attribute it to Cartaret's mother, Sarah.

69. Elizabeth is listed in the *A Report of the Records Commission of the City of Boston Containing Boston Births from AD 1600 to AD 1800* (Boston: Rockwell and Churchill, City Printers, 1894), 60.

70. See Judith S. Graham, *Puritan Family Life: The Diary of Samuel Sewall* (Boston: Northeastern University Press, 2003).

71. *Early Piety, Exemplified in Elizabeth Butcher of Boston, who was born July 14th 1709 and died July 13th 1718. Being Just Eight Years and Eleven Months Old* (Boston: Printed by S. Kneeland, for Samuel Gerrish, 1725), 2. It is worthy of note that, by the eighteenth century, reading in bed was considered a slovenly practice, as Jacqueline Pearson documents in *Women's Reading in Britain 1750–1835* (Cambridge: Cambridge University Press, 1999), 169.

72. Janeway and Mather, *A Token for Children,* 21.

73. White, *A Little Book for Little Children,* 4.

74. *Early Piety,* 15.

75. Sarah Rede, *A Token for Youth, Or Comfort to Children Being the Life & Christian Experience of the Wonderful Workings of the Spirit of God on Cartaret Rede* (Boston: Reprinted and Sold by Bartholomew Green, 1729), 9.

76. Janeway and Mather, *A Token for Children,* 51.

77. *The Compleat Scholler,* no page number.

78. Rede, *A Token for Youth,* no page number.

79. *A Legacy for Children: Being Some of the Last Expressions, and Dying Sayings, of Hannah Hill, Juris of the City of Philadelphia, in the Province of Pennsylvania, Aged 11 Years and Near 3 Months* (Philadelphia: Printed by Andrew Bradford, 1717), 22.

80. Rede, *A Token for Youth,* 11.

81. White, *A Little Book for Little Children,* 60–71.

82. Janeway and Mather, *A Token for Children,* 15.

83. Ibid., 11.

84. Ibid., 6.

85. White, *A Little Book for Little Children,* 76.

86. Janeway and Mather, *A Token for Children,* 119–20.

87. Ibid., 123.

88. Both quotations are from Mather, *The Religion of the Closet,* 13.

89. See, for instance, Fliegelman, *Prodigals and Pilgrims.*

90. Sereno E. Dwight, vol. 1 of *The Works of President Edwards: With a Memoir of His Life* (New York: S. Converse, 1829), 110.

91. William Cooper, introduction to *Jonathan Edwards, The Distinguishing Marks of a Work of the Spirit of God* (Boston: Printed and sold by S. Kneeland and T. Green, 1741), ix.

92. Jonathan Edwards, *A Faithful Narrative of the Surprising Work of God in the Conver-*

sion of Many Hundred Souls in Northampton (Elizabeth-Town, NJ: Printed by Shepard Kollock, 1790), 36.

93. William Rand, *The Late Religious Commotions in New-England Considered* (Boston: Printed by Green, Bushell, and Allen, for T. Fleet in Cornhill, 1743), 5.

94. Robert Hamlett Bremner, ed. *Children and Youth in America, 1600–1865* (Cambridge, MA: Harvard University Press, 1970), 131.

95. Rand, *The Late Religious Commotions*, preface, 18. Rand's congregation took part in the Awakening anyway and he was dismissed in 1745 for his opposition.

96. Bremner, *Children and Youth*, 131–32.

97. More recent historians have questioned accounts such as Bremner's that argue for large and lasting political effects of the Awakening. See James F. Cooper Jr., "Enthusiasts or Democrats? Separatism, Church Government, and the Great Awakening in Massachusetts," *The New England Quarterly* 65.2 (1992): 265–83.

98. Rand, *The Late Religious Commotions*, Preface 10.

99. Ibid., 24–25, 5, 31.

100. Ibid., 31–32. Definitions paraphrased from the *Oxford English Dictionary.*

101. This famous line appears in Jonathan Edwards, *Some Thoughts Concerning the Present Revival of Religion in New-England* (Boston: Printed and sold by S. Kneeland and T. Green, 1742), 163–64.

102. Ibid., 185–86.

103. Ibid., iv.

104. T.H. Breen and Timothy Hall, "Structuring Provincial Imagination: The Rhetoric and Experience of Social Change in Eighteenth-Century New England," *American Historical Review* 103.5 (1998), 1428.

105. Edwards, *Some Thoughts Concerning the Present Revival*, 154; Jonathan Edwards, *A Treatise Concerning Religious Affections* (Boston: Printed for S. Kneeland and T. Green, 1746), 5.

106. Edwards, *A Treatise Concerning Religious Affections*, 19–20.

107. Jonathan Edwards, *An Humble Inquiry into the Rules of the Word of God* (Boston: Printed & sold by S. Kneeland, 1749), 4–5.

108. Ibid., 1.

109. Williams, *The True State of the Question*, 3.

110. Dwight, *The Works of President Edwards: With a Memoir of His Life*, 1:305.

111. Ibid., 1:300, 1:306.

Chapter 2 • *Affectionate Citizenship*

Epigraphs. George Washington, "Farewell Address," in *American State Papers: Documents, Legislative and Executive of the Congress of the United States* (Washington, DC: Gales and Seaton, 1832), 1:35, and "From the Charleston Courier," *Weekly Visitor, or Ladies' Miscellany.* 3.43 (1805): 339.

1. *The Child's New Play-Thing: Being a Spelling-Book Intended to Make the Learning to Read a Diversion instead of a Task* (Boston: Printed by J. Draper, for J. Edwards in Cornhill, 1750), 73.

2. See, for instance, Lawrence Stone, *The Family, Sex and Marriage in England, 1500–1800* (New York: Harper & Row, 1979), and Jay Fliegelman, *Prodigals and Pilgrims: The American*

Revolution against Patriarchal Authority, 1750–1800 (Cambridge: Cambridge University Press, 1985).

3. Although Locke was not the only thinker who played a part in redefining political subjectivity, he was a major figure whose influence on the nation's founders has been well established. See Bernard Bailyn, *The Ideological Origins of the American Revolution* (Cambridge: Harvard University Press, 1967), 27, for an account of Locke's influence on American Revolutionary thought. Though this chapter identifies Locke as a key figure in the early American politics of childhood and citizenship, I do not attempt to contradict Bailyn, J. G. A. Pocock, and others who considered that the founders were influenced by republican as much as Lockean liberal thought. I would suggest, rather, that, as they were embraced in the United States, Locke's theories are not as distinct from republican theory as is often claimed. In fact, the internal tensions within Locke's system, as Rogers Smith has argued, often allowed readers "to graft onto it elements of quite different political outlooks." See Rogers Smith, *Civic Ideals: Conflicting Visions of Citizenship in U.S. History* (New Haven: Yale University Press, 1997), 1. Locke's underlying theory of affectionate citizenship provided early Americans with a particular means of merging the strains of liberal and republican political theory, since affection was compatible both with republican notions of self-sacrifice and civic feeling and with liberal ideals of consent and private identification with national narratives. I join with scholars who have argued that classical liberal and republican ideas cannot be fully understood as separate in this period. See, for instance, Elizabeth Dillon, *The Gender of Freedom: Fictions of Liberalism and the Literary Public Sphere* (Stanford: Stanford University Press, 2004), 143.

4. Michael Warner, *Letters of the Republic: Publication and the Public Sphere in Eighteenth-Century America* (Cambridge, MA: Harvard University Press, 1990).

5. Lauren Berlant, *The Queen of America Goes to Washington: City Essays on Sex and Citizenship* (Durham: Duke University Press, 2002), 5.

6. Ibid.

7. Warner, *Letters of the Republic*, 73.

8. Noah Webster, "On the Education of Youth in America," *Essays on Education in the Early Republic*, edited by Frederick Rudolph (Cambridge, MA: Belknap Press of Harvard University Press, 1965), 65.

9. Benedict Anderson, *Imagined Communities: Reflections on the Origin and Spread of Nationalism* (London: Verso, 1983), 15.

10. John Tebbel, *A History of Book Publishing in the United States*, vol. 1, *The Creation of an Industry* (New York: R. R. Bowker, 1972), 190.

11. John Locke, *Two Treatises of Government*, edited by Peter Laslett (Cambridge: Cambridge University Press: 1988), 142.

12. Ibid., 347.

13. Ibid., 142, 323.

14. Ibid., 308.

15. Thomas Paine, *Common Sense* (Printed for the Perusal of the Inhabitants of the Thirteen United Colonies, 1776), 30.

16. Holly Brewer, *By Birth or Consent: Children, Law and the Anglo-American Revolution in Authority* (Chapel Hill: University of North Carolina Press, 2005).

17. Lesley Ginsberg, "Of Babies, Beasts, and Bondage: Slavery and the Question of Citizenship in Antebellum American Children's Literature," in *The American Child: A Cultural*

Studies Reader, edited by Caroline F. Levander and Carol J. Singley (New Brunswick: Rutgers University Press, 2003), 91.

18. Nancy Isenberg, *Sex and Citizenship in Antebellum America* (Chapel Hill: University of North Carolina Press, 1998), 23–24.

19. Locke, *Two Treatises*, 177.

20. Ibid., 304, 307.

21. Locke, *An Essay Concerning Human Understanding*, 85.

22. Locke, *Two Treatises*, 325.

23. Thomas, *Civic Myths*, 9.

24. Locke, *Two Treatises*, 308.

25. Gillian Brown, *The Consent of the Governed: The Lockean Legacy in Early American Culture* (Cambridge, MA: Harvard University Press, 2001), 29.

26. Locke, *Two Treatises*, 304.

27. Ibid.,353.

28. Ibid., 342.

29. Ibid., 318.

30. See Anthony Ashley-Cooper, Third Earl of Shaftesbury, *An Inquiry Concerning Virtue or Merit* (Manchester: Manchester University Press, 1977).

31. Francis Hutcheson, *Essay on the Nature and Conduct of the Passions and Affections. With Illustrations on the Moral Sense* (London: Printed for A. Ward, 1742).

32. David Shields, *Civil Tongues and Polite Letters in British America* (Chapel Hill: University of North Carolina Press, 1997), xvi.

33. Paine, *Common Sense*, 24.

34. Revolutionary Political Cartoon, unknown author and date.

35. Paine, *Common Sense*, 18.

36. Thomas Paine, *Rights of Man* (Oxford: Published by Printed for J.S. Jordan, 1791), 9.

37. Paine, *Common Sense*, 23.

38. Ibid., 48. Emphasis added.

39. John Locke, *Some Thoughts Concerning Education*, edited by Ruth W. Grant and Nathan Tarcov (Indianapolis: Hackett Publishing, 1996), 112.

40. Ibid., 109.

41. Ibid., 109–10.

42. Ibid., 209.

43. See, for instance, Samuel F. Pickering, *John Locke and Children's Books in Eighteenth-Century England* (Knoxville: University of Tennessee Press, 1981).

44. Seth Lerer, *Children's Literature: A Reader's History, from Aesop to Harry Potter* (Chicago: University of Chicago Press, 2008), 105–6.

45. Jean-Jacques Rousseau, *Émile, or, On Education*, translated by Barbara Foxley (New York: Everyman Paperbacks, 1993), 92.

46. Patricia A. Crain, *The Story of A: The Alphabetization of America from the* New England Primer *to* The Scarlet Letter (Stanford: Stanford University Press, 2000), 86.

47. Ibid., 65.

48. Holbrook Jackson, *The Anatomy of Bibliomania* (New York: Charles Scribner's Sons, 1934), 188.

49. Richard and Maria Edgeworth, *Practical Education* (New York: J. F. Hopkins, 1801), 62.

50. *The Renowned History of Giles Gingerbread* (Worchester: Isaiah Thomas, 1786), 17.

51. Ibid., 20.

52. Noah Webster, *The American Spelling Book: Containing, an Easy Standard of Pronunciation.* (Hartford: Printed by Hudson and Goodwin, 1788), viii.

53. *The Renowned History of Giles Gingerbread,* 31.

54. Many children's books bill themselves as a parent or sibling's "gift" to a younger family member, including *The Mother's Gift, The Father's Gift, The Brother's Gift,* and *The Sister's Gift.* In his *Sermons to Young Women* (New York: Published by M. Carey in Philadelphia and I. Riley in New York, 1809), 43, James Fordyce presents himself as an affectionate "brother" to his young female readers, even though writers like Jane Austen later ridicule him for his patronizing tone.

55. Though Locke's tutor was explicitly male, the feminization of authority here is not coincidental. The significance of children's affections in the narrative of citizenship enabled women, particularly mothers and mother surrogates, to appear frequently as governing agents, crucial for transitioning the child's love from maternal bodies to the nation itself. Locke himself makes the case for women's domestic authority in *Two Treatises* by pointing out that the fifth commandment, which had traditionally been read only to apply to fathers, also affords power to mothers. As Linda K. Kerber has suggested in *Women of the Republic: Intellect and Ideology in Republican America* (Chapel Hill: University of North Carolina Press, 1997), female "governess" figures such as the "republican mother" gained particular authority in the eighteenth century, though their power was contingent on the ultimate transfer of authority from parent to law. Accordingly, as *The Governess* progresses, Teachum becomes distant, representational, and abstract as an authority figure.

56. Mary Kelley, *Learning to Stand and Speak: Women, Education, and Public Life in America's Republic* (Chapel Hill: University of North Carolina Press, 2006), 17.

57. The right to vote varied by state, but all states had property requirements until the 1830s. Between 10 and 80 percent of white men might have been considered eligible to vote. In certain states, such as New Jersey, women and black men could vote from 1776 to 1807.

58. Sally Ripley, Manuscript Diary, July 29, 1799. Courtesy of the American Antiquarian Society.

59. Kelley, *Learning to Stand and Speak,* 51.

60. M. O. Grenby, *The Child Reader: 1700–1840* (Cambridge: Cambridge University Press, 2011), 60.

61. Ibid., 55.

62. Ripley's diary indicates that she read all of these types of books both in school and at home. Sixteen-year-old Charlotte Sheldon also read several of these types of books and even translated Rousseau's *Émile.* See Sheldon, *Diary of Charlotte Sheldon, May, 1796, in Chronicles of a Pioneer School from 1792 to 1833, Being the History of Miss Sarah Pierce and Her Litchfield School,* edited by Emily Noyes Vanderpoel and Elizabeth C. Barney Buel (Cambridge, MA: Harvard University Press, 1903). See also Martin Brückner, *The Geographic Revolution in Early America: Maps, Literacy, and National Identity* (Chapel Hill: University of North Carolina Press, 2006), for an account of how geography textbooks were used to teach boys and girls about politics.

63. Sarah Fielding, *The Governess; or Little Female Academy* (London: Printed for A. Millar, 1749), 13. Sarah was the sister of noted author, Henry Fielding.

64. Ibid., ix.

65. Ibid.

66. This posture toward readers in texts may actually indicate an expansion and diversification of readership. As Patrick Brantlinger points out in *The Reading Lesson: The Threat of Mass Literacy in Nineteenth-Century British Fiction* (Bloomington: Indiana University Press, 1998), 15, the appeals to "dear reader" in the eighteenth and nineteenth novels are likely an attempt to reduce "the mass reading public to manageable size, providing the illusion, at least, of individual proximity and cooperation."

67. Their univocal consent stems from the eighteenth-century's intense interest, explored by Locke and others, in the process by which the individual's "free" consent to governance makes one voice out of many. American educators were explicitly concerned with even minute details of the reading experience, such as pronunciation, so that individual readers could represent a united nation of readers. This effort can be seen most readily in the attempt to standardize American pronunciation in reading, casting readers as citizens who embody unified consent to citizenship through their univocal reading. In its eleventh edition by the time *The Governess* was first printed in the United States, Noah Webster's *The American Spelling Book: Containing, an Easy Standard of Pronunciation* (Providence: Printed by John Carter, 1789), was advertised as going "very far towards demolishing all the odious distinctions occasioned by provincial dialects."

68. Fielding, *Governess*, 6.

69. Ibid., 25.

70. Ibid., 38, 40.

71. Ibid., 44.

72. See James Marten, *Children and Youth for a New Nation* (New York: New York University Press, 2009), for a number of examples.

73. Fielding, *Governess*, 43.

74. Ibid., 72.

75. Ibid., 74.

76. See, for instance, "Epitome of Boulanger's *Enquiry into the Origin of the Despotism of Oriental Governments*," *The Gentleman and Lady's Town and Country Magazine* 1 (1784): 5. The author writes, "The monarchs of the East have been always represented as the arbitrary sovereigns of the fate of those whom they govern; and their subjects as slaves destined from their birth to an abject vassalage, equally mortifying and deplorable."

77. There is evidence that despite stereotypes, American lawmakers took a relatively balanced view toward Muslims in the early nation. According to Denise Spellberg, early American congressmen departed from "the master narrative, which historically conflated the adherents of Islam as a collective of foreigners synonymous with despotic rulers [and] oppressed subjects" to create "a new definition of Muslims as individuated persons with the rights of citizens." See Spellberg, "Could a Muslim be President? An Eighteenth-Century Constitutional Debate," *Eighteenth-Century Studies* 39.4 (2006): 485–508.

78. Fielding, *Governess*, 86.

79. Ibid., 105.

80. Ibid., 145.

81. For example, Jennifer Desiderio's dissertation, "'To Collect, Digest, and Arrange': Authorship in the Early American Republic, 1792–1801," PhD Diss., Ohio State University, 2004, argues that Foster instructs her child readers to become monitorial authors.

82. Hannah Webster Foster, *The Boarding School* (Boston: I. Thomas and E. T. Andrews, 1798), 9.

83. Ibid., 11.

84. Ibid.

85. Warner, *Letters of the Republic*, 62.

86. Foster, *Boarding School*, 67.

87. Ibid., 24.

88. Ibid., 125, 179.

Chapter 3 • Child Readers of the Novel

Epigraphs: Ahimaaz Harker, *A Companion for the Young People of North America* (New York: Printed by J. Holt, at the Exchange, 1767), and *Journal of William Maclay, United States Senator from Pennsylvania, 1789–1791*, 89.

1. See Daniel I. O'Neill. "John Adams versus Mary Wollstonecraft on the French Revolution and Democracy," *Journal of the History of Ideas* 68.3 (2007): 451–76.

2. John Adams and Abigail Adams, *Adams Family Correspondence*, edited by L.H. Butterfield (Cambridge, MA: Belknap Press of Harvard University Press, 1963–73), 370.

3. Rogers Smith, *Civic Ideals: Conflicting Visions of Citizenship in U.S. History* (New Haven: Yale University Press, 1997), 138.

4. Holly Brewer, *By Birth or Consent: Children, Law and the Anglo-American Revolution in Authority* (Chapel Hill: University of North Carolina Press, 2005), 135.

5. Thomas Hobbes, *Leviathan; Or the Matter, Form, and Power of a Commonwealth, Ecclesiastical and Civil* (London: George Routledge and Sons, 1886), 95.

6. Quoted in Brewer, *By Birth or Consent*, 135.

7. Amy L. Elson, "Ex Parte Crouse," *Encyclopedia of Children and Childhood in History and Society*, edited by Paula S. Fass. www.faqs.org/childhood/Ke-Me/Law-Children-and-the .html.

8. As Jared Gardner argues in "The Literary Museum and the Unsettling of the Early American Novel," *ELH* 67.3 (2000): 743–71, early American novels are necessarily both ideological *and* subversive, due to their structure.

9. Julia Stern, *The Plight of Feeling: Sympathy and Dissent in the Early American Novel* (Chicago: University of Chicago Press, 1997), 9.

10. Samuel Richardson, *Pamela; or, Virtue Rewarded* (London: Printed for Harrison and Co., 1786), iii.

11. William Hill Brown, *The Power of Sympathy: or, The Triumph of Nature* (New York: Penguin Books, 1996), 5; *The History of Constantius & Pulchera* (Boston, 1794), v; and Susanna Rowson, *Charlotte: A Tale of Truth* (Philadelphia: Printed for Matthew Carey, 1794), v, and *Monima, or The Beggar Girl* (New York: Printed by P.R. Johnson, for I. N. Ralston., 1802), iii.

12. Cathy N. Davidson, *Revolution and the Word: The Rise of the Novel in America*, expanded ed. (Oxford: Oxford University Press, 2004), 188.

13. Rodney Hessinger, *Seduced, Abandoned, and Reborn: Visions of Youth in Middle-Class America, 1780–1850* (Philadelphia: University of Pennsylvania Press, 2005), 5.

14. Davidson, *Revolution and the Word*, 139.

15. The argument that novels are primarily subversive becomes less convincing when we

notice that novelists themselves are responsible for creating and perpetuating warnings about such works of fiction. For instance, Susanna Rowson's *Mentoria; or the Young Lady's Friend* (Philadelphia: Printed for Robert Campbell by Samuel Harrison Smith, 1794), maintains that novel reading a self-indulgent act, motivated by excessive passions and base appetites. But oddly, in spite of the potential danger of romantic stories, Mentoria gives her charges a large collection of love letters (not included for the reader's perusal), which she calls "a school for lovers." It seems strange that a presumably well-meaning governess would give her young charges what she sees as the most dangerous kind of reading that a young girl can have, an observation substantiated by her decision not to make the letters available for Rowson's actual child reader. This strategy demonstrates symbolically the many ways in which bad reading, rather than an external threat, was already *internal* to the project of educating citizens.

16. Davidson, *Revolution and the Word*, 134.

17. Child novel readers have been overlooked in part because studies of this activity have often focused on subscription lists, which do not list ages. While it seems unlikely that many subscribers would have been children due to their limited financial resources, there is some evidence that children bought individual titles and had access to books borrowed from circulating libraries. This latter finding is significant because circulating libraries have been assumed to be the purview mostly of middle- and upper-class adult men. Yet a letter-writing book written by Noah Webster includes samples in which children discuss visiting these libraries and selecting books. Though more work is needed to establish the frequency of children's library use, circulating libraries may have been one of many ways that children would have had access to novels.

18. John Tebbel, *A History of Book Publishing in the United States*, vol. 1, *The Creation of an Industry* (New York: R.R. Bowker, 1972), 145.

19. Mary Kelley, introduction to Catharine Maria Sedgwick, *Hope Leslie, or, Early Times in Massachusetts*, edited by Mary Kelley (New Brunswick: Rutgers University Press, 1987), xvii.

20. Ripley, Manuscript Diary. Notably, Sally reads these books in defiance of *Bennett's Letters*, which, as she notes in her diary, warned against young people's reading novels. Though she does not answer Bennett explicitly, she flags each of the above texts explicitly as "a novel."

21. Some of the children mark slight differences between "child" and "juvenile." For instance, Ripley writes on her thirteenth birthday that she is now in her "juvenile" years. Yet Sally still reads children's books after this event. Lydia Maria Child, writing in 1831, also makes clear that teens were understood at least partially as children: "Children, especially girls, should not read anything without a mother's knowledge and sanction; this is particularly necessary between the ages of twelve and sixteen, when the feelings are all fervent and enthusiastic, and the understanding is not strengthened by experience and observation." See Child, *The Mother's Book* (Boston: Carter and Hendee, 1831), 92. All of these readers were well below the average marriage age of twenty-two or twenty-three cited by Davidson. In the nineteenth century, children's status as novel readers continued; fan letters number children among the readers of nearly all of the most popular novels, such as *The Lamplighter*, *The Wide Wide World*, *Our Nig*, and *Uncle Tom's Cabin*. A reader from this period, Ella Gertrude Thomas, at age fourteen in 1848, observes "I have no novels to read. I wish that it were possible for me to refrain from reading one for six months or a year. I am confident I could study much better." See *Secret Eye: The Journal of Ella Gertrude Clanton Thomas, 1848–1889*, edited

by Virginia Ingraham Burr (Chapel Hill: University of North Carolina Press, 1990), 77. See also essays by Elizabeth Nichols and Mary Kelley in *Reading Acts: U.S. Readers' Interactions with Literature, 1800–1950*, edited by Barbara Ryan and Amy Thomas (Knoxville: University of Tennessee Press, 2002), and Susan S. Williams, "'Promoting an Extensive Sale': The Production and Reception of *The Lamplighter*," *The New England Quarterly*. 69.2 (1996): 179–200.

22. M. O. Grenby, *The Child Reader: 1700–1840* (Cambridge: Cambridge University Press, 2011), 114.

23. Rowson, *Charlotte: A Tale of Truth*.

24. Ala Alryyes, *Original Subjects: The Child, The Novel, and The Nation* (Cambridge: Harvard University Press, 2001), 122.

25. William Sullivan, *The Political Class Book* (Boston: Richardson, Lord, and Holbrook, 1830), 94.

26. Karen Sánchez-Eppler, *Dependent States* (Chicago: University of Chicago Press, 2005).

27. Sullivan, *The Political Class Book*, 94.

28. Nancy Isenberg, *Sex and Citizenship in Antebellum America* (Chapel Hill: University of North Carolina Press, 1998), 23.

29. John Locke, *Two Treatises of Government*, edited by Peter Laslett (Cambridge: Cambridge University Press: 1988), 307.

30. Quoted in Grenby, *The Child Reader*, 48.

31. Michael Grossberg, "Children and the Law," *Encyclopedia of Children and Childhood in History and Society*, edited by Paula S. Fass. www.faqs.org/childhood/Ke-Me/Law-Children-and-the.html.

32. Isenberg, *Sex and Citizenship*, 25.

33. "On Novel-Reading," *The Atheneum; or, Spirit of the English Magazines* 4.2 (1818): 60.

34. Isenberg, *Sex and Citizenship*, 23.

35. See Davidson, *Revolution and the Word*, 154, for a discussion of Brown's status as the first American novelist.

36. Thomas Paine, *Common Sense* (Printed for the Perusal of the Inhabitants of the Thirteen United Colonies, 1776), ii.

37. Ibid., 19.

38. William Hill Brown, *The Power of Sympathy: or, The Triumph of Nature* (New York: Penguin Books, 1996), 10.

39. Ibid., 9.

40. American editions of these works include Philip Dormer Standhope Chesterfield, *Letters Written by the Late Right Honourable Philip Dormer Stanhope, Earl of Chesterfield, to His Son, Philip Stanhope, Esq* (New York: Printed by J. Rivington and H. Gaine, 1775); John Gregory, *A Father's Legacy to His Daughters* (New York: Printed by Shober and Loudon, in Maiden-Lane, for Samuel Loudon, at Hunter's-Quay, 1775); and Hannah Chapone, *Letters on the Improvement of the Mind. Addressed to a Young Lady* (Boston: Printed for Isaiah Thomas at Worcester, 1783).

41. Brown, *Power of Sympathy*, 11, 13.

42. Marquis Caraccioli, *Advice from a Lady of Quality to Her Children; in the Last Stage of a Lingering Illness*, translated by S. Glasse (Newbury-port, MA: Printed by John Mycall, for William Green at Shakespeare's Head, Boston, 1784); Noah Webster, *A Grammatical*

Institute of the English Language (Hartford: Printed by Hudson & Goodwin, for the author, 1783); Johann Wolfgang von Goethe, *The Sorrows and Sympathetic Attachments of Werther; a German Story* (Philadelphia: Printed and Sold by Robert Bell, 1784).

43. Brown, *Power of Sympathy*, 81.

44. Ibid., 14, 94, 97.

45. Elizabeth Maddock Dillon, "The Original American Novel; Or, the American Origin of the Novel," in *A Companion to the Eighteenth-Century English Novel and Culture,* edited by Paula R. Backscheider and Catherine Ingrassia (Hoboken: Wiley-Blackwell, 2005), 253.

46. Brown, *Power of Sympathy*, 92.

47. Paine, *Common Sense*, 16.

48. Brown, *Power of Sympathy*, 62.

49. Ibid., 63.

50. Homi K. Bhabha, "Introduction: Narrating the Nation" in *Nation and Narration,* edited by Bhabha (London: Routledge, 1990), 4.

51. Brown, *Power of Sympathy*, 11.

52. Ibid., 11, 18.

53. Ibid., 34.

54. Locke, *Two Treatises,* 304.

55. John Adams, Letter to John Taylor, April 15, 1814.

56. Brown, *Power of Sympathy*, 20, 21.

57. Ibid., 22, 20–21.

58. Ibid., 23.

59. Ibid.

60. Ibid., 57.

61. Ibid., 1.

62. Charles Downer Hazen, *Contemporary American Opinion of the French Revolution* (Baltimore: Johns Hopkins Press, 1897), 168.

63. Ibid., 218.

64. Ibid., 219.

65. Ibid., 184.

66. Alexander Graydon, *Memoirs of a Life; Chiefly Passed in Pennsylvania* (Harrisburg, PA: Printed by John Wyeth, 1811), 335.

67. George Gibbs, *Memoirs of the Administrations of Washington and John Adams* (New York: William Van Norden, 1846), 1:134. Quoted in Hazen, *Contemporary American Opinion,* 204.

68. Quoted in Hazen, *Contemporary American Opinion,* 278.

69. Royall Tyler, *The Algerine Captive* (London: Printed for G. and J. Robinson, 1802), 47.

70. Susanna Rowson, *The Fille de Chambre* (Philadelphia: Printed for H. & P. Rice, no. 50, High-Street; and J. Rice & Co. Market-Street, Baltimore, 1794), 66.

71. Alexis de Tocqueville, *Democracy in America,* translated by Arthur Goldhammer (New York: Library of America, 2004), 685.

72. Hannah More, *Strictures on the Modern System of Female Education* (Boston: Printed for Joseph Bumstead, 1802), 134–35.

73. See Steven Mintz, *Huck's Raft: A History of American Childhood* (Cambridge, MA: Belknap Press of Harvard University Press, 2006), 53–74.

74. Edgeworth and Edgeworth, *Practical Education*, 285.

75. Joseph Dennie, "Shall I Liken This Generation? It is Like Unto Children," *The Port-Folio.* 1.45 (1801): 355.

76. Ibid.

77. Tabitha Gilman Tenney, *Female Quixotism*, edited by Jean Neinkamp and Andrea Collins (Oxford: Oxford University Press, 1992), 3.

78. Ibid., 93

79. Christopher Looby, *Voicing America: Language, Literary Form, and the Origins of the United States* (Chicago: University of Chicago Press, 1996), 1.

80. Tenney, *Female Quixotism*, 78.

81. Ibid., 316.

82. Joseph Dennie, "The Lay Preacher: The Fashion of this World Passeth Away," *The Port-Folio* 3.36 (1803): 281.

83. Tenney, *Female Quixotism*, 57.

84. Ibid., 77.

85. Elson, "Ex Parte Crouse."

86. Michael Grossberg, "Children and the Law," *Encyclopedia of Children and Childhood in History and Society*, edited by Paula S. Fass. www.faqs.org/childhood/Ke-Me/Law-Children-and-the.html.

87. Ibid.

88. Quoted in ibid.

89. Tenney, *Female Quixotism*, 281.

90. Elizabeth Barnes, *States of Sympathy: Seduction and Democracy in the American Novel* (New York: Columbia University Press, 1997), 43.

91. Tenney, *Female Quixotism*, 104.

92. Ibid., 297.

93. Sánchez-Eppler, *Dependent States*, 71.

94. Tenney, *Female Quixotism*, 3.

95. Ibid.

96. Aman Garcha, *From Sketch to Novel* (Cambridge: Cambridge University Press, 2009), 40.

97. See, for instance, Michael Warner, "Irving's Posterity," *ELH* 67 (2000): 773–99.

98. Washington Irving, *The Sketch Book of Geoffrey Crayon, Gent.* (New York: Dodd, Mead and Company, 1954), 354.

99. Ibid., 356.

100. Mary Wollstonecraft, *Thoughts on the Education of Daughters* (London: Printed for J. Johnson, 1787), 3.

101. J. B. C., "The Genius and Writings of Washington Irving," *The American Whig Review* 6 (1850): 608.

102. Quoted in "Review: Washington Irving," *The New-York Mirror. A Weekly Gazette of Literature and Fine Arts* 2 (1824): 70.

103. Ibid., 70.

104. Terrence Martin, "Rip, Ichabod and the American Imagination," in *Washington Irving: The Critical Reaction*, edited by James W. Tuttleton (New York: AMS Press, 1993), 59, argues that Ichabod is marked as childlike due to his propensity to swallow anything, but that "growing up involves learning what not to swallow, in every sense of the word."

105. Irving, *Sketch Book*, 383.

106. Washington Irving, *Salmagundi* (New York: Literary Classics of the United States, 1983), 146.

107. Irving, *Sketch Book*, 208.

108. Ibid., 383.

109. Ibid., 384.

110. Henry Longfellow, Extract from "Resolutions upon the Death of Irving," in *Life of Henry Wadsworth Longfellow* (Boston: Ticknor and Co., 1886), 12.

111. "Books of the Week," *Literary World* 5 (1849): 128.

112. Homer B. Sprague, ed., *Six Selections from Irving's Sketch-Book, with Notes, Questions, Etc. for Home and School Use* (Boston: Ginn and Co. Publishers, 1898).

113. Ibid., 165.

114. Amanda B. Harris, *American Authors for Young Folks* (Boston: Lothrop Publishing Company: 1887).

115. Ibid., 11–12, 18, 280.

116. J. B. C., "The Genius and Writings of Washington Irving," 607.

117. Irving, *Sketch Book*, 57.

118. Ibid., 16.

119. Ibid., 129.

120. Ibid., 30, 46.

121. In general, crayons were not associated with children until the 1890s, a transition that might have happened partially as a result of the text's transformation into a children's book.

122. Harris, *American Authors for Young Folks*, 24.

123. Edgeworth and Edgeworth, *Practical Education*, 113.

124. Irving, *Sketch Book*, 2.

125. Later, Irving's vision of the imaginative liberties of childhood was especially appealing to a post–Civil War generation of American writers such as Mark Twain, Thomas Aldrich, and William Dean Howells, who associated boyhood, not adulthood, with freedom. It is no coincidence that the two imaginative stories, "Rip" and "Sleepy Hollow," became the most frequently reprinted tales in the late nineteenth century, appearing in large, colorful editions. This generation viewed Ichabod not as a satirical figure representing the nation's childishness, but as a ridiculous old man from whom every boy might easily rebel. As a reflection of his newfound age, he gets much larger and more sinister in illustrations.

Chapter 4 • *Reading for Social Profit*

Epigraphs. "The Love of Reading in Children," *Common School Assistant; a Monthly Paper, for the Improvement of Common School Education.* 1.4 (1836): 29; Lydia Maria Child, *The Mother's Book* (Boston: Published by Carter, Hendee and Babcock, 1831), 93.

1. *The Exhibition of Tom Thumb, Being an Account of Many Valuable and Surprising Curiosities which He Has Collected in the Course of His Travels, for the Instruction and Amusement of the American Youth* (Worcester, MA: Isaiah Thomas, 1787), 49.

2. Ibid.

3. Ibid., title page.

4. David Paul Nord, "Benevolent Books," in *An Extensive Republic: Print, Culture, and Society in the New Nation, 1790–1840*, vol. 2 of *A History of the Book in America* series, edited by Robert A. Gross and Mary Kelley (Chapel Hill: University of North Carolina Press, 2010), 229.

5. For historical accounts of these changes, see both *An Extensive Republic*, cited above, and Scott E. Casper, Jeffrey D. Groves, Stephen W. Nissenbaum, and Michael Winship, eds., *The Industrial Book, 1840–1880*, vol. 3 of *A History of the Book in America* (Chapel Hill: University of North Carolina Press, 2007).

6. Anne Scott Macleod, *American Childhood: Essays on Children's Literature of the Nineteenth and Twentieth Centuries* (Athens: University of Georgia Press, 1996), 89.

7. For some accounts of actual children's economic participation, as well as its fictive representation, see, for instance, Karen Sánchez-Eppler, "Playing at Class," in *The American Child: A Cultural Studies Reader*, edited by Caroline F. Levander and Carol J. Singley (New Brunswick: Rutgers University Press, 2003), 40–62.

8. Holly Brewer, *By Birth or Consent: Children, Law and the Anglo-American Revolution in Authority* (Chapel Hill: University of North Carolina Press, 2005), 232.

9. Michael Grossberg, "Children and the Law," *Encyclopedia of Children and Childhood in History and Society*, edited by Paula S. Fass. www.faqs.org/childhood/Ke-Me/Law-Children-and-the.html.

10. Macleod, *A Moral Tale: Children's Books and American Culture, 1820–1860* (North Haven, CT: Archon Books, 1975), 28.

11. See, for instance, Warner's account of the rise of liberal citizenship and aesthetics in *Letters of the Republic*.

12. Macleod, *A Moral Tale*, 467.

13. J. G. A. Pocock, *The Machiavellian Moment: Florentine Political Thought and the Atlantic Republican Tradition* (Princeton: Princeton University Press, 2003), 464.

14. Ibid., 487, 486.

15. See Benjamin Barber, *Consumed: How Markets Corrupt Children, Infantilize Adults, and Swallow Citizens Whole* (New York: Norton, 2007).

16. Pocock, *Machiavellian Moment*, 464.

17. See Daniel T. Rodgers, *Contested Truths: Keywords in American Politics since Independence* (Cambridge, MA: Harvard University Press, 1998), 30, for an assessment of Bentham's lack of influence in the United States.

18. Adam Smith, *An Inquiry into the Nature and Causes of the Wealth of Nations* (Philadelphia, Thomas Dobson, 1789), 153.

19. Pocock, *Machiavellian Moment*, 490.

20. "The Love of Reading in Children," 29.

21. Patrick Brantlinger, *Fictions of State: Culture and Credit in Britain, 1694–1994* (Ithaca: Cornell University Press, 1996), 29.

22. Ibid., 41, 22.

23. Cathy D. Matson and Peter S. Onuf, *A Union of Interests: Political and Economic Thought in Revolutionary America* (Lawrence: University Press of Kansas, 1990), 14.

24. *Virginia Journal and Alexandria Advertiser* (1785): 2.

25. See Benjamin Franklin, *Advice to a Young Tradesman* (Boston: Sold by Benjamin Mecom, 1762), 2.

26. "The Brief Remarker," *The Academician* 1.13 (1818): 198. Current historians of the book trade have confirmed nineteenth-century educators' perceptions that they were living in a "reading age." For instance, in *Reading Becomes a Necessity of Life: Material & Cultural Life in Rural New England, 1780–1835* (Knoxville: University of Tennessee Press, 1989), 28, William Gilmore states that there was "an explosion in the volume and variety of printed material available to read" between 1785 and 1835, including "a vast expansion of both sacred and secular reading matter across all vehicles of printed communication." This expansion of the book market also coincided with large increases in literacy rates.

27. In "Die Perioden der Lesegeschichte in der Neuzeit. Das statistische Ausmass und die soziokulturelle Bedeutung der Lektüre," in *Archiv für Geschichte des Buchwesens* 10 (1970): 945–1002. Rolf Engelsing claimed that the nineteenth century marked the rise of "extensive reading," in which readers became more widely read but less attentive to their books, contrasting with an earlier generation of faithful readers of a smaller number of literary texts. Though many current scholars have noted rightly that these two kinds of reading are not mutually exclusive, educators of the period noticed and marked a similar shift.

28. "Sabbath School Libraries," *American Sunday School Magazine* 3 (1826): 316.

29. "The Brief Remarker," 198–99.

30. For scholarship on the history of the museum in England and America, see Tony Bennett, *Birth of the Museum: History, Theory, Politics* (London: Routledge, 1995), and Joel J. Orosz, *Curators and Culture: The Museum Movement in America, 1740- 1870* (Tuscaloosa: University of Alabama Press, 2002).

31. *Exhibition of Tom Thumb*, 5.

32. Gardner, "The Literary Museum and the Unsettling of the Early American Novel," 754.

33. "Peale's Museum," *The Port-Folio* 4.9 (1807): 297.

34. *Exhibition of Tom Thumb*, 49.

35. The *Oxford English Dictionary* cites this meaning of "portfolio" beginning in 1848, but "folio" meant an account book much earlier.

36. Phillip Connell, "Bibliomania: Book Collecting, Cultural Politics, and the Rise of Literary Heritage in Romantic Britain," *Representations* 17 (2000): 25.

37. *Exhibition of Tom Thumb*, 49.

38. Ibid., 6–7.

39. Ibid., 7.

40. Jacqueline Reiner, *From Virtue to Character: American Childhood 1775–1850* (New York: Twayne Publishers, 1996), xi.

41. Jane Tompkins, *Sensational Designs: The Cultural Work of American Fiction, 1780–1860* (Oxford: Oxford University Press, 1985), 83.

42. Jennifer Jordan Baker, "Cotton Mather's Theology of Finance," *Arizona Quarterly* 56.4 (2000): 15.

43. John Locke, *Two Treatises of Government*, edited by Peter Laslett (Cambridge: Cambridge University Press, 1988), 299.

44. Connell, "Bibliomania," 27.

45. Ibid., 25–27.

46. Ibid., 25. See also James Bunn, "The Aesthetics of English Mercantilism," *New Literary History* 11 (1890): 314.

47. See Reiner, *From Virtue to Character,* for an account of this movement.

48. Stephen Rachman, "Shaping the Values of Youth: Sunday School Books in Nineteenth-Century America," *Michigan State Digital Library.* http://digital.lib.msu.edu/projects/ssb/documents/essay.pdf

49. The fourteenth annual report of the American Sunday School Union (1838), 23, lists a variety of these types of books in their catalogue.

50. "Sunday-School Libraries," *The American Sunday School Magazine* 5 (1828): 28.

51. This method was pioneered by British Sunday school founder Robert Raikes and subsequently used in Joseph Lancaster's monitorial system and the British colonial Madras system developed by Andrew Bell.

52. "Sunday Schools and the American Sunday School Union," *The American Journal of Education* (1865): 712.

53. Third annual report of the American Sunday School Union (1827), iv.

54. Quoted in Betsy Rodgers, *Cloak of Charity: Studies in Eighteenth-Century Philanthropy* (London: Methuen and Co., 1949), 58.

55. Paper money, which was issued partly to pay war debts, was notorious associated with artificiality. Made often of old rags and paper waste, this money had what David Hume termed "fictitious value." See Hume, *Essays and Treatises on Several Subjects* (London: A. Millar, 1764), 328. Fears about paper money were widespread following the American Revolution. The United States lacked a national monetary system until the Coinage Act of 1792 and had multiple state currencies until the National Currency Act in 1863. State currencies were sometimes valueless because states could not pay their debts. At various times between 1780 and 1840, paper money could not easily be traded for specie. See David Anthony, "Banking on Emotion: Financial Panic and the Logic of Male Submission in the Jacksonian Gothic," *American Literature* 76.4 (2004): 719–47, and Cheryl Hinds, "Brown's Revenge Tragedy: Edgar Huntly and the Uses of Property," *Early American Literature* 30.1 (1995): 51–70.

56. *The Boys' Scrap-Book* (Philadelphia: American Sunday School Union, 1839).

57. "Dialogue for Sabbath School Children; Part First," *The Guardian, or Youth's Religious Instructor* 2.7 (1820): 232.

58. "Sunday Schools," *The Religious Intelligencer* 10.41 (1826): 647.

59. "Reward Tickets," *The American Sunday School Magazine* 4 (1827): 103.

60. Fourth annual report of the American Sunday School Union (1828), iii.

61. Nord, "Benevolent Books," 229.

62. The competing Sunday School Union of the Methodist Church called these donors an "assault" on the sovereignty of the church and decided to promote sales of their tracts by the different method of offering free gifts of extra tracts to those who purchased in bulk. See "Sunday School Library Books," *The Methodist Magazine and Quarterly Review* 13.3 (1831): 353, and "A Premium for New Auxiliary Sunday Schools, with Libraries," *Christian Advocate and Journal and Zion's Herald* 5.47 (1831): 187.

63. For instance, *The American Sunday School Magazine* notes that the libraries are intended to "give to children and youth, and indeed to all, a cheap and early access to all the books which they can read." "Sabbath School Libraries," 317.

64. Seventh annual report of the American Sunday School Union (1831), 27.

65. Tenth annual report of the American Sunday School Union (1834), 17.

66. According to the fourteenth annual report of the New York Tract Society (1839), 39, a more profitable enterprise of "volumes" and "family libraries" brought in more revenue.

67. James Eastburn, "The Second Annual Report of the New-York Sunday School Library," *The Evangelical Guardian and Review* 2.3 (1818): 137.

68. Third annual report of the New York Tract Society (1830), 14–15.

69. See Melissa J. Homestead, *American Authors and Literary Property, 1822–1869* (Cambridge: Cambridge University Press, 2005).

70. Quoted in Homestead, *American Authors and Literary Property*, 79.

71. James Lawrence Whittier, Manuscript Diary. Courtesy of the American Antiquarian Society.

72. Fifth annual report of New York Tract Society (1830), 58.

73. Third annual report of the New York Tract Society (1827), 28.

74. J. W. "Why Don't You Have a Library Connected with Your Sunday School?" *Christian Register and Boston Observer* 15.52 (1836): 206.

75. "Important Project: Sunday School and Youth's Library," *Christian Advocate and Journal and Zion's Herald* 7.5 (1832): 18.

76. "The Books We Read," *Hours at Home; A Popular Monthly Instruction and Recreation* 9.3 (1869): 242.

77. "Presentation of the General Tom Thumb at the Court of St. James," *Spirit of the Times; A Chronicle of the Turf, Agriculture, Field Sports, Lite* 14.9 (1844): 100.

78. "General Tom Thumb," *Niles' National Register* 18.10 (1845): 149.

79. See, for example, the multiple advertisements placed by bookstore and lottery office, Burtus and Crane, in *Weekly Visitor, Or the Ladies Miscellany* in 1805, or similar advertisements by Thomas and Whipple in *Merrimack Magazine and Ladies Literary Cabinet* in 1806.

80. J. Horner, *The Silver Penny; or New Lottery Book for Children* (New Haven, CT: Sidney's Press, 1805), 5.

81. Ibid., 17, 22.

82. E. S. "On Making a Lottery-Book of the Bible," *The Panoplist, and Missionary Magazine* 12.3 (1816): 109.

83. Edgeworth and Edgeworth, *Practical Education*, 126.

84. Rambler, "A Letter Containing a History of an Adventurer of Lotteries," *The Evening Fire-Side, or Literary Miscellany* 1.15 (1805): 116–17.

85. S. S. "The Lottery," *The New Monthly Magazine and Literary Journal* 2.11 (1821): 530.

86. Ibid., 531.

87. Jean-Paul Sartre, *The Imaginary: A Phenomenological Psychology of the Imagination* (New York: Taylor and Francis, 2004), 125.

88. Ibid. For a similar discussion of the imagination, see also Elaine Scarry, *Dreaming by the Book* (New York: Farrar, Strauss & Giroux, 1999).

89. S. S. "The Lottery," 531.

90. Ibid., 532.

91. Horner, *Silver Penny*, 11.

92. "History of a Gold Dollar," *Merry's Museum, Parley's Magazine, Woodworth's Cabinet, and the Schoolfellow* 35 (1858): 144.

93. Ibid.

94. Lydia Sigourney, *Letters to Young Ladies* (New York: Harper & Brothers, 1836), 148.

95. *Oxford English Dictionary*. The prevalent images in eighteenth- and nineteenth-century children's literature of conjuring boxes and budget boxes that store valuable items

may have been precursors to the still and mechanical toy banks that arose in the Civil War era and proliferated in the latter half of the nineteenth century.

96. John Aiken and Anna Barbauld, *Evenings at Home; Or, The Juvenile Budget Opened* (London: J. Johnson, 1792), 3.

97. In "Literacy, The Rise of an Age of Reading, and the Cultural Grammar of Print Communications in America, 1735–1850," *Communication* 11 (1988): 23–46, William J. Gilmore notes that money was a common trope to describe knowledge: "Knowledge was always referred to concretely, likened to coins and notes comprising holdings of a savings bank" (36).

98. "What Is a Thought Worth?" *The Guardian; Or Youth's Religions Instructor* 6.4 (1824): 126.

99. Sigourney, *Letters to Young Ladies*, 146–47.

100. Ibid., 247.

101. Ibid., 159, 222, 47.

102. Ibid., 724.

103. Hannah More, *Strictures on the Modern System of Female Education* (Boston: Printed for Joseph Bumstead, 1802), 238.

104. Anthony, "Banking on Emotion," 721.

105. See Nina Baym's Introduction to Maria Cummins, *The Lamplighter* (New Brunswick: Rutgers University Press, 1988), ix.

106. See Sánchez-Eppler, *Dependent States*, 72–76.

107. Nina Baym, *Woman's Fiction: A Guide to Novels by and About Women in America, 1820–1870* (Ithaca: Cornell University Press, 1978), 17.

108. In her introduction to *The Lamplighter*, Baym notes that *The Wide, Wide World* "established the category of the best seller as we know it today, and thus revolutionized the publishing industry. It went through fourteen printings in two years."

109. Susan Warner, *The Wide, Wide World* (New York: G. P. Putnam and Company, 1852). See, for instance, the discussion on page 140 between John and Ellen about the pure pleasures of the moon that are lost to rich people who "make and trade of pleasure."

110. Catharine Maria Sedgwick, *The Poor Rich Man and the Rich Poor Man* (New York: Harper and Bros., 1836), 154.

111. Theodore Sedgwick, *Public and Private Economy* (New York: Harper and Bros., 1836), 14.

112. Ibid., 17.

113. Sedgwick, *Poor Rich Man*, 11.

114. Ibid., 13, 114.

115. Ibid., 112, 14.

116. Ibid., 112, 15.

117. Quoted in Homestead, *American Authors and Literary Property*, 88.

118. Sedgwick, *Means and Ends; Or Self-Training* (Boston: Marsh, Capen, Lyon and Webb, 1839), 237.

119. Sedgwick, *Poor Rich Man*, 28.

120. Ibid., 178.

121. Ibid., 31, 39–40.

122. Ibid., 39–40, 178.

123. Even if they were not required to required work outside of the home, children were integral to the family economy. Children carried out household tasks, such as cleaning, cook-

ing, soap making, laundry, and sewing. Female children had the duty of learning to manage the household, as circumstances like a parent's death might have required them to take over the family finances.

124. Harriet Farley, "Editorial," *The Lowell Offering* 3 (March 1843): 144.

125. Ibid., 144.

126. Almira, "The Spirit of Discontent," *The Lowell Offering* 1.4 (1841): 111.

127. Farley, "Editorial," 143–44.

128. The suicides of two factory workers in 1844 were perhaps a result of this fragmentation. See A. G. A., "Editorial," *The Lowell Offering* 4.9 (1844): 212–16.

Chapter 5 • Natural Citizenship

Epigraph. Mary Allen Ware, Manuscript Diary. April 26, 1838. Courtesy of the American Antiquarian Society.

1. Benjamin B. Kendrick, "The Journal of the Joint Committee of Fifteen on Reconstruction," PhD Diss., Columbia University, 1914.

2. *Congressional Globe* (May 30, 1866), 2890–91.

3. Ibid., 2890.

4. Ibid.

5. See Eugene Genovese, *Roll, Jordan, Roll: The World the Slaves Made* (New York: Vintage Books, 1976).

6. "Books for Children," *The American Annals of Education* (1828), 100.

7. Quoted in John Nietz, *Old Textbooks: Spelling, Grammar, Reading, Arithmetic, Geography, American History, Civil Government, Physiology, Penmanship, Art, Music, as Taught in the Common Schools from Colonial Days to 1900* (Pittsburgh: University of Pittsburgh Press, 1961), 58.

8. See Caroline Levander, *Cradle of Liberty: Race, the Child, and National Belonging from Thomas Jefferson to W. E. B. Du Bois* (Durham: Duke University Press, 2006), and Lesley Ginsberg, "Of Babies, Beasts, and Bondage: Slavery and the Question of Citizenship in Antebellum American Children's Literature," in *The American Child: A Cultural Studies Reader*, edited by Caroline F. Levander and Carol J. Singley (New Brunswick: Rutgers University Press, 2003), 85–105. Notably, in earlier forms of patriarchalism and before the invention of chattel slavery, slaves had not been uniquely characterized as children. Rather, childhood was understood as a status that anyone could and did assume. See Holly Brewer, *By Birth or Consent: Children, Law and the Anglo-American Revolution in Authority* (Chapel Hill: University of North Carolina Press, 2005), 355: "Africans were compared to children occasionally, as were all subjects within patriarchal theory." When the social contract was introduced, connections between children and slaves became more common, in that both were barred from being full citizens, but it was not until the nineteenth century that children and slaves became closely connected in the patriarchal justification for slavery.

9. Frederick Douglass, "What to a Slave Is the Fourth of July?" in *My Bondage and My Freedom* (New York and Auburn: Miller, Orton, and Mulligan, 1855), 441.

10. Jessica Enoch, *Refiguring Rhetorical Education: Women Teaching African American, Native American, and Chicano/a Students, 1865–1911* (Carbondale: Southern Illinois University Press, 2008), 46.

11. Mary Pilkington, "The Faithful Slave; Or the Little Negro Boy," in *Tales of the Her-*

mitage Written for the Instruction and Amusement of the Rising Generation (Philadelphia: Published by James Thackeray, H. Maxwell printer, 1800), 149.

12. Ibid, 150–51.

13. African American newspapers demonstrate that free blacks were familiar with the faithful slave genre and used the concept of choice to open up possibilities not mentioned by the children's stories. In Douglass's paper, he uses the faithful slave motif as the centerpiece for a joke that highlights the limitations on the choices usually offered by the stories: "'Sancho,' said a dying planter to his slave, 'for your faithful services, I mean to do you honor; I will leave it in my will that you shall be buried in my family ground.' 'Ah! Massa,' answered the slave, 'Sancho no good be buried there. Sancho rather hab de oney or de freedom; besides, if the debil come in the dark to look for Massa, he make do mistake, and [take] this poor nigger [instead].'" By having Sancho ask for money and freedom instead of the dubious honor of being a faithful slave to the death, Douglass's version highlights the radical potentials that are silenced by the children's versions. See "Sancho," *Frederick Douglass's Paper* (August 31, 1855). Another version attributed to Herman Melville and published in *The Liberator* further dramatizes the limited choice offered by the faithful slave motif by depicting a master who shoots his faithful slave when he jokingly consents to die rather than remain enslaved. See Melville, "The Magnanimity of a Slave in Contrast with his Master," *The Liberator* 2.5 (February 4, 1832): 18.

14. Slaveholders often staged displays of paternalism by handing out clothes on the front steps of their plantation houses, a performance of charity and deference in which slaves would usually participate so that they could receive the supplies they urgently needed.

15. Quoted in Brewer, *By Birth or Consent*, 135. See also Rogers Smith, *Civic Ideals: Conflicting Visions of Citizenship in U.S. History* (New Haven: Yale University Press, 1997), 159.

16. To avoid the conclusion that citizenship was compelled rather than chosen, many politicians and judges maintained that children, even if they were naturalized, were not firmly citizens. Expatriation bills in Congress in the 1810s and 1860s suggested that children could leave their country if they so desired. Yet it is likely that few children had the resources to do so. Furthermore, as Rogers Smith points out, federal judges were not particularly likely to support expatriation rights. See Smith, *Civic Ideals*, 156–57. Meanwhile, concepts of blood inheritance also continued to shape laws and practices related to both citizenship and slavery, as children often followed the condition of their parents.

17. Jean-Jacques Rousseau, *Émile, or, On Education*, translated by Barbara Foxley (New York: Everyman Paperbacks, 1993), 7.

18. Jean-Jacques Rousseau, *The Social Contract*, translated by Maurice Cranston (New York: Penguin Classics, 1968), 49.

19. Ibid.

20. Rousseau, *Émile*, 3.

21. Carol A. Mossman, *Politics and Narratives of Birth: Gynocolonization from Rousseau to Zola* (Cambridge: Cambridge University Press, 1993), 181.

22. Ala Alryyes, *Original Subjects: The Child, the Novel, and the Nation* (Cambridge, MA: Harvard University Press, 2001), 72, 74.

23. Jean-Jacques Rousseau, *The Confessions*, translated by J. M. Cohen (New York: Penguin, 1953), 529–30.

24. Robert Wokler, *Rousseau: A Very Short Introduction* (Oxford: Oxford University Press, 1995), 116.

25. Ibid., 117.

26. Geraint Parry, "*Émile*: Learning to Be Men, Women, and Citizens," in *The Cambridge Companion to Rousseau*, edited by Patrick Riley (Cambridge: Cambridge University Press, 2001), 252, 263.

27. Ibid., 266.

28. Tzvetan Todorov, *Frail Happiness: An Essay on Rousseau*, translated by John T. Scott and Robert D. Zaretsky (University Park: Pennsylvania State University Press, 2006), 64.

29. Judith N. Shklar, *Men and Citizens: A Study of Rousseau's Social Theory* (Cambridge: Cambridge University Press, 1969), 6.

30. Rousseau, *Correspondance Générale de J-J. Rousseau*, edited by T. Dufours and P. Plan (Paris: Armand Colin, 1924–1934), vii, 233. Translated in Roger D. Masters, *The Political Philosophy of Rousseau* (Princeton: Princeton University Press, 1976), xiii.

31. Rousseau, *The Social Contract*, 86–87.

32. Mossman, *Politics and Narratives of Birth*, 166.

33. Ibid., 181.

34. Rousseau, *Émile*, 194.

35. Ibid., 152.

36. Sir Thomas Browne, *Religio Medici* (London: Printed for Andrew Crooke, 1642).

37. Rousseau, *Émile*, 54.

38. It is perhaps significant that Rousseau's most succinct discussion of the book of nature comes not in the voice of the tutor but of the priest. See Rousseau, *Émile*, 270. Although many scholars have taken the book of nature to be Rousseau's ultimate solution to the problem of society's misalignment with nature, his choice to put this revelation in the voice of the priest, not the tutor, allows him to subtly suggest that nature and culture are not reconcilable without recourse to the supernatural belief in nature's divine creation. Rousseau's depiction of the priest appears to be sincere, but religion ultimately does not play a major part in Émile's upbringing. Rather, throughout the educational portions of the text, Rousseau's tutor takes the place of God as the force that attributes meaning to the natural world and whose will directs that of Émile.

39. Rousseau, *Émile*, 88.

40. William Godwin, *The Enquirer: Reflections on Education, Manners, and Literature* (London: G. G. and J. Robinson, 1797), 120.

41. Rousseau, *Émile*, 173.

42. Ibid., 183.

43. Ibid., 501, 502.

44. Ibid., 512, 518, 520, 512.

45. Ibid., 197.

46. Ibid., 4.

47. Troy Boone, "Jean-Jacques Rousseau," *Representing Childhood*, www.representing-childhood.pitt.edu/rousseau.htm.

48. Rousseau, *Émile*, 65.

49. It is perhaps no coincidence that a popular French automaton following *Émile*'s publication, designed by Maillardet, was a child. The automaton is now housed at the Franklin Institute in Philadelphia.

50. Rousseau, *Émile*, 28.

51. Benjamin Rush, *A Plan for the Establishment of Public Schools and the Diffusion of*

Knowledge in Pennsylvania (Philadelphia: Printed for Thomas Dobson, 1786), 27. Samuel Goodrich underscores the importance of creating automatic habits in children in his civic textbook, *The Young American: Book of Government and Law; Showing Their History, Nature and Necessity. For the Use of Schools* (New York: William Robinson, 1842), 8–9: "To these several strands, which are braided together, and constitute the motives to obedience, we may add that of habit."

52. See "Education," *The Port-Folio* 1.5 (1813), 463–76. The Lancaster system closely resembled the Madras system, which was developed by Britons as part of the colonial government in India.

53. Ibid., 466.

54. "The Academician No. IX," *The Academician* 1.8 (1818): 113. While eighteenth-century spelling books, which John Nietz has called "omnibus textbooks," had comprised an entire school curriculum, the new nineteenth-century spelling books came to be composed almost entirely of tables of unmired words. Critics of these books feared that many children did not learn beyond the mechanical "skeleton" of the language. See for instance, S. S. G., "The Vitalizing Process in Teaching," *The Massachusetts Teacher* 3.7 (1850): 209: "a child [cannot] realize any advantage from saying, for instance, aitch-a-tee, as a necessary antecedent to saying hat." See also "Methods of Teaching Spelling," *Massachusetts Teacher and Journal of Home and School Education* 15.5 (1862): 189, which refers to spelling books as "nonsense columns."

55. Nietz, *Old Textbooks*, 18–20.

56. In the sixteenth annual report of the American Tract Society (New York: 1841), 42, the editors relay comments from their distributors, including a comment from S. S. White, who reports from Pittsburgh: "I have often found families very poor, without a book in the house, with the exception of a Bible and a spelling-book; and some had no Bible." Wealthier families were hardly better off. See the fifteenth annual report of the American Tract Society (New York: 1840), 47, in which Mr. R. Taylor had been similarly shocked to find that in western Pennsylvania, "Many families of wealth are found which have not a half dozen books; and large numbers in comfortable circumstances have nothing but the Bible, a spelling-book, and an English Reader!"

57. Daniel Adams. *The Understanding Reader* (Leominster, MA: Printed by Adams & Wilder, 1804), iii.

58. Though it is unclear how many children used these machines, or even how many existed, many articles describe and bemoan their outrageous claims. See "The Academician No. IX," 115: "Men may profess to teach languages and sciences in 48 lessons, by wooden machines, or some other silly contrivances, but their pretensions will deceive the illiterate only . . . Luckily . . . for these empiries, the citizens do not hesitate to liquidate their bills."

59. "Article 3—No Title," *The Common School Journal* 7.12 (1845): 190.

60. "*Worth Thinking of,*" *New York Observer and Chronicle* 18.39 (1840): 156.

61. "Modern Improvement," *The Ladies Port-Folio* 1.18 (1820): 142.

62. See, for instance, John Murray, "Mr. Stevenson's Reading Party," *Overland Monthly and Out West Magazine* 15.88 (1890): 421, in which a father instructs his children on how to read naturally: "The moment you saw that comma, Charley, you brought up your voice with a jerk, and it made your reading sound mechanical and not natural. If you were *talking* the sentence, probably you would make no pause whatever."

63. "Modern Improvement," 142.

64. Ralph Waldo Emerson, "Self-Reliance," in *The Norton Anthology of American Literature*, edited by Nina Baym et al. (New York: Norton, 2003), 1168, and Ralph Waldo Emerson, "Speech at the Kansas Relief Meeting in Cambridge, Wednesday. Evening, September 10, 1856," in vol. II of *The Complete Works of Ralph Waldo Emerson*, edited by J. E. Cabot (Cambridge, MA: Printed at the Riverside Press, 1883), 245.

65. Henry David Thoreau, *Walden*, in *The Norton Anthology of American Literature*, edited by Nina Baym et al. (New York: Norton, 2003), 1862–63.

66. Ripley, Manuscript Diary, May 7, 1800. The exhibitions were also a popular form of entertainment, attended by ordinary adult citizens, who could weigh for themselves critics' emerging arguments that children's reading was evidence of the decline of American citizenship. While Ripley is conscious of this criticism, other young people, such as fifteen-year-old James Fiske, seem to have enjoyed the examinations and even attended them for fun when they were not participants. See Fiske, Manuscript Diary, February 5–25, 1837. These accounts suggest a genuine curiosity and enthusiasm among the general public that sometimes contrasted with the views of critics.

67. Fanny Fern (Sara Willis Payson), "Children's Rights," in *Fern Leaves from Fanny's Portfolio* (Auburn and Buffalo, NY: Miller, Orton, and Mulligan, 1854), 188, 189.

68. William Lloyd Garrison, Letter in *Narrative of the Life of Frederick Douglass*, 9.

69. "Education," *The Atheneum; or, Spirit of the English Magazines* 13 (1823), 406.

70. "Anecdotes of Children in Infant Schools," *Western Luminary* 3.52 (1827), 409. As Jane Tompkins and Anna Mae Duane have both noted, slaves and children are often paired in nineteenth-century sentimental literature, which often protests the ways in which both are made powerless and vulnerable by the institutions of the period.

71. It is almost certain that Emerson read *Émile*. As Gilbert F. LaFreniere writes in "Rousseau and the European Roots of Environmentalism," *Environmental History Review* 14 (1990), 61: "There are numerous . . . quotations from Rousseau's writings and references to Rousseau scattered through Emerson's journals, notebooks and letters, leaving little doubt that he was . . . in touch with Rousseau's ideas for decades."

72. Ralph Waldo Emerson, "Politics" in *Emerson's Prose and Poetry*, edited by Joel Porte and Saundra Morris (New York: Norton, 2001), 213.

73. Emerson. "Politics," 214. As with most discussions of "youth" in this period, it is unclear how young these citizens are. While "civilian" traditionally referred to a scholar of Civil Law, it also referred to nonmilitary personnel, which included primarily women and children under age sixteen.

74. Ralph Waldo Emerson, *Emerson in His Journals*, edited by Joel Porte (Cambridge, MA: Belknap Press of Harvard University Press, 1982), 223.

75. Ibid., 224.

76. Emerson, "Politics," 215.

77. Ibid., 216–17. For a full discussion of the political meaning of nature and especially weather, see Eduardo Cadava, *Emerson and the Climates of History* (Stanford: Stanford University Press, 1997).

78. Ralph Waldo Emerson, "Nature," in *Essays. Second Series* (Boston: Philips, Samson, and Co., 1850), 178.

79. Emerson, "Politics," 221.

80. Ibid., 214.

81. Ralph Waldo Emerson, "Nature," in *Emerson's Prose and Poetry*, edited by Joel Porte and Saundra Morris (New York: Norton, 2001), 39.

82. Emerson, "Nature," in *Emerson's Prose and Poetry*, 29. Emerson further theorized on page 35 that children's uses of language held the key to restoring the forgotten links between word and thing: "Most of the process [by which language describes natural experience] is hidden from us in the remote time when language was framed, but the same tendency may be daily observed in children. Children and savages use only nouns or names of things, which they continually convert into verbs, and apply to analogous mental acts."

83. Emerson, "Self-Reliance," 1164.

84. Judith Plotz, *Romanticism and the Vocation of Childhood* (New York: Palgrave, 2001), 7.

85. Ralph Waldo Emerson, "History," in *Emerson's Prose and Poetry*, edited by Joel Porte and Saundra Morris (New York: Norton, 2001), 120.

86. See Michael Paul Rogin, *Fathers and Children: Andrew Jackson and the Subjugation of the American Indian* (New York: Knopf, 1975).

87. Emerson, "Self-Reliance," 1164–65.

88. Ibid., 1174.

89. Emerson, "Nature," in *Emerson's Prose and Poetry*, 39.

90. Emerson, "Politics," 219.

91. Ibid.

92. Emerson, "Self-Reliance," 1165.

93. Ibid., 1173. See Elizabeth Hewitt, *Correspondence and American Literature, 1770–1865* (Cambridge: Cambridge University Press, 2004), for a further discussion of Emerson's political model in "Friendship" and "Love."

94. Emerson, "Self-Reliance," 1171.

95. Emerson, "Politics," 219. Emphasis added.

96. Emerson, "Self-Reliance," 1164.

97. Plotz, *Romanticism and the Vocation of Childhood*, 25.

98. Hewitt, *Correspondence and American Literature*, 63.

99. Ibid.

100. See Elizabeth Peabody, *Record of Mr. Alcott's School* (Boston: Roberts Brothers, 1874), 31.

101. Ibid., 32, 33.

102. Mary Allen Ware, Manuscript Diary. April 26, 1838. Courtesy of the American Antiquarian Society.

103. Ralph Waldo Emerson, "The Uses of Natural History" *Reading the Roots: American Nature Writing Before* Walden, edited by Michael P. Branch (Athens: University of Georgia Press, 2004), 275.

104. As Angela Sorby has argued, still another way of making children's reading "natural" in the nineteenth century was through the instructional method of "sounding out" rather than spelling out words: "This method of teaching reading produced language as a somatic experience, located not outside the body but within it; language could be figured as a natural part of the self, and that linguistically determined self could in turn be figured as a natural part of a national imagined community." See Sorby, *Schoolroom Poets: Childhood, Performance, and the Place of American Poetry, 1865–1917* (Lebanon: New Hampshire University Press, 2005), xxx.

105. "Art III—Practical Observations on the Education of the People," *The North American Review* 23.52 (1826): 64.

106. Johann Heinrich Pestalozzi, *How Gertrude Teaches Her Children*, translated by Lucy E. Holland and Francis C. Turner (London: Swan Sonnenschein and Co., 1900), 163. Pestalozzi later abandoned the idea of the mother's book, claiming that it was too difficult to actually realize his idea for its contents. See Charles Monaghan and E. Jennifer Monaghan, "Schoolbooks," in *An Extensive Republic* for an account of the effects of the Pestalozzian movement on American schoolbooks.

107. Pestalozzi, *How Gertrude Teaches Her Children*, 161.

108. Ibid., 146.

109. The next best thing to the object—the image—became more indispensable to the idea of a children's book as the crude woodcuts and simple design of early children's books gave way to large, bright, and colorful pictures, often of plants, animals, and birds. Though these colorful texts could not be had by all readers, various means of adding color to printed texts, such as stenciling and lithography, meant that images more frequently accompanied texts and that representations could potentially become more closely allied to the natural objects that they represented.

110. *The Illustrated Alphabet of Birds* (Boston: Crosby, Nichols, and Company, 1853), no page number.

111. Ibid., no page number.

112. *The Aviary; Or Child's Book of Birds* (New York: Kiggins and Kellogg, undated), 5.

113. Ibid.

114. Ibid., 8.

115. *The Illustrated Alphabet of Birds*, no page number.

116. *The Anti-Slavery Alphabet* (Philadelphia: Printed for the Anti-Slavery Fair by Merrihew & Thompson, 1847), no page number. Emphasis added.

117. Ibid., no page number.

118. "Suggestions to Parents: Books for Children," *The American Journal of Education* 3.2 (1828): 100–101.

119. *Natural History; or Uncle Philip's Conversations with the Children about Tools and Trades Among Inferior Animals* (New York: Published by Harper & Brothers, 1835), 206.

120. Ibid., 148.

121. Eugene Genovese, *Roll, Jordan, Roll: The World the Slaves Made* (New York: Vintage Books, 1976), 3–6.

122. See Caroline Levander, "'Let Her White Progeny Offset Her Dark One': The Child and the Racial Politics of Nation-Making," *American Literature* 76.2 (2004): 225. See also Levander, *Cradle of Liberty*.

123. "Story of Philip Brusque," *Robert Merry's Museum* (September 1841), 85.

124. Ibid., 85–86.

125. "Story of Philip Brusque," *Robert Merry's Museum* (October 1841), 101.

126. Ibid., 102–3.

127. Goodrich, *The Young American*, frontispiece.

128. "Story of Philip Brusque," *Robert Merry's Museum* (October 1841), 102.

129. Goodrich, *The Young American*, i–ii.

130. Bercovitch and others have expounded on this tension as it relates to *The Scarlet Letter* (1850), but Hawthorne's children's literature was an equally rich venue for his explorations.

Sacvan Bercovitch, *The Rites of Assent: Transformation in the Symbolic Construction of America* (New York: Routledge, 1993), 194. See also R. W. B. Lewis, *The American Adam: Innocence, Tragedy and Tradition in the Nineteenth Century* (Chicago: University of Chicago Press), 1955.

131. Nathaniel Hawthorne, *A Wonder Book for Boys and Girls* (Boston: Houghton Mifflin, 1892), 3.

132. Ibid., 3, 141.

133. Ibid., 79.

134. Ibid.

135. Nathaniel Hawthorne, *Grandfather's Chair: True Stories from History* (London: Standard Book Company, 1931), 186.

136. Hawthorne, *A Wonder Book*, 6.

137. Ibid., 76.

138. Ibid., 124.

139. See Ginsberg, "Of Babies, Beasts, and Bondage."

140. Ann Preston, "Howard and His Squirrel," From *Cousin Ann's Stories for Children* (1849), included in Deborah C. De Rosa, *Into the Mouths of Babes: An Anthology of Abolitionist Children's Literature* (Westport, CT: Praeger Publishers, 2005), 165.

141. Quoted in Deak Nabers, *Victory of Law: The Fourteenth Amendment, the Civil War, and American Literature, 1852–1867* (Baltimore: Johns Hopkins University Press, 2006), 91.

142. Douglass, *Narrative of the Life of Frederick Douglass*, 43.

143. Ibid., 42.

144. Ibid., 40.

145. *The Anti-Slavery Alphabet*, no page number.

146. See Douglass, *Narrative of the Life of Frederick Douglass*, 43.

147. Anna Mae Duane, *Suffering Childhood in Early America: Violence, Race, and the Making of the Child Victim* (Athens: University of Georgia Press, 2010), 132.

148. Nabers, *Victory of Law*, 5–6. Nabers has shown that the perceived relationship between nature and the law changed significantly in the period between the Somerset case outlawing slavery in England in 1772 and the sectional conflicts in antebellum America.

Conclusion • The Legacy of the Fourteenth Amendment

1. "Extension of the Elective Franchise to the Colored Citizens of the Free States," *New Englander and Yale Review* 5.20 (1847): 522. Emphasis mine.

2. *Congressional Globe* (June 8, 1866), 3033.

3. "The Proposed Compromise: The Slave Emancipated Shall Be the Citizen Enfranchised," *The Independent* 18.896 (1866), 4.

4. Mark Twain, *The Adventures of Huckleberry Finn* (New York: Penguin Classics, 2002), 42.

5. See Jane Smiley, "Say It Ain't So Huck: Second Thoughts on Twain's 'Masterpiece.'" *Harper's Magazine* 292.1748 (1996), 61–67.

6. Nancy Isenberg, *Sex and Citizenship in Antebellum America* (Chapel Hill: University of North Carolina Press, 1998), 49.

7. Ibid., 192.

8. Mary Celeste Kerney, "Coalescing: The Development of Girl Studies," *NWSA Journal* 21.1 (2009): 6.

9. Peggy Cooper Davis, *Neglected Stories: The Constitution and Family Values* (New York: Hill and Wang, 1997), 85.

10. Michael Grossberg, "Children and the Law," *Encyclopedia of Children and Childhood in History and Society*, edited by Paula S. Fass. www.faqs.org/childhood/Ke-Me/Law-Children-and-the.html.

11. Barbara Bennett Woodhouse, *Hidden in Plain Sight: The Tragedy of Children's Rights from Ben Franklin to Lionel Tate* (Princeton: Princeton University Press, 2008), 3.

12. For instance, January 6, 2011, Republicans Steve King, Phil Gingrey, Rob Woodall, and Gary Miller of California introduced H.R. 140, the Birthright Citizenship Act of 2011, to the House Judiciary Committee. The act, if passed, would declare that the Fourteenth Amendment does not apply to the children of illegal aliens, except when a parent is actively serving in the U.S. military. See "U.S. State Lawmakers Target 'Birthright' Citizenship," *The Star Online*, http://thestar.com.my/news/story.asp?file=/2011/1/6/worldupdates/2011-01-06.

13. *Congressional Globe* (May 30, 1866): 2890.

14. Ibid., 2891.

15. The judges in the case declared that Indians and the children of foreign diplomats should not be included as citizens based on the jurisdiction clause, showing some remaining limitations to the notion that citizenship was natural and universal.

16. Peter Schmidt, *Sitting in Darkness: New South Fiction, Education, and the Rise of Jim Crow Colonialism, 1865–1920* (Jackson: University Press of Mississippi, 2008), 113.

17. Frederick Douglass, *Narrative in the Life of Frederick Douglass, An American Slave, Written by Himself,* in Douglass, *Autobiographies*, edited by Henry Louis Gates (New York: Library of America, 1994), 70.

18. Ralph Waldo Emerson, *Uncollected Lectures by Ralph Waldo Emerson*, edited by Clarence Gohdes Jr. (New York: Rudge, 1832), 41–42.

19. Lynn A. Casmier-Paz, "The Effects of Literacy in English Slave Narratives," PhD Diss., University of Pittsburgh, 1998.

20. See Saidya Hartman, *Scenes of Subjection: Terror, Slavery, and Self-Making in Nineteenth-Century America* (Oxford: Oxford University Press, 1997).

21. Francis A. March, "Spelling Reform," *Princeton Review* (January–June 1880): 127.

22. "English Reviews," *The Methodist Quarterly Review* 33 (April 1881): 362.

23. See Julia Mickenberg, *Learning from the Left: Children's Literature, the Cold War, and Radical Politics in the United States* (Oxford: Oxford University Press, 2006).

24. "Columbus Day," *The Youth's Companion* 65.46 (1892): 608. The phrase, "under God," was added in the 1950s.

25. It is beyond the scope of this book to consider contemporary portrayals of children's imaginary citizenship. However, literature would be one place to continue the investigation about what a meaningful idea of children's and adults' citizenship might be. We live in an era in which the divisions between children's and adults' literature are becoming, once again, especially blurry; millions of adults read books that are directed at children, such as the Harry Potter series, which notably features a powerful child. This particular series required the *New York Times* to make a separate bestseller list for children's books to avoid them taking over the adult list, raising the questions of what political binaries such texts preserve and dissolve. Although such children's texts, like children, do not define public policy, they represent a vision of humanity that has captured the imagination of readers and an arena through which child and adult citizens might meet and contend with their common interests.

26. Thomas Spence, *The Rights of Infants; Or, the Imprescriptable Right of Mothers to such a Share of the Elements as is sufficient to enable them to suckle and bring up their Young. In a Dialogue between the Aristocracy and a Mother of Children* (London: Printed for the Author at No. 9 Oxford Street, lately removed from No. 8 Little Turnstile. 1797), no page number.

27. Amartya Sen, *Development as Freedom* (Oxford: Oxford University Press, 2001); Martha Nussbaum, *Women and Human Development: The Capabilities Approach* (Cambridge: Cambridge University Press, 2001).

28. Scott Keeter, Juliana Horowitz, and Alec Tyson, "Young Voters in the 2008 Election," *Pew Research Center Publications*, accessed November 2, 2010. http://pewresearch.org/pubs/1031/young-voters-in-the-2008-election.

29. James W. Loewen, *Lies My Teacher Told Me: Everything Your American History Textbook Got Wrong* (New York: Touchstone, 1995), 277.

30. Most recently, see children's participation in the Occupy movement. "'Children's Brigade' Joins Occupy Wall Street on Two-Month Anniversary," *Huffington Post*, accessed November 21, 2011. http://www.huffingtonpost.com/2011/11/17/children-occupy-wall-street-education_n_1100408.html.

Bold page numbers refer to figures

Adams, Abigail, 96
Adams, Daniel, 186
Adams, John, 96, 109, 114, 146, 219n8
Aesop's Fables, 147, 181
affection, 40, 108, 159, 173, 176; authority and, 112, 117–20; education and, 75, 136, 152, 185, 188; Great Awakening and, 36, 55–62; law and, 27, 97; slavery and, 175, 187, 196. *See also* affectionate citizenship
affectionate citizenship, 63–95, 113, 169; children's literature and, 14, 232n3; consent and, 20–21, 30; Lockean liberalism and, 105
affectionate reading, 44, 62, 128
affectionate republic, 29
Aiken, John, 157
Alcott, A. Bronson, 191–93
Aldrich, Thomas, 241n125
Alien and Sedition Acts (1798), 98
alphabet books, 38–39, 76–77, 152, **153**, 154, 192–97
Alryyes, Ala, 102, 178
Althusser, Louis, 21–22
American Civil War, 196; citizenship and, 8–10, 29, 130, 168. *See also* Reconstruction
American Revolution, 17, 39, 119, 123–24, 200; affection in, 76, 105, 108; children's dissent and, 86, 115, 118; citizenship and, 7, 27, 65; gender in, 69, 96; Great Awakening's impact on, 36, 58; paper money in, 146, 244n55; reading and, 109, 128; role of child in, 2–4, 13–14
American Sunday School Union, 145, 147–49

Anderson, Benedict, 6–7, 67
Anderson, Nick, 206
"anchor babies," 29, 206, 210
Anthony, David, 159
Anti-Slavery Alphabet, 194–95
Ariès, Philippe, 10, 221n33, 221n37
Ashley-Cooper, Anthony, 72
Augustine, St., 154
Austen, Jane, 234
automata, 167, 184–93, 249n49
The Aviary; Or the Child's Book of Birds, 194

bad readers, 28, 98–100, 104–13, 116–17, 125–26
Baier, Annette C., 31
Bailyn, Bernard, 232n3
Baker, Jennifer Jordan, 142
Balibar, Étienne, 19–20
Barbauld, Anna Laetitia, 115, 157
Barber, Benjamin R., 132
Barnes, Elizabeth, 122
Barnum, P. T., 150–51
Baxter, Richard, 49
Baym, Nina, 160, 246n108
Bell, Andrew, 244n51
Bennett, John, 93
Bennett, Tony, 243n30
Bentham, Jeremy, 136, 242n17
Bercovitch, Sacvan, 221n26, 253n130
Berlant, Lauren, 2, 10, 21, 26, 65
Bewick, Thomas, 161, 229n51
Bhabha, Homi, 108
Birthright Citizenship Act (2011), 255n12

Blake: or, the Huts of America, 202

book eating (bibliophagia), 77, 129, 188

Boone, Troy, 184

Bowen, Daniel, 140

Boyer, Paul S., 220n15

Brantlinger, Patrick, 138, 235n66

Breen, T. H., 59

Bremner, Robert, 58, 231n97

Brewer, Holly, 38, 69, 220n13, 225n4; on
boundaries of childhood, 11, 13–14, 247n8;
on children's economic practices, 133; on
Halfway Covenant, 34; on Locke, 4

Brooks, Thomas, 46

Brown, Gillian, 26–27, 74, 225n18; on children's freedom, 3, 14, 69, 71

Brown, Matthew P., 226n23

Brown, William Hill, 28, 48, 102, 238n35;
The Power of Sympathy, 94, 100, 105–13

Browne, Sir Thomas, 180

Brückner, Martin, 234n62

Bunn, James, 143

Bunyan, John, 15–16, 21

Burder, George, 228n41

Butcher, Elizabeth, 51–53, 55

Cadava, Eduardo, 251n77

Calvinism, 46, 58

capitalism, 140, 161, 165–66; children as capitalists, 156, 162; citizenship and, 134, 136–38;
expansion of, 28, 145. *See also* economics;
Panic of 1819; Panic of 1837

Caraccioli, Marquis, 106, 112

Casmier-Paz, Lynn A., 213

catechisms, 15–16, 52, 148, 224n2, 225n7;
Mather's, 50, 226n21; patriarchal nature of,
37–42

censorship, 115

Chapone, Hannah, 106

Child, Lydia Maria, 131, 157, 173, 237n21

childhood: boundaries of, 11, 13–16, 103,
243n26, 247n8; as metaphor, 38–41, 95–98;
political history of, 10–14

children, 81, 220n13, 220n15, 232n3; as aligned
with slaves, 13, 169–70, 172, 176, 247n8,
251n70; as aligned with women, 103–4,
112; as authors, 4, 24, 90, 93; as automata,
185–93, 249n49; as book eaters (bibliophagia), 77–78; boy readers, 48; church

membership of, 26–27, 34–35, 57–62;
citizens as, 2–5, 18–19, 22, 64, 68, 94,
124–30; citizenship defined through, 1–10;
closet reading of, 42–46, 52, 56–57, 228n37;
contemporary representations of, 255n25,
256n30; conversion narratives of, 53–57;
dissent of, 86, 96, 41–50, 113–123; economic
practices of, 131–67, 216, 242n7, 246n123;
feral, 194; Fourteenth Amendment and,
29–30, 206–17; French Revolution and,
113–15, 118, 178, 221n33; girl readers, 17–18,
52, 91–92, 100–101, 237n21; Lacan on,
220n22; Locke on, 19, 68–76, 105, 180–81,
228n43; as mini adults, 221n37; novel readers, 61, 96–130, 237n17, 237n21; race and,
173–76, 212–13; readers as, 107–12; religious
communities and, 32–62, 229n49; rights of,
3–5, 26–31, 97, 115, 187; role in history, 1,
10, 14, 85; role in politics, 65–66; Rousseau
on, 177–85; studying, 23–26, 237n17. *See
also* alphabet books; citizenship: imaginary; citizenship: natural; diaries; literature
(children's); Locke, John; pedagogy; spelling
books; United Nations Convention on the
Rights of the Child (1989)

The Child's New Play-Thing, 63, 221n29

choice, 11, 14, 50, 116; defining citizenship, 4,
8; in reading, 54, 110, 115, 125; in religion,
27, 34, 44, 225; slavery contrasted with, 170,
173, 175, 248n13; social contract and, 82, 97,
185. *See also* consent

citizenship, 108, 116–23, 220n14, 235n67,
255n15; age and, 103, 110–11, 220n15; alternative definitions of, 31, 215–16; citizens as
children, 2–5, 124–30; economic, 28–29,
131–67; Emerson on, 179, 214; gender and,
4–7, 65, 80–82, 88–93, 111–12, 172; Hawthorne on, 167, 171–72, 179, 198–201; ideology and, 20, 23, 28; imaginary, 6–11, 14, 25,
223n87, 255n25; immigrants and, 29–30,
170, 172, 206, 210–11; infantile, 2, 17–18, 21,
26, 65; legal versus literary, 27, 32, 220n22;
natural, 29–30, 105, 168–205; and naturalization, 97, 169, 176, 190, 205, 211; novels
and, 101, 112–13; race and, 20–22, 69, 81, 97,
169, 190, 247n8; Republican versus Federalist definitions of, 95–100; Rousseau on, 29,
171, 176–85, 221n33; slavery contrasted with,

69, 84, 98, 130, 247n8, 248n16; subjecthood contrasted with, 12–13, 18–23, 36–41; suffrage and, 20, 203–4; teaching, 38, 79–94. *See also* affectionate citizenship; consent; Constitution (U.S.); Fourteenth Amendment; law; Locke, John; social contract theory

Civil Rights Act (1868), 168–69

Civil Rights Act (1964), 207

Civil War. *See* American Civil War

Clapp, David, 24

Clark, Beverly Lyon, 18

Cobbett, William, 114

Cohoon, Lorinda B., 223n87

Coke, Sir Edward, 12

Coleman, William H., 23–25

collecting, 147, 150, 160; books, 141, 155; curiosities, 131, 141–43, 157, 226n25; letters, 54, 93, 236n15. *See also* scrapbooks

Colley, Thomas, **73**

colonialism, 2, 26–27, 32–33, **73**, 250n52; colonial government, 67, 79; print culture and, 38, 41, 46, 62, 89, 226n23. *See also* empire

The Columbian Orator, 102, 212

Connell, Phillip, 141, 143

consent, 66–67, 102, 171–72, 214, 216; affection and, 30, 60, 62; age of, 4, 103; defining citizenship, 8–9, 22, 25–27, 31, 167; Fourteenth Amendment and, 210–11; gender and, 69, 96; Locke on, 12, 64–65, 71–72, 75, 232n3, 235n67; race and, 69, 212; religion and, 33, 43–44, 225n4; social contract and, 6, 14, 19–20; slavery and, 203, 248n13; suffrage and, 207. *See also* choice

Constitution (U.S.), 7, 20, 66, 105; definition of citizenship, 4, 26, 169, 210; race and gender in, 172, 209. *See also* Fourteenth Amendment

Cooper, James Fenimore, 17

Cooper, William, 57

Cotton, John, 40

Cowan, Edgar, 211

Cowan, Frank, 168–69

Cowles, Julia, 102

Cox, Caroline, 3

Crain, Patricia A., 77, 225n18

The Crayon Reading Book, 127

The Cries of London, 147

Cummins, Maria Susan, 17, 159, 237n21

Darley, Felix O. C., 124

Darley, Matthew, **3**

Davidson, Cathy N., 5, 25–26, 101

Davis, Peggy Cooper, 209

Day, Angel, 226n25

Day, Thomas, 185

Defoe, Daniel, 14, 17, 129, 180, 182

Dennie, Joseph, 115–16, 141

De Rosa, Deborah, 202

Desiderio, Jennifer, 235n81

diaries, 4, 80, 225n7; representation of reading practices in, 24, 102, 187, 234n62, 237n20

DiGiromalo, Vincent, 3

Dillon, Elizabeth, 107

dissent, 8, 16, 98; children's, 86, 96, 113–21; gender and, 96; political, 12–13; religious, 39–42

Douglass, Frederick: on citizenship, 167, 171–72; on slavery, 187, 202–3, 223n87, 248n14

Duane, Anna Mae, 14, 203, 221n28, 251n70

Dwight, Sereno E., 57, 61

Eastburn, James, 149

economics, 9–10, 21, 130; children's practices, 131–67, 216, 242n7, 246n123; credit, 136–39, 141–42, 152, 154; currency, 135, 142–43, 146, 156–65, 244n55; economic citizenship, 28–29, 131–67. *See also* capitalism; Panic of 1819; Panic of 1837

Edgeworth, Maria, 77, 115, 129, 154–55, 158

Edgeworth, Richard, 77, 115, 129, 154–55, 158

Edwards, Jonathan, 27, 32, 36, 57–61

Elbert, Monika, 224n89

Ellsworth, Oliver, 97

Emerson, Ralph Waldo, 155, 173, 186, 200, 204; on children's citizenship, 179, 214; on citizenship (general), 29, 167, 176, 198; on education, 188–89, 212; on language, 252n82; Rousseau and, 251n71

empire, 79, 109, 138. *See also* colonialism

Engelsing, Rolf, 243n27

England, 17, 86, 114, 129; citizenship, 9, 11–14, 106, 221n33; economics, 136, 145; English books in United States, 89–90, 100–101, 132; language politics, 78, 87; parental metaphor, 2, **3**, 4, 108; slavery, 174

English Civil War, 8, 11

Enoch, Jessica, 173

The Evening Fire-Side, or Literary Miscellany, 155

Ex parte Crouse (1838), 121–22

Federalists, 28, 113, 115; views on children's citizenship, 95–98, 121. *See also* Adams, John; Dennie, Joseph; Tenney, Samuel; Washington, George

feminism, 31, 124, 209. *See also* gender

Fern, Fanny. *See* Payson, Sara Willis (Fanny Fern)

Fielding, Henry, 102

Fielding, Sarah, 27, 67–68, 79–92, **83**

Filmer, Sir Robert, 11–12, 37–39, 42

Fiske, James, 102, 251n66

Fliegelman, Jay, 2–3, 14, 26–27, 69, 100

Follen, Eliza Lee Cabot, 202

Fordyce, James, 234n54

Foster, Hannah Webster, 28, 48, 235n81; *The Boarding School,* 67–68, 79–80, 88–94; *The Coquette,* 88, 94, 111, 116, 120

Foucault, Michel, 70

Fourteenth Amendment: definition of citizenship, 8, 10, 29–30, 130, 167, 168–72; gender and, 191; legacy of, 206–17, 255n12; slavery and, 203–5

France, 28, 101, 113, 142, 184–85

Franklin, Benjamin, 139, 146, 186

French Revolution, 118, 178, 197; images of children in, 96–97; views of in United States, 113–16

Fuller, Margaret, 192

Garcha, Aman, 123

Gardner, Jared, 140, 236n8

Garrison, William Lloyd, 187

gender, 23, 26, 33, **73**, 98, 129–30, 184; J. Adams on, 96; authority and, 82, 85; bad readers and, 116–17; boy readers, 15, 26, 48, 55, 173–75, 189–90; citizenship and, 4–7, 65, 80–82, 88–93, 172; economics and, 158–59, 165–66; Emerson on, 189–90; Fourteenth Amendment and, 190–91, 209; girl readers, 17–18, 52, 100–101, 237n21; Great Awakening and, 36, 49; Irving on, 241n125; Locke on, 13, 68–69, 234n55; manhood, 113; Quak-

ers on, 40; sexuality and, 47, 119, 122, 124; slavery and, 223n87; social contract theory and, 80–83; suffrage and, 170, 234n57; women aligned with children, 5, 12, 102–4, 110–12, 120. *See also* feminism; patriarchy

Genet, Edmond-Charles (Citizen), 113–14

Genovese, Eugene D., 197

Gibbs, George, 114

Gilmont, Jean-François, 36

Gilmore, William J., 228n46, 243n26, 246n97

Ginsberg, Lesley, 69, 172, 202

Godwin, William, 182

Goodrich, Samuel, 10, 17, 171–72, 249n51; on citizenship, 179, 197–98; *The Tales of Peter Parley about America,* 1–2; *The Young American,* **199**

Gopnik, Alison, 30

Graydon, Alexander, 114

Great Awakening, 34–36, 43, 57–62, 231n95, 231n97

Gregory, John, 106

Grenby, M. O., 23, 81, 102, 223n77

Grossberg, Michael, 104, 121, 133, 209–10

Gubar, Marah, 23

Halfway Covenant, 33–34, 43, 60, 225n6

Hall, David D., 16–17, 226n23, 227n28

Hall, Timothy, 59

Harris, Amanda B., 128–29

Hartman, Saidya, 213

Hatchett, Harley, 1–2, 24

Hawthorne, Nathaniel, 115, 159, 253n130; on children's citizenship, 167, 171–72, 179, 198–201

Henderson, John B., 208

Henley, Harriot, 89

Hewitt, Elizabeth, 9, 191, 252n93

Hill, Hannah, 54

history, 5, 9, 105, 115, 243n30; children's role in, 1, 10, 14; of children's imaginary citizenship, 8, 21, 26, 31, 94, 215; of children's literature, 16; of children's natural citizenship, 29, 170–71; pedagogy and, 92, 154, 157; textbooks, 81, 121, 144, 216. *See also* natural history

The History of Constantius and Pulchera, 100

The History of Little Goody Two Shoes, 17, 27, 67, 76–77, 117

The History of Little King Pippin, 48,
   229nn51–54
Hobbes, Thomas, 97
Homestead, Melissa, 163
Horner, J., 151–52, **153**
Howard, Jacob, 169–71
Howells, William Dean, 241n125
Hume, David, 244n55
Hutcheson, Francis, 72

ideology, 2, 12, 15, 161, 164; capitalism and, 36,
   136, 138; citizenship and, 20, 23, 28
The Illustrated Alphabet of Birds, 193–94
immigrants, 8, 97, 213; "anchor babies" discourse, 29, 206, 210; citizenship of, 29–30,
   170, 172, 206, 210–11; naturalization of,
   176, 205
Immel, Andrea, 221n32
Irving, Judge John, 149, 163
Irving, Washington, 157, 241n125; *The Sketch
   Book of Geoffrey Crayon, Gent.*, 17, 28,
   123–30
Isenberg, Nancy, 69, 103–4, 122, 209

Jackson, Andrew, 133–34, 190
Jackson, Holbrook, 77
Janeway, James, 16–17, 230n68; *A Token for
   Children*, 44, 51–52, 54–56, 227n28
Jefferson, Thomas, 9, 65

Kant, Immanuel, 19
Keach, Benjamin, 16, 222n54, 229n49
Keithe, George, 49
Kelley, Mary, 80–81
Kerber, Linda K., 234n55
Kerney, Mary Celeste, 209
Kline, Daniel, 221n32

Lacan, Jacques, 220n22
Lancaster system of education, 185, 244n51,
   250n52
language, 79, 102, 105, 118, 171; affection and,
   76–78, 93; citizenship and, 18, 20–21, 214;
   Emerson on, 191, 252n82; nature as, 29,
   252n104; patriarchal nature of, 27, 35–38,
   42–45, 67, 225n18; pedagogy of, 5, 9; politics of, 86–87, 185; religious, 53, 56, 132;
   revolutionary, 108–9, 128, 178; Rousseau on,

180, 182, 184; seduction through, 122–23;
   slavery and, 201–3. *See also* alphabet books;
   spelling books
law, 18, 22, 25, 78, 93, 95; affection and, 20–21,
   27, 63–64, 66–68, 118–19; age in, 102–4,
   122; common, 4, 29, 97, 120–21, 176, 208;
   economics and, 133–34, 159–60; election, 13,
   32–33, 220n13; Emerson on, 188–91; Filmer
   on, 37–38, 42; Hawthorne on, 198–200;
   W. Irving on, 125–26; Jefferson on, 9, 65;
   literacy, 32–33, 224n2; Locke on, 19, 70–71,
   78, 88; natural, 168–69, 171, 181, 191–92,
   197; origin of, 91–92; religious, 43, 46;
   replacement for parents, 70–71, 75–77, 99,
   120–21, 234n55; Rousseau on, 179–83; slavery in, 203–4; teaching of, 5–7, 81, 182–83;
   utilitarianism and, 136; women in, 69, 96,
   209. *See also* Alien and Sedition Acts (1798);
   citizenship; Civil Right Act (1868); Civil
   Rights Act (1964); consent; Constitution
   (U.S.); *Ex parte Crouse* (1838); Fourteenth
   Amendment; Locke, John; Naturalization
   Act (1790); Reconstruction; republicanism; rights; Rousseau, Jean-Jacques; social
   contract theory; suffrage; United Nations
   Convention on the Rights of the Child
   (1989); *United States v. Isaac Williams*
   (1799); *United States v. Wong Kim Ark*
   (1898)
Lennox, Charlotte, 116
Lerer, Seth, 76
letters, 51, 106–7, 117–18, 157, 236n15; of John
   and Abigail Adams, 96; of children, 54,
   91–93; collections of, 140, 223n80; of fans,
   237n21; in popular publications, 24; in
   religion, 46, 50
Levander, Caroline F., 2, 19, 129, 172, 197,
   247n8
literary museums, 139–44, 147
literature (children's), 64, 102, 227n28, 245n95;
   canon of, 126–27; children's conversion
   narratives, 27, 34, 44, 50–54; development
   of, 9, 14–18; economics in, 136, 154, 162;
   Hawthorne's children's books, 198, 253n130;
   Locke on, 61–62, 75; as parental stand-in,
   66–67; slavery in, 173; voice in, 84. *See also*
   alphabet books; censorship; diaries; language; letters; literature (general); lottery

literature (children's) (*cont.*)
  books; metaphors; novels; primers; reading;
    republic of letters; sketches (short stories);
    spelling books
literature (general), 4–5, 120, 129, 150, 154,
    208; book collecting and, 143; boundary
    between children's and adults', 17–18, 98,
    255n25; children in, 11, 14, 68; contrasted
    with law, 26, 32, 34, 65–66, 95, 97, 173;
    nation-building and, 8–9, 21; sentimental
    literature, 155–56, 251n70. *See also* alphabet
    books; censorship; diaries; language; letters;
    literature (children's); lottery books; meta-
    phors; newspapers; novels; primers; reading;
    republic of letters; sketches (short stories);
    spelling books
Locke, John, 135, 142, 180–81, 228n43; on
    affection, 68–75, 105, 232n3; on children,
    3–4, 19, 27, 103; on citizenship, 12–14, 215;
    on education, 16, 61–62, 64–66, 117, 119–20,
    124; on equality, 109; on freedom, 90, 95,
    130, 177, 235n67; on gender, 234n55; on
    madness, 223n85; Romanticism and, 171;
    on social contract, 40, 79–84
Lockridge, Kenneth, 33
Loewen, James W., 216
Longfellow, Henry, 127
Lord Chesterfield, 106
lottery books, 132, 137, 146, 150–57, **153**
The Lowell Offering (magazine), 165–66,
    247nn124–28
Luther, Martin, 11, 36

Maclay, William, 95
Macleod, Anne Scott, 132–35
Madison, James, 146
March, Francis A., 213
Marten, James, 224n1
Martin, Terrence, 240n104
Mather, Cotton, 16–17, 59–61, 225n6, 227n33,
    228n46; *Cares about the Nurseries*, 39–40; on
    children's reading, 27, 34–36, 42–51, 56–57,
    226n23, 227n28; on closet reading, 228n37;
    on government, 226n21; on race, 225n7; in
    The Sketch Book of Gregory Crayon, Gent.,
    123–26
Mather, Increase, 43, 50, 226n21
Matson, Cathy D., 139

Mein, John, 85
Melville, Herman, 248n13
metaphors, 43, 68, 95–96, 141, 182; for child-
    hood, 2, 7–9, 11–18; for economics, 132, 150,
    156, 163; patriarchal, 32; for readers, 38–39,
    42, 97; religious, 46, 50, 55, 228n46; revolu-
    tionary, 69, 73; for slavery, 172, 177, 187, 201
methodology, 23–26, 237n17
M'George, William, 186
Mickenberg, Julia, 213–14
Middlemarch (Eliot), 17
Mill, John Stuart, 136
Minor, Virginia, 209
Mintz, Steven, 3, 26–27, 115
Monaghan, Charles, 253n106
Monaghan, E. Jennifer, 33, 44–46, 224n3,
    253n106
Monima, or the Beggar Girl (Read), 100
More, Hannah, 114–15, 159
Morse, Jedidiah, 89
Mossman, Carol A., 178–79
Murray, John, 250n62

Nabers, John, 204, 254n148
Native Americans, **73**, 172, 190, 206, 255n15
natural history, 144, 167, 192, 196–98, 202
*Natural History, or Uncle Philip's Conversations
    with the Children about Tools and Trades
    among the Inferior Animals*, 195, **196**
Naturalization Act (1790), 97, 176
New, Elisa, 15
Newbery, John, 17, 61, 67, 76–77, 131
New England Primer, 14, 34, 38–42, **39**, **41**;
    politics in, 226n21; religion in, 47–48,
    225n18
*The New Monthly Magazine and Literary
    Journal*, 155
newspapers, 4, 24, 126, 144, 195, 248n13
Nietz, John, 250n54
Nord, David Paul, 132, 148
novels, 57, 81, 184, 235, 237n20; abolitionist,
    202; agency in, 25–26; audiences, 4–5, 17;
    child readers of, 61, 96–130, 237n17, 237n21;
    children's citizenship in, 28, 94; circulation,
    67; dissent in, 4–5; epistolary, 54; politics of,
    236n8, 236n15; quixotic, 105, 116–27; seduc-
    tion, 49, 98, 104–5; sentimental, 159
Nussbaum, Martha, 216

Obama, Barack, 2, 10

Occum, Samson, 76

Onuf, Peter S., 139

Owen, Robert Dale, 193

Paine, Thomas, 7, 13, 95, 105, 119; on parent-child political metaphor, 69, 72–74, 108

Panic of 1819, 135

Panic of 1837, 135

The Panoplist, and Missionary Magazine, 154

Parley's Magazine, 1–2, 5

patriarchy, 8, 64, 81, 97–99, 110; charity in, 145; colonialism and, 2; W. Irving on, 123, 129; language and, 27; Locke on, 70–71; patriarchal subjecthood, 11–13, 18–22, 25, 31–32, 66–68; religion and, 15–16, 33–45, 54–57, 229n49; resistance to, 31, 61, 124, 209; Rousseau on, 177; slavery and, 29, 169–70, 175, 187, 247n8; women and, 95–96

Payson, Sara Willis (Fanny Fern), 187

Peabody, Elizabeth, 192

Peale, Charles Willson, 140

Pearson, Jacqueline, 230n71

pedagogy, 5, 15, 94, 113, 154, 214; of affection, 74–75; books as teachers, 126–29, 167, 172, 186; Emerson on, 188–89; failure of, 107; W. Irving on, 123–30; Locke on, 16, 61–62, 64–66, 117, 119–20, 124; methods, 185; Rousseau on, 178–85; slavery and, 174–75, 203, 212, 225n7; teaching citizenship, 38, 79–94; teaching economics, 139–40, 165; teaching language, 77–78; teaching law, 5–7, 81, 136, 182–83; teaching reading, 9–10, 17, 21; voice and, 84. *See also* alphabet books; catechisms; history: textbooks; primers; spelling books; Sunday schools

Perry, Gerraint, 178

Pestalozzi, Johann, 185, 193, 253n106

Pfieger, Pat, 23

Pilkington, Mary, 173–76

Plotz, Judith, 189, 191

Pocock, J. G. A., 134–38, 232n3

The Political Class Book, 102

Pollock, Linda, 221n32

premium certificates, 132, 143–52, **145**

Preston, Ann, 202

primers, 34, 63, 227n28; circulation of, 4, 16, 101–2, 226n23

Protestant Reformation, 11, 36, 38–39

Quakers (Society of Friends), 40, 48–49

race, 190, 202–3, 234n57; in children's literature, 172–76, 195–97; citizenship and, 20–22, 69, 81, 97, 169; Fourteenth Amendment and, 207–8, 211–13. *See also* colonialism; empire; Native Americans; slavery; whiteness

Rachman, Stephen, 144

Raikes, Robert, 244n51

Rand, William, 57–59

reading, 68, 85, 115–16, 151, 227n28; adult/child boundary, 15–16, 103, 243n26, 243n27; affectionate, 64, 67, 71, 79, 93–94; agency and, 90, 128; bad, 28, 98–100, 104–13, 125–26; of boys, 15, 26, 48, 55, 173–75, 189–90; closet, 42–46, 52, 56–57, 228n37; economics and, 132, 139–44, 150, 154–59; of girls, 17–18, 52, 91–92, 100–101, 237n21; Locke on, 75–76, 181; nationalism and, 62; natural, 166–72, 190, 193, 252n104; of newspapers, 4; of novels, 28, 102, 236n15, 237n20; patriarchy and, 13, 36–41; reading public, 1, 17–18, 165, 235n66; religious, 27, 39–62, 47–56; resistant, 123; Rousseau on, 76, 179, 182; slavery and, 201–3, 212–13; studying reading public, 23–26, 237n17; teaching of, 9–10, 174–75, 185–87, 235n67; of women, 5, 18. *See also* alphabet books; book eating (bibliophagia); censorship; diaries; language; letters; literature (children's); literature (general); lottery books; newspapers; novels; primers; republic of letters; sketches (short stories); spelling books; tract societies

Reconstruction, 169, 204, 213

Rede, Cartaret, 51–54

Reiner, Jacqueline, 142

religion, 81, 100, 137, 161, 225n4; Anglicanism, 38; Baptists, 229n49; Catholicism, 11, 36, 38; children's participation in, 10, 15–16, 26–27, 32–36, 57–62; conversion narratives, 53–57; economics and, 132, 144, 150; Islam, 244n62; nature and, 180–81; Pledge of Allegiance and, 255n24; politics and, religion (*cont.*)

11–13, 37–39, 222n49; printing and, 148, 163, 225n18, 228n46; reading and, 41–52, 154; Rousseau on, 249n38. *See also* catechisms; Edwards, Jonathan; Great Awakening; Half-way Covenant; Mather, Cotton; Mather, Increase; Protestant Reformation; Quakers; Sunday schools

The Renowned History of Giles Gingerbread, 67, 76–78, 117–18, 124

republicanism, 19, 28, 81, 105, 133–35; children's literature and, 62; citizenship and, 6–7, 21, 64–65; economics and, 9, 130; Lockean liberalism contrasted with, 232n3; print culture of, 66, 89; "republican machines, " 185–86, 212–13; republican virtue, 107–8, 122. *See also* Republicans (political party)

Republicans (political party), 96–97, 113–14. *See also* Jefferson, Thomas; Madison, James

republic of letters, 17, 23

Richardson, Samuel, 17, 100, 102, 121

rights, 58, 173, 225n6; of children, 3–5, 26–31, 97, 115, 187; citizenship and, 6–8, 18–20, 121; Fourteenth Amendment and, 168–70, 203–17; Locke on, 64, 181; loss of, 8, 11, 13–14; of men, 124; of Muslims, 235n77; natural, 9, 68; of poor people, 164; property, 71, 135; in religious communities, 33–34, 58–61; of women, 80–81, 96, 104, 191, 223n87. *See also* United Nations Convention on the Rights of the Child (1989)

Ripley, Sally, 4, 80, 187, 234n62, 237n21; on reading practices, 102, 237n20

Robert Merry's Museum, 1–2, 23, 25, 187, 219n4

Robinson, R. R., 171–72

Rodgers, Daniel T., 242n17

Rousseau, Jean-Jacques, 167, 173, 200, 204–5; on children's citizenship, 29, 171, 176–85, 221n33; compared with Emerson, 188, 191, 251n71; on education, 76, 193, 212; on law, 189–90; on religion, 249n38

Rowlandson, Mary, 50, 154

Rowson, Susanna, 100, 114, 121, 236n15

Rush, Benjamin, 17, 185–86

Sánchez-Eppler, Karen, 26, 103, 122, 160, 242n7

Sartre, John Paul, 155–56

Schmidt, Peter, 212

scrapbooks, 147

Sedgwick, Catharine Maria, 17, 102, 160–65

Sedgwick, Theodore, 161

Sen, Amartya, 216

de Sévigné, Marie de Rabutin-Chantal, 93

Sewall, Edmund Quincy, 4

Sheldon, Charlotte, 234n62

Shields, David, 72

Shklar, Judith N., 179

Sigourney, Lydia, 157–60

Singley, Carol J., 2

sketches (short stories), 123–30. *See also* Irving, Washington

slavery, 22, 118, 167, 247n8, 248n14; as aligned with childhood, 13, 169–70; *Anti-Slavery Alphabet*, 194–95; in children's literature, 5, 172–76, 195–97, 201–3; citizenship contrasted with, 69, 84, 98, 130; in the Constitution, 105; Emerson on, 190; Fourteenth Amendment and, 203–8, 211–13; imaginary citizenship and, 4, 29; metaphor of, 68, 111, 187; Paine on, 108; patriarchy and, 29, 169–70, 175, 187, 247n8; Rousseau on, 177, 181, 183

Smith, Adam, 136–37, 146

Smith, Rogers, 96–97, 232n3

social contract theory, 79, 136, 203, 211, 247n8; affection and, 64–67; children's role in, 27, 97; citizenship and, 25, 169–71; consent and, 6, 31; Emerson on, 188; Jefferson on, 9; patriarchy contrasted with, 19–20; Rousseau on, 176–85, 188; state of nature, 42, 71, 81, 177, 181, 183; women in, 80–83. *See also* Locke, John; Rousseau, Jean-Jacques

Society of Friends. *See* Quakers

Sorby, Angela, 252n104

Sorrows of Young Werther (Goethe), 106, 109

Spellberg, Denise, 235n77

spelling books, 212–13, 250n54

Spence, Thomas, 215

Sprague, Homer, 127

S. S., 155–56

S. S. G., 250n54

Stanton, Elizabeth Cady, 209

Stern, Julia, 99

Stoddard, Samuel, 60

suffrage, 66, 89, 234n57; citizenship and, 20, 203–4; gender requirements, 81, 170,

209; property ownership requirements, 13, 134; racial requirements, 207–8; religious communities and, 34–35; young voters, 2, 210, 216

Sunday schools, 133, 143–52, 159, 244n51, 244n62

Sunday School Union, 148–49

Taylor, R., 250n56

Tebbel, John, 67, 102

Tenney, Samuel, 116

Tenney, Tabitha Gilman, 28, 94, 116–25

Thomas, Brook, 22, 70

Thomas, Ella Gertrude, 102, 237n21

Thomas, Isaiah, 4, 17, 67, 131–33

Thompkins, Jane, 251n70

Thompson, Jane, 142

Thoreau, Henry David, 155, 186–87

Thorne, Harley, 1

Tierney, Nathan, 6

Tocqueville, Alexis de, 114

Todorov, Tzvetan, 179

tract societies, 144, 148–50, 186, 244n66, 250n56

Trimmer, Sarah, 103

Trumbell, Jenny, 102

Twain, Mark, 17, 146–47, 208, 241n125

Tyler, Royall, 114

Tyndale, William, 45

United Nations Convention on the Rights of the Child (1989), 29–30, 210

United States v. Isaac Williams (1799), 97

United States v. Wong Kim Ark (1898), 211

Vernon, Caleb, 52, 54

Ware, Mary Allen, 168, 192

Warner, Michael, 6, 20, 64–66, 91, 93, 242n11

Warner, Susan, 17–18, 160, 237n21, 246n108, 246n109

War of 1812, 134

Washington, George, 39–40, 63, 95, 105, 114, 123

Watson, Noah, 113

Webster, Noah, 114, 146, 185, 237n17; on affectionate citizenship, 20, 66; *American Spelling Book*, 17, 78, 212, 235n67; *Grammatical Institute*, 106, 108

White, S. S., 250n56

White, Thomas, 45–46, 52, 54–56, 227n28, 228n37

Whitefield, George, 59

whiteness, 20–22, 69, 81, 97, 195–97, 225n7

Whitman, Elizabeth, 11–12, 117

Whitmore, Michael, 221n33

Whittier, James Lawrence, 149

Williams, Solomon, 32, 60

Wittgenstein, Ludwig, 6

Wollstonecraft, Mary, 124–25

Woodhouse, Barbara Bennett, 210

Woolf, Virginia, 17

The Youth's Companion (magazine), 5, 214